THE ROLE AND STATUS OF INTERNATIONAL HUMANITARIAN VOLUNTEERS AND ORGANIZATIONS

LEGAL ASPECTS OF
INTERNATIONAL ORGANIZATION

VOLUME 12

The titles published in this series are listed at the end of this volume.

THE ROLE AND STATUS OF INTERNATIONAL HUMANITARIAN VOLUNTEERS AND ORGANIZATIONS

The Right and Duty to Humanitarian Assistance

Yves Beigbeder

MARTINUS NIJHOFF PUBLISHERS

DORDRECHT/BOSTON/LONDON

Library of Congress Cataloging-in-publication Data

Beigbeder, Yves.
    The role and status of international humanitarian volunteers and
organizations: the right and duty to humanitarian assistance / Yves
Beigbeder.
        p.   cm. -- (Legal aspects of international organization ; 12)
    Includes index.
    ISBN 0-7923-1190-6
    1. International relief. 2. Disaster relief. 3. Humanitarianism.
4. Voluntarism. 5. Non-governmental organizations.   I. Title.
II. Series.
HV553.B45 1991
361.3'7--dc20   91-10642

ISBN 0-7923-1190-6

Published by Martinus Nijhoff Publishers,
P.O. Box 163, 3300 AD Dordrecht, The Netherlands.

Sold and distributed in the U.S.A. and Canada
by Kluwer Academic Publishers,
101 Philip Drive, Norwell, MA 02061, U.S.A.

In all other countries, sold and distributed
by Kluwer Academic Publishers Group,
P.O. Box 322, 3300 AH Dordrecht, The Netherlands.

Printed on acid-free paper

Printed in the Netherlands

To all the national and international humanitarian volunteers and workers, the Red Cross delegates, the doctors, nurses and other health care personnel who have offered their skills and their knowledge, given their time and sometimes their life in order to provide emergency relief and care to those in need

TABLE OF CONTENTS

viii

PART II. NEUTRALITY OR POLITICIZATION? DISCRETION OR DISCLOSURE?   135

ACKNOWLEDGEMENTS

I wish to thank all the organizations' representatives who have given some of their time, and have helped me to obtain relevant information and documentation. In particular, my thanks are extended to members of the International Committee of the Red Cross and of the League of Red Cross and Red Crescent Societies in Geneva for their useful advice and assistance in finding reference material. Members of the "French Doctors" (Médecins Sans Frontières, Médecins du Monde, Aide Médicale Internationale) associations, and other non-governmental organizations have also been very cooperative.

Finally, the editing skills and willing assistance of Mandy Eggleston are, again, as for previous books, gratefully acknowledged.

Note.

In order to avoid repetitive "his/her", "him/her", the use of the masculine gender in this book is deemed to apply equally to men and women except when a contrary intention is evident from the context.

The author has written this book in a personal capacity: the views and conclusions are his own responsibility.

FOREWORD

In the present stage of international relations, communication between organized human societies is developing on the alternate (and even sometimes simultaneous) basis of sheer violence, rational mutual interests and altruistic solidarity: war, cooperation and *humanitarian assistance* reflect the main facets of such ambiguous—if not contradictory—intercourse. The book written by Dr. Yves Beigbeder, a former WHO official and today a distinguished contributor to the specialized literature on international organization, deals with the last (but not the least) of those three facets. For scholars, it comes out as a timely as well as seminal study.

Immediate expressions of moral solidarity and material assistance rushing from all over the world in reaction to recent natural and/or man-made disasters (such as hunger in Africa, Chernobyl, earthquakes in Armenia, Iran, etc.) bear witness to the fact that humanitarian issues are a growing international concern in an interdependent world, which is actually turning out into the "global village" once prophesied by Marshall MacLuhan. This largely explains the fact that the General Assembly of the United Nations has issued calls for a "New International Humanitarian Order" and that the essentials of such a concept have already been outlined by the Independent Commission on International Humanitarian Issues—a global expert body comparable to the Brandt Commission on development issues, to the MacBride Commission on communication issues, to the Maitland Commission on telecommunication issues or to the Brundtland Commission on environmental issues. Moreover, and as significantly, humanitarian matters represent a standing top-ranking item on the transregional (Europe/North America) East-West relations agenda for more than a decade: since 1975, the implementation of the Helsinki Final Act provisions on human rights and "humanitarian" cooperation has consolidated an actual "right" of interference in internal affairs, which has eventually been institutionalized under the form of a special mechanism operating within the "Conference on Human Dimension" of the Conference on Security and Cooperation in Europe. Within this context, the relevance of a study on *The Role and Status of International Humanitarian Volunteers and Organizations* appears self-evident.

Dr. Beigbeder's book provides a thorough analysis of the complex interplay between the main several governmental, intergovernmental, non-governmental and individual forces operating within the contemporary humanitarian network — as well as the major issues involved: discretion vs. disclosure, neutrality vs. politicization, right and duty to humanitarian assistance vs. national sovereignty... The value of what actually amounts to a handbook is enhanced by the multidisciplinary approach used by the author. Although the study is political science-oriented, it contains historical information on "dead" international institutions such as the International Relief Union, UNRRA and the International Refugee Organization; it also makes room for developments on the legal status of NGOs, international volunteers and medical missions.

Chapter 11 of the book addresses a central problem: conflict between the vital imperative of humanitarian assistance and the blunt reality of national sovereignty. Although the author recognizes that the implementation of human rights regimes has triggered a right of intervention, he does not conclude in favour of such a right in the humanitarian field. All readers may not share his cautious stand. After all, the dichotomy between human rights and humanitarian law has only historical — that is to say contingent — roots: its legitimacy becomes questionable once its implementation has adverse effects on the protection of individuals. Moreover, if we admit (along with the recommendations of the Independent Commission on International Humanitarian Issues) that for the time being Nation-States cannot be superseded, but that their behaviour should be "humanized", one should then insist that governments recognize that the legal duty of non-interference stops where the risk of non-assistance begins. In summary, the reader will find in Chapter 11, as in other parts of the book, real food for thought.

PROFESSOR VICTOR-YVES GHEBALI
Graduate Institute of International Studies — Geneva

INTRODUCTION

"To prevent and alleviate human suffering wherever it
may be found"
(Excerpt from the Red Cross Fundamental Principle of
Humanity)

On 17 December 1989, Romanians started fighting for their freedom. The consequent losses in human lives, the number of the wounded, together with the shortages in medicaments, foodstuffs, and other basic necessities, as well as admiration
felt for those who risked, and often lost, their lives in order to overthrow a hated
tyranny, triggered a vast movement of international solidarity.

The French associations "Médecins sans Frontières" and "Médecins du Monde"
were the first to ship emergency medical equipment by plane on 22 December, followed by teams of volunteer doctors and nurses. The French Government sent three
medical teams and a field hospital with surgeons and anaesthetists specialized in
military surgery. The French "Secours Catholique" released 8 million French
Francs to prepare and send family food packages of 5 kilos.

The Governments, National Red Cross Societies and non-governmental organizations (NGOs) of other Western countries shared in the assistance movement: the
United Kingdom, Austria, the Federal Republic of Germany, Italy, Belgium, Nordic
countries. The Swiss Government donated one million Swiss Francs to the Red
Cross. Japan gave $ one million and Monaco one million Francs. The United States
sent directly to Romania medical equipment and medicaments for $250,000 and
$500,000 to the International Committee of the Red Cross (ICRC).

Eastern European countries were also prompt in giving assistance: the USSR
sent medical supplies by plane, trains and trucks and offered 6,000 hospital beds in
Moldavia. Poland, Hungary, Czechoslovakia and Yugoslavia also sent medicaments, blood and food.

Two planeloads were sent by Morocco.

In order to deal with the afflux of international aid, a coordinating committee
was set up on 26 December in Bucarest, composed of representatives of the

1

Romanian Ministry of Health, the World Health Organization (WHO) and the ICRC, to stock and deliver medical equipment and evaluate needs.

On 28 December, the U.N. General Assembly adopted unanimously a resolution calling upon States and International Financial Institutions to provide emergency humanitarian aid to Romania. UNESCO proposed to participate in the country's efforts in the fields of education and culture. The European Economic Community granted a credit of Ecu 6,5 million for medical assistance and the supply of food-stuffs.

On 29 December, the non-governmental organizations considered that the emergency phase had been dealt with successfully. Priority should henceforth be given to mid- and long-term assistance. Donations in cash should replace donations in kind, in order to adjust better to the Romanians' real needs.

The NGOs wanted to prevent a repetition of the "Armenian Syndrome", where an excess of assistance, both in volunteer personnel and supplies, and a rivalry between helping nations and organizations, had clogged communications and transportation and had failed to respond, in part, to real needs[1].

This recent example of "applied humanitarianism" is typical of modern large-scale relief operations, with its quick reaction to the event, be it a natural disaster or a man-made emergency. It shows the interaction of the main actors in the humanitarian network: the generous "man-in-the-street" donator, the resources of donor governments, the exhortation, coordination and support given by intergovernmental organizations (IGOs), the operational intervention of the NGOs with the support of their permanent staff and of their volunteers, and the will and capacity of the assisted country to receive and distribute help. It also illustrates some of the problems of humanitarian intervention, in particular, the more or less mediatized appeal of humanitarian crises on the potential donors, the necessary coordination of relief assistance, the need for efficient management and professionalism on the part of the voluntary agencies and the extension of short-term emergency external assistance into long-term training, development and self-reliance.

Humanitarianism has been defined by the Independent Commission on International Humanitarian Issues[2] as "a basic orientation towards the interests and welfare of people". Its perspective takes a long-term view of human welfare and one of its essential dimensions is solidarity with future generations. Humanitarianism is "an ethic of human solidarity" based on the following values:

— respect for life
— a responsibility for future generations
— protection for the human habitat

[1] *Le Monde*, 26, 28, 29, 30 December 1989.
[2] *Winning the Human Race? Report of the Independent Commission on International Humanitarian Issues*, Zed Books Ltd, London/New Jersey, 1988, pp. 3 and 12.

— altruism nurtured by a sense of mutual interest and a recognition of human dignity and worth.

The principle of humanity is a long-standing and entrenched principle of international law. It is employed in various ways: it may refer to the protection of combatants and non-combatants in war conditions under the "Law of The Hague" or the "Law of Geneva"; it may denote an approach that emphasizes protection and assistance to the individual as opposed to politically influenced considerations; it may be used in a broad, generic sense: to relieve human suffering and to help in the realization of human needs.

The internationally established norms on human rights, particularly those defined in the Universal Declaration of Human Rights and the International Covenants, the 1951 Convention and the 1967 Protocol relating to the status of refugees, the Geneva Conventions of 1949 and the Protocols Additional thereto, the 1989 Convention on the Rights of the Child, form the backbone of the normative framework established by the international community to determine minimum standards of humane treatment and of human solidarity.

As noted by the U.N. Secretary-General[3], while the essential normative and institutional frameworks exist, the main problem that occurs in practice is the failure to implement existing norms, which may stem either from unawareness of their existence, deliberate disregard of their provisions, non-adherence to certain parts of the normative system through the non-ratification of treaties, or lack of education, training and dissemination of information.

One of the seven fundamental principles of the Red Cross is the principle of humanity. As defined in a Red Cross document:

"Humanity: The Red Cross, born of a desire to bring assistance without discrimination to the wounded on the battlefield, endeavours — in its international and national capacity — to prevent and alleviate human suffering wherever it may be found. Its purpose is to protect life and health and to ensure respect for the human being. It promotes mutual understanding, friendship, cooperation and lasting peace amongst all people"[4].

This principle, which recalls the origin of the Red Cross movement, broadens the concern of humanitarians from wounded soldiers to all suffering humanity, from whatever causes its suffering occurred. It also defines the ultimate aim of humanitarianism as peace in the world, through respect for the human being, i.e. respect for human rights.

The U.N. Charter also associates humanitarianism with human rights: it sets as one of the purposes of the U.N. "to achieve international cooperation in solving

---

[3] U.N. Doc. A/40/348, *New International Humanitarian Order — Report of the Secretary-General submitted pursuant to General Assembly resolution 38/125*, 9 Oct. 1985, p. 42.

[4] *International Red Cross Handbook*, 12th Ed., Geneva, July 1983.

4

international problems of an economic, social, cultural or humanitarian character, and in promoting and encouraging respect for human rights and for fundamental freedoms (U.N. Charter, Art. 1.3).

The protection of life, health and human rights as a condition for peace is one of the tenets of humanitarianism. For a Red Cross official[5], modern humanitarianism is an advanced and rational form of charity and justice: it acts to care for suffering individuals and it also tries to prevent suffering. Charity is an expression of Christian morality and is synonymous with love for one's neighbour.

For another writer[6], humanitarians represent the consciences of the rich countries of the world. Religion and charity require that the rich give to the poor. The rich's sense of guilt of having too much when the poor suffer from poverty and ill-health will be alleviated by a donation or by voluntary service. The humanitarian acts, not for any personal gain, but because he is moved by a regard for the welfare of others. At the same time, he may derive religious, moral or psychological satisfaction from his altruism.

While originally humanitarianism was identified with a religious and/or moral "do-gooder" ethic, it later became associated with the defence and support of the underprivileged and the promotion of the economically, socially or politically oppressed or underrepresented. Thus humanitarians, like human rights activists, become politicized when they need to protect the individual from the power of the State[7].

International Humanitarian Assistance

For the U.N. Secretary-General[8], the following have been identified as acute humanitarian problems that require attention and that lend themselves to solutions within the scope of humanitarian organizations: hunger and starvation, health and environmental conditions, massive unemployment, massive illiteracy, the situation of women and children, genocide, arbitrary and summary executions, torture, enforced or involuntary disappearances, slavery and slavery-like practices, armed conflicts, weapons that cause unnecessary human suffering, situations of gross violations of human rights, disrespect for basic standards in the area of human rights, humanitarian law, refugees and disaster relief, mass exoduses and displacements, migrant workers and non-citizens, natural and man-made disasters, population questions, vulnerable groups whose survival is threatened, racial and religious

[5] *The Fundamental Principles of the Red Cross—Commentary*, Jean Pictet, Henry Dunant Institute, Geneva, 1979.

[6] *Imposing Aid*, B.E. Harrell-Bond, Oxford University Press, 1986, p. 68.

[7] "Humanitarian Intervention: Lessons from the Nigerian Civil War", L. S. Wiseberg, *Human Rights Journal*, Vol. VII-1, 1974, Pedone, Paris, pp. 80–81.

[8] U.N. Doc. A/40/348, p. 40.

intolerance, the drug problem and regions or countries in need of special humanitarian assistance.

For the purposes of this book, this extensive list will be reduced generally to the problems of natural and man-made disasters and refugee relief and to volunteers and organizations dealing with such problems. Organizations dealing with human rights, such as Amnesty International and the International Commission of Jurists, are not included, even though the promotion and defence of human rights is closely related to humanitarian action and humanitarian law.

The term "humanitarian assistance" will therefore be employed as equivalent to disaster relief or relief assistance. Disasters will be considered as emergency situations in which there is an urgent need for international assistance to relieve human suffering.

As noted by Kent[9], human suffering may be caused by various external agents, such as man-made and natural disasters. Man-made events, such as internal or external conflicts, may result in casualties, inadequate or no medical care of the wounded, the ill-treatment of prisoners of war, the flight of refugees, the dispersion of families, famine, epidemics.

Natural disasters include three broad types:—the "sudden onset" variety, like earthquakes, cyclones, volcano eruptions and floods, which give little warning before they strike. "Creeping disasters", like insect infestation, droughts and famine, are more readily predictable. "Chronic disasters", such as soil erosion and deforestation, have no specific time limit.

To these two categories, Kent adds technological disaster agents (for example, a nuclear reactor breakdown) and ecological disaster agents.

It is estimated[10] that from 1965 to 1974 disasters occurred at a world-wide rate of about once a week, killing more than 3,5 million people and affecting more than 400 million. These disasters caused material damage in the tens of billions of U.S. dollars, and necessitated almost $5,3 billion for disaster assistance within the affected countries and $1,6 billion of assistance from the international community. The total flow in international emergency assistance, both in cash and in kind, is estimated at $1.42 billion in 1986 –1987, and $1.6 billion in 1988 –1989.

In general, the impact of disasters falls largely on those countries which are least able to bear it—the Third World countries. It has been estimated that 95 percent of disaster-relief deaths occur in those countries. The proportional economic burden is also much higher in those countries because of the disruptive impact of disasters on already hard-pressed economic and social development efforts in countries suffering from inadequate administrative structures, lack of material resources, untrained personnel, corruption and other ailments. In many disaster-prone developing coun-

[9] R.C. Kent, *Anatomy of Disaster Relief*, Pinter, 1987, pp. 2 and 3.

[10] *Evaluation of the Office of the U.N. Disaster Relief Coordinator*, U.N. Doc. JIU/REP/80/11, Geneva, Oct. 1980, p.1, and U.N. Doc. A/45/271,E/1990/78 of 1 June 1990, Office of the U.N. Disaster Relief Coordinator, *Report of the Secretary-General*, para.18.

tries, disaster losses more than cancel out any real economic growth and amount to many times the value of foreign development assistance.

When a disaster exceeds the resources available to handle it within a country, an appeal for outside aid is made, which generates "international relief (humanitarian) assistance".

Relief assistance falls into three basic categories: assistance in kind, financial contributions and the services of trained personnel. Assistance in kind refers to the supplies and materials needed for the relief operation, depending on the nature of the disaster. It may include food, clothing, medicines, blankets, temporary shelters, hospital equipment, vehicles or equipment needed for search and rescue. Financial contributions may help in meeting cash expenses in a relief operation, or they may serve to buy equipment or supplies. Personnel may include doctors, nurses and other health specialists, logistics experts, administrative staff, coordinators. It includes the provision of facilities to transport both equipment and supplies, and international relief workers. As noted by Macalister-Smith[11], all categories of assistance are to meet the immediate needs of the victims, and not to serve commercial or other purposes.

International humanitarian assistance is distinguished from foreign aid by its concentration on the relief of victims, and in most cases, by its emergency character.

Kent[12] has identified three stages of disaster relief. The relief provided during the first stage, the emergency phase, entails measures to ensure the immediate survival of victims. The second stage is the rehabilitation phase. Having dealt with the immediate needs of victims, relief tends to help the community to assume again its normal functions. This phase involves such assistance as materials to rebuild housing, provision of seeds to produce crops, equipment to dig wells etc.

Post-rehabilitation, the third phase of disaster relief, overlaps with general approaches to development. In theory, in this phase, efforts are made to reduce the vulnerabilities which a disaster agent may have exposed. For natural disasters, it may involve the creation of barriers against flood-prone rivers, the setting-up of structures at central or local level to promote pre-disaster planning and coordination, the building up of health facilities, the training of health personnel in emergency care etc.

International relief assistance involves a humanitarian effort, increasingly accepted as an international responsibility to alleviate the suffering of disaster victims. Secondly it involves a managerial effort to plan, finance, staff, supply, coordinate, implement and evaluate the assistance operations. Thirdly, since international relief assistance is mainly directed to Third World countries, it involves a development task as an integral part of national development.

---

[11] Peter Macalister-Smith, *International Humanitarian Assistance — Disaster Relief Actions in International Law and Organization*, Martinus Nijhoff Publishers, Henry Dunant Institute, Geneva, 1985, p. 4.
[12] Kent, op.cit., p. 12.

Assessment of Relief Assistance

According to Kent[13], there are six crucial aspects of disaster relief that ultimately determine the strengths and weaknesses of any single operation: preparedness, prediction, assessment, appropriate intervention, timely intervention and coordination.

The U.N. Disaster Relief Office (UNDRO) has promoted preparedness measures in disaster-prone countries, including practical ways to organize relief units, to prepare paramedical facilities and to establish early warning systems. The Jamaica's Office of Disaster Preparedness and Emergency Coordination, established in 1980 with UNDRO assistance, has designed a "National Disaster Plan" for emergencies caused by earthquakes, hurricanes, oil spills and transport incidents.

Prediction may apply in a few specific cases. For instance, livestock sales, grain prices and population movements give indications of famine onsets, together with more sophisticated technology, such as satellite observation. However, there are many disasters which cannot be predicted.

Since the late 1970s, greater attention has been given to practical assessment techniques, which attempt to make clear demarcations between types of disasters and their impacts. The growing capacity to assess the needs of victims will hopefully eliminate or decrease the negative effects of unplanned, hasty, uncoordinated, ill-adjusted *ad hoc* relief efforts. Emergency assessment also applies in refugee assistance. Satellites can provide an evaluation of damage and population movements. Greater stress is also placed on the need of relief workers to adjust to the social structure and culture of the stricken community. Community participation is valuable and necessary in all aspects of emergency aid.

Appropriate intervention refers to making lists of supplies to be used in an emergency, appropriate to local communities. The need to purchase food or equipment locally or regionally, rather than to import them from donor countries has been stressed. In the case of refugees, sociologists have underlined the need to rebuild community life and stimulate educational and economic opportunities, rather than giving them ill-considered hand-outs: relief has to be matched by refugee involvement.

A timely intervention is dependent on complex political, logistical, financial and human resources factors. It requires a decision on the part of donors to intervene in this or that country, to collect and ship promptly the necessary equipment and supplies, to draft, train and send volunteers, to overcome export and import customs and immigration requirements, to travel on inadequate or unsafe infrastructures. It also requires a decision on when to stop aid.

Finally the need for more effective coordination of relief aid in the recipient country and at the international donor level has become evident, as noted before. The lack of coordination has caused the duplication of aid, waste, the delivery of

---

[13] Kent, op.cit., p. 21–28.

unwanted products, competition of relief agencies, and in general an inefficient relief assistance and a loss of credibility for some of the relief agencies.

Landmarks of International Humanitarian Assistance

While individual humanitarian feelings and aid are as old as humanity itself, one can identify the charitable Christian orders of the Middle Age as the first group efforts to care for the wounded and the sick on an international basis. Among them, the Order of the Knights of St. John of Jerusalem (later the Order of Malta) was founded in the 12th Century to give religious and hospital care to Christian crusaders in Jerusalem. In the 20th Century, the Order of Malta, while never abandoning its mission to defend Christendom, continues its charitable assistance by running hospitals, giving emergency relief in case of disasters, assisting refugees, caring for leprosy patients and running health-related courses (see Chapter 6).

Christian missionaries were sent overseas primarily to convert the pagans, but they also attempted to "educate" the natives and to give health care. The first mission societies were established in the 17th century. New mission agencies continued to be created throughout the 18th and 19th centuries, culminating in the first decade of the 20th[14].

The creation of the "Religious Society of Friends" (Quakers) dates back to the 17th century in England. Its declaration against war was issued in 1660. The Quakers have had long experience of relief work following wars and natural calamities (see Chapter 6).

In 1839, the "British and Foreign Anti-Slavery Society" was created, five years after the emancipation of slaves in British colonies. It is the world's oldest human rights organization.

The first secular voluntary organization providing medical aid was the American Medical Association, founded in 1847.

Jewish welfare agencies were set up to support the flow of Jewish immigrants to Palestine: the "Alliance Israélite Universelle" in 1860, the "World ORT Union" in 1880, the "Jewish Colonization Association" in 1891.

In 1865, William Booth, an ordained Methodist minister, created the Salvation Army in England. It is now at work in 91 countries. As a religious denomination, its objects are the advancement of the Christian religion, education, the relief of poverty and other charitable pursuits.

[14] Jorgen Lissner, *The Politics of Altruism — A Study of the Political Behaviour of Voluntary Development Agencies*, Lutheran World Federation, Geneva, 1977, Table F, The emergence of non-governmental aid organizations 1650–1970, p. 59.

The Roman Catholic "Caritas Internationalis" movement started with the foundation of "Caritas Germany" in 1897. In the 1980s, 120 autonomous national organizations are members of the international confederation directed by its statutes "to spread charity and social justice in the world" (see Chapter 6).

As noted by Macalister-Smith[15], secular humanitarianism of the 19th century can be traced to the natural law theorists of the 17th century, who recognized a distinction between combatants and non-combatants and emphasized some moderation in war and the advisability of humane behaviour—and to 18th century publicists, such as E. de Vattel and J.J. Rousseau.

The creation of the Red Cross in 1863 at the initiative of Henry Dunant (see Chapters 2, 3, 4, 9, 10 and 11) led to the adoption of the Geneva Conventions for the protection of victims of international war and the formation of a universal movement, made up of national secular voluntary relief organizations, and their federation, the League of Red Cross Societies, founded in 1919.

The Red Cross movement is at the origin of the development of modern humanitarianism through the action of NGOs.

In 1914, the "Commission for Relief in Belgium" (CRB) was set up to give humanitarian assistance to civilian populations of occupied Belgium and Northern France, as a U.S. initiative, with the agreement of Germany and the Allied Powers. CRB was an international NGO with some IGO characteristics. It was a working and successful experiment which served as a blueprint for the conception and management of later large scale humanitarian operations (see Chapter 1).

In 1919, Eglantyne Jebb set up "Save the Children Fund" (SCF) to help starving Austrian children after the First World War. Its present network includes 21 autonomous SCF organizations around the world, the SCF Alliance (see Chapter 5).

Other religious organizations also developed between the two World Wars.

Following a World Missionary Conference in Edinburgh in 1910, the "International Missionary Council" brought together in 1921 foreign missionary societies and national Christian councils. This Council and other movements led to the decision in 1937 to form a "World Council of Churches", although its actual creation was delayed for 11 years by World War II (see Chapter 6).

In 1923, a "Lutheran World Convention" was founded in Eisenach, Germany, a forerunner for the "Lutheran World Federation", which was effectively created in 1947 (see Chapter 6).

In 1927, the "International Relief Union" (IRU) was set up as an IGO in charge of coordinating relief efforts in the event of disasters, of giving financial and operational assistance and to promote international law in this field. Although IRU was never operational as a relief agency, it prepared the way for more effective inter-governmental efforts to give and coordinate relief after World War II (see Chapter 1).

---

[15] Macalister-Smith, op.cit., p. 9.

The Second World War and its aftermath saw the flowering of international humanitarianism, as a somewhat chaotic "non-system". Specialized bodies of the U.N. and both secular and religious organizations were created as IGOs and NGOs to meet initially war-related needs, then relief and development needs, particularly in the Third World.

The Actors in the International Relief Network

Kent[16] has argued that there is no international relief system *per se*, as the diverse set of actors displays little structural interdependence, nor does it share a common boundary, other than the fact that each component may on occasion contribute to the relief process. Even when focused on a relief operation, these components rarely share a set of common institutional goals. On the other hand, Kent notes that an international relief network has emerged

> that is loose, unpredictable, but at least reflects a consensus about the nature of disaster relief and which institutions might be available for relief work. This network is devoid of any institutional framework, lacks coherent goals, reflects few patterned relationships, yet points to a variety of transnational and functional linkages which have emerged probably more out of informal contacts than from formal institutional arrangements.

This network is characterized by an intense web of communications between IGOs, between NGOs and between IGOs and NGOs. It is also characterized by a large degree of transnationalism (less nationalist orientation of relief participants) and specialization of organizations.

Who are the actors of this network?

The receiving governments, authorities and people of the "afflicted" nations, with their suffering, their pride, their sovereignty, but also their own national resources.

The donor governments which, in terms of the volume of resources provided for international relief, are by far the network's most significant components. Donor governments provide bilateral and multilateral assistance. Their assistance may be provided directly or through the IGOs and the NGOs.

The global and regional IGOs, which include mainly various U.N. bodies.

And finally the complex world of the NGOs on which we will focus, as international volunteers, except for the U.N. volunteers, work mainly for NGOs.

As the international relief network involves a constant interaction of all the actors, and more particularly of the IGOs and NGOs, we will review in a First Part the role and characteristics of the two types of organizations. We will also consider prevailing trends concerning the role of NGOs and the role of volunteers.

---

[16] Kent, op.cit., pp. 68–69.

In a Second Part, we will review the activities of a few selected NGOs to ascertain whether the original neutrality and discretion principles of the international humanitarian pioneer, the Red Cross, is shared by other NGOs, and whether humanitarian organizations should consider, or not, the protection of human rights as one of their functions, in addition to their basic relief role. We will first recall the traditional principles and practices of the ICRC and identify recent challenges to the Red Cross "dogma" of neutrality, discretion and silence. We will then consider the role and practices of different types of NGOs, including the "British Charities", the religious Agencies, Medical Volunteers and the U.N. Volunteer Programme. This selection of NGOs is clearly not exhaustive: among the numerous humanitarian voluntary agencies, a choice had to be made, at the risk of being unfair and/or incomplete.

In a Third Part, we will review the legal status of humanitarian NGOs and consider whether international volunteers should have an international legal status in order to assure their protection, in the interest of humanitarian relief programmes. We will then examine more specifically the protection of the volunteer doctor. Finally, we will assess the need for new international regulation to formalize a proclaimed "right of humanitarian intervention".

PART I

HUMANITARIAN ASSISTANCE AND VOLUNTARISM

International humanitarian assistance is based on the contributions of governmental, intergovernmental and non-governmental entities, as well as contributions from individuals. The effectiveness of the international humanitarian network is dependent on the financial and material resources made available to these entities, their access to the victims, their technical performance, their interest and dynamism, their ability to cooperate at the international and local levels, and to build on separate and sometimes specialized efforts.

In Chapter 1, the role and characteristics of intergovernmental organizations will be considered, and in Chapter 2, the role and characteristics of non-governmental organizations. In Chapter 3, the nature and evolution of national and international voluntarism.

As an introduction to these Chapters, the role of states, as the main actors on the international scene, will be mentioned briefly, although the main focus of this book is on international humanitarian volunteers and non-governmental organizations.

The Role of States

Countries may be arbitrarily separated into those which need and receive international relief assistance, and those which provide this assistance. This distinction may become blurred when some donor countries call for international aid in some specialized areas, and when recipient countries assist others, within their capacities.

Recipient Countries

Governments are responsible for the governance, administration and welfare of their own people. In case of natural or man-made disasters and emergencies, the national authorities are those who should initiate, manage, coordinate, implement and evaluate relief operations. U.N. resolutions on humanitarian assistance constantly reaffirm "the sovereignty, territorial integrity and national unity of states and ... that it is up to each state first and foremost to take care of the victims of natural disasters and similar emergency situations occurring on its territory"[1].

If a country needs external assistance, in view of insufficient resources or capacity, its government may request it, on a bilateral or multilateral basis, or it may accept such assistance, in funds, equipment and supplies, or in manpower (international medical or other relief workers). No state, intergovernmental or non-governmental organization can impose external aid on an afflicted country, whatever its needs are. Most developing countries, which are likely to need external assistance, stress the international law principle of national sovereignty and reject any overt or covert attempts to establish a "right and duty" of international humanitarian intervention" considered to be a gross interference in the domestic affairs of those states (see Chapter 11).

Some countries may be reluctant to ask for and receive external assistance for reasons of national pride: "we can manage". They may reject assistance from some countries or intergovernmental organization (IGO) for political, ideological or religious reasons.

Countries torn by civil war may suspend or reject external aid in the fear that it may reinforce and legitimize the rebels, as in Biafra in the late 1960s. In January 1990, the Secretary-General of the U.N. expressed concern to Ethiopia's President Lieutenant Colonel Mengistu Haile Mariam, about the threat of a major famine, and urged him to cooperate with relief agencies. Concern over Ethiopia's reluctance to allow these agencies to distribute food to millions of people facing starvation was shared by relief officials, the U.S. administration and other donors[2].

Donor Countries

Most Official Development Assistance (ODA) is provided by countries members of the Organization for Economic Co-operation and Development (OECD), the "Club of Rich Nations". As a percentage of gross national product, in 1988, the more generous countries were Norway (1.12 percent), the Netherlands (0.98), Denmark (0.89), Sweden (0.87), France (0.73), Finland (0.59), Canada (0.50). The percentage of Japan, Switzerland and the U.K. was 0.32 and that of the U.S.A., 0.20. The average ODA by OECD countries in 1988 was 0.35 percent[3]. Two-third of ODA is provided bilaterally, one-third through multilateral institutions.

A number of "Northern" governments have created departments to deal specifically with disaster assistance, within or separately from, development assis-

---

[1] U.N. General Assembly resolution 43/131 of 8 December 1988.

[2] *International Herald Tribune*, 18 January 1990.

[3] *OECD Report, Development Assistance Committee*, 1989.

tance departments. For instance, the Disaster Unit in the U.K. Overseas Development Administration, the Emergency and Humanitarian Aid Section in the Netherlands Ministry of Foreign Affairs[4].

The Swedish International Development Authority (SIDA) has a Disaster Relief Section in its NGO Division. Swedish government assistance to the development of Third World countries grew out of the international experience of Swedish NGOs, such as trade unions, Christian missionary societies, producer and consumer cooperatives, youth and women's movements, humanitarian aid organizations. In the 1940s, they requested government support and they were invited to influence the formulation of the official programme of development cooperation. In 1952, a central Swedish Committee was formed with representatives of voluntary organizations and of the government. In 1962, SIDA was founded. Its board of directors includes a number of NGO representatives. About 10 percent of public assistance funds are used for NGO projects[5].

The OECD countries' average of state support to NGOs, as a percentage of ODA, was 5.3 percent in 1986: it was 14 percent in Switzerland, 11.1 percent in the U.S.A., 9.9 percent in Canada, 6.5 percent in the Federal Republic of Germany— only 0.3 percent in France[6]. Several donor countries have created government-NGO liaison units: for instance, the Canadian Council for International Cooperation, the DANIDA (Danish International Development Agency) Secretariat, the Norwegian Catastrophe Committee[7].

As recent examples of bilateral aid in emergency situations, in July 1989, President Bush approved a $2 million U.S. contribution in response to the appeal for Lebanon sponsored by the International Committee of the Red Cross, to provide emergency medical and relief supplies. In addition, American NGOs provided more than $14 million in food assistance. France granted $7 million in September 1989, also to Lebanon[8].

The contributions of donor governments in development and relief assistance is therefore a major and essential one, both in bilateral and multilateral aid, the latter through financial and other support to IGOs and NGOs. IGOs are almost entirely dependent on the obligatory and voluntary contributions of member states. NGOs of OECD countries received significant government subsidies for the financing of individual projects, from 50 to 100 percent, besides government and IGO subventions to their regular budget[9].

---

[4] *Anatomy of Disaster Relief—The International Network in Action*, Randolph C. Kent, Pinter Publ., 1987, p. 53.

[5] "Democracy as a Force for Development and the Role of Swedish Assistance, by Ernst Michanek, in *Development Dialogue*, Uppsala, 1985/1.

[6] *Voluntary Aid for Development, The Role of Non-Governmental Organizations*, OECD, Paris, 1988, p. 83.

[7] Kent, op.cit., p. 48.

[8] *Daily Bulletin*, U.S. Mission (Geneva), No. 139, 26 July 1989 and *Le Monde*. 10–11 September 1989.

[9] *Voluntary Aid*, op.cit., p. 86.

CHAPTER 1

THE ROLE AND CHARACTERISTICS OF THE INTERGOVERNMENTAL ORGANIZATIONS

Since World War II, together with the creation and growth of global and regional intergovernmental organizations (IGOs), humanitarian relief activities have been increasingly entrusted to specialized intergovernmental bodies, or relief tasks have been added to organizations' basic constitutional activities in the social and economic fields.

The expansion of international relief assistance through IGOs has responded to chronic or recurrent needs created by military, political, economic and social problems, or by natural disasters, mostly in Third World countries. Better communications made these needs better and more quickly known in all parts of the world, while technical and medical progress, and more efficient transportation methods enabled relief to be brought more quickly to those in need.

The relatively new realization of an interdependent world and a spirit of solidarity between the rich and the poor countries have developed this trend. Most rich countries have accepted an obligation to assist afflicted countries on a bilateral and multilateral basis.

Although the largest resources are given through bilateral aid, donor governments want to show their international solidarity and generosity, and improve their public international image by supporting the humanitarian activities of IGOs.

Recipient countries generally favour untied multilateral aid as, in contrast with bilateral assistance, multilateral aid does not create political and/or economic dependence and obligations towards one specific country.

Characteristics of IGOs

Created and financed by Member states, IGOs benefit from government support and share some of governments' authority and prestige. The IGOs and their staff have a legitimate international status, recognized in constitutions, international conventions and host agreements.

IGOs are structured, organized bureaucracies which ensure permanency and continuity of action. Global IGOs are present in most countries through their accredited regional or country representatives and offices. IGOs have access, on request, to their member countries. They communicate officially with the member states' government authorities in their capitals and through the governments' permanent delegations to the IGO.

IGO governing bodies formulate, approve and publicize international policies and strategies which enjoy global (or regional) legitimacy and serve as objectives and guidelines for countries and NGO action. For instance, the "Health For All by Year 2000" slogan, adopted by the World Health Assembly in 1977 (Resolution WHA30.43) and the recommendations of the joint WHO/UNICEF report of the International Conference on Primary Health Care held at Alma-Ata in September 1978, were adopted by other U.N. agencies and most NGOs as the basis for public health strategies and programmes at the global, national and local level (WHO Resolution WHA32.30, May 1979).

Some IGOs are financed by member states through assessed contributions, which gives them a relatively stable income, except for withholdings and delayed payments by some states. Some IGOs are financed in part, or totally, by voluntary contributions, which makes them more dependent on donors and more responsive to their demands. Their capacity to attract voluntary government and private funds will depend on their past performance record, their reputed impartiality, their ability to respond quickly to emergencies, their particular specialized competence, their known management skills, their financial accountability and integrity. It will also depend on the relative mediatization and politicisation of emergencies, their "attractiveness" to public opinion. NGOs, which depend entirely on voluntary contributions, are subject to similar constraints.

While IGOs provide order and continuity, their bureaucratic nature may tend to slow or stall progress, to stifle initiatives, to discourage innovation.

The intergovernmental structure of IGOs implies that they are dependent on the agreement of governments to provide assistance to their populations. Decisions on major or sensitive issues can only be taken by IGO secretariats after formal or informal clearance by governing bodies, or by important, or directly concerned, member states. IGO secretariats have to accept and implement decisions of their governing bodies, even if these decisions are politically motivated, controversial, or technically unsound.

The bureaucratic and diplomatic nature of IGOs explains, although it does not always justify, the international secretariats' political and operational caution, their fear of antagonizing Member states, which may paralyse or sterilize their humanitarian action and subject them to media criticisms of "cowardice", partiality and politicization. IGOs are necessarily conformist, in contrast with the NGOs freedom to either agree and conform, or to disagree, or to rebel against governments' politics, action or inaction. IGOs are bound by their constitutions, their statutes and mandates, they are more or less closely controlled by their intergovernmental governing bodies, and they are monitored closely by some of their member states.

Diplomatic and bureaucratic structures are needed in international relations generally, and in international relief in particular, provided that notice is taken of their strengths and limitations.

One limitation is that the role of most IGOs is of an advisory and not operational nature: WHO representatives and field workers advise governments, they do not run hospitals. Some UNHCR staff consider themselves as "diplomats". IGO staff raise and distribute funds, formulate programmes, obtain governments' agreements to activities, but they do not usually do the "dirty work", the direct contact with the afflicted people, the care and education: the "dirty work" is mainly done by the international and indigenous NGOs: however, some UNHCR, UNICEF, WHO and World Food Programme field workers share in the "daily grind" of direct, personal assistance.

The following summary includes the main past and present IGOs which have had, or have now, a "full-time" or "part-time" humanitarian role: the mandate of some IGOs, like that of the U.N. High Commissioner for Refugees, is entirely dedicated to humanitarian assistance, while the mandate of others, like that of the World Health Organization, includes "emergency assistance" as only one of many other functions.

For existing organizations, their recent role in emergency relief operations and their interaction with non-governmental organizations (NGOs) will be underlined, without attempting to give a complete and detailed description of all the IGOs' history, structure and programmes.

An original and pioneering effort to organize intergovernmental and nongovernmental cooperation in the humanitarian field during World War I was carried out by the Commission for Relief in Belgium between 1914 and 1919. A hybrid entity, the Commission was a "general" relief NGO, with IGO characteristics.

Other predecessors to existing U.N. bodies were all concerned with refugee protection and assistance and dealt mostly with European refugees: The League of Nations Nansen Office (1921–1930), the ineffective International Relief Union (IRU — 1927–1966), the U.N. Relief and Rehabilitation Administration (UNRRA — 1943–1948), and the International Refugee Organization (IRO—1948–1952).

The present refugee organizations include the U.N. Relief and Works Agency for Palestine Refugees in the Near East (UNRWA), established in 1949, and the U.N. High Commissioner for Refugees (UNHCR), established in 1951, "temporary" organizations which are likely to continue their work as long as refugees remain an international problem.

Outside the U.N. family, the International Organization for Migration (IOM) has organized migration movements (under other names), since 1952.

Created in 1946, the U.N. Children's Fund's (UNICEF) mandate for assistance to children in developing countries is essentially humanitarian, although it has expanded into development assistance. The World Health Organization (WHO), established in 1948, has an "emergency assistance" function, among others, and it cooperates closely with UNICEF in health care programmes.

The World Food Programme (WFP), by its nature, has responded to emergency needs since 1961.

Other U.N. organizations, such as U.N. Educational, Scientific and Cultural Organization (UNESCO), the Food and Agriculture Organization of the U.N. (FAO), the International Labour Organisation (ILO), the World Meteorological Organization (WMO), the U.N. Environment Programme (UNEP), have emergency preparedness and response activities, with direct or indirect humanitarian impact.

The Office of the U.N. Disaster Relief Coordinator (UNDRO), created in 1971, has been given a directing and coordinating function as focal point in the U.N. system for disaster relief matters. UNDRO is represented in the field by U.N. Development Programme (UNDP) resident representatives. UNDP also sponsors the U.N. Volunteer Programme, which has recently been involved in emergency relief work.

Regional IGOs, such as principally the European Economic Community (EEC), and others, including the Organization of American States (OAS), the Organization of African Unity (OAU), the Association of South East Asian Nations (ASEAN), also play a role in international relief work.

The Commission for Relief in Belgium (CRB)

During World War I, the first large scale international operation of humanitarian assistance was undertaken on behalf of the civilian populations of occupied Belgium and northern France, in response to the threat of famine in that region. The relief operation dealt with a population of 9 million people, without means of income, cut off from their sources of supply, in a territory of 20,000 square miles under German control. Macalister-Smith[1] relates this extraordinary and successful humanitarian venture.

The CRB was created by Herbert Hoover in 1914, with the preliminary agreement of the U.S.A., France and the U.K.,—and Germany. Germany agreed to grant complete freedom of movement for CRB staff within Belgium.

The CRB was accountable to the Western Allies for the fulfilment of German guarantees regarding the protection and equitable use of supplies. It was accountable to the German government for the conduct of a strictly humanitarian relief operation for the benefit of Belgian and French civilians.

Between 1914 and 1919, the CRB procured, shipped and supervised the distribution of relief supplies sufficient to maintain the protected population at subsistence level, and it also supported welfare services.

As noted by Macalister-Smith:

The CRB was an organization without precedents in international relations. It

---

[1] The author is indebted to Peter Macalister-Smith's book on *International Humanitarian Assistance — Disaster Relief Actions in International Law and Organizations*, M. Nijhoff/Henry Dunant Institute, Geneva, 1985 in particular for the information and assessment on the CRB, the League of Nations work for refugees, the IRU, UNRRA and the IRO. Detailed references to this book are made hereunder.

appeared to be an *ad hoc* private international organization on a temporary basis, but in the performance of its functions the Commission possessed many of the attributes of state institutions. It negotiated and concluded agreements at the highest level, and enjoyed important immunities granted by the belligerents. Its representatives in military occupied regions operated with wide powers and privileges, and it flew its own flag and issued its own passports. The CRB operated a large fleet of ocean vessels and canal boats, and by its existence and in the actual discharge of its relief functions it assumed the fundamental responsibility of providing for the basic needs of a whole population.

...In particular, the Commission's political neutrality and operational independence, and its director's capacity to negotiate directly and impartially with all sides involved, indicate minimum requirements for any relief operation or relief organization. The level of international cooperation developed by the CRB in its global network of procurement offices and supporting charitable organizations was also a valuable precedent for the conduct of future relief programmes[2].

In summary, the CRB was a temporary international NGO with some IGO attributes. No doubt the precedent of the International Committee of the Red Cross, which has similar characteristics of a hybrid NGO/IGO, served as an example when the CRB mandate was elaborated. In turn, later humanitarian organizations and operations have benefitted from the experience acquired by the CRB venture.

The League of Nations

On 20 August 1921, the League of Nations appointed Dr. Fridtjof Nansen, the Norwegian scholar, explorer and philanthropist, as the High Commissioner for Russian Refugees. Most original refugees resulted from the Russian Revolution of 1917, but additional numbers from other European sources converted the initially "temporary" programme into a permanent activity: a process which has often applied to "temporary" U.N. bodies in the humanitarian and other fields. The competence of the Commissioner was later extended to cover Armenians, Assyrians, Assyro-Chaldeans and Turks, and to refugees from the Near East.

The Red Cross Societies and other charitable organizations, as well as a number of governments, had initiated international refugee work during the first World War. A Conference of such NGOs, convened by the ICRC and the League of Red Cross Societies had then brought the question of refugee protection to the attention of the Council of the League of Nations.

On the death of Dr. Nansen, in 1930, the Nansen International Office for Refugees was created by a resolution of the Assembly of the League of Nations, as an autonomous body responsible for the exercise of functions of humanitarian assistance. In 1933, a new High Commissioner for Refugees Coming from

---

[2] Macalister-Smith, op.cit., pp. 10–12.

24

Germany was appointed. In 1938, both offices were closed, and a new High Commissioner for Refugees under the Protection of the League of Nations was appointed: he was to coordinate humanitarian assistance provided by other organizations.

The Evian Conference of 1938, convened at the initiative of President F.D. Roosevelt to deal with political and economic questions arising from the exodus of refugees from Germany and Austrian set up the Intergovernmental Committee on Refugees, headed by the High Commissioner.

World War II interrupted the League of Nations' activities in the field of refugee work[3].

The International Relief Union

In 1927, an International Conference adopted the Convention and Statute of a new IGO, the International Relief Union (IRU)[4].

IRU was created through the desire of nations "to render aid to each other in disasters, to encourage international relief by a methodical coordination of available resources, and to further the progress of international law in this field". IRU's objectives were primarily "in the event of any disaster due to 'force majeure', the exceptional gravity of which exceeds the limits of the powers and resources of the stricken people,—to furnish to the suffering population first-aid and to assemble for this purpose funds, resources and assistance of all kinds,—to coordinate the efforts of other relief organizations in the event of any disaster,—to encourage the study of preventive measures against disasters,—and to induce all peoples to render mutual international assistance" (Art. 2 of the IRU Convention). The two main principles of the IRU were respect for the territorial sovereignty of member states and non-discrimination in assistance. The IRU was granted legal personality as well as certain immunities, facilities and privileges for its establishment and personnel. Such privileges and immunities also extended to all organizations, including NGOs, acting on behalf of the IRU.

The ICRC and the League of Red Cross Societies were to supply the permanent central service of the IRU, under the direction of the IRU Executive Committee. This would have subordinated the independent Red Cross to the authority of an IGO, an unlikely arrangement.

After 30 states adhered to the Convention, the first meeting of the IRU General Council was held in 1933, a fateful year for Germany and Europe. Inadequate

[3] Gilbert Jaeger's Chapter on "Participation of NGOs in the activities of the UNHCR", in *Pressure Groups in the Global System*, Peter Willetts, Ed, Pinter Publ.,1982, p. 171. See also A. LeRoy Bennett's *International Organizations*, Third Ed., Prentice-Hall, 1984, pp. 287–288 and Macalister-Smith, op.cit., pp. 15–16.
[4] Macalister-Smith, op.cit., pp. 18–21, 95–96.

funding, the economic depression, the political conflicts and increasing tension, and World War II, prevented the IRU from giving effective relief. Its work was in practice limited to scientific studies.

The IRU formally disappeared as an organization in the later 1960s, when some of its functions and assets were transferred to UNESCO.

The U.N. Relief and Rehabilitation Administration (UNRRA)

UNRRA was created by an international agreement signed by representatives of more than 40 governments in November 1943[5]. It therefore preceded the later (1945) creation of the U.N. itself. The "United Nations" of UNRRA were those 26 countries whose representatives had signed the "Declaration by United Nations" of 1 January 1942, pledging their governments to continue fighting together against the Axis Powers, Germany, Italy and Japan.

UNRRA's three main tasks were relief, rehabilitation and resettlement of certain groups of displaced persons. The relief of victims of war in any area under the control of any of the United Nations, included the production, transportation and provision of food, fuel, clothing, shelter and other basic necessities, medical and other essential services. UNRRA was an organization for charitable relief through international cooperation.

Like later refugee organizations, UNRRA was financed by governments on a voluntary basis. The independence of UNRRA representatives was protected by immunities and the transport of its supplies benefitted from priorities. The formal establishment of missions in recipient countries was preceded by the conclusion of a detailed agreement between the government concerned and UNRRA.

The organization operated from 1943 to 1948. Its peak staffing, in 1946, amounted to 3,400 employees at its headquarters and at its London regional office, plus 24 country missions with staff ranging from 1,300 in China to 10 in the Ukraine, an additional 17 regional shipping and procurement officers, numerous short-term diplomatic missions, as well as a separate displaced persons operation with a staff of 5,000.

From 1943 to 1947, UNRRA furnished almost $4 billion worth of supplies for relief and rehabilitation. Recipient governments were required to sell most of the supplies and use the funds for UNRRA-approved rehabilitation projects. UNRRA delivered the goods to the countries, but internal distribution was the responsibility of the receiving state, although UNRRA maintained surveillance over the process. The approach was one of self-help and internal responsibility with external assistance. The U.S. was the chief donor, supplying more than two-thirds of the goods and money.

UNRRA served a vital purpose in helping the war-devastated countries of

---

[5] Macalister-Smith, op.cit., pp. 12–14.

Europe and Asia to meet their immediate relief needs of food, clothing and medical supplies at the survival level, to prevent starvation and the spread of infectious diseases. It helped from 9 to 14 million displaced persons (according to varying estimates) return to their homes. Nevertheless, more than a million displaced persons remained, most of whom sought resettlement rather than repatriation[6].

While the CRB was a NGO, UNRRA had the status of an IGO. While the CRB worked in "enemy-occupied" territories, UNRRA only worked in liberated areas. In both cases, however, the humanitarian operational cooperation concept was applied internationally: the mobilization of resources on a voluntary basis and their distribution in accordance with needs.

Although UNICEF was the more direct successor of UNRRA ($34 million of residual assets were transferred to UNICEF), UNRRA's projects in the field of agriculture and health were transferred respectively to FAO and WHO. More broadly, UNRRA's experience and some of its staff contributed to other U.N. bodies (IRO and UNHCR) and to the Intergovernmental Committee on Migration (now IOM).

The International Refugee Organization (IRO)

The International Refugee Organization (IRO) was established in August 1948 by a Resolution of the U.N. General Assembly (Resol. 62(I) 1946) to succeed the existing international organizations engaged in assisting and repatriating refugees, displaced persons and prisoners of war, of whom there were, initially, some twenty-one million scattered throughout Europe. The tasks of the IRO were mainly the protection and resettlement of those refugees and displaced persons who were reluctant to return to their homelands either because they had lost all ties there, or because of a well-founded fear of persecution.

The IRO was intended as a temporary specialized agency of the U.N. whose primary objective was to seek solutions to the problems of refugees and displaced persons still living in camps, mostly in Austria, Germany and Italy. Like the UNRRA, the IRO was essentially a field agency conducting its own assistance activities with the help and support of local authorities and voluntary agencies.

In its $4\frac{1}{2}$ years of existence, the IRO assisted over 1,619,000 refugees and displaced persons and operated over 670 refugee centres. Most refugees and displaced persons were re-settled in the U.S.A., Canada, Australia and Latin America.

As most of the refugees and displaced persons were fleeing Soviet-occupied Eastern Europe, political controversies affected IRO's work: Western countries maintained that the refugees could choose between repatriation to their countries of origin or resettlement to asylum countries, while the USSR maintained that the IRO was required to promote repatriation. It followed that the Soviet Union and other

---

[6] LeRoy Bennett, op.cit., p. 235 and Harold K. Jacobson, *Networks of Interdependence — International Organizations and the Global Political System*, 2nd Ed., A.A. Knopf, New York, 1984, p. 340.

Eastern European States were bitterly critical of the IRO, which contributed to its closure and to the creation of the UNHCR as a "non-political" body.

The IRO's operations ceased on 1 March 1952[7].

The U.N. High Commissioner for Refugees (UNHCR)

Creation and Mandate

The mandate and activities of the UNHCR are wholly humanitarian in the specialized field of international refugees' protection and assistance. They are in part of a legal nature (international protection) and in part of an operational nature. The latter category of activities, on which we will focus, is carried out in close association with humanitarian NGOs. In view of its limited financial and staffing resources, the UNHCR needs and uses the complementary support and action of NGOs in order to fulfil its operational mandate.

The Office of the UNHCR is a subsidiary organ of the U.N. General Assembly established under Article 22 of the Charter to assume responsibility for international action in favour of refugees, upon the demise of the IRO. As an *ad hoc*, semi-autonomous body within the administrative and financial framework of the U.N., its sponsors wanted the new body to be capable of acting independently, remaining as far as possible outside the political considerations with which the U.N. secretariat has to deal. Paragraph 2 of its Statute states that

> The work of the High Commissioner shall be of an entirely non-political character: it shall be humanitarian and social ...

However, as the causes and consequences of refugee problems are highly political, on a national and international basis, the UNHCR, like other IGOs, has not been immune to political pressures and crises.

The recent conflict between the UNHCR and Somalia is symptomatic of some of the problems of humanitarian assistance: should an IGO exert control over relief supplies provided to a government by international aid?

In October 1988, High Commissioner Jean-Pierre Hocké decided to gradually end all assistance programmes to Ethiopian refugees in Somalia. The Somalia government was being suspected of :—corruption with regard to the generous budget ($30 to 35 million annually),—swollen estimates of the number of refugees in Somalia (840,000),—forced military recruitment of refugees. On 5 August 1989, the UNHCR representative, Mr. Abdallah Saied, was expelled from Somalia. The suspension of the regular programme of UNHCR and the World Food Programme (WFP) became effective in October 1989.

In a conciliatory and humanitarian move, the U.N. Secretary-General launched

---

[7] Macalister-Smith, op.cit., pp. 35–36, Randolph C. Kent, *Anatomy of Disaster Relief—The International Network in Action*, Pinter Publ., 1987, pp. 37–38,—UNHCR *Information Paper*, pp. 1–2.

in February 1990 an "Extraordinary Interim Emergency Programme for Somalia", which was to provide emergency relief assistance to 140,000 refugees for six months. The UNHCR would use its "good offices" with donors to obtain resources.

Like that of the other U.N. organizations, the mandate of the UNHCR is universal: it is called on to protect refugees whoever and wherever they may be.

The competence of the UNHCR applies to refugees as defined under its Statute, for persons in refugee-like situations, including displaced persons due to man-made disasters[8].

According to Kent[9], the UNHCR extends its "good offices" to assist non-statutory refugees when it feels that governments will accept such non-mandated involvement.

Yet should governments show any sign that the UNHCR might be overstepping the mark, the organization will retreat into the most conservative and prudent approach to fulfilling its responsibilities.

Which IGO would do otherwise, at the risk of damaging its relationships with one or several of its member states? Furthermore, the UNHCR's financial dependence on voluntary contributions makes it particularly susceptible to pressures by the main Western donor governments.

On the other hand, this is one of the areas where NGOs can, and do, ignore diplomatic fiats, at the risk of being expelled from the host country, but without other diplomatic or financial implications. On the contrary, the image of an NGO may benefit from an act of independence, for purely humanitarian reasons, in relation to donor or recipient countries.

The two main functions of the UNHCR are the protection of refugees and the seeking of permanent solutions to their problems. The Office assists governments and, subject to the approval of the governments concerned, private organizations (NGOs) to facilitate the voluntary repatriation of the refugees, or their assimilation within new national communities.

As recognised by the XXIVth International Conference of the Red Cross, the UNHCR has a primary function in the field of international protection and material assistance to refugees, persons displaced outside their country of origin and returnees[10].

However, except in special circumstances, its material assistance activities are conducted through national or local authorities of the country concerned, other

---

[8] *Le Monde*, 16 Nov. 1988, 6–7 Aug. 1989, 1 Nov. 1989, 16 March 1990, *U.N. Press Release* SG/SM/1085 of 16 Feb.1990. U.N. Doc.A/40/348 of 9 Oct. 1985: *New International Humanitarian Order, Report of the Secretary-General Submitted Pursuant to General Assembly resolution 38/125*, pp. 20–21.

[9] Kent, op.cit., p. 91.

[10] *International Red Cross Handbook*, Geneva, 12th Ed., July 1983, p. 665.

U.N. organizations, NGOs or private technical agencies. Such activities include emergency relief, assistance in voluntary repatriation or local integration, resettlement to other countries, counselling, education and legal assistance.

Relations with other IGOs

Since 1988, UNDP has continued to administer various projects on behalf of the UNHCR, in countries where the UNHCR is not represented.

WHO has financed the costs of health coordinators or consultants for refugee missions. The WFP meets the majority of refugees' basic food aid needs. UNESCO assists in refugee education, UNICEF in primary health care, water supply and basic sanitation, and in vaccination programmes.

Cooperation is also achieved with the International Fund for Agricultural Development, the World Bank, UNIDO, the U.N. Volunteer Programme, UNDRO, FAO and others.

At the regional level, cooperation is carried out with the Organization of African Unity, the Arab League, the Organization of American States, the Council of Europe, the European Community and others[11].

Relations with NGOs

As an integral part of the U.N., the UNHCR grants to NGOs the consultative status that each of them has with the Economic and Social Council, i.e. Category I, II and Roster[12]. At the same time, the UNHCR, in an essentially pragmatic attitude, cooperates with any organization if it considers that such cooperation is beneficial to refugees and provided that the cooperation is carried out for humanitarian and social, non political, purposes.

As noted by Jaeger[13], the NGOs represent the organized expression of interested public opinion, as well as field workers who can make informal and close contact with the individual refugee and his family.

The UNHCR establishes contractual relationships with the NGOs under varying terms. Some contracts are financed entirely by the UNHCR, while, in other cases, the NGO makes a contribution in personnel, relief supplies (medicaments, foodstuffs) and/or in cash. The supplementing role of the NGOs is more evident in material assistance. NGOs frequently distribute food, clothing and blankets, organize health and sanitation services and initiate or assume full responsibility for the process of integration.

The UNHCR needs the agreement of the recipient government to provide opera-

---

[11] U.N. Doc. A/44/12, 1989, *Report of the U.N. High Commissioner for Refugees*, pp. 36–40.

[12] For 1989, see U.N. Doc. *1989/NGO List*, Parts I and II.

[13] Jaeger, in Willetts, op.cit., pp. 171–178.

30

tional assistance. NGOs contracted by the Office are also subject to the agreement, or consent, of the government concerned. Some governments are reluctant to allow NGOs to deal with refugee programmes in view of their sensitive political implications.

A few examples of UNHCR/NGO interaction follow, related to 1987-1988 activities.

In Zambia, UNHCR assistance projects to 146,100 refugees have been implemented through NGOs under the overall supervision of the Ministry of Home Affairs, Zambian Office of the Commissioner for Refugees. UNHCR has provided approximately 85 percent of the total budget, the remaining 15 percent being covered by some of the major agencies, usually to cover salaries of their international staff and administrative or operational support costs. The principal agencies were: — the Lutheran World Federation, the Catholic Secretariat of Zambia, the Save the Children Federation (U.S.A.), the Christian Council of Zambia, the two Federations of Employers, Zambia Red Cross Society (with the assistance of the League of Red Cross and Red Crescent Societies), Médecins Sans Frontières (MSF/France), the African National Congress, the South West African People's Organization, the Young Men's Christian Association.

In Honduras, Caritas, the Comita Evangelico de Desarrollo y Emergencia Nacional, the Mennonite Central Committee, Catholic Relief Services and MSF/France have provided multi-purpose assistance on behalf of Salvadorian and Guatemalan refugees.

In Malaysia, a National Task Force within the Prime Minister's Department acted as the government's focal point on matters related to the Vietnamese refugee programme. The Malaysian Red Crescent Society was UNHCR's sole operational partner for this programme, and was assisted by personnel seconded by several organizations, such as MSF/France, World Concern, Ecoles Sans Frontières, the Jesuit Refugee Service. The Malaysian Muslim Welfare Organization was UNHCR's implementing partner for the programme of local integration of Indo-Chinese Muslims[14].

In countries where no NGO coordinating structure exists, UNHCR should take the lead in encouraging NGOs to set up their own coordinating committee and mechanisms[15].

In Geneva, regular contacts with NGOs is maintained through UNHCR participation in the monthly Emergency and Disaster Coordination Meeting, held at the headquarters of the League of Red Cross and Red Crescent Societies. UNHCR also organizes briefing and consultation sessions with NGOs, as well as training workshops on emergency management[16].

---

[14] U.N. Doc. A/AC.96/708 (Part I, II, IV), *UNHCR Activities financed by voluntary funds, Report for 1987–1988 and Proposed Programmes and Budget for 1989, Africa, Latin America and the Caribbean, Asia and Oceania.*

[15] UNHCR *Handbook for Emergencies,* pp. 175–176.

[16] U.N.Doc. A/44/12,1989, pp. 40–41.

Some sixty NGOs were represented by observers at the Thirty-Ninth Session of the Executive Committee of the High Commissioner's Programme held in Geneva, 3–10 October 1988, including the International Committee of the Red Cross (ICRC), the League and the International Council of Voluntary Agencies[17].

Budget and Staffing

Total expenditures in 1988 were $565 million, including approximately $20 million financed by the U.N. regular budget, essentially for administrative costs, and $545 million as voluntary funds. 1978 expenditures were $134.7 million.

For 1988, governments (mainly the U.S.A., Japan, the Federal Republic of Germany, Italy, Sweden, Denmark, Canada—no Socialist State) contributed $428 million, IGOs (mainly the European Community) $47 million, NGOs and other donors $7 million. Almost half of the expenditures went to refugee programmes in Africa[18].

UNHCR budget is mainly dependent on states' voluntary contributions which, in turn, depend mainly on the good will and interest of Western donors and on the capacity of the Commissioner to attract funds.

At 31 December 1988, UNHCR employed 2,170 staff members, including 738 professional and 1432 general service staff. 77 percent were assigned away from the UNHCR Geneva headquarters[19]. UNHCR staffing in 1982 was 1,349 staff members.

In November 1989, Thorvald Stoltenberg, a Norwegian diplomat, was elected by the General Assembly, upon nomination of the U.N. Secretary-General, to replace Jean-Pierre Hocké (Switzerland) as High Commissioner for a four-year period beginning 1 January 1990.

Appointed High Commissioner in January 1986, J.P. Hocké seemed to be ideally suited for the post. Delegate of the ICRC in Nigeria in 1968, he became Director of Operations of the Committee in 1973, and, in 1975, he was named to the Committee's three member Directorate. His downfall (he resigned on 25 October 1989) resulted from criticisms of his "autocratic" management style, and the alleged misuse of funds for his own first-class air travel. During the UNHCR Executive Committee meeting of 5-13 October 1989, the organization was experiencing its most serious financial crisis at a time when the High Commissioner was personally embarrassed by media accusations. Hocké had lost the confidence of some of the powerful members of the Committee and had critics among his own staff. There was also tension between the High Commissioner and the U.N. Secretary-General. His resignation became unavoidable.

---

[17] U.N. Doc. A/AC.96/721 of 13 Oct. 1988.

[18] U.N. Doc. A/44/12, 1989, Annex.

[19] U.N. Doc. ACC/1989/PER/R.11 of 20 July 1989, *Personnel Statistics.*

On 2 November 1990, T. Stoltenberg unexpectedly resigned to become his country's foreign minister, leaving the organization in some disarray[20].

Evaluation

An internal self-evaluation system was introduced in UNHCR in 1980. Since 1988, self-evaluations have been prepared for all major operational activities, with the introduction of field statement of objectives for each country. Evaluations include recommendations for the improvement of programmes[21].

A 1984 Joint Inspection Unit (JIU) report[22] gave both praise and criticism to UNHCR activities in South-East Asia between 1979 and 1983.

The report stated that UNHCR had weathered a major refugee crisis in the region with the concerted support of the international community. This was an impressive achievement, representing the most large-scale intercontinental movement of refugees in UNHCR history. Success was also achieved in its resource mobilization endeavours.

On the other hand, the report underlined weaknesses in the administration and financial operations of field offices, performed mostly by inexperienced local clerical staff with little training and experience in UNHCR administrative policies and procedures. This required a strengthening of the organization and staffing of UNHCR field offices, including the assignment of experienced headquarters staff to reinforce field offices when needed.

Another JIU report on "The Role of the UNHCR in Africa" (Doc. JIU/REP/86/2) identified similar weaknesses in the management of field offices and the need for its strengthening.

When the General Assembly decided to continue the Office of the UNHCR for a further five years from 1 January 1989 (Resolution 42/108 of 7 December 1987), it acknowledged:

— the need for concerted international action on behalf of the increasing numbers of refugees,

— the outstanding work performed by the Office in providing international protection and material assistance to refugees and displaced persons as well as in promoting permanent solutions to their problems,

---

[20] *Le Monde* of 28 Oct. 1989, UNHCR *Refugees* of Nov. 1989, Quaker U.N. Office in Geneva *Newsletter*, Oct.-Dec. 1989. According to *Journal de Genève* of 31 March/1 Apr. 1990, a U.N. Inquiry Committee concluded that Mr. Hocké had not violated any regulation concerning the use of UNHCR funds. This was confirmed by the Danish Auditing Court: *Tribune de Genève*, 3 Oct. 1990. On T. Stoltenberg's resignation, see *Le Monde*, 4–5 Nov. 1990.

[21] U.N. Doc. A/AC.96/709 of 24 Aug. 1988, *Overview of UNHCR Activities, Report for 1987–1988 Submitted by the High Commissioner*, pp. 32–33.

[22] JIU/REP/84/15 in U.N. Doc. A/40/34, 1985, *Report of the Joint Inspection Unit.*

— the effective manner in which the Office had been dealing with various essential humanitarian tasks entrusted to it.

A World Council of Churches representative stated in December 1989, when T. Stoltenberg was elected as High Commissioner, that a strong UNHCR was needed. He added that the church, as one of the very few international bodies with a global constituency, and as an advocate for refugees, must play a major role in discussions of the future international refugee system. UNHCR must work more closely with the churches[23].

No doubt, other international NGOs share such views and demands, and also want a closer association with the UNHCR.

Current Problems

UNHCR ended 1989 with a unprecedented deficit of $38 million. While estimates of funding needed in 1990 amounted to some $702 million, voluntary contributions from mostly Western countries were expected to be limited to $378 million. In 1980, when there were seven million refugees, UNHCR had four times as many resources for each refugee as it had for 1990, to deal with 15 million refugees. At its 41st Session in October 1990, the Executive Committee of the UNHCR approved a programme target of $345.5 million for 1991 general programmes.

Donors' "compassion fatigue" explains in part the agency's financial problems. Official and public attitudes in Western countries have become negative towards a perceived unending flow of people from the Third World, fleeing not political persecution, but seemingly motivated by economic reasons, attracted by the wealthy North. Economic austerity in industrialized countries has also limited external financial aid.

Compassion fatigue also affects refugee acceptance in first-asylum and settlement countries.

For instance, in April 1990, the UNHCR protested against Malaysia's repeated denial of first-asylum of Vietnamese boat people, in violation of a June 1989 international agreement.

In the same month, advances by Burmese troops against rebellious ethnic minorities along the Thai border, created a new refugee problem, with thousands of Burmese seeking shelter and assistance in Thailand. Thailand put pressure on the UNHCR and relief agencies not to recognize the Burmese as refugees or give them aid. The Thais complained of a refugee "overload": 300,000 Cambodians and thousands of Vietnamese and Laotians: "Are we to shelter everybody?"

In Western Europe, acceptance rates of refugees, in 1989, averaged from 7 to 14 percent of all asylum seekers. Since the mid-1980s, policies described as "human

[23] WCC *Ecuview*, "The Church and Refugees", EPS 89.12.89.

deterrence" have been adopted in the region, including increasingly restrictive admission requirements. These new policies respond to public protests against the surge of legal and illegal immigrants, leading at times to minority but vocal rejection racist movements or demonstrations.

The previous High Commissioner, T. Stoltenberg, said in Canada

Charity is fine, but it is not enough. Refugees must be accepted as a political issue for the refugee-producing countries, the first-asylum countries and the donor countries.

Optimistically, he saw the warming of East and West relations as a harbinger of hope for the vast number of refugees in the world. He was then hoping that one candidate for a "peace dividend" would be an augmented refugee assistance budget. Although this expectation has not materialized yet, it was hoped that the election of Mrs. Sadako Ogata (Japan) to succeed Stoltenberg in January 1991 would restore the morale of the staff and regain the confidence of donor governments[24].

The U.N. Relief and Works Agency for Palestine Refugees in the Near East (UNRWA)

In 1948–1949, about three quarters of a million Palestinians became refugees in the Near East, following the creation of the State of Israel and the Arab-Israeli conflict. The number of registered refugees was more than 2.2 million on 30 June 1988.

On 8 December 1949, the U.N. General Assembly voted by Resolution 302 (IV) to set up UNRWA to carry out relief and works programmes for the Palestine refugees. UNRWA, a subsidiary organ of the General Assembly began operations on 1 May 1950. Its headquarters was originally in Beirut. It was transferred to Vienna in 1978.

The competencies of UNHCR and UNRWA do not overlap: refugees registered with UNRWA and receiving its assistance are excluded both from the competence of the UNHCR by paragraph 7(c) of the Statute, and from the terms of the 1951 Convention Relating to the Status of Refugees, by Art. 1(D)[25].

From a body largely devoted to meeting the emergency relief needs of a population displaced by the 1948 war, the Agency has evolved into one primarily concerned with the administration of quasi-governmental services of public education, public health and social welfare. Concurrently with this evolution, the Agency is still required to meet urgent needs of Palestine refugees affected by the periodic upheavals taking place in the region.

---

[24] *International Herald Tribune* of 28 March 1989, U.N. *Press Release* SI/06/90 of 2 April 1990, *Globe and Mail* of 10 April 1990, *New York Times* of 17, 18 Apr. 1990, *International Herald Tribune* of 14 Apr. 1990. The budgetary decisions of the UNHCR's Executive Committee, at its 41st Session, are in UNHCR Press Release Ref/1660 of 5 Oct. 1990. UNCHR Press Release REF/1663 of 21 Dec. 1990.

[25] Macalister-Smith, op.cit., p. 47.

As a result of the Israeli military action in Southern Lebanon in March 1978, about 67,000 Palestine refugees were temporarily displaced. An UNRWA emergency programme, launched with the help of the European Community, nine governments and several voluntary agencies, provided the displaced families with emergency assistance in the form of food, blankets and clothing[26].

In 1986 and 1987, UNRWA provided essential supplies of food and medicines to civilians besieged in Lebanese camps.

In 1987–1988, UNRWA expanded its relief and supplementary feeding programmes, its health centres and other medical facilities. On the other hand, vocational, technical and teacher training programmes in the occupied territories of the West Bank and the Gaza Strip were disrupted. Since early 1980, UNRWA basic education schools in the West Bank, normally attended by some 36,000 young Palestinians, have been closed by the Israeli authorities for "reasons of military security".

Between July 1988 and June 1989, Palestine refugees were confronted with emergencies in Lebanon, the West Bank and the Gaza Strip. In particular, in the occupied territories of the West Bank and Gaza Strip, the *intifidah* and the Israeli response thereto continued to affect virtually all UNRWA activities. Agency premises were violated more often than before and a number of local staff were arrested and detained without charges[27].

Consultations between UNRWA and NGOs were held in February 1986 at Amman, Jordan under the joint sponsorship of the UNRWA and the International Council of Voluntary Agencies. UNRWA was urged to expand its cooperation with NGOs, both those able to contribute funds to support programmes, and those interested in a more active role in the region.

Budget and Staffing

Since its creation, UNRWA has faced continued budget deficits, in view of its budgetary dependence on voluntary contributions, varying degree of donors' support, and variations in the value of currencies.

The Agency's income for 1988 was $206.1 million. Budget estimates for 1989 were $227.4 million. In addition, supplementary budgets to cover emergency operations amounted to $43.8 million. The main contributors (pledged contributions) for the 1989 budget were the U.S.A. (27 percent of the total budget), Sweden, Italy,

---

[26] *Basic Facts about the U.N.*, 1980, p. 79.

[27] U.N. Doc. A/43/13, 1988, *Report of the Commissioner-General of the UNRWA*, 1 July 1987–30 June 1988 and U.N. *Press Release* DH/379 of 29 March 1989. U.N. Doc. A/44/13, 1989, *Report of the Commissioner-General of the UNRWA*, 1 July 1988–30 June 1989, pp. 1–3. The tense relations between UNRWA and Israel were again demonstrated in November 1990, when the representative of Israel told the U.N. General Assembly Special Political Committee that the annual report of UNRWA was biased and unbalanced against Israel: see U.N. *Press Release* DH/760, 2 Nov. 1990.

Norway, Canada, the Federal Republic of Germany. The European Community's contribution was approximately $26.4 million, and the U.N. regular budget share, $7.8 million[28].

As of 31 December 1988, UNRWA employed 108 international staff members (98 professional, 10 general service) under regular U.N. employment conditions. It also employed, under special employment conditions, more than 18,000 locally recruited "area staff", the majority of whom are Palestine refugees. Area staff included, UNRWA is the largest body in the U.N. system.

A number of UNRWA area staff have been subjected to arrests and detention by the Israeli Defence Forces,—and more generally, UNRWA has been accused of serving as a Palestine Liberation Organization base. A few UNRWA area and international staff members have been abducted by "unknown elements" in Lebanon: eight such abductions were recorded by August 1989[29].

In 1983, the Joint Inspection Unit found that the agency, in cooperation with UNESCO and WHO, had developed an effective organization for humanitarian assistance in its three main programmes, education, health and relief services[30].

Over the years, UNRWA has come to be considered as a semi-permanent agency of the U.N. system. It will continue its humanitarian activities until a solution to the Palestinian problem has been found. In the meantime, its activities are subject to all the political, military, economic, social, financial and human rights uncertainties and challenges of the enduring conflict.

The International Organization for Migration (IOM)

IOM is not a U.N. agency, but it is a specialized intergovernmental body of 35 member countries and seventeen observer states. IOM is mainly a Western organization composed of the U.S.A., Australia, Israel and twelve Western European countries (not including the U.K. and France), ten Latin American countries, three Asian and one African countries. It is a non-political (but Western-oriented) and humanitarian organization, with a predominantly operational mandate and a strong interest in Latin America. It promoted "freedom of movement" as one of the basic human rights.

Founded in 1951, the organization (first named Intergovernmental Committee for European Migration (ICEM), then Intergovernmental Committee for Migration (ICM) in 1980, then IOM in 1989) commenced operations in 1952, with its headquarters in Geneva.

---

[28] U.N. Doc. A/44/13, Addendum, 17 Oct. 1989.

[29] *U.N. Special*, Geneva, Aug. 1989. In March 1990, Yasir Kazmuz, Palestinian Director of an UNRWA refugee camp in the occupied West Bank was killed by Arabs who accused him of being an Israeli informant and of embezzling U.N. funds. UNRWA "was not aware of any work-related allegations or complaints about his behaviour": International Herald Tribune, 29 March 1990.

[30] U.N. Doc. JIU/REP/83/8.

Initially, the most immediate task entrusted to the new organization was that of carrying out the movement of large numbers of persons who had freely chosen to migrate from Europe to overseas countries but did not possess the means to do so. Transport was then given the highest priority in the programme of its activities. At the same time, there remained the major problem of resettling several hundreds of thousands of refugees displaced by the war or by post-war political problems. The IRO's demise had created a gap and the new organization also had to deal with the movement and resettlement of the refugees. The organization later changed its priorities from transport to services. The primary goal was no longer to relieve Europe of the burden of a surplus population, but to further the development of other regions by providing them with the qualified professional and skilled personnel needed.

At present, the IOM has the following main functions:

— the handling of orderly and planned migration to meet specific needs of emigration and immigration countries;
— the processing and movement of refugees, displaced persons and other persons in need of international migration services to countries offering them resettlement opportunities;
— the transfer of qualified human resources to promote the socio-economic advancement of developing countries;
— the provision of a forum to states, intergovernmental and non-governmental organizations to exchange views and experiences on international migration issues.

Since 1952, IOM has assisted more than four million persons (three million refugees and one million national migrants). For refugees, IOM provides medical services, language and cultural orientation courses. For national migrants, it provides counselling, placement and integration.

In all migration activities, IOM arranges for reliable transportation at substantially reduced costs, and seeks, in close cooperation with governments and other agencies, to finance the movement of refugees and migrants.

IOM cooperates with the UNHCR, other U.N. organizations and regional IGOs. It also cooperates with NGOs as important partners in the refugee and migration field. Voluntary agencies are the link between the individual seeking international assistance to resettle, and persons and institutions willing to accept them in new homelands. IOM cooperates with the League of Red Cross and Red Crescent Societies, the World Council of Churches, the Lutheran World Federation, the Norwegian Refugee Council, the International Confederation of Free Trade Unions, the International Council of Voluntary Agencies, the International Catholic Migration Commission, among others.

IOM programmes are implemented by its international and locally-recruited staff totalling, at the end of 1988, 745 persons: 128 at its Geneva headquarters and 617 in 44 field offices worldwide.

IOM's 1989 budget amounted to $129.6 million, of which $117 million were for operations and $12.6 for administrative costs. In 1989, IOM staff were to deal with 158,200 refugees and migrants. The administrative budget is funded by assessed contributions according to a percentage scale: in 1989, the U.S.A. contribution was 33.33 percent, the Federal Republic of Germany and Italy, 10.57 percent. The operational part of the budget is paid by voluntary contributions: the biggest contribution for 1989 was $6 million by the Federal Republic of Germany, $2.750.000 by the U.S.A., $2.715.OOO by Italy.

IOM's Director-General is James N. Purcell, Jr. (U.S.A.), appointed in 1988.

In 1989, IOM has handled the flow of Soviet refugees to the U.S.A., it has cooperated with the Orderly Departure Programme which processes Indochinese refugees and reeducation camp detainees legally permitted to leave for the U.S.A.

To help developing countries meet their immediate needs for highly skilled persons, IOM has developed specific Migration for Development programmes. Since 1964, the organization has transferred over 42,000 highly qualified specialists and technicians to developing countries. In 1983, IOM created the Centre for Information on Migration in Latin America in Santiago, Chile.

In September 1990, IOM organized an international airlift, with financial and operational support from several donor countries, to repatriate Bangladeshi, Filipino, Pakistani and Sri Lankan nationals stranded in Jordan, following Iraq's invasion of Kuwait[31].

The U.N. Children's Fund (UNICEF: Originally the U.N. International Children's Emergency Fund)

UNICEF was created on 11 December 1946 by the U.N. General Assembly (Resolution 57(I) as a temporary organization, to be financed from the residual assets of UNRRA and from voluntary contributions. In 1953, UNICEF was extended for an indefinite period (Resolution 802(VII) of 6 October 1953).

During its early years, UNICEF resources were devoted largely to meeting the emergency needs of children in post-war Europe for food, drugs and clothing. Its mandate and activities extended later to the developing world.

The major field of UNICEF work is child health services with the objective of reducing infant and young child mortality and morbidity and promoting child growth and development. Working closely with WHO, the main UNICEF goal is to

---

[31] See IOM (previously ICM) publications, including *ICM 1988, Programme and Budget for 1989*, Doc. MC/1609, ICM Doc. MC/1631 of 13 Oct. 1989, "Continued Effectiveness of the Organization in view of New Challenges", *Report of the Director-General* on the implementation of Resolution No. 749 (LVII) of 26 May 1988. U.S. Mission *Daily Bulletin*, Geneva, EURG_1 of 29 Nov. 1989, "Effective migration increasingly important, U.S. tells IOM". On the international airlift from Jordan, see IOM *Press Release* No. 670 (1990).

help countries expand their primary health care system, e.g. maternal and child health services, sufficient and accessible water supply, adequate sanitation and health and nutrition programmes.

Since 1982, UNICEF and WHO have promoted the "GOBI-FFF" principles. This represented the championship of low-cost measures which could result in fewer child deaths and a better quality of life for children without any massive injection of economic resources.

GOBI stands for growth monitoring, oral rehydration therapy to combat diarrhoeal related illness, breast-feed to combat malnutrition, and immunization to stave off six child diseases. FFF stands for better feeding, family spacing and female education. Together, these principles and practices have been called the Child Survival and Development Revolution, CSDR.

UNICEF activities utilize materials among which are many items which can be usefully diverted to meet emergencies in disaster areas, or which can be drawn from an emergency stockpile in the UNICEF warehouse in Copenhagen (UNIPAC). The UNICEF Executive Director has a cash reserve at his disposal for rapid use in emergencies, and can divert funds from regular programmes to emergency operations with the agreement of the government concerned. In consequence, while UNICEF's main interest after a disaster lies in the medium-term restoration and long-term development of services to children and mothers, it is geared to provide substantial emergency assistance for these vulnerable groups. UNICEF can also undertake procurement of relief supplies on behalf of UNDRO, other U.N. agencies, and other relief organizations.

For example, in 1984, UNICEF assisted 21 countries hit by disasters: 14 in Africa, 5 in Asia, one in the Middle East and one in the Americas. The organization spent $4.3 million from the Executive Director's Emergency Relief Fund, and channelled special contributions amounting to $25 million for shelter, medicaments, water supply, equipment, food supplements and other essentials. A joint effort was launched with WHO in Nepal to help avert an epidemic of meningitis. Vaccines, syringes, needles and spare parts for pedo-jets were lifted from UNIPAC at a cost of $50,000.

In 1986, UNICEF provided relief for victims of—cholera in several African countries,—malaria in Sao Tome and Principe,—typhoons and floods, in Bolivia, Jamaica, Madagascar, Vietnam,—earthquakes, in El Salvador.

In 1988, 16 out of 43 African countries met with natural disasters. Hurricanes devastated Nicaragua and Jamaica. floods inundated 75 percent of Bangladesh, leaving an estimated 45 million people affected in 64 districts: damage to housing, agriculture and infrastructure was estimated in billions of dollars. In all, 43 countries absorbed a total of $32.2 million from the UNICEF emergency programme[32].

In 1990, more than 60,000 Liberians, mostly women and children, fled to Côte

---

[32] UNICEF *Annual Report, 1985*, UNICEF *Facts and figures, 1987*, UNICEF *Annual Report, 1989*, p. 35.

d'Ivoire and Guinea as a result of intense tribal strife in their country. UNICEF diverted $80,000 from its regular health programme to respond to an urgent appeal made by the Ivorian Minister of Health. This amount was used to provide essential drugs, oral rehydration salts, blankets, soap and kitchen utensils. NGOs were associated with this relief programme.

In April 1990, UNICEF called for a three-day cease-fire in Lebanon in order to vaccinate all children of less than one year. A similar UNICEF-sponsored cease-fire had been obtained in 1987[33].

Cooperation with NGOs

UNICEF cooperates actively with NGOs in the field, through its cadre of experienced country staff, in a variety of activities, especially at the grassroots level in rural areas and in deprived urban settings. In recent years, and particularly since 1987, there has been growing programme involvement by NGOs in such programmes as nutrition, water supply and sanitation, primary health care, child immunization, AIDS prevention through health education campaigns, family self-reliance, women's activities and non-formal education. In addition to mobilizing community support and participation in such fields, women's organizations and other NGOs are often useful in overcoming obstacles in project implementation, particularly when government administrative structure in districts or provinces is new or understaffed.

In emergency situations, UNICEF works closely with the International Committee of the Red Cross (ICRC), the League of Red Cross and Red Crescent Societies and a large number of voluntary relief agencies. Some of UNICEF's NGO partners are Rotary International, Save the Children Alliance, the Red Cross organizations, the World Organization of Scouts, the World Council of Churches etc.

The NGO Committee on UNICEF represents more than 160 international organizations in consultative status.

1988 was a year of growth and consolidation of UNICEF collaboration with NGOs. In most UNICEF-assisted countries, international, national or regional NGO networks continued to provide vital access to children in need and those most difficult to reach. For instance, in Columbia, Haiti, Peru and Senegal, UNICEF developed local and regional NGO "Alliances" across the spectrum of health and education, training for rural women, water and sanitation and women's development[34].

---

[33] U.N. *Press Release*, SI/05/90 of 19 March 1990, *Le Monde*, 5 April 1990.

[34] UNICEF *Annual Report, 1988, Annual Report, 1989*, p. 47.

Budget and Staffing

UNICEF is financed by voluntary contributions from governments, organizations and individuals. Government contributions provide the major portion of the budget: 75 percent in 1986, 70 percent in 1988. The major governmental contributions were in 1988, in decreasing order, the U.S.A., Italy, Norway, Canada, the U.K., Denmark, Japan and Switzerland. Also in 1988, the major non-governmental contributions were received from Canada, the Federal Republic of Germany, U.S.A., France, the Netherlands, Japan and Switzerland.

UNICEF income was $313 million in 1980, $390 in 1985, and $709 million in 1988. On 31 December 1988, UNICEF employed 3,941 staff members (1,473 professional, and 2,468 general service), of whom 20 percent were assigned to its New York headquarters, 40 percent in its 92 field offices, and 40 percent in country projects[35].

The World Health Organization (WHO)

WHO was established on 7 April 1948 as a U.N. specialized agency, with headquarters in Geneva. Its objective is "the attainment by all peoples of the highest possible level of health".

WHO is mandated to be the directing and coordinating authority on international health work. Its field of work includes strengthening health services, epidemiological and statistical services, the eradication of diseases, the improvement of nutrition, sanitation, maternal and child health, health education, mental health, international health regulations and standards.

Article 2(d) of its Constitution states that one of the functions of WHO

shall be ... to furnish appropriate technical assistance and, in emergencies, necessary aid upon the request or acceptance of governments.

In emergency relief operations, WHO acts as the "check point" for the health and medical assistance required: it is concerned with the provision of medicaments and other medical supplies, the prevention and control of communicable diseases caused or aggravated by the disaster, the provision of technical advice regarding medical equipment and supplies offered by donors, and the provision of technical assistance and advice regarding public health matters such as drinking water supply and malnutrition. At country level, WHO representatives assist the local authorities in assessing the requirements of personnel, medical supplies and equipment to prevent or minimize health hazards to disaster victims. WHO can furnish technical personnel and limited amounts of emergency supplies and can also assist in measures of disaster prevention and rehabilitation.

---

[35] UNICEF *Annual Report, 1989*, pp. 50–53, U.N. Doc. ACC/1989/PER/R.11 of 20 July 1989.

Until the beginning of the 1980s, WHO's main disaster activity was relief. Gradually, the emphasis has changed to disaster preparedness and response, support to national training, assessment of health situations and needs, and coordination of large scale disaster operations. The focus remains on developing countries.

WHO's work on country projects is normally carried out in cooperation with the headquarters units concerned and the WHO Regional Office responsible for all programme activities in a specific geographical area.

In 1982–1986, WHO was involved in the establishment of the Afghan refugee health programme in Pakistan, prior to the transfer of the programme to the UNHCR.

In 1987–1988, WHO assisted Angola and Bangladesh (flood management: health sector emergency plans),—Ethiopia (drought and famine: health facilities),—Iran (Afghan refugee health services),—Mozambique, Sudan, Botswana, China, India, Indonesia, Lebanon, Madagascar, Malawi, Mali, Somalia.

Close collaboration was maintained with UNDRO, the UNHCR, UNICEF, the League of Red Cross and Red Crescent Societies and other relief agencies dealing with emergency situations[36].

WHO's Relations with NGOs

In accordance with Article 71 of its Constitution, WHO

> may, on matters within its competence, make suitable arrangements for consultation and cooperation with non-governmental international organizations and, with the consent of the government concerned, with national organizations, governmental or non-governmental.

The objectives of the WHO's collaboration with NGOs are to promote the policies, strategies and programmes approved by the governing bodies, to collaborate in jointly agreed activities, and to ensure the harmonizing of intersectional interests in a country, regional or global setting.

On 20 May 1985, the World Health Assembly appealed to NGOs to support the WHO Strategies of "Health For All by the Year 2,000", to encourage self-care and self-help groups at the community level for the effective implementation of primary health care and to establish national coordinating mechanisms, such as national councils of NGOs, to provide a focal point for non-governmental activities in health and health-related fields. It called on governments to promote the partnership approach by involving NGOs in policy formulation, planning, implementation and evaluation of the national Health For All strategies (Resolution WHA38.31).

In January 1990, 164 NGOs were in official relations with WHO.

---

[36] WHO Doc. PCO/EPR/89.3, *Emergency Preparedness and Response, Annual Report 1988* and PCO/EPR/89.5, *Programme 1989–1991*, May 1989.

A number of these NGOs are research and science oriented and work on the setting of standards and guidelines. Some have a strong network of national societies which spread information and encourage the cross-fertilization of ideas and experience. Others raise funds. Some are operational in countries, besides an advocacy and information role.

Among the latter are included the International Union against Tuberculosis and Lung Diseases, Helen Keller International, Inc. (prevention of blindness), the Aga Khan Foundation (community-based health care), the International Council of Women (nutrition, health education, child care), the African Medical and Research Foundation International (AMREF: see Chapter 7), the Christian Medical Commission of the World Council of Churches (see Chapter 7).

The International Committee of the Red Cross collaborates with WHO mainly in carrying out missions related to emergencies and in training courses on the health aspects of disaster preparedness and management. The League of Red Cross and Red Crescent Societies and its national societies collaborate with WHO on emergency preparedness and response, health laboratory technology, blood transfusion services, AIDS prevention and control, diarrhoeal diseases[37].

Budget and Staffing

In July 1989, a Division of Emergency Relief Operations (ERO) was established at WHO headquarters to replace the former, smaller, Emergency Preparedness and Response Unit.

The new Division consists of three units: Emergency Preparedness and Response, Food Aid Programme, and Relief Programmes. It is staffed by twelve staff members: one Director, eight professional and three general service staff.

The funds available for emergencies in 1988-1989 were:

— Regular WHO funds	$ 576,000
— Donations	$5,740,300
— Total	$6,316,300

The World Food Programme (WFP)

The joint U.N.-FAO World Food Programme (WFP) was established in Rome by parallel resolutions of the U.N. General Assembly and the FAO Conference in 1961. Its objectives are: to establish international procedures for meeting emergency food needs and emergencies inherent in chronic malnutrition; to assist in preschool and school feeding projects; and to implement food-for-work pilot projects

---

[37] WHO Doc. EB85/36 of 22 January 1990.

as an aid to economic and social development. WFP has offices in 83 developing countries.

Pledges to the programme are made in the form of commodities, cash or services, with the aim that cash and services pledged should together amount to at least one third of the total. In 1989, the total development commitments amounted to $575 million, plus $93 million for emergency operations. WFP total expenditures on all projects were valued at $874 million in 1988, and $712 (provisional figure) in 1989, including $206.5 million for emergencies.

WFP's main task is to furnish foodstuffs in support of economic and social development projects in developing countries. These projects are designed to increase food production, improve nutritional standards, promote human development and reduce rural poverty. Much of the aid is directed to the rural areas of low-income, food-deficit countries in the form of "food for development". In addition, substantial resources are available to meet emergency food needs, some of which can be furnished from project food stocks already in a disaster stricken country. WFP also purchases and ships food needed in emergencies on behalf of donor governments, UNDRO, UNEP or the stricken countries themselves. WFP staff may assist, if and when required, in coordinating the reception and utilization of food aid received from all sources.

During 1986 and 1987, the importance of food aid as a development resource was made clear by the fact that it constituted ten percent of all official development aid (20 percent in Sub-Saharan Africa). WFP was responsible for 25 percent of global food aid. WFP is now the largest source of multilateral assistance after the World Bank Group, providing fully one third of all resources transferred through the U.N. system.

In 1989, nearly 8.4 million people in 24 countries received emergency food assistance through WFP. A total of 46 emergency operations were approved, involving 259,000 tons of food. Afghan refugees in Pakistan and Iran, and those affected by war in Afghanistan itself, were assisted with an additional 225,000 tons of food through WFP[38].

In November 1989, WFP urged donors to ship food aid to Northern Ethiopia to prevent starvation of more than 1.7 million people in the coming year, due to a serious drought: in 1984, more than one million Ethiopians died during the famine. In response to this appeal, the Lutheran World Federation with its Orthodox and Catholic partners in the Joint Relief Partnership in Ethiopia, initiated food shipments[39].

In January 1990, WFP announced that it would provide emergency food aid worth $8 million to Ethiopian drought victims and refugees, and over $8 million more to Mauritanian refugees, Algerian earthquake victims and Mozambicans[40].

---

[38] WHO Publication *The Work of WHO, 1986–1987*, p. 34 and World Food Programme, *1990 Food Aid Review*, pp. 13, 47, Tables 1, 3 and 5.

[39] *Lutheran World Information*, Nov. 1989, No. 11, p. 12.

[40] U.N. *Press Release* DH/562 of 10 January 1990.

Clearly, the ability of WFP to respond to disaster food needs depends on the resources (food surpluses) which governments or other IGOs (such as the European Community) are prepared to make available to the international community. It depends also on the capacity of WFP to attract funds and donations and to ensure effective and prompt delivery. WFP has now significantly grown in status and importance in the global food aid system. It has also developed as the *de facto* logistics arm of the U.N. in disaster situations.

The U.N. Educational, Scientific and Cultural Organization (UNESCO)

Besides its main programmes and activities, UNESCO has a role in disaster prevention, and a role in disaster relief in its own domaine, which is not of immediate humanitarian concern. UNESCO is concerned mainly with the scientific and technical aspects of disaster prevention in respect of earthquakes, volcanic eruptions, landslides and avalanches, and also with some aspects of flood prevention. Its studies of the causes and mechanisms of natural phenomena lead to definitions of vulnerable zones and to estimations of the risks to life and property in such zones. They may also lead in some cases to effective forecasting and warning of occurrence of potentially disastrous phenomena. UNESCO can send scientific and technical missions to the sites of natural disasters, immediately after their occurrence, in order to elucidate their causes and to assess their effects, with a view to improving protection against future disasters. It can also assist in the rehabilitation and reconstruction of educational or scientific institutions and cultural monuments that have suffered damage from disasters[41].

For instance, in 1988, UNESCO provided $100,000 for the re-building of educational establishments following floods in Bangladesh, $200,000 to finance education projects for population fleeing from civil war areas in Mozambique. In Nepal, a joint mission by UNESCO and the U.S. Geological Service investigated *in situ* the causes of the earthquake of 21 August 1988. $100,000 were provided for the initial rebuilding of school buildings[42].

The Food and Agriculture Organization of the U.N. (FAO)

FAO's mandate, as a U.N. specialized agency, is to raise the levels of nutrition in member states, to improve the production and distribution of all food and agricultural products and to improve the condition of rural people. It provides technical assistance in all areas of food and agriculture in the developing countries.

---

[41] This summary is taken from the League of Red Cross and Red Crescent Societies *Red Cross Disaster Relief Handbook*, Annex 4. Parts of summaries concerning ILO, WMO, UNEP and UNDP (see below) have also been taken from the same document.

[42] *1988 at UNESCO*, UNESCO Doc., 1989, p.19.

FAO is frequently called on to help farmers resume production after floods, fires, outbreaks of livestock diseases or other emergencies. When disaster strikes, the FAO representative assesses needs in close collaboration with the local authorities and other U.N. agencies. At government request, emergency missions make detailed assessments of damage and losses, and prepare assistance projects for external funding.

FAO, through the Global Information and Early Warning System for Food and Agriculture, also monitors the factors that affect food production and alerts governments and donors to potential food shortages. Through its co-sponsorship, with the U.N., of the World Food Programme, FAO oversees the provision of food aid when shortages occur.

The organization's disaster relief assistance is coordinated by its Office for Special Relief Operations. Since 1976, about $48 million have been spent on emergency operations[43].

The International Labour Organisation (ILO)

ILO can make contributions in the early phase of rehabilitation and reconstruction by undertaking projects of accelerated vocational training of all types of construction workers. In the longer term, ILO may also assist in the rehabilitation, retraining and placement of persons disabled or displaced by a disaster(41).

The World Meteorological Organization (WMO)

WMO is concerned with the planning and coordination of the establishment of the international warning system for dangerous meteorological and hydrological phenomena, in particular through its programmes of the World Weather Watch and Operational Hydrology. It is concerned with the implementation of projects in developing countries to strengthen their technical and technological capabilities to issue warnings and to develop, together with the League and UNDRO, appropriate counter-measures against destructive natural phenomena, such as tropical and extra-tropical storms, floods and storm surges. WMO is involved in community preparedness through a joint WMO/ESCAP Committee on Typhoons and Tropical Cyclones in the Bay of Bengal, and similar WMO committees for the Western Indian Ocean. Its work in disaster prevention mainly concerns floods, but it also conducts activities in the evaluation of tropical storm risks, drought and other meteorological phenomena which can cause disasters (41).

---

[43] *FAO, What it is, what it does*, 1986, p. 6.

The U.N. Environment Programme (UNEP)

This programme includes natural disasters as a priority area. Related activities concern the survey, analysis and application of existing knowledge in the field of disaster prevention and mitigation, and the development and dissemination of new knowledge and improved techniques. Such activities are carried out in cooperation with UNDRO, WMO and UNESCO. UNEP is also concerned with the disaster implications of human settlements and habitat, and arid lands (41).

The Office of the U.N. Disaster Relief coordinator (UNDRO)

The multiplicity of U.N. organizations having a complete or partial relief role, the competition among them, the occasional overlapping or excess of assistance gave rise to concerns among donor countries in the General Assembly in the late 1960s.

On 14 December 1971, the General Assembly approved the establishment of the Office of the U.N. Disaster Relief Coordinator (UNDRO) and defined his mandate (Resolution 2816(XXVI).

UNDRO was to be the focal point in the U.N. system for disaster relief matters. The Coordinator was

> to mobilize, direct and coordinate the relief activities of the various organizations of the U.N. system in response to a request for disaster assistance from a stricken state.

The "directing and coordinating" function given to an Office in the U.N. secretariat was, not unexpectedly, resented and opposed by other U.N. bodies (such as UNICEF) or U.N. specialized agencies, always wary of losing their autonomy in their specialized field, their freedom of decision and perhaps some of their resources in favour of the U.N., perceived as hegemonic and not always as effective as some of the technical organizations.

The creation of UNDRO could also have alienated the Red Cross organizations, proud of their pioneering and leading role, long and recognized experience in relief assistance, as well as the voluntary non-governmental organizations, which reject any obvious link with and dependence on, governments and intergovernmental organizations.

The General Assembly resolution diplomatically recognized the "vital role in international relief played by the International Red Cross and other voluntary societies" as well as the assistance provided by the UNDP, the IBRD, UNICEF, UNHCR and the WFP. In practice, close collaboration is maintained between the League of Red Cross and Red Crescent Societies and UNDRO on all disaster-related matters. During disaster emergencies, the League and UNDRO exchange information and ensure that duplication is avoided in their respective requests for international assistance. The League is also consulted before projects of U.N. assistance to governments in pre-disaster planning are initiated[44].

In fact, neither fears nor expectations that UNDRO would play a directing role in international relief assistance were fulfilled: besides the intractable difficulties of such a mandate, UNDRO's status, authority, financial and staffing resources are totally inadequate to this task.

UNDRO is not an organization: it is an "Office" within the U.N. secretariat, based in the U.N. Office at Geneva. Directed by a Coordinator with the rank of Under-Secretary-General, its overall staffing grew from an original six to 57 staff members (29 professional and 28 general service) in 1989. Its original annual budget was $330,000. For 1988-1989, its expenditures amounted to:

— Regular budget	$ 7,299,400
— Trust Funds	$ 42,249,403
Total:	$ 49,548,803[45]

For 1990–1991, $6,910,700 were approved as appropriation from the U.N. regular budget. five UNDRO posts have been eliminated for the biennium, a 30.9 percent reduction in line with the overall staffing cuts mandated by the Group of 18 and the General Assembly. Estimates for extra-budgetary resources amounted to $3.5 million[46].

UNDRO's mandate, as spelt out in several U.N. resolutions[47], includes:

— mobilization and coordination of emergency relief from U.N. agencies and from the international community in general, to provide timely and effective assistance to disaster-stricken countries;
— to provide precise information as to relief requirements in disaster emergencies;
— to maintain a clearing house in Geneva for the exchange of information and for the matching of needs with supplies and services from donor sources;
— disaster preparedness, which involves activities designed to raise the level of pre-disaster planning, including disaster assessment and relief management capability in disaster-prone developing countries;
— disaster prevention, to promote the study, prediction and mitigation of natural disasters through appropriate measures, including collection and dissemination of information on relevant scientific and technological developments.

Those various tasks can be grouped into relief coordination, disaster preparedness and disaster prevention. While the most appropriate balance between these three categories of functions is still the object of debates, UNDRO's coordinating role is

---

[44] See *Red Cross Disaster Relief Handbook*, Annex 4.

[45] U.N. Doc. A/45/271, E/1990/78 of 1 June 1990, *Office of the U.N. Disaster Relief Co-Ordinator, Report of the Secretary-General.*

[46] U.N. *Press Release* GA/AB/37 of 8 Nov. 1989.

[47] U.N. General Assembly resolutions 3243(XXIX), 36/225, 37/144, 38/202 and 39/207.

considered the more important: since 1976, the Office has established a "60-30-10" per cent ratio in these respective roles, although some of the functions overlap[48].

General Assembly resolution 2816(XXVI) refers to assistance in cases of natural disaster and "other emergency situations" or "other disaster situations".

"Other emergency or disaster situations" has not been clearly defined in the mandate of UNDRO. Is the role of UNDRO limited to natural disasters, or does it extend to man-made disasters?

A clear distinction has been made in the 1978 Memorandum of Understanding between UNHCR and UNDRO, which essentially gives UNDRO responsibility for coordination of relief assistance in all situations, and for all refugees, other than those involving deliberate man-made disasters (war, civil strife and genocide).

In recent activities, the distinction between natural and man-made disasters has become fuzzy, particularly because of problems resulting from mixed disaster situations, such as famine occurring during or after a civil war. In practice, UNDRO has been involved in both types of disasters.

UNDRO's Recent Activities

In 1986–1987, UNDRO was involved, to varying degrees, in 110 disaster situations. Major disasters included cyclonic storms and floods in Bangladesh, the release of toxic gas from Lake Nyos in Cameroon, an earthquake in El Salvador, floods in Bolivia, Haiti and in Peru, drought in Ethiopia and in the Sudan, armed conflict and floods in Lebanon, a cyclone in Madagascar, in Vanuatu and in the Solomon Islands, drought/destabilization in Mozambique, a typhoon in Vietnam, a forest fire in China, an earthquake in Ecuador, a tidal wave in the Maldives, civil strife in Democratic Yemen and a wide-spread locust threat in Africa.

In these disaster situations, UNDRO mobilized and coordinated relief assistance, provided an independent assessment of damage and needs and kept the donor community informed of developments.

In its function of mobilizing funds, UNDRO organized a meeting in Geneva in March 1987 convened by the U.N. Secretary-General on humanitarian assistance to Mozambique. The meeting, which was chaired by the U.N. Disaster Relief Coordinator, was attended by the Prime Minister of Mozambique and by representatives of 53 governments, 2 intergovernmental organizations, 14 agencies of the U.N. system and 37 non-governmental organizations. 19 donor governments and one IGO pledged relief contributions in an amount of approximately $209 million.

The capacity of the Office to respond to emergency needs was enhanced by the use of the UNDRO warehouse at Pisa, with the support of the main donor, the Government of Italy and other donors. The warehouse was constructed at the site of the U.N. Supply Depot at Pisa. It became operational early in 1986 and has accom-

---

[48] U.N.Doc. JIU/REP/80/11, Oct. 1980, para. 30.

50

modated a wide range of standard relief goods in sectors such as shelter, logistics equipment and water supply. Its location at the Pisa airport, which can accommodate any type of aircraft, makes it suitable for dispatching relief supplies to disaster-stricken developing countries at short notice. The operations of the warehouse, operating in complement with UNIPAC (UNICEF Packing and Assembly Centre) at Copenhagen, have been expanded, following donations from Norway and Finland. Japan is expected to contribute to these operations.

In disaster mitigation, UNDRO provides staff who advise and assist national authorities in developing a programme and calendar and in identifying sources of funding.

In the Asian region, the focal point for disaster mitigation activities of UNDRO is the Asian Disaster Preparedness Centre, established in January 1986 at the Asian Institute of Technology in Bangkok.

In the field of disaster information, UNDRO has developed a computerized system for distribution of disaster situation reports (SIREPS). A new information network for international disaster management (UNIENET) has been launched, through which members of the world-wide disaster management community can have direct contact with each other. The network provides them with background and operational disaster-related information. In 1988-1989, 150 users subscribed to the system, representing 10 U.N. organizations, and 60 other entities (IGOs and NGOs, universities and research centres, private voluntary agencies and individuals)[49].

In 1989, UNDRO airlifted to flooded Djibouti water-pumping and pesticide-spraying equipment to contain the risk of malaria, as well as emergency relief supplies for the worst-affected people. This operation was financed by a contribution of $500,000 to UNDRO from the Italian government. Italy also financed an UNDRO shipment of medicines for Lebanon, for a value of $800,000; to be distributed through the Lebanese Red Cross, Caritas Internationalis and the Lebanese NGO Amel. Both shipments were flown from the Pisa warehouse[50].

In September 1989, UNDRO sent a disaster preparedness planning mission to Armenia. The mission's six experts considered pre-disaster planning measures for such hazards as earthquakes, floods and mudflows, landslides as well as industrial accidents. The costs were assumed by a contribution from the Federal Republic of Germany[51].

In October 1989, the European Community granted $1.5 million to UNDRO to finance three emergency aid programmes to Lebanon. Relief materials (blankets, mattresses, stoves, lamps etc.) will be distributed to 20,000 families through NGOs: the Middle East Council of Churches, World Vision International, the Knights of Malta, the Farah Social Foundation, Makassed and the High Council of Shiahs and

[49] U.N. Doc. A/45/271, op.cit.
[50] U.N. *Press Releases* SI/12/89 of 8 May 1989 and ND/256/Rev.1 of 23 Aug. 1989.
[51] U.N. *Press Release* ND/257 of 12 Sept. 1989.

Sanabel. The Save the Children Foundation (U.S.A.) will control a sanitation programme[52].

In November 1989, UNDRO airlifted relief supplies for the victims of an earthquake in Algeria: financing came from the Italian government, OPEC, the U.S. Foreign Disaster Assistance and the Belgian Air Force[53].

In October-November 1989, UNDRO and the government of the USSR organized a Training Seminar on Earthquake Disaster Management in Moscow, attended by 21 representatives of disaster-prone developing countries. This seminar, as well as two previous ones, were financed by a Soviet contribution[54].

Since 1986, UNDRO has organized three meetings of National Emergency Relief Officials to improve cooperation in providing relief assistance to disaster victims.

The last meeting, held in October 1989, was attended by representatives of 18 donor countries and six U.N. agencies. The meeting recommended that there should be unified appeals for aid and concerted relief programmes. It called on donor governments to provide funding as well as the services of relief experts to assist UNDRO in conducting field assessment of damage and relief needs, in view of UNDRO's limited staff resources.

A post-operation evaluation procedure developed in consultation with officials of the National Emergency Relief Services had identified some of the typical, recurrent problems of international disaster assistance:

— some agencies do not automatically inform UNDRO of their relief programmes in affected countries;
— some agencies do not share their evaluations of their own evaluations with other partners;
— appeals for international assistance are sometimes delayed by the reluctance of local authorities to admit their difficulties in handling the situation;
— relief supplies should only be sent after real needs have been assessed[55].

On 1 and 2 March 1990, UNDRO convened a meeting of NGOs in Geneva: representatives from 30 NGOs, including the ICRC and the League, attended. The local purchasing of relief goods was again recommended and the usefulness of emergency stockpiles confirmed.

The NGO representative endorsed the use of "disaster management teams" in disaster-prone countries to provide collective judgement on damage and relief requirements and stressed the need to communicate with the mass media at an early stage of any disaster relief operation[56].

---

[52] U.N. *Press Release* ND/258 of 3 Oct. 1989.
[53] U.N. *Press Releases* ND/263, 2 Nov., ND/265, 20 Nov. 1989
[54] U.N. *Press Release* ND/262 of 26 Oct. 1989.
[55] U.N. Doc. A/43/375 of 1 June 1988, pp. 8, 9 and U.N. *Press Release* ND/261 of 25 Oct. 1989.
[56] U.N. *Press Release* ND/270 of 5 March 1990.

On 11 December 1987, the U.N. General Assembly designated the 1990s as the International Decade for Natural Disaster Reduction, beginning on 1 January 1990 (Resolution 42/169). A secretariat for the Decade was established at UNDRO's headquarters in Geneva. Over these ten years, nations are asked to give special attention to programmes designed to reduce loss of life, property damage and economic and social disruption caused by natural disasters[57].

Assessment of UNDRO

In 1980, the Joint Inspection Unit (JIU) made a critical assessment of UNDRO's performance, after eight years of activities[58].

JIU found that the implementation of UNDRO's mandate had been hampered by its imprecise nature and UNDRO's inability to establish a leadership role. JIU stated that other U.N. system organizations had not accepted UNDRO's leadership. Donor countries had been increasingly critical of its performance. Disaster-prone countries wanted more direct contacts and innovation from UNDRO. Voluntary agencies also wanted more UNDRO leadership: links with the disaster research community and the media had been limited. JIU also criticized a "tightly centralized style" of internal management.

The JIU report recommended confining UNDRO's role to "sudden" natural disasters in order to "sharpen (UNDRO's) performance", with an emphasis on information-sharing and catalytic leadership, to stress the importance of disaster preparedness and prevention, — to reduce UNDRO's staffing and have UNDRO report to the UNDP Governing Council.

In December 1981, the U.N. General Assembly reaffirmed the mandate of UNDRO as the focal point of the U.N. system for disaster relief coordination and called for the strengthening and improvement of the capacity and effectiveness of the Office (Resolution 36/225). It urged all appropriate U.N. bodies to cooperate closely with UNDRO. It decided that in disaster-stricken countries, the U.N. resident coordinator should convene meetings of the concerned U.N. and Red Cross bodies and voluntary agencies, with the approval of the host country, to plan, monitor and take immediate action. It also decided that, when an exceptional or complex natural disaster or other disaster situation requiring system-wide actions existed, the Secretary-General would designate, at the international level, a "lead entity" among the U.N. organizations, including UNDRO.

The latter could be interpreted as a sign of distrust in the Coordinator's capacity to deal with "exceptional or complex" disasters, such situations being clearly in UNDRO's mandate.

---

[57] U.N. *Press Release* ND/267 and *UNDRO News*, Jan. Feb. 1988.
[58] U.N. Doc. JIU/REP/80/11, Oct. 1980, *Evaluation of the Office of the U.N. Disaster Relief Coordinator.*

On the other hand, by-passing UNDRO may be justified first by the prestige of an appointment by the Secretary-General himself, particularly if the appointee is himself a well-known personality with international experience who can obtain support and funds. Secondly, an UNDRO official might have to deal with a variety of tasks, while the "lead entity" could concentrate fully, full-time, on his mission.

In addition to responding to immediate emergencies, the role of the Special Representative of the Secretary-General is to formulate and implement a long-term strategy for bringing together multilateral and bilateral efforts to deal with particular threatening situations. In executing his strategy, the Special Representative solicits within the U.N. system and beyond, via donor meetings or by other means, the money, services and material required to meet the crisis.

In the case of aid to Afghanistan, after the Soviet troop withdrawal, the Secretary-General appointed Prince Saddrudin Aga Khan as his Special Representative and Coordinator of "Operation Salam". The Coordinator established a division of labour as follows: the U.N. High Commissioner for Refugees was responsible for the repatriation of refugees, the World Food Programme was primarily responsible for the delivery and distribution of food, the FAO was to oversee the rehabilitation of agriculture, WHO and UNICEF were to deal with health, UNFPA with mother and child health and midwife training, UNESCO with education and UNDP with planning and rural public works. NGOs would be involved in these programmes. The Special Representative also engaged in fund-raising: by October 1988, $800 million had been pledged for the Afghanistan programme, including $600 million donated by the USSR. Since 1989, the U.S. contributions in cash and kind to "Operation Salam" amounted to some $27 million[59].

James P. Grant, Executive Director of UNICEF was Special Representative for the "Operation Lifeline Sudan" since April 1989. He was responsible for the first phase of the operation that involved the establishment, organization and coordination of activities designed to move 120,000 tons of food and other emergency commodities to areas of the Sudan that became inaccessible during the rainy season. Michael Priestley replaced Grant in October 1989: he was to implement the second phase, involving the provision of large-scale emergency and rehabilitation assistance to enable the displaced sectors of the population to sustain themselves until the next harvest[60].

The Secretary-General has also appointed a Special Representative for the coordination of humanitarian assistance programmes for Cambodia, Shah Kibria[61].

---

[59] U.N. *Press Release* AFG/21 of 12 Oct. 1988. See also *The Challenge of Relevance: the U.N. in a changing world environment*, D.J. Puchala and R.A.Coate, the Academic Council on the U.N. System, 1989–5, p. 98, and the U.S. *Daily Bulletin*, Geneva, EURG-1, 1 May 1990.

[60] U.N. *Press Release* DH/503 of 4 Oct. 1989. The Sudan Operation met with major difficulties: considerable logistical and security problems, linked with the civil war. Some critics said that the U.N. programme started late and was overly ambitious: *International Herald Tribune*. See also U.N. *Press Release* DH/591 of 1 March 1990: the Sudan Government agreed that relief operations could resume.

[61] U.N. *Press Release* DH/489 of 14 Sept. 1989.

Other Special Representatives have been appointed by the U.N. Secretary-General for the coordination of assistance programmes to Ethiopia, Lebanon, Mozambique and Somalia.

The U.N. General Assembly Resolution 43/131 of 8 December 1988 formally recognized that U.N. humanitarian assistance operates through a dual system. One is the cooperation of IGOs, governments and NGOs with UNDRO for short-term, run-of-the-mill, relatively "routine" natural disasters. The other channel, by-passing UNDRO, is an *ad hoc* mechanism set up by the U.N. Secretary-General in the coordination of aid, mainly by the appointment of a Special Representative, dealing with major, long-term, complex programmes.

The expansion of such *ad hoc* mechanisms stems in part from the wish of the United Nations' headquarters to maintain close control over such complex, and often politically sensitive, operations. The U.N. headquarters considers that it can initiate stronger interagency coordination in New York than in Geneva: for instance, the New York-based "African Emergency Task Force", an interagency advisory body, deals with all emergencies in Africa: it meets once a month in New York. The exception to the New York localisation of *ad hoc* operations management is the Afghanistan "Operation Salam", based in Geneva.

On 29 August 1990, the U.N. Secretary-General requested the U.N. Disaster Relief Coordinator to coordinate humanitarian programmes undertaken by the U.N. system during the Gulf Crisis.

On 12 September, the Secretary-General relieved the Coordinator of this mission, which he entrusted to Sadruddin Aga Khan, the Coordinator for U.N. Humanitarian and Economic Assistance relating to Afghanistan. The Gulf coordination involved UNDRO, UNHCR, UNICEF, WHO, WFP, UNRWA, UNDP,—the League of Red Cross and Red Crescent Societies, IOM and a number of NGOs.

Again, the Secretary-General's appointment of a Personal Representative, to replace the U.N. Disaster Relief Coordinator, could only be interpreted as a sign of distrust in UNDRO's capacity to deal with the "multifaceted nature" and the magnitude of the humanitarian challenge of the Gulf Crisis, in particular relation to third-country nationals.

In fact, the Secretary-General's decision was announced following bitter criticism of the way UNDRO was handling the humanitarian efforts on the Iraqi-Jordanian border. According to the *U.N. Observer* (October 1990), many countries, including Sweden, Jordan and India, complained that UNDROs 'efforts to help the people, most of them living in the desert without shelter and food, were poorly coordinated.

The "dual process" demonstrates that neither the U.N. leadership, nor major donor governments, are prepared to give major responsibilities in this field to UNDRO..

In spite of this increasing challenge to UNDRO's mandate and responsibilities, it appears that UNDRO itself has somewhat matured since the 1980 JIU critical report, as shown by the funds recently entrusted to it by donors, governments and IGOs such as the European Community.

A few member states' support for UNDRO was expressed during the debates in the fifth Committee in November 1989: Mr. Monthe, Chairman of the Committee for Programme and Coordination emphasized the importance and high priority to be given to UNDRO. The delegates from Morocco and Bangladesh also stressed the importance of UNDROs' activities[62].

The U.N. Development Programme (UNDP)

Under U.N. General Assembly resolution 2816(XXVI) of December 1971, the UNDP resident representatives were asked to coordinate relief operations at country level. In accordance with a memorandum of understanding between UNDP and UNDRO signed in 1979, these officials, stationed in 112 developing countries, represent the U.N. Disaster Relief Coordinator in those countries. They should take an active part on behalf of UNDRO by directing "relief committees" in disaster-afflicted states. They provide a channel for requests from governments on all disaster-related matters. When disasters strike, with assistance if necessary from staff dispatched by UNDRO, they lead the U.N. team in the assessment of emergency needs and the local coordination of aid from the U.N.system and other international sources. UNDP also undertakes disaster-related projects and may provide financial aid to emergency programmes. It may adapt country development programmes to the needs of rehabilitation and reconstruction following a disaster. In addition, UNDP undertakes or participates with UNDRO in disaster preparedness projects.

The effectiveness of the UNDP resident representatives or coordinators depends on their own competence and interest in the field of emergencies. Kent[63] has noted that UNDP

> had shown little predisposition "to give disaster work a high development priority", for such work—from UNDP's perspective—often raised sensitive issues for both donor and recipient governments that could complicate the all-important longer-term relations between UNDP and host governments.

The essential mission of UNDP resident representatives or coordinators is to coordinate development programmes in their country of assignment: they may not be particularly qualified nor interested in disaster work, which calls for different skills.

The total UNDP income for 1988 amounted to $1.2 billion, of which $33.2 million were spent on health projects and $22.7 on population, humanitarian aid and human settlements. In 1988, the main contributors to UNDP voluntary programme (those which gave more than $80 million) were the U.S.A., Sweden, the Netherlands, Norway, Japan and Denmark.

---

[62] U.N. *Press Release* GA/AB/37 of 8 Nov. 1989. On the Gulf Crisis, see U.N. *Press Releases* ND/287 of 30 Aug. 1990 and DH/723 of 12 Sept. 1990, and the *U.N. Observer*, Vol. 12, No.10, Oct. 1990.

[63] Kent, op.cit., p. 59.

As of 31 December 1988, UNDP was employing 6,331 staff members (1492 professional and 4,839 general service), 80 percent of whom were serving away from the New York headquarters.

A senior adviser on grass-roots and NGO matters was first appointed in UNDP in 1984. In January 1987, an NGO Division was established at UNDP headquarters, with a yearly allocation of $1 million. As part of its effort to encourage grass-roots approaches to development and to expand in-country cooperation among the governments of developing countries, UNDP field offices and NGOs, UNDP launched the Partners in Development Programme in 1988, with a budgetary allocation of $2.5 million to support indigenous NGOs innovative community-based projects. In 1988, 37 field offices gave support of up to $25,000 each for 101 such projects in such areas as primary health care, education, income and employment generation. Steps were also taken in 1988 to establish the Africa 2000 Network, a programme linking Africa-based grass-roots organizations and NGOs in a continent-wide effort to combat environmental degradation and promote ecologically sustainable development[64].

In 1988, UNDP gave emergency grants and coordinated the international relief response in Bangladesh, where floods swept through much of the country. Assistance was also extended to Nepal (earthquake) and Jamaica (hurricane). In Bangladesh, $50,000 was allocated for the purchase of cattle vaccines and animal feed. An additional $5.8 million was earmarked for housing and agricultural reconstruction. In Nepal and Jamaica, $50,000 grants were given for essential supplies and transport. In flood-ravaged Sudan, UNDP coordinated supply deliveries and joined the World Bank in drawing up a $407 million relief plan.

UNDP has cooperated with the Office of the Coordinator for U.N. Humanitarian and Economic Assistance Programmes relating to Afghanistan to help develop a relief, rehabilitation and reconstruction strategy for that country. In 1988, UNDP made available $12 million in assistance to help NGOs work effectively in the Afghan resettlement process[65].

The U.N. Volunteers Programme (UNV)

The U.N. Volunteers programme is the sole volunteer-sending organization in the U.N. system. It was established on 1 January 1971 by the U.N. General Assembly (Resolution 2659(XXV) of 7 December 1970) under UNDP. The purpose of this programme is to channel, at relatively low cost, professionally qualified men and women, on a volunteer basis, into development assistance activities calling for middle- and upper-level operational expertise. In 1988, 1,500 U.N. volunteers were serving in 100 developing countries. About 100 of them have assisted the most

[64] U.N. Doc. DP/1989/23 of 27 Feb. 1989.
[65] UNDP *World Development Annual Report—1988*, pp. 1, 16 and 17.

seriously affected African countries in the implementation of an emergency rehabilitation assistance programme. Thus the UNV programme has recently added some humanitarian activities to its basic development mandate.

This Programme will be considered in more detail in Chapter 8[66].

Regional Intergovernmental Organizations

Among the many regional intergovernmental organizations, the role of the European Economic Community in emergency aid is important. Its relations with NGOs are also well defined and developed.

The European Economic Community (EEC)

The European Economic Community, as one of the several "Clubs of Rich Nations", makes a significant contribution to international relief, both by direct assistance of the Community to a recipient country, and/or by contributing to IGOs and NGOs humanitarian programmes.

EEC relief is provided:

— through the emergency assistance provisions of the Lomé Conventions to States of the African, Caribbean and Pacific group,
— to any beneficiary, under the provisions for cash payments in the Community budget,
— and as special food aid.

Several EEC bodies deal with international relief: the Emergency Services Section, the Emergency Relief and Humanitarian Assistance Unit and the Food Aid Committee. Decisions relating to finance humanitarian assistance are taken by the EEC Commission in accordance with Article 205 of the Treaty of Rome which enables the Commission to implement the budget.

During 1989, the Commission gave emergency aid for victims of disasters in developing countries and other non-member countries at a total cost of ECU 38,606,000. A significant portion of this aid went to victims of drought and civil war in Africa, particularly in Sudan, Mozambique and Ethiopia.

On 31 December 1989, the Community granted a $9.5 million assistance to send medicaments, food and material to Lebanon. This decision was based on the report of an experts' mission who went to Lebanon to assess the population's needs. The Community had specified that this emergency assistance should benefit "all populations victims of the events, without discrimination and in a balanced way"[67].

---

[66] UNDP Doc. *The U.N. Volunteers—An Overview*, December 1988.

[67] *XXIIIrd General Report on Activities of the European Communities*, 1989, paras. 890, 891. *Le Monde*, 10, 11 Sept. 1989.

Cooperation between the EEC and NGOs began in 1976 with the aim of adding a new dimension to the Community's development policy. By this cooperation, the Community wanted to express Europe's solidarity at a non-official level towards the poorest sections of the population in the Third World.

The voluntary agencies within the EEC Member states established in 1982 an "Emergency Coordinating Committee" under the "Liaison Committee of Development Non-Governmental Organizations" to the EC.

In 1988, the Community's contribution for various NGO activities was ECU 266.4 million. Some of its main elements were as follows:

— ECU 109.3 million for food aid, plus
— ECU 4.8 million for the purchase of foodstuffs by NGOs
— ECU 79.8 million for co-financing, including operations to raise public awareness of development issues in EC countries
— ECU 29.9 million for emergency aid
— ECU 29.9 million for aid to the victims of apartheid[68].

In its cooperation with NGOs, the Community undertakes to respect their pluralism and their independence.

"Cofinancing" by the EEC of aid and development projects in the developing countries undertaken by European NGOs jointly with local partners is subject to conditions set under budget Article 941:

In order to be eligible for cofinancing, the NGO must satisfy the following conditions:

1. It must be established as an autonomous, non-profit-making NGO in a member state of the EEC;
2. It must have its head office in one of the member states of the EEC;
3. Its head office must be the effective decision-making centre for all co-financed projects;
4. The bulk of its human and financial resources must be of European (Community) origin.

Projects eligible for cofinancing are those which:

— directly meet the economic and social development needs of the people concerned, in particular the basic needs of the poorest sections of the population;
— are aimed at increasing the indigenous development capacity of the beneficiaries;
— involve the beneficiaries as partners at all stages of the project, namely design, implementation, management and post-execution operation.

Special attention is accorded to projects which reinforce development structures in

[68] *Commission of the European Communities, Commission Report on Cooperation with European NGOs in fields concerning developing countries (1988 exercise)*, Doc. SEC(89)1575 of 17 Oct. 1989.

the developing countries, particularly grassroots organizations and their networks, which do not have access to support from a network of organizations outside the developing countries, so that they are better able to perform their tasks for the benefit of the people concerned[69].

871 NGOs are in relationships with the EEC Directorate-General for Development (NGO Section). Most recognized NGOs are found in France (169), followed by the U.K. (124), Belgium (97), Italy (96) and the Federal Republic of Germany (95).

From 1976 to end 1988, the Community contributions to NGOs totalled ECU 342.2 million, allowing 3,080 projects to be cofinanced in developing countries. These projects were undertaken with 409 NGOs in 117 developing countries.

In the same period, 43 percent of the funds were allocated to African countries South of the Sahara, 31 per cent to Latin America, 10 percent to Asia, 5 percent to the Mediterranean area and 1 percent to the Pacific area. Almost half of the funds were allocated to developing countries with a per capita GNP of less than $500.

The Organization of American States (OAS)

The OAS has set up a small relief coordinating office and an Inter-American Emergency Fund. The OAS Pan-American Health Organization, which also acts as the WHO Regional Office for the Americas, has designed a disaster preparedness and response programme, including training elements, which has become a global model[70].

Other regional intergovernmental organizations, such as the Organization of African Unity and the Association of South East Asian Nations, have programmes and activities in respect of disaster planning and response.

Humanitarian assistance budget expenditures (or income) in 1988 of selected IGOs are shown in Table 1.1.

---

[69] *Commission of the European Communities, Directorate-General for Development, General Conditions for the Cofinancing of Projects undertaken in developing countries by NGOs — Budget Article 941*, 1 January 1988.

[70] WHO Doc. PCO/EPR/89.5 of May 1989.

60

Table 1.1. Humanitarian Assistance Expenditures (or income) of Selected Intergovernmental Organizations in 1988 (in million of $)

World Food Programme (a)	874.
UNICEF (b)	709.
UNHCR (c)	565.
UNRWA (d)	206.1
EEC (e)	173.9
IOM (f)	106.2
UNDRO (g)	24.7
UNDP (h)	22.7
WHO (i)	3.1

Sources:

(a) WFP *1990 Food Aid Review*.

(b) UNICEF *Annual Report 1989*.

(c) U.N. Doc. A/44/12, 1989, Annex. Later annual budgets have been sharply reduced: the proposed 1991 budget is at $345.5 million.

(d) Income figure—see U.N. Doc. A/44/13 Add. 17 Oct. 1989.

(e) ECUs have been converted in $ at November 1990 rate of exchange. EEC Doc. SEC (89)1575 of 17 October 1989, *Commission Report* on cooperation with European NGOs in fields concerning developing countries (1988 exercise).

(f) *ICM 1988—Programme and Budget for 1989*, Doc. MC/1609.

(g) Based on half of biennium 1988-1989 expenditures: U.N. Doc. A/45/271.E/1990/78 of 1 June 1990.

(h) UNDP expenditures on population, humanitarian aid and human settlements: UNDP *World Development Annual Report—1988*.

(i) Based on half of funds available 1988–1989: WHO Doc. PCO/EPR/89.5 of May 1989.

CHAPTER 2

THE ROLE AND CHARACTERISTICS OF NON-GOVERNMENTAL ORGANIZATIONS

Besides governments and intergovernmental organizations (IGOs), non-governmental organizations (NGOs) play a significant and increasingly recognized role in the international humanitarian network. NGOs initiate humanitarian action independently, assess needs, call for funds, send relief teams, provide equipment, medicaments, foodstuffs and other material to recipient populations.

NGOs also act in relation with IGOs, by supplementing or complementing IGO-initiated and funded programmes, as indispensable operational partners: without NGOs field work, many IGOs could not implement their programmes nor use all their funds.

The Red Cross organizations have a special, privileged position in the overall humanitarian network, and among NGOs. The Red Cross created in 1863 the first international relief system, and initiated and promoted international humanitarian law. The creation of the League of Red Cross Societies in 1919 served to federate National Red Cross Societies and to coordinate their international relief work in situations of peace.

The International Committee of the Red Cross (ICRC) was the first international body to define the basic principles of international humanitarian law during conflicts. It remains as a respected humanitarian thinktank, a promoter in the field of international humanitarian law, the monitor of the Red Cross Conventions, a fund-raiser and an actor in relief action.

The League of Red Cross and Red Crescent Societies is the only secular international NGO with a quasi-universal geographical network of national societies in 149 countries. It provides funds, personnel and supplies with the assistance of the donor Societies, and in cooperation with the recipient country's National Society.

Through the Geneva Conventions and the resolutions of the International Conferences of the Red Cross, the Red Cross organizations enjoy official legal legitimacy and diplomatic recognition from all participating governments. In their past and present international and national programmes, Red Cross organizations generally benefit from the prestige of the Red Cross and protection accorded to the Red Cross emblem.

In the last decades, many other NGOs, at the national and at the international levels, have assumed humanitarian tasks in cooperation with the Red Cross organizations, or separately from them. The extraordinary proliferation of NGOs in general, and particularly of those concerned with relief assistance and development, and the international recognition of the value of their contribution is a phenomenon specific to the late Twentieth Century.

In a first section of this Chapter, we will recall the composition and mandate of the organizations of the Red Cross system, their main characteristics as well as some of their recent activities. Issues concerning the Red Cross principles of neutrality and impartiality and the practice of discretion will be considered in Chapter 4.

In a second section, the role and main characteristics of the other (non-Red Cross), more typical NGOs will be examined.

In a third section, some of the bodies and mechanisms created for the coordination of NGOs will be reviewed.

The legal status of humanitarian NGOs and the protection of humanitarian volunteers will be reviewed in Chapter 9.

The International Red Cross and Red Crescent Movement

The International Red Cross and Red Crescent Movement is composed of the ICRC, the National Red Cross and Red Crescent Societies and the League of Red Cross and Red Crescent Societies. Each component of the Movement is independent, although they should all act in accordance with the Fundamental Principles of the Movement and cooperate with each other.

It is a transnational movement or network linked by common principles, a common name and, initially, a common emblem, the Red Cross, now a dual emblem, the Red Cross and the Red Crescent. It has no "chief", but each component has functional responsibilities and act together in some of its functions. The powers of the International Conference of the Red Cross for decision-making and for ensuring unity between the components are limited[1].

The seven Fundamental Principles of the Movement, e.g. Humanity, Impartiality, Neutrality, Independence, Voluntary Service, Unity and Universality were proclaimed by the XXth International Conference of the Red Cross in Vienna in 1965 (Resolution No. IX). These Principles are specific to the Red Cross Movement and must be respected by all its components. The revised text adopted in 1986 is in Table 2.1.

---

[1] *Statutes and Rules of Procedure of the International Red Cross and Red Crescent Movement*, adopted by the Twenty-Fifth International Conference of the Red Cross at Geneva in October 1986, pp. 5 and 6. The Statutes were first adopted in 1928, then revised in 1952. In *International Review of the Red Cross*, Jan.–Feb. 1987.

The Preamble to the Statutes of the International Red Cross and Red Crescent Movement has proclaimed that the National Red Cross and Red Crescent Societies, the ICRC and the League "together constitute a worldwide humanitarian movement", e.g. the International Red Cross Movement[2].

The components of the Movement meet at the International Conference of the Red Cross and Red Crescent with the States Parties to the Geneva Conventions of 27 July 1929 or of 12 August 1949, normally every four years.

Table 2.1. The fundamental principles of the international red cross and red crescent movement.

Humanity
The International Red Cross and Red Crescent Movement, born of a desire to bring assistance without discrimination to the wounded on the battlefield, endeavours, in its international and national capacity, to prevent and alleviate human suffering wherever it may be found. Its purpose is to protect life and health and to ensure respect for the human being. It promotes mutual understanding, friendship, co-operation and lasting peace amongst all peoples.

Impartiality
It makes no discrimination as to nationality, race, religious beliefs, class or political opinions. It endeavours to relieve the suffering of individuals, being guided solely by their needs, and to give priority to the most urgent cases of distress.

Neutrality
In order to continue to enjoy the confidence of all, the Red Cross may not take sides in hostilities or engage at any time in controversies of a political, racial, religious or ideological nature.

Independence
The Movement is independent. The National Societies, while auxiliaries in the humanitarian services of their governments and subject to the laws of their respective countries, must always maintain their autonomy so that they may be able at all times to act in accordance with the principles of the Movement.

Voluntary Service
It is a voluntary relief movement not prompted in any manner by desire for gain.

Unity
There can be only one Red Cross or one Red Crescent Society in any one country. It must be open to all. It must carry on its humanitarian work throughout its territory.

Universality
The International Red Cross and Red Crescent Movement in which all Societies have equal status and share equal responsibilities and duties in helping each other, is worldwide.

Source: Compendium of Reference Texts on the International Red Cross and Red Crescent Movement, Geneva, 1990, p. 8. This revised text is contained in the Statutes of the Movement. It was adopted by the XXVth International Conference of the Red Cross, Geneva, 1986.

[2] *Ibid,* p.5.

The International Committee of the Red Cross (ICRC)

In 1863, Henry Dunant and four other citizens of Geneva founded the "International Committee for Relief to the Wounded", known as the ICRC since 1875. In 1864, an international conference in which the representatives of 16 States participated adopted the first Geneva Convention.

As an independent humanitarian organization and as the founding body of the Red Cross, the ICRC's role is mainly to maintain and disseminate the Fundamental Principles, to recognize National Societies, to undertake the tasks incumbent upon it under the Geneva Conventions, to monitor the application of international humanitarian law applicable in armed conflicts, to ensure the protection of and assistance to military and civilian victims. In brief, the ICRC is essentially a promoter, guarantor, custodian and monitor of international humanitarian law. It is also an important actor in international relief and medical assistance.

The ICRC's Role in International Humanitarian Law

As a neutral and independent institution and intermediary between parties to international or non-international armed conflicts, the ICRC may take any humanitarian initiative within its role, in order to bring protection and assistance to the victims of these situations.

Following the original 1864 Geneva Convention, the ICRC has been instrumental in enlarging and updating humanitarian law and having it adopted by States. As noted by Armstrong[3]

> The invariable sequence of events has seen an *ad hoc* action by the ICRC develop into a general practice that later achieved the status of a customary norm in international law and was finally codified by treaties and conventions.

The current international treaties in force are the four 1949 Geneva Conventions which demand respect for human beings in time of armed conflict and provide that persons not directly participating in the hostilities, such as the wounded, the sick, medical personnel, chaplains, prisoners of war and civilians in enemy or occupied territory, shall be protected.

The States party to the Conventions pledge to:

— care for friends and enemies alike;
— respect every human being, his honour, family rights, religious convictions and the special rights of the child;
— prohibit inhuman or degrading treatment, the taking of hostages, mass extermination, torture, summary executions, deportations, pillage and the wanton destruction of private property;

---

[3] J.D.Armstrong, "The International Red Cross Committee and Political Prisoners", *International Organization*, Vol. 39, No.4, Autumn 1985, p. 621.

— authorize ICRC delegates to visit prisoners of war and civilian internees, and to interview without witnesses persons in detention.

The 1949 Conventions have been supplemented by the two 1977 Additional Protocols applicable in the event of international armed conflict and non international armed conflict.

By November 1990, there were 164 States party to the Conventions, 97 States party to Protocol I, and 87 to Protocol II. Further reference to the "Conventions" will imply "Conventions and Protocols", unless specified otherwise in the text.

The ICRC continues to promote the development of international humanitarian law by initiating studies and conferences, in consultation with experts.

The Conventions and Protocols commit those States which have ratified them, or which have acceded to them, to specific humanitarian obligations. At the same time, their provisions confer on the ICRC certain rights:—the right to take action, such as the right to visit prisoners of war and civilian persons protected by the Fourth Geneva Convention—the right to make proposals to States, such as to offer its services. The Movement's Statutes recognize that the ICRC has a right of humanitarian initiative in situations not covered by the Conventions or their Protocols.

Within its role under humanitarian law, the ICRC's Central Tracing Agency obtains and records information which might enable dead, wounded or missing persons, prisoners of war and civilian persons protected by the Fourth Geneva Convention, to be identified and to pass information to families.

The Relief Role of the ICRC

Other ICRC activities include assistance to war disabled, assistance to war victims by providing medical care, setting up hospitals and rehabilitation centres, assistance to civilians by providing material aid, such as food, shelter and clothing.

In principle, the ICRC undertakes material and medical aid programmes only in cases of armed conflict and internal disturbances and tension, and only providing it can:

— carry out on-the-spot checks on the urgency of the victims' needs;
— make local surveys to identify the categories and numbers of people requiring assistance;
— organize and supervise relief distributions[4].

Assistance to victims of natural disasters and epidemics is a responsibility of the League, not of the ICRC.

In accordance with the "Principles and Rules for Red Cross Disaster Relief"[5], the prevention of disasters, assistance to victims and reconstruction are the respon-

---

[4] *1988 Annual Report, ICRC*, p.9.
[5] *International Red Cross Handbook*, 12th Ed., July 1983, pp.488–494.

sibility of the public authorities. In principle, Red Cross help is of an auxiliary and complementary nature and operates basically in the emergency phase. Depending on circumstances and available resources, the Red Cross may undertake longer-term assistance programmes.

Since the end of War World II, medical activities have diversified. While care of the wounded and the supply of medicines and medical equipment remain the top priority in countries in conflict, other activities now include disease prevention, nutrition programmes, water purification and public hygiene.

The ICRC: A Swiss Institution

The ICRC is a Swiss Association created under Article 60 and following of the Swiss Civil Code: as such, it enjoys Swiss legal personality. It is a private, independent NGO, exclusively composed of Swiss nationals.

The ICRC's supreme policy-making body is the Assembly, composed of the ICRC members: the ICRC coopts its members (from fifteen to twenty-five) from among Swiss citizens.

The institutions' field operations and administration are managed by its headquarters in Geneva, and by delegations set up in or sent to areas of conflict throughout the world. In 1990, the ICRC staffing consisted of more than 600 employees at its headquarters, plus 700 delegates working in field delegations, of whom about 100 were seconded by National Red Cross Societies. In addition, 4,000 local collaborators assisted the ICRC in field activities. They are generally nationals of these countries.

As the ICRC mission and activities are international and not limited to, nor oriented towards Switzerland, questions have been asked since shortly after its creation whether the ICRC should not become an international, multinational secretariat, like the secretariats of IGOs, and like the secretariat of the League. The composition of the ICRC Assembly, by cooptation of eminent Swiss citizens has allowed close functional and personal relationships between ICRC leaders and Swiss governmental authorities, particularly in the development of humanitarian law for armed conflicts. The ICRC hosts preparatory meetings, and presents working documents to the diplomatic conferences called and chaired by the Swiss government, which is the official depository for the Geneva Conventions. Observers have alleged that the cultural, intellectual and political "symbiosis" between the Swiss government and ICRC leaders has influenced ICRC positions and decisions, particularly in periods of high political and military tensions, when politically-sensitive decisions to intervene, or not to intervene, to take or to avoid public positions, had to be taken.

Those who favour the *status quo* argue that the ICRC's extraordinary role on the international scene is directly related to Switzerland's own unique status, and to the ICRC's own relationship with the Swiss government. The Red Cross principle of neutrality is consonant with the international neutral status of Switzerland.

Switzerland's abstention policy, its non-participation in the two World Wars, its non-participation in the United Nations, are deemed to have facilitated the humanitarian activities of the ICRC as a neutral intermediary. To internationalize the ICRC would introduce political controversies in its midst, and hence put an end to an impartial protection for victims of conflict. It would introduce problems of "equitable geographic representation" which have been major irritants in the staffing of most IGOs and have caused criticisms of favouring a "good" nationality to the detriment of qualifications. A multinational staff might also have less respect for discretion than the Swiss.

Switzerland's reputation as a safe country for diplomacy, its peaceful internal politics, its geographic position, its communications, transportation and financial facilities all support and reinforce the value of a Swiss ICRC. Switzerland has given the ICRC a partial diplomatic status: for instance, the Swiss government has given the ICRC a declaration guaranteeing the inviolability of the ICRC buildings and grounds, as if they were diplomatic, or IGO, property,—the inviolability of the ICRC's information about foreign countries has also been guaranteed,—ICRC delegates on mission are entitled to a Swiss diplomatic passport[6].

Forsythe[7] suggests that the all-Swiss Committee is an asset to ICRC work, because that body is widely associated with responsible and conscientious activity. Indeed the Swiss well-earned reputation for hard work, integrity and pragmatism can only reflect favourably on the image of a humanitarian Swiss institution.

The Swiss government is the main government contributor to the ICRC budget: in 1988, its contribution amounted to one fourth of all governments' contributions.

The ICRC considers[8] that independence, neutrality and impartiality are based on its three special characteristics:

— its members are coopted, thereby excluding any kind of external influence;
— its members are all of the same nationality, thereby preventing governments from influencing the ICRC in taking its decisions;
— being Swiss, its members are citizens of a country which is bound by neutral status in perpetuity.

In terms of organizational efficiency, the Swiss members of the ICRC have a common appreciation of issues and a common approach to problem-solving and decision-making: decisions can be made more quickly by a "uninational" than by a multinational and multicultural group.

In practice, the ICRC seeks a Swiss monopoly only over its headquarters staff and personnel engaged in Red Cross protection: only Swiss personnel will undertake detention visits and other sensitive diplomatic matters. On the other hand, the

[6] Armstrong, op.cit., p. 641, — David P. Forsythe, *Humanitarian Politics: The International Committee of the Red Cross*, The Johns Hopkins University Press, 1977, p. 9.

[7] Forsythe, op.cit., pp. 207–208.

[8] *The ICRC, the League and the Report on the Re-Appraisal of the Role of the Red Cross*, Geneva, 1979, p. 53.

ICRC does not seek a Swiss monopoly on Red Cross personnel engaged in assistance missions: such personnel is provided in part by the multinational League, which draws its staff from National Societies.

Those in favour of internationalizing the ICRC generally allege that it would make the organization more acceptable to governments and that

> an international body would be more aware of the world and responsive to its problems than an Assembly selected from a small, affluent European country with a Christian tradition[9].

Some have argued that the ICRC's overclose relationship with the Swiss government may influence the Committee by the same attitudes found in Swiss governmental circles, attitudes more concerned with governmental rights, national sovereignty, diplomatic relations and law than with humanitarian values *per se*.

A more recent argument might be that such a close link between an international humanitarian organization and Switzerland might no longer be desirable at a time when the country's moral respectability and international renown had been the object of criticisms[10].

Another speculative question is whether Switzerland might, at some future date, join the European Community and the United Nations (in reversal of the Swiss people's rejection of U.N. membership in the referendum of March 1986), and whether such participation might affect Switzerland's neutrality, and in consequence, affect the neutral image of the ICRC.

The Tansley Report (8) concluded in 1975 that the ICRC should continue to be constituted as in the past. In its comments to the Report, in 1979, the ICRC shared the view that to internationalize the Committee would mean to introduce political controversies in its midst and hence put an end to an impartial protection, the only valid protection, for victims of conflicts. The Committee realized that it was the wish of almost all States which entrust it with duties under the Geneva Conventions to maintain its Swiss composition.

Indeed, the XXVth International Conference of the Red Cross confirmed this assumption in adopting Article 5.1 of the Statutes of the International Red Cross and Red Crescent Movement, which refers to the Swiss composition of the ICRC.

In order to avoid a Swiss parochialism and to counterbalance the need for its uninationality, the ICRC agreed with the Tansley Report that it should seek the advice of non-Swiss authorities from around the world in situations or problems confronting it. It would not thereby lose anything of its essential independence but

---

[9] D.D. Tansley, *Final Report: An Agenda for the Red Cross*, Geneva, 1975, quoted by Armstrong, op.cit., p. 641.

[10] According to *Newsweek*, 27 March 1989, "problems of money-laundering by international drug traffickers have cracked the secretive world of Swiss banking". One of the first casualties was Swiss Justice Minister Elizabeth Kopp. *Le Monde* referred to the "chipped" Swiss respectability (26–27 March 1989).

would be better prepared to act for the greatest benefit of the victims whom it is its mission to protect.

Whether or not the ICRC has, in the past, been overoriented to the Swiss establishment and whether or not the ICRC has appeared to consider itself "more Swiss than Red Cross", it is in the interest of the Red Cross and Red Crescent Movement and in the interest of the victims under ICRC protection that the ICRC should retain its Swiss nature and composition, based on history, tradition, long practice, organization's culture and common values as well as on its Statutes.

The ICRC is and will remain "different" from the typical international organizations. Its internationalism is demonstrated and guaranteed, not by a multinational staff, but by a strict respect for the Fundamental Principles of impartiality, neutrality and independence.

The dual responsibility of the ICRC and of the Swiss Government for the protection of ICRC delegates is discussed in Chapter 9.

Recent Activities of the ICRC

In 1988, the ICRC was active in 88 countries in Africa, Latin America, Asia, the Middle East and Europe, providing protection and assistance for the victims of armed conflict and internal disturbances and tension.

In 1988, ICRC delegates visited prisoners of war and "security detainees" in 830 places of detention in 36 countries. The purpose of these visits was to inspect the material and psychological conditions of detention and the treatment accorded to prisoners, provide detainees with relief if required (medicines, clothing, toilet articles), and, if necessary, ask the authorities to take steps to improve the detainees' treatment and living conditions.

The activities of the ICRC Central Tracing Agency included the following:

— almost 1.5 million Red Cross messages were exchanged, most of them in relation to the Iraq-Iran conflict;
— more than 78,000 requests for tracing missing persons were processed;
— 2,283 travel documents were provided;
— 652 family reunifications and 4,865 repatriations were organized.

The ICRC dispatched a total of 77,291 tons of relief materials (not including medical supplies), worth Sw.F. 65 million, to 39 countries. This included relief supplies purchased by the ICRC (18,680 tons) and supplies made available by donor governments (58,644 tons).

The costs of medical assistance amounted to Sw.F. 11.5 million. In addition, the ICRC sent 274 medical and paramedical personnel (doctors, surgeons, male and female nurses, physiotherapists, prosthesists, nutritionists, public health specialists and medical administrators) to take part in missions. Of these, 132 were seconded to the ICRC by the National Red Cross Societies of 19 countries (most of them from Western countries).

A few examples of specific ICRC activities in 1988 follow:

— in August 1988, the ICRC repatriated 3,789 prisoners of war and civilian internees detained by Somalia and Ethiopia in connection with the Ogaden conflict;
— in Zaire, delegates visited regularly over 300 security detainees in 42 places of detention in Kinshasa and other parts of the country;
— a workshop for the production of prostheses and other orthopaedic fittings was set up in Ho Chi Minh City for the many Vietnamese war amputees[11].

In January 1989, the ICRC stepped up its airlift of relief supplies to Southern Sudan, in the first phase of a relief operation for the victims of conflict and famine. It extended its large-scale operation in Afghanistan, setting up bases outside Kabul, to reach more victims of the conflict.

In April, the ICRC extended its assistance programme for civilians affected by the conflict in Mozambique. The ICRC was the only organization working in zones not fully controlled by the Mozambican government.

On 10 April, the ICRC repatriated a group of 66 wounded, sick or elderly Iraqi prisoners of war from Iran to Iraq, as a result of a unilateral decision taken by Iran. Since the Gulf conflict began in 1980, the ICRC has repatriated over 2,100 Iranian and Iraqi prisoners of war: more than 100,000 were still held by the two sides (until August 1990) and should have been repatriated without delay after the cease-fire of 20 August 1988, according to the provisions of the Third Geneva Convention.

In October 1989, the ICRC completed a four-week visit to detainees in Jordan: two delegates and a doctor saw 3,280 prisoners in six rehabilitation centres and one military detention centre. The visits take place every 18 months.

In November, the ICRC regional delegation visited 17 security detainees in Togolese prisons. Most of the detainees were arrested after an attempted coup in September 1986, and were last seen by ICRC delegates in October that year.

Also in November, for the first time since 1976, the ICRC was able to visit detainees held in Sri Lanka.

In December, the ICRC organized a major emergency operation in Romania, with the ICRC headquarters in Geneva and delegates in the field coordinating the efforts of around 20 National Societies. In January 1990, the ICRC was given permission to visit detainees held in Romania as a result of the "Revolution".

In the domain of international conventions, the ICRC welcomed the declaration of a high-level Conference on chemical weapons held in Paris in January 1989, where representatives of 149 countries pledged not to use chemical weapons and urged the U.N. Conference on Disarmament to conclude a convention as soon as possible to ban their production and storage, and bring about the destruction of existing stocks. The ICRC has long been opposed to these weapons. In 1918, it stated that they were "a method of warfare which could only be described as crimi-

[11] *1988 Annual Report—The ICRC Worldwide.*

nal". The ICRC had taken an active part in the work leading to the adoption of the Geneva Protocol of 1925 which prohibits their use in international armed conflicts[12].

The Budget of the ICRC

In 1950, the ICRC budget expenditures amounted to Sw.F. 4.5 million,—in 1970, 15.6 million,—in 1980, 142 million. In 1988, its overall expenditures totalled Sw.F. 349 million, comprising Sw.F. 102.9 million for the regular budget and Sw.F. 246.1 million for special budgets. Africa accounted for the largest share of ICRC expenditures (43 percent). Operational expenditures including material and medical assistance totalled 59 percent of the 1988 budget. Protection expenditures accounted for 17.3 percent of the budget.

The main government contributions for 1988 were from:

— Switzerland	Sw.F. 45.6	million
— U.S.A. Sw.	F. 41.3	million
— Canada Sw.	F. 16	million
— Federal Republic of Germany	Sw. F. 14.2	million

The European Community provided Sw.F. 6.9 million in emergency aid and Sw.F. 6 million in food aid.

The main contributions from National Societies were from Sweden, Japan, Libya and the Netherlands[13].

National Red Cross and Red Crescent Societies

Within ten years of the creation of the ICRC, National Red Cross Committees (now Societies) had been established in 22 European countries. The Movement then spread to other parts of the world. In 1990, there were 149 National Societies, with more than 250 million members, grouped in the League.

National Societies are the basic units of the Red Cross Movement. They support the public authorities in their humanitarian tasks. Within their own countries, they are autonomous national organizations, providing a framework for the activities of their voluntary members and their staff.

They provide emergency relief assistance on a national and international basis, to assist the victims of armed conflicts as provided by the Geneva Conventions, as well as the victims of natural disasters and other emergencies.

They are to disseminate international humanitarian law[14].

---

[12] ICRC *Bulletins*, February, April, May, December 1989, January 1990.

[13] *1988 Annual Report, ICRC*.

[14] *Statutes and Rules ...*, op.cit., Art.3), 4).

The recognition of National Societies by the ICRC is subject to strict conditions (see Table 2.2), which include:

— only one Red Cross or Red Crescent Society may be recognized in one state;
— they must have an autonomous status;
— they must respect the Fundamental Principles of the Movement and be guided in their work by the principles of international humanitarian law.

Table 2.2. Conditions for recognition of National Red Cross and Red Crescent Societies

1. Be constituted on the territory of an independent State where the Geneva Convention for the Amelioration of the Condition of the Wounded and Sick in Armed Forces in the Field is in force.
2. Be the only National Red Cross or Red Crescent Society of the said State and be directed by a central body which shall alone be competent to represent it in its dealings with other components of the Movement.
3. Be duly recognized by the legal government of its country on the basis of the Geneva Conventions and of the national legislation as a voluntary aid society, auxiliary to the public authorities in the humanitarian field.
4. Have an autonomous status which allows it to operate in conformity with the Fundamental Principles of the Movement.
5. Use the name and emblem of the Red Cross or Red Crescent in conformity with the Geneva Conventions.
6. Be so organized as to be able to fulfil the tasks defined in its own statutes, including the preparation in peace time for its statutory tasks in case of armed conflict.
7. Extend its activities to the entire territory of the State.
8. Recruit its voluntary members and its staff without consideration of race, sex, class, religion or political opinions.
9. Adhere to the present Statutes, share in the fellowship which unites the components of the Movement and co-operate with them.
10. Respect the Fundamental Principles of the Movement and be guided in its work by the principles of international humanitarian law.

Source: Statutes of the International Red Cross and Red Crescent Movement (adopted by the Twenty-fifth International Conference of the Red Cross at Geneva in October 1986), Art. 4.

The National Societies were originally created for service in time of war, to help the army medical personnel care for the wounded and the sick. After World War I, their role expanded in medico-social activities: the creation of hospitals, nursing schools, education programmes in child care and public health, pioneering ambulance, mountain and sea rescue services, providing first aid training, caring for the elderly and the handicapped, and youth programmes. National Societies also promote or run blood transfusion services.

Since World War II, National Societies in industrialized countries have initiated drug addiction, unemployment and delinquency-related programmes. In developing countries, National Societies have engaged in basic health education, intensive vaccination campaigns, training for medical and social administrators.

The National Societies also provide relief and social services to refugees and, more generally, to the victims of natural disasters.

Typically, National Societies are national NGOs, although their links with governments in a number of countries make them quasi-official organizations.

Forsythe[15] has submitted that the Red Cross Movement has been "nationalized" to a great extent:

> The National Red Cross Societies, once recognized, have been free to adopt the dominant values of the nation.

After recognition, the ICRC can exercise almost no control, and very little influence, over the composition and activities of a National Society. The ICRC has never withdrawn its recognition of a National Society.

It is indeed very difficult for a National Society to be really independent from its government. One reason is that the National Red Cross tends to be part of the "establishment", and its leaders are often appointed by the government[16]. Some National Societies perform quasi-governmental functions, such as blood collection and transfusion, first aid duties, or training nurses. Most Societies are funded in part by public funds. Finally, in the field of international humanitarian protection, it is difficult for a National Society to oppose government policies or practices with regard to political, religious or ethnic minorities, or in the face of armed rebellion.

The international character of National Societies is only maintained by the thread of a common ideal, common principles and their formal belonging to the International Red Cross Movement. It is reinforced by the more substantial experience of joint international relief activities with the ICRC, the League and other National Societies.

The League of Red Cross and Red Crescent Societies

One of the leaders of the American Red Cross, Henry P. Davison, convened an international medical conference in 1919 at which he proposed

> to federate the Red Cross Societies of the different countries into an organization comparable to that of the League of Nations, in view of a permanent worldwide crusade to improve health, prevent sickness and alleviate suffering.

On 5 May 1919, the League was founded in Paris. Since 1939, its permanent home has been in Geneva, in a location at some distance from that of the ICRC.

---

[15] Forsythe, op.cit., pp. 15, 16, 18.

[16] For instance, the appointment of Georgina Dufoix, Socialist "Chargée de mission" to the French President of the Republic, as President of the French Red Cross Society, in April 1989, has been criticized for introducing partisan politics into an "autonomous" National Society. In fact Mme Dufoix was well qualified to lead the French Red Cross out of its morale, management and financial crisis, without jeopardizing its independence: *Le Monde*, 28 Apr. 1989, *Journal du Dimanche*, 30 Apr. 1989, *Libération*, 9 May 1989.

The Red Cross peacetime programme was consecrated by Article 25 of the League of Nations Covenant, which read:

> The members of the League of Nations agree to encourage and promote the establishment and cooperation of duly authorized voluntary National Red Cross organizations, having as purposes the improvement of health, the prevention of disease and the mitigation of suffering throughout the world[17].

The League is an international NGO, a federation of 149 National Societies. While it is an independent organization, separate from the ICRC, it is a component of the Red Cross Movement, which is to abide by the Red Cross Fundamental Principles and by the Principles and Rules adopted by the International Conference in the field of relief action. The League is required to cooperate with the other components of the Movement, and, in particular, to maintain frequent regular contacts with the ICRC in order to coordinate their activities.

The main functions of the League are:

— to act as the permanent body of liaison, coordination and study between the National Societies and give them assistance;
— to bring relief by all available means to all disaster victims;
— to assist the National Societies in their disaster relief preparedness, in the organization of their relief actions and in the relief operations themselves;
— to assist the ICRC in the promotion and development of international humanitarian law;
— to be the official representative of the member Societies in the international field[18].

The League acts as the information centre for the Red Cross regarding situations caused by disasters and coordinates at the international level the assistance provided by the National Societies and the League or channelled through them.

The League's Activities

The League has participated with the League of Nations in the creation, in 1922, of the International Committee for Relief to Russia, then suffering from famine. The ICRC and the League provided relief following the 1923 earthquake in Japan, and floods in China in 1931.

More recently, in 1959–1961, the League sent an international staff of 180 persons from 16 National Societies and obtained funding to assist in the rehabilitation of Moroccans who had been poisoned by mineral oil. The League distributed relief supplies to Algerian refugees in Tunisia and Morocco, between 1958 and 1962. In 1960, under ICRC leadership, the League and National Societies sent 28

---

[17] *Red Cross and Red Crescent—Portrait of an International Movement*, 1989, p. 15,—*The League of Red Cross and Red Crescent Societies, 1919–1989*, 1989, pp. 3–4.

[18] *Statutes and Rules . . .* , op.cit., Art. 6.

teams (totalling 100 persons) of doctors, nurses and other personnel from 20 countries to give medical aid to the newly independent Congo (now Zaire).

Between 1984 and 1986, the League distributed food in 21 African countries, feeding around 2 million famished people with the help of 250 expatriate delegates and thousands of national Red Cross volunteers[19].

In 1988, the League launched a record 51 international emergency appeals in aid of 6.2 million victims of earthquakes, floods, drought and famine, hurricanes, cyclones and typhoons, landslides, epidemics, insect plagues, economic depression, ethnic violence and insecurity in 41 countries. Cash contributions received for operations and programmes amounted to Sw.F. 76.3 million,—cash, kind and services contributions were estimated as totalling Sw.F. 110.7 million. 140 delegates were recruited directly by the League or through National Societies and assigned to the disaster areas. The League's supplies service arranged the purchase and despatch of some 50,000 tons of relief supplies and the forwarding of goods stocked in the League's regional disaster warehouses.

In 1989, the League launched 39 international emergency appeals, seeking Sw.F. 54 million for 2.5 million victims of natural disasters and other emergencies, in 33 countries. The League's biggest relief operation was in earthquake shattered Armenia. Cash contributions received for operations and programmes amounted to Sw.F. 81.6 million. Secretariat expenditures amounted to almost Sw.F. 23 million. At the end of 1989, the League had 188 employees[20].

Coordination Between the ICRC and the League

Insofar as the ICRC, the National Societies and the League are all parts of the International Red Cross Movement, and as neither the ICRC nor the League can claim or assume an overall leadership role over the other components, there is a compelling need for cooperation and coordination, as integration of those independent bodies is not desired.

Armstrong[21] notes that the distinction between the ICRC, on the one hand, and the League and National Societies, on the other, is "carefully maintained", especially by the ICRC, for two main reasons. The first is the difference of functions between the two organizations—ICRC, the international guardian of humanitarian law and the neutral intermediary—the National Societies' national health work and the League's international relief work. The second reason is that the ICRC's reputation for strict impartiality might be endangered if it found itself in too close a relationship with National Societies identified too closely with their government's policies. In 1979, the ICRC rejected a proposal that it should share a building, or at

---

[19] *The League, 1919–1989*, op.cit., and *1960 Annual Report—ICRC*.

[20] The League *Review*, 1988 and 1989.

[21] Armstrong, op.cit., pp. 616–617.

least a common site with the League, mainly because of the "type of mandate" it had received from governments. The League had been in favour of the proposal, mainly because it would have demonstrated convincingly to the public the unity of the International Red Cross[22].

Other reasons, such as the different cultures of the two institutions (one Swiss, one multinational), competition or rivalry for programmes and funds, personal characteristics of top or middle-level managers, may also explain the resistance to a closer union or integration of the two institutions.

While the ICRC has its own mandate and responsibilities in the field of humanitarian law and protection, both the ICRC and the League have relief assistance functions: hence, there is a potential area for conflicts of leadership and competence between the two, and possible overlapping of assistance, and a compelling need for clarification of their respective responsibilities and roles.

In principle, the ICRC has responsibility for international assistance during armed conflicts while the League is concerned with peacetime natural disaster situations.

However, the League's components, the National Societies, have a dual national and international assistance role: they assist victims of armed conflicts as provided in the Geneva Conventions *and* victims of natural disasters and other emergencies, while their coordinator, the League, is supposed to deal only with the latter: here lies another possible source of conflict, or confusion.

Cooperation is based on statutory texts and on practice[23].

The ICRC cooperates at the highest policy-making levels, the International Red Cross Conference and the Council of Delegates.

Members of the International Conference, the supreme deliberative body for the Movement, include delegations from the ICRC and the League, in addition to delegations from National Societies and from the States Parties to the Geneva Conventions. The trustee of the International Conference between two Conferences, the Standing Commission includes representatives of both the ICRC and the League (including the Presidents of both organizations), in addition to representatives of National Societies. One of the functions of the Standing Commission is to

promote harmony in the work of the Movement and, in this connection, coordination among its components.

The Council of Delegates is the body where the representatives of National Societies, the ICRC and the League meet to discuss matters which concern the Movement as a whole.

---

[22] *Report on the Re-Appraisal of the Role of Red Cross*, op.cit., pp.44–45.
[23] *Statutes and Rules . . .*, op.cit.: see in particular Statutes, Art. 1.2, 3.3, 5.2 d), 5.3 b), 6.4 i), 7, 9.1, 10.6, 13, 17.1, 18.3 a).

Article 7 of the Statutes requires that the components of the Movement "shall cooperate with each other" and in particular, that the ICRC and the League

> shall maintain frequent regular contact with each other at all appropriate levels so as to coordinate their activities in the best interest of those who require their protection and assistance.

The 1969 Agreement between the ICRC and the League contained a number of provisions for cooperation, particularly in the field of relief.

On 20 October 1989, a new Agreement was concluded between the ICRC and the League[24]. *Inter alia*, it provides that:

— the ICRC and the League will coordinate their respective methods for relief preparedness;
— in addition to their cooperation in training medical and paramedical staff, the ICRC and the League will work together to standardize the supplies and medical equipment used in relief operations;
— in situations of international or other armed conflict, the ICRC will assume the general direction of international Red Cross and Red Crescent actions;
— in situations of peace, the League will coordinate the relief work of National Societies following any major disaster;
— in other situations requiring action by a specifically neutral and independent institution, the ICRC will assume the general direction of Red Cross and Red Crescent international action;
— the Presidents of the ICRC and the League will meet as often as they deem useful;
— the Directorate and staff of the ICRC and the Secretary General and staff of the League will cooperate in daily routine matters;
— in countries where both institutions are present, ICRC and League delegates will maintain contact and cooperate.

These provisions formalize past practices[25] and also reflect a need and sincere wish for closer cooperation between the two institutions.

In the past, the ICRC and the League have occasionally cooperated in joint appeals and operations. For instance, they made joint appeals for aid in March/April 1975, in favour of displaced persons from Cambodia, and North and South Vietnam. A Working Group, the "Indochina Bureau", was formed in Geneva to coordinate, execute and administer Red Cross international relief operations in those countries under the supervision and direct authority of the League and the ICRC. In 1979, they formed a task force for South-East Asia to supplement the relief operations conducted by governments and the UNHCR.

---

[24] *Compendium of Reference Texts on the International Red Cross and Red Crescent Movement*, Geneva, 1990, "Agreement between the ICRC and the League of Red Cross and Red Crescent Societies", 20 October 1989, pp. 45–59.
[25] *Report on the Re-Appraisal...*, op.cit., pp. 41–42.

The current thinking is that the origin of appeals and the responsibility for operations should be clearly identified, in part to establish accountability in relation to donors, and in part for reasons of effectiveness: instead of joint appeals and joint management, one organization only (the ICRC or the League) should call for funds and be fully responsible for the management of the operations.

Coordination of Red Cross Organizations with Other Organizations

Three years after the creation of the U.N., in 1948, the XVIIth International Red Cross Conference recommended that the Red Cross components exercise "the greatest care" in regulating their relationship with intergovernmental, governmental and non-governmental organizations.

Almost two decades later, this caution, related to the political conflicts of the Cold War in the U.N., had given way to a more positive attitude of cooperation with U.N. organizations, while safeguarding the unique status of the Red Cross, its freedom of action and its universality[26].

There is now an active interaction between the Red Cross organizations and the U.N. organizations concerned with relief, and with other national and international NGOs.

Internationally, the ICRC and the League maintain close cooperation with UNDRO. Training events have been jointly organized and contacts are permanent on relief operations. Contacts are maintained both centrally and in the field, on a practical level, with WHO, UNICEF, WFP, FAO, WMO, UNDP and with certain regional organizations such as ESCAP (U.N. Economic and Social Commission for Asia and the Pacific) and PAHO (Pan American Health Organization), among others[27].

In Geneva, a regular process of working cooperation between the main international relief NGOs has been in operation since 1972: the "Licross/Volags" Steering Committee for disasters was founded by the League, Catholic Relief Services (CRS), the Lutheran World Federation (LWF), the World Council of Churches (WCC) and Oxfam. The Steering Committee meets twice a year in rotating locations: its members are the chief executives of these NGOs. A policy-making body, it has contacts with the heads of secretariats of IGOs, including the Secretary-General of the U.N. and may submit joint policy statements to U.N. organizations. The secretary of the Steering Committee, appointed jointly by its members, is located at the League.

A sub-committee of the Steering Committee meets monthly at the League to

---

[26] *International Red Cross Handbook*, op.cit., pp. 616–617: Stockholm 1948, Resol.XVIII and Executive Committee, 84th Session, Geneva 1964, Resol. No. 31, approved by the Board of Governors, XXVIIIth Session, Vienna 1965.

[27] *Report on the Re-Appraisal...*, op.cit., pp. 36–37.

enable relief operations officers of each member organization, together with IGOs, to review current disaster situations and exchange information: it is called the "Meeting of International Agencies on Disaster Information". Its membership is broader than that of the Steering Committee: in 1990, its membership included the ICRC, the League, the International Council of Voluntary Agencies, the American Joint Distribution Committee, Caritas Internationalis, Catholic Relief Services, Food for the Hungry International, International Civil Defence Organization, the International Save the Children Alliance, the Quaker U.N. Office, the Lutheran World Federation, the World Alliance of YMCAs, the World Council of Churches, World Vision International. Representatives of IGOs also attend: UNDRO, UNDP, UNHCR, UNICEF, WHO, FAO, IOM. Copies of minutes of the meetings are sent to the Australian Overseas Disaster Response Organization, to the French Permanent Mission in Geneva, to the Commission of the European Communities, to the U.N. in New York, to Oxfam and Tearfund. Short reports are made informally by NGO and IGO officials on current or planned operations in specific countries or areas, appeals for funds, refugee movements and other important issues. The main value of these monthly meetings lies in their informal nature, which provides a free exchange of information[28].

In 1979, the ICRC and the League noted that most of the management problems in disaster assistance are met at the national level. It was therefore essential that the National Society coordinate its activities with other national agencies and international organizations active in disaster situations in order to ensure the optimal use of available resources. If no such coordination was initiated by the government, the Red Cross, thanks to its special position, could play an important role in this field.

While the responsibility for national Red Cross planning lies with the National Society, the League may assist by despatching planning delegates or funds[29].

These positions of principles do not necessarily resolve all coordination problems at the national or local level, which involve NGOs outside the Red Cross purview, IGOs and national government agencies. The lack of a clear "lead agency coordinator", in the absence of a decisive recipient government coordinating body, remains a serious handicap to the effectiveness of relief operations.

In practice, several IGOs and NGOs have, or have acquired, a specialized competence in particular fields of relief assistance, which they apply in disaster situations: complementarity then becomes a substitute for coordination.

The "Real" Non-Governmental Organizations (NGOs)

We have seen that the ICRC, although legally established as a NGO, has a mandate and responsibilities in relation with governments, in particular with regard to the

---

[28] Information obtained from a member of the Steering Committee on 26 Sept. 1989.

[29] *Report on the Re-Appraisal ...*, ibid.

formulation and monitoring of international humanitarian law, which distinguishes it from the "real" (non-Red Cross) NGOs. The nature of some of the activities of National Red Cross and Red Crescent Societies, in close association with their government, gives them a quasi-public status, even though they are also legally established as NGOs.

For the purpose of this book, international humanitarian NGOs will be defined as non-governmental, autonomous, non-profit organizations, initiated by private citizens for a stated international relief assistance purpose, supported mainly by voluntary contributions in cash and kind from private purposes.

The term "NGO" will be used, in preference to "private voluntary organizations" (PVOs), a term more commonly used in the U.S.A.

Our focus is on international, rather than national NGOs, or more precisely on national NGOs which have developed international activities. However, some of our general comments about NGOs may apply to both national and international NGOs, or only to one type, depending on the context. Our focus is also on humanitarian NGOs: however, in view of the close connection between relief assistance and development, due to the need to expand emergency assistance into mid-term and long-term development plans, in view of the fact that some relief organizations also have a development role, part of our general review will include both humanitarian and development NGOs.

The legal nature of NGOs will be considered in Chapter 9.

General Comments on NGOs

The non-governmental nature of NGOs distinguishes them from IGOs, organizations created and directed by governments, and dependent on them. The fact that NGOs are created and managed by private individuals asserts, in principle, their claim to autonomy and independence from government authority, provided that they respect national legislation and regulations concerning their establishment and management. NGOs have mainly developed in political democracies, where the freedoms of association and expression are guaranteed and legally protected from government interference.

Financing NGOs activities mainly by private individual or group contributions will avoid an excessive reliance on the generosity and goodwill of the NGO's government, which could jeopardize the political and programme independence of the NGO. On the other hand, contributions by IGOs, organizations representing a collectivity of states, for specific projects, is not likely to affect the NGO's independence, provided that the projects fall within the mandate and policies of the NGO.

The motivation of these organizations is purely philanthropic, thus excluding any profit motive: funds are to be used essentially for the mandated relief and assistance, limiting administrative and fund-raising expenditures to the minimum.

The requirement that a NGO must be a formally established, organized and relatively permanent body excludes one-time fund-raising campaigns with a time-limited objective.

The Union of International Associations has set up a number of criteria for defining international NGOs covering aims, membership, structure, governance, finance and activities. The aim must be genuinely international in character, with the intention to be active in at least three countries. The membership of individuals and collectives must be drawn from at least three countries and must be open to any appropriately qualified individual or entity in the organization's area of operation. The constitution must provide for a formal structure which allows periodical elections of a governing body and officers and for a permanent headquarters. There should be a rotation of headquarters and officers among the various member countries at designated intervals. Substantial financial contributions to the budget must come from at least three countries. No attempt must be made to make profits for distribution to members of the NGO. Finally, there must be available evidence for current activities: NGOs not reporting for over five years are considered as "dissolved" or "dormant".

The U.N. Economic and Social Council applies broader criteria:

Any international organization which is not established by intergovernmental agreement shall be considered as a non-governmental organization... including organizations which accept members designated by government authorities, provided that such membership does not interfere with the free expression of views of the organization[30].

The first NGOs involved in foreign aid were the religious missions. According to Lissner[31], the oldest mission agency is the Canadian Society "Les Soeurs de la Congrégation de Notre-Dame" in Montréal, founded in 1653 and still active in education and literacy training in Latin America. Feld and Jordan[32], identify the "World's Evangelical Alliance", founded in 1846, as the first international NGO. The "World Alliance of Young Men's Christian Associations" (YMCA) was the first international NGO to settle in Geneva, in 1855, now the site of hundreds of NGOs.

The growth of IGOs and INGOs since World War II has been spectacular. The Union of International Associations has recorded

— in 1951, 123 IGOs and 832 NGOs
— in 1960, 154 IGOs and 1,255 NGOs
— in 1972, 280 IGOs and 2,795 NGOs
— in 1981, 1,039 IGOs and 9,398 NGOs

---

[30] ECOSOC Resol. 288(X) of 27 Feb. 1950 and 1296(XLIV) of 25 June 1968.

[31] Jorgen Lissner, *The Politics of Altruism—A Study of the Political Behaviour of Voluntary Development Agencies*, Lutheran World Federation, Geneva, 1977, p.58.

[32] Werner J. Feld and Robert S. Jordan, *International Organizations—A Comparative Approach*, 2nd Ed., Praeger, 1988, p. 26.

— in 1990, 1,856 IGOs and 16,208 NGOs[33].

It is estimated that from 400 to 500 international NGOs are involved in humanitarian activities.

In development terms, the 1980s have been called the decade of the NGOs:

> From relative obscurity a decade ago, NGOs have suddenly found themselves catapulted into international respectability. Donor governments and multilateral institutions now routinely pay tribute to their presumed capacity to reach the poor, and to the qualities of innovation and flexibility which are supposed to characterize NGO work[34].

Indeed the Chairman of the Organization for Economic Cooperation and Development (OECD) Development Assistance Committee, Mr. Joseph C.Wheeler, recognized in 1988 the mutually supporting roles among official and non-official organizations:

> To us on the official side, the NGO sector represents an educator of our publics, an aspect of our support, the origin of some of our policy, a welcome financial contribution, the source of insights on methodology and a vehicle for administering a portion of our official assistance[35].

The growth of NGOs and the recognition of the value of their contribution has been attributed to such factors as:

— governmental and intergovernmental budget constraints leading to alternative ways of financing development and assistance programmes;
— ideological views that social and economic programmes and development should not be totally controlled by donor and recipient government leaders and bureaucrats;
— the failures or failings of government-planned programmes, which have led to a pragmatic search for alternative approaches to development;
— the increasing technical competence of NGOs, evolving from classic voluntary, do-gooder enterprises, to more professional, specialized, effective organizations.

Although NGOs are diverse, they can be categorized according to their type of activity and their role.

---

[33] *Yearbook of International Organizations, 1989–1990*, Appendix 7: numbers include conventional and other international bodies, A through G. Including only "conventional international organizations" (A through D), there were 293 IGOs and 4,646 NGOs in 1990: see *Transnational Associations*, 1990, No. 4, pp. 220–221.

[34] Tim Brodhead, "NGOs: In One Year, Out the Other ?" in *World Development*, "Development Alternatives: the Challenge to NGOs", Vol. 15, Supplement, 1987, p.1.

[35] *Voluntary Aid for Development : The role of NGOs*, OECD, Paris, 1988, p. 5.

Typology of NGOs' Functions

In 1977, Lissner classified 1,502 NGOs into eight groups[36]:

— mission agencies
— Church-related agencies
— secular voluntary agencies
— educational institutions
— student welfare organizations
— Jewish welfare agencies
— labour and business organizations and foundations
— umbrella organizations.

Brodhead and O'Malley[37] have identified three broad functional categories: service delivery, innovation and advocacy. In the first category lies the bulk of traditional NGO activities: for instance, in the health field, developing and experimenting with low cost forms of primary health care, the running of hospitals and clinics, medical care for refugees, immunization programmes, developing and implementing rural water systems and other sanitation projects.

NGOs' innovation role refers to their development of new responses to meet needs, new products, more appropriate technologies, new processes.

The advocacy role of NGOs is represented by campaigns on agrarian reform, health education activities, the promotion of breast feeding. Advocacy may be related to the particular mission and philosophy of the NGO, its religious or secular nature, its ideological beliefs, its technical orientation and approach (emergency relief, "sustainable" development, community involvement).

These categories are not mutually exclusive: some NGOs may combine relief action with innovation and advocacy, while some voluntarily restrict themselves to only one or two roles.

Another distinction is between NGOs which work exclusively within industrialized countries (Northern national NGOs)—donor NGOs based in the North but working internationally (international NGOs),—and Third World indigenous NGOs. Some of the latter, like Church agencies in the Third World, may be affiliated with, subordinated to and subsidized by, world-wide Northern organizations.

Korten[38] has identified three "generations" of NGOs' voluntary development action: relief and welfare, small-scale local development and sustainable systems development.

---

[36] Lissner, op.cit., pp. 32–33.

[37] Tim Brodhead and Jeff O'Malley, "NGOs and Third World Development: Opportunities and Constraints", WHO Doc. GPA/GMC(2)/89.5, Add.1, Dec. 1989.

[38] David C. Korten, "Micro-Policy Reform—The Role of Private Voluntary Development Agencies", in *Community Management—Asian Experience and Perspectives*, Korten Ed., Kumarian Press, 1986, pp. 313–315.

Many of the larger international NGOs such as Catholic Relief Services, CARE, Save the Children, Oxfam and World Vision began as charitable relief organizations, relying on private contributions to deliver welfare services to the poor and afflicted throughout the world. Relief efforts were and remain an essential and appropriate response to emergency situations, which demand immediate and effective humanitarian response.

However useful it may be, relief and welfare assistance, such as the direct delivery of food, health care and shelter,only address symptoms: they do not attempt to identify or correct root causes of poverty, ill health, famine, nor to engage in planning and prevention. They usually are *ad hoc* emergency responses to humanitarian crises.

The "second generation" is essentially based on small-scale, community development projects aimed at self-reliance. In the 1970s, NGOs came to recognize that sustainable improvements in the lives of Third World populations depend on increasing their capacity to meet their own needs with their own resources. Thus many NGOs started to promote and fund local development activities in areas such as primary health care (as recommended by WHO and UNICEF), improved farming practices, local infrastructure, and other community development activities.

Such NGOs programmes have, in some countries, been resisted or controlled by governments, which saw them as competitive with their own public development programmes, and feared that independently-created local organizations might compete with, or oppose official doctrine or ideology.

NGOs realized that supporting the isolated community-based projects depended on systems linking local public and private organizations, in order to integrate local initiatives into a national development system.

In some countries, independent local groups may not be legally recognized, or their local income-generating activities may be in conflict with State agencies monopolies or they may be discouraged by central bureaucracies.

In such instances, the "third generation" NGOs will assume a catalytic role involving collaboration with government and other public and private institutions, to initiate new policies and institutional linkages that enable self-sustaining local private initiative. Third generation strategies cast the NGO into the role of catalyst of broader policy and structural change. It may involve direct lobbying at policy levels by influential personalities, sponsorship of policy research, public education campaigns, the advocacy of needed reforms in public policies. For Northern NGOs, it may even involve an advocacy role on macro-economic decisions and official aid assistance with governments of the industrialized countries.

For Elliott[39], the third generation of NGOs is the "empowerment and conscientization" approach, which sees poverty as the result of political processes. In this

---

[39] Charles Elliott, "Some Aspects of Relations between the North and South in the NGO Sector", in *World Development*, 1987, op.cit., pp. 57–68.

view, the international NGO seeks to establish relationships with local institutions, local NGOs and communities that enable the latter to become empowered to confront the politics and processes that impoverish them. According to the author, the techniques used by NGOs for the empowerment of local communities have to be located within an envelope of parameters determined by governments.

Siedentopf[40] links empowerment to the assumption that the public sector, in particular at the local level, will not be able to grow and to provide for extensive services in the future. But there is evidence, in a number of developing countries, that people at local levels have taken significant initiatives, either on their own or when motivated by a catalytic agent from the outside:

— in organizing themselves under local leadership;
— in identifying their specific development needs and effectively articulating them;
— in formulating development plans to meet those needs and mobilizing available resources;
— in drawing up action plans and collective decisions to implement them;
— in bargaining and liaising with relevant government agencies to demand resources and to utilize them effectively for development purposes.

This empowerment of the people model is based on people-centred values and development is defined as a process requiring as its primary resource human commitment and creativity. Organizations are built gradually from the bottom up rather than the top down. Their primary resources are creative, committed and knowledgeable people.

With these objectives in mind, NGOs seem to be capable of and willing to fill gaps which exist due to scarce financial and personnel public resources at the local government level...

With regard to international cooperation and activities of international NGOs, it was emphasized that although this cooperation was welcome, preserving national and local identity was necessary to guarantee that rural programmes remain indigenous, relevant and responsive to people's aspirations and needs.

What is the ultimate purpose of Elliott's rather ambiguous "empowerment" of local communities? If poverty is the result of government action or inaction, unjust social and economic structures, if the objective is economic and social justice, would it be appropriate and legitimate for the NGOs to incite the "empowered" communities to rebel against the government authorities and existing political, economic and social structures by more or less radical methods?

For instance, Swedish assistance supports the "Third System", the voluntary organizations representing the people and its force for development as a factor

---

[40] Heinrich Siedentopf, "Decentralisation for Rural Development: Government Approaches and People's Initiatives in Asia and the Pacific", in *Planning and Administration*, 1989–2, p.10.

alongside the two other power groups: the state, which has demonstrated both superpotency and impotence, and the commercial system. The Third System represents a power of liberation and development.

Swedish assistance is not neutral: it promotes democracy as a force for development, freedom of association, freedom of information, human rights, national liberation and social liberation from domestic dictatorship. The "second liberation" (the first having been achieved through decolonisation), by peaceful or violent means, comes from within and from under, but it may be speeded up and facilitated by external support[41].

The "social justice" objective of the World Council of Churches, under the influence of the "liberation theology", may have justified, in certain countries, civil disobedience or civil war.

What kind of change, and how much change should "conscientization and empowerment" promote ? A limited economic progress (a self-financing community), a limited health progress (primary health care assumed by locally-trained health assistants), or locally-imposed, illegal, agrarian reform, or armed revolt against corrupt or incompetent local or national politicians or military junta chiefs?

The International Council of Voluntary Agencies (ICVA), one of the main cooperation bodies of international NGOs, and certainly not labelled as radical or revolutionary, pointed out in 1984 that many of the early development initiatives addressed the symptoms, not the causes of poverty:

> It is increasingly apparent that the causes of poverty and underdevelopment do not derive so much from lack of funds or technology, as from the oppression of the poor through complex social structures, both locally and internationally. It is also recognized that much development aid in the past has been essentially counterproductive to the best interests of the very poor. It is, therefore, essential that NGO programmes should not be used in ways that strengthen such structures or processes, but rather should reinforce social change[42].

Some NGOs dedicated to welfare and relief can be classified as purely first generation organizations. Some NGOs initially engaged in welfare and relief have expanded their activities into local community development, without relinquishing their original role. Some "development" NGOs are strictly second generation organizations. Some NGOs with first and second generation activities have always engaged in advocacy, and some have recently attempted to promote empowerment. One organization may well pursue all three strategies simultaneously in response to different situations in different locations or countries.

Many NGOs are not homogeneous entities with clear, constant, policies: classi-

---

[41] Ernst Michanek, "Democracy as a Force for Development and the Role of Swedish Assistance", in *Development Dialogue*, 1985:1, pp. 59–60, 67–68.

[42] International Council of Voluntary Agencies (ICVA), "Relations between Southern and Northern NGOs: Effective Partnerships for Sustainable Development"—1989 (unpublished internal document).

fying them in one or the other category can only be indicative and often transient. The role of selected NGOs will be described in Part II of this book.

NGOs and Governments

Lissner[43], has proposed a classification of 6 different NGO roles in relation to governments, in a spectrum ranging from the subservient to the subversive. His finding, in 1966, that there were very few "pure" examples of categorized roles, or attitudes, is still true now, as a particular NGO may adopt different roles in different situations. While Lissner was referring to the relations between a NGO and its own government, his categorization has been extended, in the following commentaries, to the NGO relation with a recipient country, with the reservation that a NGO may have one role in relation to its own government and a different one in relation to a recipient country.

1. The "subservient" role requires the NGO to accept any government request, with no critical questions asked. The NGO would thus be fully loyal to its own country's foreign policy objectives and directives, and it would fully respect the host country's laws, directives and priorities,—or it could be subservient to one or to the other.

   While a NGO's loyalty to its own country is to be expected, its subordination to his country's government "instructions" does not tally with an essential characteristic of NGOs, their independence from government control. Such independence is related to the NGO's degree of financial dependence on government subsidies, as well as to other non-financial factors, such as the NGO's political and/or ideological adhesion to the government's views, a possible full or partial symbiosis of the NGO leadership and the country's politicians and elites, government's pressures on the NGO to conform. •

2. The NGO "partnership" role is one of complementing or supplementing donor governments' programmes. Rather than a relationship of domination or rivalry, government and NGO cooperate willingly. Partnership may also extend to the relation between the NGO and the recipient government.

3. The "compensatory" role concept emphasizes the importance of NGOs helping people who have become victims of governmental mistakes, unwillingness and/or inability to help. While the NGO realizes the government's inadequacy, it does not openly criticize the government.

4. The "corrective" role is characterized by a conviction that NGOs are "the voice of the voiceless": the NGOs have expertise, they have information about human suffering in various parts of the world, and for this reason, they are responsible for defining needs and pressuring governments into correcting harmful or unsat-

---

[43] Lissner, op.cit., pp. 206–216.

isfactory policies. This role could also be construed as "constructive advocacy".

5. The "disobedient" role is adopted by NGOs that put a premium on their own values and are indifferent to legalism. The ultimate loyalty of the NGO is not to positive law, which may be unjust, inhumane or obsolete, but to religious or moral principles concerning justice and human solidarity. Disobedience is directed against a specific law or act of government. It grows out of a concern for the values of the NGO and by a hope that publicity and public pressure will change the law or reverse the decision in question. The attitude of the NGO is reformist, not revolutionary.

6. Finally, the "subversive" role takes disobedience one step further, as the conflict between the values of the NGO and the existing political order will justify outright confrontation. This role has been assumed by NGOs involved in assistance to victims of human rights violations, or assisting populations fighting against their own government in "just" liberation wars. Such assistance has often been provided without regard to governments' laws and prohibitions, on the grounds of divine or religious aspirations which transcends human laws, or on the basis of a "right of humanitarian intervention" and a "duty of assistance to persons in danger", the "French Doctors" ethic of extreme urgency (see Chapter 11).

Most NGOs have adopted a partnership and compensatory role in relation with donor and recipient governments. Only a few, in exceptional circumstances, decide to take illegal or even subversive public positions, at the risk of legal sanctions, expulsions, or even physical threats or attacks against their personnel's safety, honour or life.

Intergovernmental organizations have no such freedom of choice: dependent on and controlled by governments, their role is to prepare and implement decisions taken by intergovernmental bodies. Their operational interventions must respect the principles of national sovereignty, national legislations as well as the national political, economic and social established order.

Internal Politics of NGOs

For Lissner[44], the political behaviour of NGOs is determined by the following three organizational considerations:

1. the desire to maximize the influence of agency values on public opinion;
2. the desire to maximize agency income;
3. the desire to maximize agency respectability and leverage.

Agency values may stem from religious or philosophical beliefs, historical traditions, social norms, personal experiences of the founders. While these values are

---

[44] Ibid., pp. 73–78.

usually, general, abstract and symbolic (the Golden Rule, social justice), and cannot be translated directly into concrete action they serve in deciding on strategy and general policies.

The agency values are influenced by the interests of the aid recipients in the Third World, the interests of the agency constituency in the donor country and the interests of the agency policy-makers themselves.

All voluntary agencies try to increase their income by appearing as attractive as possible to the actual and potential contributors, individuals, private or public entities. Public appeals for funds will build on the agency's contribution to humanitarian assistance, its cost-effectiveness, in response to concrete, demonstrated needs. They may be addressed to "old" supporters, by emphasizing continuity, or to new, potential contributors, by stressing new ventures. "Charity business", nowadays, uses the same marketing methods to attract funds as those used to sell soap or cars.

Organizational resources are the third determinant of agency behaviour: financial assets, qualified manpower, prestige and goodwill. The agency makes use of these resources in order to maximize its organizational respectability and leverage vis-à-vis other agencies, voluntary, governmental and intergovernmental bodies.

In practice, fund-raising by Northern NGOs may come into conflict with or distort agencies' values and respectability, as shown by the following study.

The "Image of Africa" Project

This project was undertaken by a number of voluntary agencies from the European Community and Africa as an evaluation of the information material on Africa produced by European media during the 1984/1985 African food crisis[45].

According to the European reports, the European public perceived the food crisis in Africa as a dramatic and catastrophic event. On the contrary,the African reports emphasize that, viewed from their perspective, the crisis was a process over an extended period of time, not an immediate happening.

Although the humanitarian feelings which motivated the massive response of the European public to images of the crisis in Africa were appreciated, the African reports reacted strongly to the fact that many Northern donors used the response to the famine in Africa as a way of furthering their own political, economic and institutional interests. More generally, food aid was seen as a means used by donors to perpetuate dependency.

In the Western media, the subject of self-development was almost totally ignored. Generally, an emotive terminology tended to show Africa and the Africans as extreme stereotypes. For instance, the campaign conducted by the Daily Mirror

---

[45] International Foundation for Development Alternatives (IFDA) *Dossier 67.* Sept. Oct. 1988. pp. 3–18.

to raise funds for Burkina Faso showed the African country inhabited by desperate, suffering families, by children dying of hunger. The response of the "dear readers" was "magnificent" and "generous".

The Northern NGO messages on the African crisis varied considerably and depended, to a certain extent, on the different ideological orientations. In most cases, the declared objectives were to highlight the less obvious causes of the famine, to analyze the role of European governments, and to provide information on long-term development policies and self-sufficiency. In fact, they had to drop this type of structured information and use the same biased, stereotyped but effective images as the press and the television. Linguistically, most of the NGO messages fell into the category "underdevelopment/aid".

The study showed that this contradiction in NGO information during the crisis springs from the material conditions in which they work. On the one hand, for many of them, survival is closely linked to collecting money from the public, which obliges them to appeal to emotions, since "people give with their hearts rather than with their heads": people were far more generous when faced with photographs of famine victims. On the other hand, NGOs are usually involved in long-term programmes and in development education, intended to provide a more complex and realistic view of problems and to challenge the stereotypes. The contradiction emerges also from the analysis of published material: in that intended for aid campaigns, there is a large percentage of photographs of victims, mostly women and children, and the image of the Africans as passive receivers of aid is emphasized. In the educational material, on the other hand, the opposite image prevails: the Africans are shown as active and participating in the development process, — attempts are made to understand what lies behind the food shortage and the operations of European and African politicians are analyzed.

Marc Nerfin[46] concluded that:

> The very campaign of unprecedented solidarity with the victims of the 1984/85 "hunger crisis" resulted in a further degradation of the representation of Africa in Western minds. Africa's perception of, and response to, the crisis were ignored, and the image projected was that of an apathetic Africa, dependent on the European "good samaritan".

He suggested that the celebration in 1991 of Cristoforo Colombo's first landing in "America" should be used for a genuine re-discovery of the Third World, by a conscientization campaign undertaken in equal partnership between South and North, for a new awareness of the other.

[46] Ibid., Editorial.

Northern and Southern NGOs in Partnership

While Northern NGOs describe their Southern counterparts as "partners", the latter allege that such arrangements are frequently a partnership between the rider and the horse[47].

Southern NGOs claim that international or donor NGOs try to influence their programme priorities and to dominate them through the power of the money. The tyranny of the project is widely seen as a creation of the donors to ensure control. Sending expensive and inexperienced Northern "experts" when qualified Southern specialists are available is also criticized.

Southern NGOs challenge the right of Northern NGOs to have an operational role: Southern NGOs should have the primary responsibility, within the NGO community, for leading the development process in their own countries. Northern NGOs should focus more on fund-raising, development education and policy advocacy, and address the alleviation of poverty in their own countries.

Southern NGOs are also criticized: some are viewed as unnecessary intermediaries with little contact with the grass-roots communities. Northern NGOs complain of the organizational weaknesses of their partners.

In order to improve relationships between Northern and Southern NGOs, the International Council of Voluntary Agencies (ICVA) recommends a search for genuine and equitable partnerships, based on a realistic division of labour.

Northern NGOs will have to recognize that the South is responsible for the development of the South, for the interpretation of development in the South and for the implementation of development in the South.

The main role of Northern NGOs in the South should be to support Southern NGOs by financing their programmes and facilitating their institutional development. This would involve a major change in the skills required by Northern NGOs in the field: rather than acting as project managers and financial controllers, they will need to develop expertise in networking, training and organizational development. Instead of being experts, they will need to become facilitators. Furthermore, Northern NGOs have a responsibility to influence policies and attitudes concerning development in their own countries.

More broadly, all external interveners (governmental and intergovernmental agencies, Northern NGOs), should involve Southern NGOs in needs assessment and programme design and evaluation, not just use them as cost-effective project implementors. Training both in technical skills and in management systems should also be supported.

Partnership is based on the premise that development is a global issue affecting both the North and the South: both parties should work together to solve the common problem. True partnership should be based on

---

[47] Developments in this section are based on the ICVA Doc. "Relations between Southern and Northern NGOs...": see Note 42.

transparency, common commitment, mutual trust, confession and forgiveness, keeping one another informed on all plans and programmes and submitting ourselves to mutual accountability and correction.

It has been said that in the 1980s, the "buzz word" of the NGO community was "partnership". Will the 1990s see "true" partnership realized[48]?

Comparative Advantages of NGOs

The greater role of, and support for, NGOs in the 1980s may be explained by their own strengths in contrast with the limitations of governmental and intergovernmental agencies' action.

As noted by Brodhead[49], official donors have turned to NGOs out of pragmatic considerations, seeing them as

more efficient conduits for development inputs than the often discredited official agencies.

NGOs, with their "human side" and public support, their targeting the poor in their programmes and their relatively low-cost management style seemed an attractive alternative.

One of the NGOs' more significant strengths is their ability to involve the intended beneficiaries of a particular project, by being closer with the people as "grass-roots" organizations.

As private voluntary organizations, NGOs are not subject directly to governmental or intergovernmental agencies' policies, rules and regulations. They are free to adjust more quickly to changing environments and circumstances than governmental and intergovernmental bureaucracies. They are smaller organizations, with flexible administrative structures, which can react promptly and effectively to emergencies.

Macalister-Smith has noted[50] that NGOs are more ready than governments to perceive disasters, to report on and respond to them. NGOs are usually the best-informed group. Voluntary agencies often have personnel on the scene before official action is taken. Their role of providing information and stimulating action by governments and IGOs reflects the fact that they are less circumscribed by restrictive objectives and regulations than official bodies.

The NGOs' independence from governments may allow them to help in situations and locations where governmental organizations are unable to intervene for

---

[48] Tim Brodhead and Herbert Copley Brent, *Bridges of Hope: Canadian Voluntary Agencies and the Third World*, North-South Institute, Ottawa, 1988, p. 141.

[49] Tim Brodhead, "NGOs: In One Year, Out the Other ?", op.cit., p. 1.

[50] Peter Macalister-Smith, *International Humanitarian Assistance—Disaster Relief Actions in International Law and Organization*, Martinus Nijhoff, 1985, p. 119.

political or other reasons. They may also identify, formulate and publicize problems and needs without excessive caution and without exclusive reliance on official, diplomatic sources of information.

The NGOs' light administrative structure and their focus on limiting non-operational expenditures makes them more cost-effective than government organizations: NGOs need not pay their permanent headquarters or field staff at international levels. Some of the NGOs employ national and/or international volunteers who receive a limited compensation for their services.

NGO personnel are deemed to be highly motivated, not by material, financial benefits, but by a spirit of humanitarian dedication, based on philosophical, religious, political or other concerns. The satisfaction of helping their fellow beings is their reward.

In a specialized field of international public health, the importance of NGOs collaboration was underscored in 1989 by Jonathan Mann, the former Director of the WHO Global Programme on AIDS:

(There is) an increasing recognition of the power and importance of community-based organizations. These... have often been pioneers, leading the way for more timid or more reluctant governments... These organizations have in common the critical ability to reach people, to deliver information people will believe and to give support where governments cannot reach or in ways that governments cannot provide. This is one of the far-reaching and practical lessons of the decade: that in AIDS programmes there is a direct relationship between the strength, diversity and involvement of community-based and NGOs and the level of success which can be achieved[51].

In May 1989, the Forty-Second World Health Assembly has acknowledged the fact that, because of their contacts with, and access to, individuals and communities, their commitment and versatility, their knowledge and experience, NGOs can make a special impact on society regarding AIDS and the needs of AIDS patients and HIV-infected persons. Many NGOs have assured rapid and appropriate support to people and communities affected by the AIDS pandemic—especially in overcoming discriminatory attitudes—thus contributing towards understanding the sensitivities and needs of those affected and to the formulation of policies and programmes relating to AIDS[52].

It is noteworthy that twelve of the 25 members of the WHO Global Commission on AIDS have had extensive personal experience with NGOs in areas such as human rights, health and development. NGO representatives attend various WHO-sponsored meetings on AIDS: meetings of Participating Parties, meetings of the Management Committee, consultation meetings on blood transfusion services. Coordinating groups of NGOs working internationally on AIDS have been created

[51] WHO Doc. GPA/GMC(2)/89.5 of 4 Dec. 1989, p.1.
[52] WHO Press Release WHA/13 of 19 May 1989.

in seven Western countries. Since 1988, WHO has given financial support to NGOs' AIDS activities with WHO-assisted national AIDS programmes in developing countries.

Limitations of NGOs

Being responsive to local needs can result in a lack of strategic direction and concern for long-term planning.

The NGOs fierce spirit of independence may affect their capacity to work together with other NGOs, IGOs and government agencies. Some resent public accountability, external evaluation and reject standardization in methods or documentation. Their diversity can make replicability of success difficult. Many NGOs, except those which have a professional base or sectoral specialization (for instance, medical associations), lack technical capacity in particular areas and management skills.

NGOs' financial dependence on voluntary contributions forces them to spend considerable time and efforts in search of resources and funds. NGOs risk having their priorities and programmes decided upon, or influenced by, the demands, interests or expectations of their private or public donors, rather than by the real needs of assisted communities.

Unattractive remunerations, difficult working conditions, lack of job security and retirement schemes in the voluntary sector may act as disincentive to talented persons whose motivation is not entirely altruistic. For such reasons, some NGOs suffer from a high turnover.

Recipient governments may distrust or be hostile towards some NGOs for various reasons: fear of political, ideological or religious activity undertaken under the guise of humanitarian or development assistance, — governments' fears that autonomous NGOs may challenge or oppose laws or public policies.

NGOs Cooperation and Coordination

In view of the multiplicity of autonomous IGOs and NGOs dealing in part, or fully, with international humanitarian assistance, and the lack of recognized, authoritative, operational leaders in this field, the need for cooperation and coordination among the agencies is blatant. Because of the independence and autonomy of the different agencies, and of their varied characteristics, objectives and motivations, none of them is in a position to assume an overall coordinating function.

As noted in Chapter 1, UNDRO's mandate to coordinate the U.N. agencies' relief activities gives it an impossible task to fulfil, either at the donors or at the recipient country levels.

The coordination of NGOs among themselves, and their coordination with

IGOs, is no easier task. NGOs are multiple and independent: they resist any attempt by governments, IGOs,or other NGOs, to be told, and even less ordered, to undertake, or not, relief activities at specific places, times, and in determined ways. Autonomy is the essence of NGO identity and coordination can only be voluntary. In most cases, coordination is even limited to voluntary cooperation.

National Coordination of NGOs

National coordination of donor NGOs is organized more or less formally in various Northern countries, with or without government support, generally in the development field, including relief assistance, or specifically for relief assistance NGOs.

For instance, the "Disasters Emergency Committee" was set up in 1963 in London to provide British aid agencies with a channel of cooperation for emergency relief overseas after large-scale disasters. The British Red Cross Society, CAFOD, Christian Aid, Oxfam and Save the Children Fund are full members (see Chapter 5).

In France, since the 1970s, most agencies of national significance are grouped in "collectifs". In 1983, France introduced a new administrative structure with the purpose of integrating NGOs more formally within national development cooperation policy, the "Commission Coopération-Développement", composed of government and NGO representatives. The Commission aims at facilitating dialogue and aid coordination between French authorities and NGOs, enabling NGOs to be more aware of official aid policies, while government officials may become better acquainted with NGO approaches and concerns.

Consultation and coordination mechanisms between NGOs and government at the national level have also been instituted in Scandinavian countries. For similar purposes, the "Australian Council for Overseas Aid", a national NGO Council, was established in 1965. In 1975, the Canadian International Development Agency established a division for cooperation with international NGOs. In 1985, New Zealand's major voluntary agencies established the "Council for International Development". In Japan, the "NGO Centre for International Cooperation" was established in 1987. In the late 1970s, consortia of Private Voluntary Agencies (PVOs) were created in the U.S.A., such as "Private Agencies in International Development"[53]. Examples abound.

In 1989, the "University/NGO Action Research NETWORK" was established under the auspices of the Northwest International Education Association, Seattle, WA. The purpose of this consortium of universities, international and indigenous NGOs is to promote joint approaches to grassroot development through partnership, and to generate support for development education in the North.

In 1990, David C. Korten created the "People-Centred Development Forum" as

[53] OECD Report, op.cit., pp. 24–25, 79–80.

a "voluntary organization that engages in research, education,networking and advisory activities to encourage and support the definition and pursuit of a people-centred development vision as a global citizen's movement"[54].

International Coordination of NGOs

Coordination is effected either by the NGOs independently, or at the initiative of, or in relation with, IGOs.

In the specific field of relief assistance, a successful example of voluntary coordination of donor NGOs at the international level is the Licross/Volags Steering Committee created in 1972 in Geneva (see pp. 78–79). The "Monthly Meetings for Disaster Relief Information Sharing", convened in Geneva also play an essential role in exchange of information and cooperation between some 16 international NGOs, 9 IGOs and two governmental offices.

Geneva is a unique centre where dozens of IGOs (including the U.N. Office at Geneva, UNDRO, UNHCR, WHO, UNICEF and UNDP Offices, UNV, IOM), the Red Cross organizations, hundreds of NGOs (including the World Council of Churches, the Lutheran World Federation, the Save the Children Alliance), and NGO cooperation groups such as the International Council of Voluntary Agencies, are represented or based.

No other city, whether New York, Paris, London, Vienna, Rome or Brussels offers the same concentration of IGOs and NGOs. In the field of relief assistance, IGO coordination, IGO/NGO coordination or NGO coordination could not be achieved (or attempted) to the same extent in any location other than Geneva.

The Conference of NGOs (CONGO) was set up by the U.N. in New York and in Geneva to safeguard the NGOs' rights of participation in U.N. meetings and committees. CONGO's sub-committees on human rights, development, women and other issues have allowed NGOs to discuss and decide on strategy, both within and outside the U.N. Briefings on forthcoming meetings are also provided by U.N. officers to NGO representatives.

In the late 1970s, institutional relationships were established between the Commission of the European Economic Community (EEC) and NGOs of EEC member countries collectively. Representatives of NGOs from the member states are involved in an annual general assembly in Brussels and in the election of a permanent EEC/NGO Liaison Committee. The Committee offers contacts among an estimated 600 European NGOs and a continuing dialogue with the Commission, as well as with the European Parliament, notably the latter's Committee on Development and Cooperation.

---

[54] Ernst W. Gohlert, "Breaking the Mold: New Thinking in International Development", Draft Paper submitted to the 31st Annual Meeting of the International Studies Association, Washington, D.C., April 10–14, 1990.

In a 1988 Report, the Organization for Economic Co-operation and Development (OECD) assessed the EEC/NGO Liaison Committee in Brussels and the International Council of Voluntary Agencies in Geneva (see below) as the most significant international consultative and liaison networks of NGOs from OECD countries, although the two bodies cover different geographic areas. International linkages remain weak between NGOs from North American and Pacific countries, and those in Europe, particularly from Latin cultures[55].

The International Council of Voluntary Agencies (ICVA)

ICVA was created in 1962 in Geneva from the merger between the "Conference of NGOs Interested in Migration", the "Standing Conference of Voluntary Organizations Working for Refugees" and the "International Committee for World Refugee Year".

One of the main purposes of the merger was to build upon the spirit of cooperation and consultation which had been fostered by the founding members in refugee matters, extending it to all areas of voluntary agency activity that could benefit from a permanent international liaison structure.

Today, ICVA brings together 86 member organizations, all of which are engaged in humanitarian or development activities. Together with the EEC/NGO Liaison Committee, ICVA is one of the most significant and effective secular permanent structures for consultation among international NGOs.

ICVA is an independent international association of non-governmental, non-profit making organizations. It does not implement relief or development projects itself, but it provides services and support to its member agencies to enable them to cooperate and perform more effectively.

One of ICVA's primary functions is to provide an international forum for the exchange of views and information among its members and other voluntary agency activities.

Another priority is the promotion of national and regional networks of voluntary agencies as an important way of strengthening voluntary action in the Third World. For instance, ICVA has been involved in the promotion of an African NGO Network and a South Asian network.

The General Assembly is ICVA's major statutory body for consultation: it meets every three years, with representatives of all member associations. The sixteen members Executive Committee decides on policy issues, such as the 1988 Policy Statement and Action Plan "Making Common Cause Internationally", calling for increased cooperation among NGOs in international development, environment and population activities.

---

[55] OECD Report, op.cit., p. 28.

ICVA maintains documentation on voluntary agencies activities in the fields of development and humanitarian assistance and disseminates such information.

ICVA's total yearly expenditures amounted to approximately Sw.F. 1.7 million in 1987-1988. Its regular programme income (membership fees and miscellaneous) amounted to Sw.F. 934,000. The main external grants were provided by the Canadian International Development Agency, the Ford Foundation, the Swedish International Development Authority, UNHCR, the Norwegian Government, the World Bank, Radda Barnen and IOM. The Australian Development Assistance Bureau made a contribution (Sw.F. 35,360) to facilitate the participation of representatives from the Third World in ICVA's activities.

ICVA has promoted the establishment of liaison committees and the organization of meetings to improve communications and coordination between NGOs and IGOs.

ICVA conveys a collective NGO view to UNHCR, through statements submitted to its Executive Committee. ICVA participates in the UNHCR/NGO Consultative Group on International Protection, and convenes meetings jointly with UNHCR, such as those of the Consultative Group on Refugee Operations. ICVA also holds consultative meetings on Palestinians with UNRWA. ICVA is a member of a Working Group of Governmental Representatives which meets regularly to plan the IOM seminars on topical migration issues and it participates in IOM's Annual Council. ICVA holds consultative meetings with UNDP and IFAD. It has contributed to the NGO input in UNCTAD VII negotiations. ICVA provides the secretariat for the NGO members of the World Bank/NGO Committee, established in 1981 to foster policy dialogue and more systematic operational collaboration between the Bank and NGOs. ICVA has been involved for some years in organizing and participating in meetings in cooperation with the OECD and its Development Assistance Committee.

ICVA has been invited to participate in meetings of the "Humanitarian Liaison Working Group". This Group is an informal body of Geneva-based Ambassadors to the U.N., who meet periodically to exchange information on humanitarian issues and organizations, such as UNHCR and UNDRO.

Representatives of UNDP, UNEP, UNCTAD, ILO, UNICEF, FAO, OECD and the World Bank have also attended meetings of the ICVA Working Group on Development Issues, as IGO guests of the voluntary agencies in a voluntary agency meeting[56].

Coordination of Relief in Recipient Countries

This coordination is, in principle, a responsibility of the country's government authorities. U.N. organizations (UNDRO, UNDP, UNHCR, WHO) and/or the Red

---

[56] ICVA *Annual Reports*, 1985–86, 1986–87, 1987–88,—*UNDRO News*, Jan.Feb. 1988,—and an interview with an ICVA representative on 4 Aug. 1989.

Cross organizations (the ICRC, National Societies, the League), or groups of other NGOs, may take the lead in supporting the government's efforts at coordination, or in setting up coordination, cooperation or information exchange bodies or mechanisms, when a government is unable or unwilling to assume the coordination task.

NGOs coordinating bodies are sometimes set up in relation to specific programmes in specific areas or countries.

For instance, the "Committee for Coordination of Services to Displaced Persons in Thailand" groups 39 NGOs in relation to the U.N. Border Relief Operation (UNBRO) and UNHCR, dealing with the 250,000 Khmer displaced persons on the Thailand-Cambodian border. The Committee participates in monthly meetings with the Thai government authorities and IGO representatives, which ensure a broad exchange of information, if not actual coordination.

About 104 NGOs assist the U.N. "Operation Salam", directed by the Coordinator for the U.N. Humanitarian and Economic Assistance Programme relating to Afghanistan. The NGOs work with Afghan refugees, returnees and displaced persons in health, education, shelter, de-mining and other fields. They are divided into two major groups: the "Agency Coordinating Body for Afghan Relief" (ACBAR) is an independent association of more than 50 NGOs based in Peshawar, formed in 1988 and operating from Pakistan inside Afghanistan. Founded also in 1988, and based in Quetta, the 15-member "Southern and Western Afghanistan and Baluchistan Association for Coordination" (SWABAC) provides services to a specific geographic area in Baluchistan and inside Afghanistan[57].

Coordination is also initiated by families of NGOs for their own members.

An ecumenical group, the "Churches Drought Action for Africa/Ethiopia", later called "Joint Relief Partnership" (JRP) was organized in 1985 to create a shared, Christian response to the relief needs in Ethiopia. Its partners are the Ethiopian Catholic Secretariat, the Ethiopian Evangelical Church/Makane Yesus, the Ethiopian Orthodox Church, the Lutheran World Federation and Catholic Relief Services.

In December 1989, the ICRC in Geneva and ICRC delegates in the field were coordinating the efforts of about 20 National Societies of the Red Cross in Romania, following the Revolution[58].

Local Coordination of NGOs

Other international bodies have a more immediate local role in helping international NGOs settle in the city and country where they decide to have their headquarters or an office. These bodies also represent the NGOs' interests with the

---

[57] Raymond J. Smyke, "NGOs Involved in Humanitarian Assistance", in *Transnational Associations*, Union of International Associations, Brussels, 1990/4, pp. 233 to 239.

[58] ICRC *Bulletin*, No. 168 of Jan. 1990, and Catholic Relief Services *Annual Report 1987–1988*.

government's authorities and exert pressure to facilitate the entry and residence of NGOs officials in the country, to grant them working permits, to reduce or eliminate taxation on the NGOs financial transactions, to try to obtain an official status for the NGOs.

Among these, the "Fédération des institutions internationales semi-officielles et privées établies à Genève" (FIIG), created in 1929 in Geneva, and the "Fédération des Associations Internationales établies en Belgique" (FAIB), created in 1949 in Brussels.

These Federations have a practical, administrative, advisory role in relation to the locally-established international NGOs and they serve as legitimate intermediaries between local authorities and the NGOs. They do not intervene in the programmes and activities of the NGOs, nor do they have any role or coordination of the NGOs work programmes.

A list of 1988 expenditures of selected international humanitarian NGOs is shown in Table 2.3.

Table 2.3. 1988 Expenditures of Selected International Humanitarian NGOs (in million of $)[a]

International Committee of the Red Cross	277.
League of Red Cross and Red Crescent Societies	87.9
American Friends Service Committee[b]	19.
Aide Médicale Internationale	0.5
African Medical and Research Foundation	13.7
Catholic Relief Services	297.
International Save the Children Alliance	200.
Lutheran World Federation[c]	101.2
Médecins du Monde	12.1
Médecins Sans Frontières/Belgium	21.
Médecins Sans Frontières/France	29.
Médecins Sans Frontières/Switzerland	0.9
Order of Malta/France	38.
Oxfam	93.7
Quaker Peace and Service	3.3
Salvation Army (U.K. Central Funds)	90.
Save the Children Fund/U.K.	80.4
World Council of Churches	55.
World Vision (International and Subsidiaries)	162.6

[a] Conversion into U.S. $ from other currencies was made at rates of exchange as of November 1990.
[b] 1987 expenditures.
[c] Only part of the organization's total expenditures was spent on international humanitarian assistance.
Source: 1988 Annual Reports of the organizations.

CHAPTER 3

NATIONAL AND INTERNATIONAL VOLUNTEERS

The "Maseru Declaration"[1] affirmed that

> voluntarism is one of the most effective instruments of development today. We believe that, if carefully nurtured, the spirit of voluntarism, so noble and yet so fragile, will continue to be a powerful force for national and international development.

The Declaration also recognized that international voluntarism is an appropriate and complementary source of technical and professional manpower to be used by countries striving for social and economic development.

What is true for development also applies to education, health, and generally social and welfare services, as well as to emergency relief operations.

Volunteers provide an additional human and technical resource in both industrialized and developing countries, as a complement to, or as a replacement for, government and intergovernmental programmes. By themselves, volunteers cannot solve all the world's problems, hunger, poverty, ignorance, ill health, intolerance, political, economic and social oppression, internal and external conflicts, natural calamities: however, they can contribute to alleviating the suffering of the sick and the poor and they can help individuals and groups, morally, psychologically and practically, to face and hopefully resolve their problems. They can also detect and deal with social and other community problems, initiate innovative schemes and alert the authorities, through their independent action, to blatant failings of social care and protection.

In the 19th century, voluntary work was often initiated by highly motivated individuals who helped identify and meet, on an unpaid basis, particular social needs, such as child welfare, health care, housing and education. Recognition followed later by the creation of public services, manned by paid employees.

Voluntarism has been for many of those who chose this approach a direct per-

---

[1] Second UNV High-level Intergovernmental Meeting on International Volunteerism and Development, Maseru, Lesotho, 16-21 Nov. 1986, U.N. Doc. UNV II/1986/REP/1/E, p. 39.

sonal assistance and support to their fellow human beings and a service to society in general;—a moral duty;—a concrete gesture of human solidarity;—a wish to do-good;—for some, a demonstration of ideological and political dedication;—a compensation for the guilt feeling of the rich and well-to-do towards the "lower classes" and the underprivileged;—for those who joined relief or development teams in Third World countries, a wish to help the poor nations, an interest in other cultures, a taste for adventure.

Voluntarism is more or less developed in different countries and regions: in its modern form, it started essentially in Western Europe and North America in the 19th century. It has been estimated that over the last 150 years, nearly 15 percent of the European population has been more or less regularly involved in volunteer work[2].

In the U.K., in France, in the U.S.A., and in other Western countries, there are millions of volunteers, offering time to work unpaid in hospitals, old people's homes, youth movements, charity shops etc.

In addition to the national volunteers working at home, some decide to help the Third World. The only statistics available on their numbers relate to "volunteers from OECD (Organization for Economic Cooperation and Development) countries serving overseas wholly or partly financed by official aid agencies". The relevant figures for 1975 and 1986 are shown in Table 3.1.

According to these statistics, official funding was provided in 1986 to over 18,000 volunteers, whether of quasi-public bodies or of NGOs, depending on the system adopted by each member country. The OECD report on "Voluntary Aid for Development" suggests that the total of volunteers of OECD countries working in developing countries with NGOs is probably several times higher.

According to a May 1990 U.N. Volunteers report, government-sponsored organizations account for an estimated 22,000 skilled international volunteer personnel serving in programmes of development cooperation. An additional 50 percent may be added by private NGO sources, or an estimated total of 33,000. More than 90 percent of those volunteers are from OECD countries. Most volunteers serve in the Least Developed Countries.

On the basis of one or the other estimate, the number of international development volunteers largely exceeds the number of U.N. staff assigned to field projects (9,448 in 1988)[3].

We will first attempt to define the term "volunteer", identify the volunteer's motivation, give a typology of organizations working with volunteers, and provide some historical elements of the evolution of voluntarism.

The characteristics of Red Cross volunteers, an important, world-wide category of humanitarian volunteers, will be reviewed, followed by indications on voluntarism in a few selected countries: the U.S.A., including the U.S. Peace Corps,

[2] European Documentation Centre concerning volunteer work in the 19th and 20th century, The Netherlands, 1989, p. 17.

[3] *Voluntary Aid for Development—The role of NGOs*, OECD, Paris, 1988, pp. 115, 153: further references to this book will be shortened to "OECD Report",—U.N. Doc. ACC/1989/PER/R.11 of 20 July 1989, *Personnel Statistics*. UNDP/U.N. Volunteers "Programme Advisory Note – The Appropriate U.N. of Volunteers in Development", May 1990.

Table 3.1. Volunteers serving overseas wholly or partly financed by official aid agencies—
1975 and 1986—Number of persons and official expenditures

	Number of persons		US$ million	
	1975	1986	1975	1986
Australia	157	257	0.1	1.5
Austria	276	260	1.3	3.5
Belgium	657	(1461)	2.2	6.2
Canada	1195	2422	10.3	20.3
Denmark	401	(465)	2.8	7.4
Finland	0	13	0	(0.1)
France	(2100)	2100	..	98.3
Germany F.R.	1720	1725	13.7	58.6
Ireland	—	575	—	1.8
Italy	504	1010	1.9	23.2
Japan	712	2434	4.1	35.4
Netherlands	687	582	9.0	17.8
New Zealand	(90)	89	—	0.5
Norway	114	204	1.1	6.4
Sweden	182	(58)	1.6	..
Switzerland	117	(357)	0.9	(2.4)
United Kingdom	1915	1745	2.1	9.2
United States	(5000)	5132	(50.0)	96.6
Total	8637	18548	51.1	373.1
Including estimates	(15827)	(20889)	(101.1)	(389.2)
() OECD Secretariat estimates				

Source: *Voluntary Aid for Development—The Role of Non-Governmental Organizations*, OECD,
Paris, 1988, Table 7 p. 153 (excerpt).

France and the U.K. The more recent employment of "senior experts" as volunteers
will also be referred to.

Finally, various proposals for Volunteer Charters will be reviewed and references will be made to various international umbrella groups of voluntary associations.

Definition of a Volunteer

The French "Centre national du volontariat" has defined five main conditions for
voluntarism[4]: the volunteer is a person who commits himself (commitment) of his
own free will (freedom of choice) without profit motive (non-profit objective) in an
organized action (belonging to a group or structure) to the service of the community (common social interest).

[4] *Le Volontariat*, M. Le Net and J. Werquin, La Documentation française, No. 4780, Paris, 1985–5,
p. 9.

Originally, as recalled by Meurant[5], the most familiar image of a volunteer was of a man or woman who carried out a specific individual voluntary service, looking after a chronically sick or lonely person. The full significance of this approach was an inter-personal relationship.

However, inter-personal voluntarism progressively evolved into a social context, in the service of the community.

The First Red Cross World Meeting on Voluntarism, in Mexico, 1983, defined a volunteer as a person who reaches the consciousness of solidarity, leading him to work with people with the objective of wakening in them their own capacity to improve the quality of their lives[6].

The role of the volunteer was then changing from that of a one-sided charitable, generous provider, into that of a facilitator, helping others to help themselves.

The Coordinating Committee for International Volunteer Service (CCIVS)[7] distinguishes voluntary service and other forms of social activities, such as benevolence and charity.

Benevolence corresponds to a deep-felt instinct in man to alleviate the pains of his fellow men and in particular of the most impoverished ones. It is an expression of the natural and social solidarity of man, either in traditional communities or in modern societies. However, benevolence, or charity, deals with the symptoms of the problems, not with their social causes.

Modern voluntary service tries to attack the roots of the ills and problems, while involving those who suffer in the process. Voluntary service is more than a useful social activity:

it presupposes an ideological and practical commitment. It requires an analysis of economic, social and human reality

> as a basis for a strategy to eliminate the causes of alienation, create the conditions for the underprivileged to take charge of their own destiny, to advance beyond present conditions and build their own future on the basis of their own values.

This sharp distinction between charity, alleged to limit its action to care and relief, and voluntary service, with its more activist and participative approach, may be overstated, as both approaches are needed, unless it is meant to show the two extremes of a spectrum.

Going further, CCIVS makes another distinction, between revolutionaries and volunteers, presumably on the premise that some activist volunteers may be

[5] Jacques Meurant, *Red Cross Voluntary Service in Today's Society*, Henry Dunant Institute, Geneva, 1985, p. 12.

[6] *Report on the First World Meeting on Red Cross Voluntary Service*, Mexico, 7–12 March 1983, The League of Red Cross and Red Crescent Societies, Geneva.

[7] CCIVS *New Trends in Voluntary Service*, Paris, undated, pp. 41–43.

tempted to join revolutionary movements, or may be assimilated to revolutionaries by suspicious governments.

For CCIVS, there is a fundamental difference between revolutionaries and volunteers. For a revolutionary, the main objective is to seize power, in order to remodel society, an objective which is not shared by the volunteer.

The revolutionary resorts principally to political and military struggle to reach its aims, while the volunteer uses only peaceful means of action. Voluntary service seeks alternatives to violence as the means to settle conflicts of interest between individuals, groups, nations.

The revolutionary's action is based on an ideology, which is the basis for his model of society.

> The volunteer, irrespective of the ideology which inspires his action, has simply to be a catalyst of the forces of change in society working towards social justice and, consequently he has to first and foremostly respect the positive values of the society he is working in. He can by no means impose his own values, his own model of society. Through an open spirit, the spirit of dialogue, the voluntary dissociates himself from a revolutionary militant.

The European Parliament, in a resolution on voluntary work voted on 16 December 1983[8], specified that:

— voluntary work is not obligatory: governments should never try to influence people's commitment to voluntary work by putting pressure on them (e.g. forcing young people to do community work in return for social security payments);
— voluntary work is (should be) socially relevant: its policy should take into account policy in related sectors, such as welfare, education, environment, cooperation on development;
— voluntary work is unpaid (this assertion will be discussed below, in the section on "Red Cross Volunteers") and there should be a clear distinction in law between spontaneous, impartial voluntary activities and paid work, to avoid any risk of voluntary work being used as a means of by-passing regulations and collective agreements and increasing moon-lighting;
— voluntary work must not compete with but may complement traditional employment structures: it should not be used to make economies in the public sector. In the choice between professional (paid) staff and voluntary workers, the interests of those who require their services must be put first;
— an infrastructure should be created to enable volunteers to carry out their activities, with a minimum of adequate and clear rules.

While the Resolution generally supports voluntary work in the European Community (EC) countries, it also expresses the fears of trade unions in industrial-

---

[8] *Official Journal of the European Communities*, No. C 10/288–290, 16 Jan. 1984.

106

ized countries that unpaid voluntary workers may assume functions which could be undertaken by paid workers, thus either leading to the abolition of paid jobs, or preventing the creation of more paid jobs. The use of unpaid volunteers may also undercut the claims of paid workers for better salaries and benefits. Political leaders in Western socialist or social welfare states have expressed similar concerns: more generally, the issue is whether all social needs should be assumed and paid by the welfare state, or whether dedicated unpaid volunteers have a legitimate role in this area.

The Volunteer's Motivation

The basic motivation of volunteers is altruistic: they have a need to help others, to feel useful and needed. They also want to belong to a group sharing the same values.

For those who work only to earn a living, volunteer service adds a qualitative value which enhances their own social and personal status. While many individuals have not enjoyed much freedom in finding employment, voluntary service is a free choice: the volunteer may choose the organization he wishes to join, the type of voluntary activities, the time he is willing to offer to these activities.

Besides the pure altruistic motivation, the volunteer's dedication has its own attractions and compensations:

— for those who have time on their hands (mothers with grown children, young retirees), to have an occupation;
— to find new interests, new activities;
— for those who are lonely, to find new friends and belong to a group, to expand one's social contacts;
— to undergo training, to learn new skills, to acquire a useful experience;
— to assume responsibilities and power and to gain recognition in a structured body and network;
— to be able to promote political, religious, social or philosophical views, shared by other members of the group;
— to feel useful by the benefits or services provided to others, in complement to the official public services;
— to remain healthy by a continued, demanding, occupation.

The motivation of international volunteers may include, in addition to the same factors, the wish to participate personally in international development or relief work, a spirit of adventure, a taste for risk and exotism, escape from professional, personal or family problems, escape from a routine life or occupation, unemployment at home.

The findings of an American study on the motivation of national volunteers, based on a sample of city-dweller volunteers, are shown in Table 3.2.

Table 3.2. The (U.S.) Volunteer's Motivation (in percentages)

	Women	Men
To help others	41	32
Personal satisfaction	27	21
To be busy	18	21
To work for a cause in which I believe	0	16
To help society	5	11
Voluntary work is career-oriented	5	0
To meet people	5	0

Source: M.C. De Carlo, R.M. Mc Conochie, "Women and Volunteering: Perceptions, Motivations and Effects", *Volunteer Administration*,Vol. 13, no. 2, 1980, p. 27.

Typology of Volunteers' Organizations

Hoekendijk has identified eight different types of organizations working with volunteers: traditional volunteer associations, professional organizations (statutory or voluntary), alternative, critical assistance and other critical activities, local volunteer initiatives, self-help groups, interest groups, unions or bonds, action groups, "mentality" movements. This typology is shown in Table 3.3.

Table 3.3. Different types of organizations working with volunteers and examples

1. Traditional Volunteer Associations

Aim: service, education, health care, youthwork etc. Professional workers are employed, exclusively in supporting functions. Coordination is done by volunteers themselves. Very often these associations or societies are dependent on fund-raising for their work. There are often strong international affiliations. Local branches often start new, innovating, projects. The basis is a Christian, humanitarian ideology.
Examples: Women associations, Church groups, youth associations, scouting, Red Cross, nature study groups, associations for displaced persons, sports, firebrigades, life boats.

2. Professional Organizations (Statutory or Voluntary)

Type 2 evolved partly from Type 1, but of late we have reached a turning point and volunteers are being called in only for supplementary tasks. Coordination is always done by professionals. The ideology of the profession also functions for the volunteers.
Examples: Community centres, youth services, educational work, information centres, creativity centres, hospitals, libraries, museums, schools.

3. Alternative, Critical Assistance and Other Critical Activities

Volunteers together with critical professional workers, as a reaction to Type 2.The first aim is structural change, secondarily personal assistance is given with strong identification with the youth, the patient, etc. It is often professional workers who, especially in the beginning, bring this about unpaid and in so doing act as volunteers. Volunteers work mostly more than half time. Mixed opinions on volunteering. Ideology: critical of existing structures.
Examples: Different "shops", health shops, school shops, women's cafes, services for youth , for families that have problems with the "caring" authorities, for runaway psychiatric patients, legal centres.

4. Local Volunteer Initiatives

When the first circle of assistance, that of friends, relations and neighbours, fails or is not sufficient, then volunteer initiatives give organized friendship, often including quite intensive help. First comes the personal help, secondly the situation that causes the trouble, which is the opposite of Type 3. Volunteers do the work, often paid coordination. Type 4 may become radical, Type 3, or professionalize like Type 2. Local independent initiatives with varying names and formats, with national federations. Ideology: pragmatic, "organized friendship".

Examples: New neighbour help groups, groups for immigrants, kindergartens, groups for young delinquents, S.O.S. telephone help, battered women houses, literacy projects, drop-in coffee bars, aids buddies, senior volunteer groups.

5. Self-Help Groups

Self-help is a kind of help, given to people in similar circumstances and based on a common experience. The aim is within the person, emancipatory. Groups exist to help with psychological and social problems. Help consists sometimes of groupwork, but very often of help by telephone, by visits etc. People who have overcome their problems help those starting to seek help. Relationships with professionals differ, but self-help groups often give them information. Ideology: "the strength is in you".

Examples: Psychological problems: bereavement, addictions, crises, victims (incest, war), patient groups, social minority groups, groups for people who have to reintegrate for a problem in the family, like parents, partners of addicts, many "anonymous" groups.

6. Interest Groups, Unions or Bonds

Unlike Type 5, they do not want to strengthen the personality, but they want to change the society which reduces human beings to problem groups. They want to improve the actual situation and to influence the mentality which pushes aside the category which organizes itself, they want a fair share of living, money, jobs, provisions. large associations might be able to afford some paid staff, the services are for a much larger group than members only. Interest groups might develop into Type 1. Ideology: a fair deal for everybody.

Example: Old-age pensioners, divorcees, minors, patient associations, ex-convicts, ex-psychiatric patients, unemployed.

7. Action Groups

Groups whose principal purpose is to change the existing conditions through political action at all levels. The action group is by definition only temporary. Concrete goals. Also help when administration fails (against famine).

Example: Local neighbourhood groups for more parks, playgrounds, safer traffic, more housing, actions against nuclear plants, factory farming, life aid, artists for Africa etc.

8. "Mentality" Movements

Longer lasting groups which cover a broad field. The aim is above all a change in mentality of larger groups of the population, as a preparation for a changing of administration towards a more humane society. They are also a base for temporary actions. Cooperation with many other organizations of all types.

Examples: Oxfam shops, peace groups, Amnesty International, social awareness groups, women's lib, environment groups, different "militants" groups, anti-racism and anti-fascism movements.

Note: Boundaries between the types and given examples differ in different countries. The same type of work can be done by different types of organizations, and the motivation and position of the volunteers differ with the type of organization.

Source: L. Hoekendijk, in Volonteurope *Journal No. 5*, p. 12.

Historical Evolution of Voluntarism

Throughout the ages, every human society has recognized the necessity of helping those in need without reference to personal gain, and has created mechanisms, either structured or informal, to give expression to this human impulse. In this sense, the concept of voluntarism as the offering of one's time, skills and services for the benefit of fellow human beings, is not a modern one.

For Christians, service to one's neighbour is a moral obligation. Similarly, the Koran commands its followers to consider it their duty to help the needy. In many African, Asian and Pacific Islands cultures, tribe members have within their closely knit economic and social systems the obligation to serve each other in case of need, bad harvest etc. In such cases, voluntarism was a social obligation, and it was limited to assisting those in close proximity: one's own family, clan, neighbourhood, or tribe.

In some parts of Africa, for example, help to one's neighbour is a natural part of daily life. If a village is threatened by an animal, a bell is rung and the population mobilized to guard the village. Or the bell is rung to help a villager who has experienced a harvest failure and needs support.

In colonial times, in Asian countries, the relationship between the central government and the local communities was either relatively weak or non-existent. The local communities were practising varying measures of self-management: community affairs were managed through the people's own efforts. These included the construction and maintenance of roads, road side shelters, irrigation systems, management of religious centres, marketing infrastructures, mutual assistance in farming and common performance of wedding or funeral rites. Schools were managed by committees elected by the people, who also contributed to their operation and maintenance. In some communities, people organized and operated their own savings and credit cooperatives, health services were often part of community management.

In newly independent Asian states after World War II, power and authority were gradually centralized and bureaucratized, in part because of their governments' political insecurity. The ruling regimes were strongly linked to the urban elites, and to national and multinational business interests. In their quest for popularity and retention of political power, the governments introduced what they considered a modern system of delivery of services to the people, on the model of the former colonial power. The new system was run by government agencies and civil servants not always familiar with the socio-economic conditions of the citizens: it replaced the traditional system of self-management through organized people's action.

In recent years, governments embarked on alternative ways to secure a greater measure of people's participation and support, with the encouragement and assistance of IGOs and NGOs[9].

---

[9] Address of Mr. Y.Y. Kim, Regional Representative, UNDP, Thailand, UNV Doc. DP/UNV/CM/1987/OSA/6/E, Consultative Meeting on Volunteer Service and Development, Geneva, 8–10 Apr. 1987.

In Europe, since 1863, the Red Cross initiated the first structured international movement of secular volunteers through its National Societies.

The devastation caused by the First World War resulted in an enlargement of the concept of voluntarism. The need to assist people in countries ravaged by war was recognized by many farsighted persons who started new organizations (for instance, "Save the Children Fund", created in 1919 to help starving Austrian children) and mechanisms enabling individuals to go and assist the victims of war in other countries. Following and expanding on the Red Cross example, internationalism then became an important element in programmes of humanitarian assistance. While, previously, people had mainly volunteered to help their own kinsmen or countrymen, the emerging volunteer movement saw increasing numbers of volunteers going beyond their own national boundaries to bring comfort to those in need.

The end of the Second World War saw yet another step in the evolution of voluntarism. Following the ravages of war and the exodus of European refugees, a new dimension was brought about by the emergence, in the 1960s, of a number of countries in Asia and Africa as independent nations, in dire need of assistance, as well as by the concern for underdevelopment in Latin American countries. For the first time, the stark reality of poverty in many Third World countries became a stimulus to action aimed at helping them to develop. This realization led to the establishment of overseas development programmes in a number of Western industrialized countries, such as the U.S.A., the U.K., France, Australia, Scandinavian countries and others. Hundreds of men and women, mostly the young, offered to go to the newly independent countries and to Latin America to assist in the task of nation building. Voluntarism took a new role, that of an agent of development, without neglecting its traditional action in war-related and natural disaster emergency relief assistance.

The better knowledge of local conditions around the world brought about by the progress of communications and quicker and cheaper transportation stimulated the development of voluntary services. The deployment of international volunteers was however hampered in some areas on account of the Cold War between East and West, regional conflicts, civil wars, political, ideological and cultural differences between volunteer organizations and recipient countries.

The current détente between East and West, the lessening of ideological differences and the end of a few regional conflicts may lead to an expansion of international voluntarism both in relief assistance and development work.

European Attitudes Towards National Voluntarism

Western and Eastern European countries provide a wide range of different political and social attitudes of governments towards voluntarism at home. Some of these characteristics affect the attitudes and activities of national volunteers sent on international missions. These characteristics may also be found in recipient countries, depending on their own traditions, the influence of the former colonial power and their current ideology and type of government.

Welfare programmes, including health and education, may be centrally organized, financed and run by state bodies, or they may be offered by private sector organizations on an optional basis. The latter may, or not, receive state subsidies and be submitted to state control.

While there may be volunteers in the state sector, most volunteers are found in the private sector organizations, ranging from large NGOs to small local groups.

In Western Europe, as analyzed by Hoekendijk[10], one may identify three political mainstreams with different positions regarding voluntarism: social democrats (or Western socialists), Christian democrats and conservative/liberals.

In the social democratic view, the state is responsible for all social services: it should organize them, finance them through taxes and provide the services to all citizens. If NGOs are involved in these services, they should be subsidized and controlled by the state. Social services should be neutral:they should not impose religious ideologies.

The state social services are manned by paid, competent professionals, at the service of the population, and particularly for those in need.

Social democratic views are generally espoused by national labour unions, some of which are close to the socialist and communist ideologies.

Volunteers are considered unnecessary, since the "Welfare State" caters to all the population's needs. Volunteers may be considered with suspicion, in view of their assuming functions without pay and thus depriving workers of paid jobs.

Critics of this view submit that the state or government cannot, or should not, do everything, — civil servants may lack the dedication, sense of initiative and personal interaction of volunteers, — the socialist equalitarian society is impersonal and alienating, — individuals and private groups should be able to take initiatives, independently from the government, and assume social functions and responsibilities.

The Christian democrat views are traditionally in favour of the NGO, as an intermediate area between the individual and the state. The state has its own responsibilities, but the community, or "civil society", the network of private organizations in which personal solidarity is expressed, is even more important. The Christian democrats believe that it is valuable to do something for your neighbour just for the love of God, or just out of charity. It is part of your duty as a citizen and as a Christian.

Critics of this view say that Christian democrats have the "lost village" in mind, the romanticized agrarian community, which has disappeared. Voluntarism in an industrialized society is a different question, with other constraints and demands.

The liberal/conservatives have a clear preference for the private sector in general, and in particular for non-governmental voluntary organizations. Their

---

[10] L. Hoekendijk, "Which work ought to be paid ?", Volonteurope, *The Journal*, No. 5, pp. 39–44.

position is totally opposed to that of the social democrats. The less state intervention and control, the better. They encourage and appreciate the private initiative of voluntary service, and criticize public expenses and waste, rigid state bureaucracies and their ineffective civil servants. They believe that volunteers should be fully qualified professionals, not "social amateurs".

Critics of this view say that you cannot rely only or mainly on private initiatives without public accountability to provide comprehensive social services to the whole population: only the impartial state can assume this overall responsibility.

In Eastern Europe (prior to the 1989 democratization), the civil society, the autonomous social intermediaries between the all-powerful state and the citizens, was destroyed, or not allowed to develop independently. "Democratic centralism", controlling all aspects of political, economic and social life, left little or no room for private and spontaneous initiatives. In the Marxist-Leninist view, there is no room for separate independent organizations, because the state is the benevolent provider of all citizens, and no conflict of interest may arise between the state (or the Communist Party, representing all citizens) and the people. All organizations, even if independent in name, are (were) controlled by the Communist Party.

A Soviet participant at a recent workshop on "Volunteer work and the State"[11], said that

> We always had NGOs, but they were not very active. The Red Cross is not active, and the churches are introvert — only dealing with spiritual matters. There is no official volunteer policy... in my country, everybody is expected to bear responsibility for the community.

Volunteer work for a "good cause" (as defined by the Party) is generally an obligation, an honour which citizens cannot refuse when asked. the "freedom to volunteer" element was essentially absent from the Soviet concept of voluntarism.

The 1989 democratic revolution in Eastern European countries, and glasnost and perestroika in the USSR have opened new prospects of "real" voluntarism in this region, with the creation of NGOs, really independent from Party and government control.

The Red Cross Volunteers

The original concept of Red Cross voluntarism is directly related to the Christian charitable inspiration and to the Western liberal political support for personal dedication and initiative, to provide direct humanitarian assistance to those in need, both in armed conflicts and in civilian relief assistance.

---

[11] Serguei Yourilin, "Volunteer work in the USSR", in *State and Civil Society: Voluntary Work in Eastern and Western Europe*, Workshop held on 2 July 1989, Volonteurope 7, Nov. 1989, the Netherlands, , pp. 23–24. See also the Introduction by J. Heinsius and J. Houben, pp. 9–12.

The Red Cross' views on voluntarism are particularly valuable on account of the world-wide experience of Red Cross organizations with volunteers over more than a century.

Voluntary service is one of the seven Fundamental Principles of the Red Cross:

The Red Cross is a voluntary relief organization not prompted in any manner by desire for gain.

As stated by Meurant[12]

the term "voluntary" is therefore the common denominator of the Red Cross as an institution, of the National Societies composing it, and of its members, groups and individuals who act in its name in time of armed conflict as well as in time of peace.

That voluntarism is one of the basic tenets of the Red Cross Movement is demonstrated by statutory texts as well as by practice.

In 1863, the year of creation of the Red Cross, the Geneva International Conference approved a resolution stating, in part, that national committees (Societies) will train, instruct and organize voluntary medical personnel, and send them to the battlefield, when they will be placed under military command[13].

In 1957, the XIXth International Red Cross Conference invited National Societies, *inter alia*, to encourage a wide participation of voluntary auxiliary personnel in the various Red Cross activities such as first-aid, disaster relief, health education, nursing, blood transfusion, care of the handicapped and old people, mental health services, fight against alcoholism, nutrition and social welfare, particularly in the field of mother and child care[14].

In 1981, the XXIVth International Conference of the Red Cross recommended to the National Societies to provide opportunities to volunteers in cooperating with the authorities and private organizations in planning health and social welfare programmes to cover the needs of the population, and in implementing plans made, and recommended to governments to support the National Societies' efforts to extend the scope of voluntary services and increase their efficiency[15].

In 1986, the XXVth Conference recommended to National Societies, in part, to facilitate making qualified personnel available for urgent humanitarian missions, and to promulgate, if they do not already have one, a national charter for volunteers specifying their rights and duties[16].

In practice, national and international Red Cross volunteers play a significant

---

[12] J. Meurant, op.cit., p. 9.

[13] *International Red Cross Handbook*, 12th Ed.,Geneva, 1983, pp. 547–548—referred to below as *Handbook*.

[14] *Handbook*, p. 675: New Delhi 1957, Resol. No. XXVII.

[15] *Handbook*, p. 613–615: Manilla 1981, Resol. No. XIX.

[16] Geneva 1986, Resol. No. XXIII.

role in Red Cross protection and relief activities, as volunteers also play an important role in the activities of most other NGOs.

The Red Cross organizations, like other humanitarian NGOs, are "volunteer" organizations in a broad sense: their employees and volunteers are not attracted by profit, material motives or career advancement prospects which may be offered in business firms, nor do they seek civil service status. They freely, voluntarily choose to work for humanitarian NGOs for altruistic purposes, in order to help the wounded, the sick, the prisoners, the refugees, the poor and the afflicted.

However, in a stricter sense, Red Cross volunteers are only a part of the establishment of the Red Cross organizations. Like other NGOs, the International Committee of the Red Cross (ICRC), the League and the National Societies need a permanent, remunerated, central staffing structure, supplemented or complemented, as necessary, by volunteers.

The central structure includes the organization's leadership, professional managers and specialists, and support clerical and secretarial personnel. Among the Red Cross professionals, there are those who support the organization itself, administrators, accountants, lawyers, documents' officers, etc., and those responsible for services, including medical and paramedical personnel, nutritionists, social workers etc.

Permanent staff are needed to ensure continuity and responsibility. They are also needed to brief, train and supervise the volunteers.

Red Cross volunteers share the same general characteristics and motivation as other volunteers, as discussed above. However they have their own specific characteristics, as part of a durable, structured Movement with specific legal, ethical and administrative policies and guidelines, including the Fundamental Principles, the Geneva Conventions, resolutions of the International Conference of the Red Cross and other statutory provisions or agreements.

Characteristics of Red Cross Volunteers

Pictet[17] has defined a volunteer as someone who works of his own free will, without external compulsion—and not necessarily one who is not paid:

> In the Red Cross world, the concept of voluntary service implies that one serves not because of any constraint but because of a freely accepted commitment...The voluntary character of the Red Cross is directly related to the principle of humanity, being in effect a means for putting that principle into effect. For the Red Cross to be able to carry out its work, it has to inspire a feeling of dedication and appeal to the best in people: its ranks must be filled

[17] Jean Pictet, *The Fundamental Principles of the Red Cross—Commentary*, Henry Dunant Institute, Geneva, 1979, pp. 70–81.

with men and women with a highly developed spirit of service...Charity and self-denial are inseparable.

Also associated with voluntary service is the "golden rule" of the Red Cross, selflessness: the Red Cross does not reap any advantage from its activities: it is only concerned with the humanitarian interest of the persons who require help.

Finally, the spirit of service is the source of the Red Cross' vital energy: to serve the Red Cross is in some respects like "taking religious vows". The glory of the Red Cross consist above all of unknown acts of heroism.

Adding a social dimension to these elements, the First World Meeting on Red Cross Voluntary Service in Mexico, in 1983, said that

a volunteer is a person who reaches a consciousness of solidarity, which leads him to work with people with the objective of wakening in them their own capacity to improve the quality of their lives[18].

Berlin and Grimoldi[19] have defined four categories of Red Cross volunteers:

— the "initial volunteer", who first joined a Red Cross organization, with only a diffuse idea of the Movement;
— the "service volunteer", who has acquired basic knowledge, training and experience in Red Cross work;
— the "professional volunteer", with 3 to 5 years' training and experience in a Red Cross organization, who are able to supervise programmes and act as instructors;
— the "volunteer professional", who has a profession outside the Movement but commits himself to do voluntary work in his spare time. This group includes doctors, nurses, social workers, engineers, etc.

Red Cross work was initially related to medical work and nursing care in war situations. It later extended to relief following natural disasters. National Red Cross Societies played the role of auxiliary to the public authorities, they undertook social work. Blood transfusion and ambulance services are examples that many Red Cross and Red Crescent Societies in all parts of the world have in common. Other services may be provided: in Algeria, the Red Crescent Society has assumed national responsibility for services to the elderly, the disabled and the 15,000 abandoned children in the country. Dealing with AIDS is now a concern for National Societies in both industrialized and Third World countries.

Societies in developing countries, especially in Africa, have linked disaster interventions to rehabilitation, environment projects and longer term development involvement. However, there have been warnings against having community-based programmes depending too much on Red Cross volunteers. The volunteer involved

---

[18] *Report on the First World Meeting on Red Cross Voluntary Service*, op.cit.
[19] *Combining Professionalism with Voluntarism*, A. Berlin and J.A. Rocha Grimoldi, Institut Henry Dunant, Geneva, Working Paper 2:88, pp. 6–7.

in decision-making and implementation must be someone from within the community, selected and maintained by the community itself, but not a Red Cross volunteer. Another objection is that a Red Cross volunteer recruited for an emergency mission may not be interested, available nor qualified to work for a long-term community development programme[20].

The extent of the Red Cross and Red Crescent relief programme depends on the responsibilities delegated to the National Society by its government or by the national relief plan, if any. As a general rule, the Red Cross and Red Crescent programme is limited to the provision of: first aid, medical and nursing care, food supplies, clothing, shelter, services for the prevention of epidemics, including health education, social welfare, tracing services and other forms of emergency assistance.

Foreign personnel provided by donor Societies are placed under the direction of the National Society of the stricken country or of the League, when the direction and execution of the relief operation have been entrusted to it[21].

Emergency relief has remained a primary task of the Red Cross Movement.

For instance, after the 1986 earthquake which destroyed large parts of San Salvador, the capital of El Salvador, over 9,000 Red Cross volunteers, mostly young people, were quickly mobilized for the relief operation. Around 5,500 were regular volunteers, already enrolled in the El Salvador Red Cross, and 3,500 were temporarily recruited for this operation. Under the supervision of experienced Red Cross staff, in 72 hours the volunteers removed the rubble and first-aid was given. 3,207 persons who had been trapped in the ruins were rescued.

Following the political and economic crisis in Panama, between April and June 1988, thousands of Red Cross volunteers, distributing food to the needy under the leadership of the Panama Red Cross, helped 17,800 families, or over 100,000 persons, to survive. In this case also, both regular and temporary volunteers contributed to the success of this operation[22].

Paid or Unpaid Volunteers?

Does voluntary service signify unpaid service? This question affects all NGOs, and not only the Red Cross organizations.

In general, national volunteers working in their home country are unpaid: they may contribute in a more or less significant way to the organization's administration and to its technical activities, as well as fund-raising, training etc.

The employment of unpaid volunteers to work abroad raises different problems: at the minimum, the organization has to pay travel expenses and a basic subsistence

[20] Ibid., pp. 10–11, 15–16.
[21] Points 9 and 23 of *Principles and Rules for Red Cross and Red Crescent Disaster Relief*, The League, ICRC, Geneva, 1986.
[22] *Combining Professionalism...*, op.cit., p. 14.

allowance during the foreign assignment. Some organizations add to these minimum requirements an additional "indemnity" (not a salary) paid at home during or at the end of the mission, social security coverage, and a separation or resettlement allowance.

For Red Cross organizations, the question as to whether the remuneration of Red Cross volunteers was in conflict with the Fundamental Principles was studied in 1950.

Until the First World War, some privileged people could devote time to relief activities without pay or refund of outlays, but economic conditions had so changed by 1950 that few people could then live without earning their livelihood. In addition, the activities of National Societies had grown and qualified staff with professional training had become increasingly necessary. The investigation conducted by the ICRC and the League showed that all National Societies consulted employed paid staff and did not consider this to be a departure from the Red Cross principles. The ICRC concluded that the question of remuneration of Red Cross personnel depended very much on economic conditions and the social structure of the country, and that it was for the National Society in each country to decide how to organize the recruitment of its staff[23].

For Pictet[24], the important thing is that the work carried out for the Red Cross "shall be" voluntary. Whether it is paid for or not is a secondary consideration.

While he agreed that it was up to each National Society to make its own rules, he felt that it would be appropriate to limit the term "volunteers" or "voluntary workers" to persons who offer their services free or for a low sum, either on a permanent or temporary basis. All those who serve the Red Cross, whether they are paid or not, should create a living and fraternal working community, a team spirit.

Rights and Obligations of Red Cross Volunteers

There is no universal standard Charter of the Red Cross Volunteer defining his status, rights and obligations. Each National Society has to define the type of "employment" relationships between the Society and the volunteer, with due regard to the International Red Cross statutory texts, the statutes of the National Society and national labour legislation.

Similarly, the status of volunteers employed by the ICRC and by the League are defined by these organizations on a similar basis.

For instance, the French Red Cross has formulated a "Charte du Volontaire bénévole dans la Croix-Rouge Française", which defines the rights and obligations of the French National Society and those of volunteers.

[23] *Voluntarism within the Red Cross*, Working Doc. submitted to the Third Conference of National Red Cross and Red Crescent Societies of the Balkan Countries, Athens, 21–27 May 1979, Doc. DD/SND-9 of 8 May 1979.

[24] Pictet, op.cit., pp. 76–77.

118

The volunteer's rights include:

1. to be clearly informed
   — of the Fundamental Principles of the Red Cross and of the Geneva Conventions,
   — of the objectives, structures and functioning of the Red Cross,
   — of the tasks to be accomplished and relations to be maintained.
2. to know clearly his employment conditions: time given by the volunteer, reimbursement or not of related expenses, personal and third-party insurance, limitations of his action, relationships and support.
3. to be given the tasks for which he is more suited, or which he wishes to assume, and to be trained for these tasks.
4. to work within the Red Cross structure and supervision, and to be helped by other Red Cross employees, including paid technical personnel, if needed.

The volunteer's obligations include:

1. to accept the Red Cross Fundamental Principles, its mission, its objectives, the spirit in which he will work and the tasks entrusted to him.
2. to know the Geneva Conventions and their scope of application.
3. to accept orientation or training in the activities or functions entrusted to him, and on-going training which may be offered in order to maintain the quality of the services.
4. to accept the supervision, teamwork (if required) and collaboration with paid technical personnel in the respect of their competence.
5. to respect "the other person", in particular by ensuring discretion and secrecy similar to professional secrecy.
6. to abide by the "Clause of Reserve" peculiar to the Red Cross:

   No oral or written statement, concerning a mission or action accomplished in the name of the Red Cross, either at the local, national or international level, shall be issued without the prior approval of the French Red Cross authority who ordered the mission or action (President of the French Red Cross, Departmental Council Président or other Red Cross Official). No French Red Cross Volunteer may refer to his Red Cross affiliation for personal motives (political, ideological, commercial...). Any violation likely to cause severe harm (to the Red Cross) may result in the suspension or dismissal of the Volunteer.

The rights and obligations of the National Society are the mirror image of the obligations and rights of the volunteer[25].

Pictet[26] said that the Red Cross is threatened by two opposite hazards: bureaucratism and amateurism, and that it must protect itself from both.

[25] Internal French Red Cross Doc.
[26] Pictet, op.cit., p. 73.

What is needed in the Red Cross organizations, and in NGOs in general, is a healthy blend of professionalism and voluntarism, where paid staff and volunteers work as a dynamic team.

A few notes follow on voluntarism in a few selected countries: the U.S.A., with some data on the U.S. Peace Corps,—France and the U.K. Recent data and comments on the voluntary sector in other Western countries (Canada, the Federal Republic of Germany, Israel, Italy, Japan, the Netherlands, Spain, and Sweden) and in Sri Lanka may be found in the British publication *Charity Trends*, 1989[27].

Voluntarism in the U.S.A.

The American concept of voluntarism corresponds in general to the European "liberal/conservative" views. Since the creation of the U.S.A., the spirit of individual initiative and private entrepreneurship has been prevalent: government intervention should be limited to its essential functions and not stifle individual or private groups' efforts. Voluntarism is an integral part of the life of the citizen. It has initiated most social welfare programmes. Business firms encourage their employees to volunteer for community work.

The President of the U.S. "Volunteer: the National Center for Citizen Involvement"[28] has expressed clearly the philosophical and pragmatic approach of American voluntarism. Kerry Ken Allen believes that the voluntary commitment of citizens and of their organizations may contribute to resolve the problems of a world where the poor doubt that they can escape from their position, while the rich suffer of spiritual poverty. The solutions will not come from above, but from creative local initiatives, relayed and amplified by complex networks: programmes of mutual aid and assistance, neighbourhood organizations, consumers' groups. Individuals have observed a significant time lag between the onset of their own individual problems and political action: feeling more and more isolated, they search for ties to link them to others and to the whole community. Everyone is a potential volunteer, and voluntarism may deal with practically all issues. The motivation of voluntarism has evolved from the notion of helping others, or even of helping them to help themselves, to the concept of mutual benefit: the volunteer fulfils his own needs and escapes from his problems to the benefit of the others. The need to belong to a group and to develop the group's relationships and resources is also important.

Based on a 1988 survey[29], the average hours volunteered per week in 1987 for all adults 18 years and older, including non-volunteers, was 2.1. There were 176.7

---

[27] *Charity Trends*, 12th Ed., Charities Aid Foundation, 1989, pp. 76–92, "The Voluntary Sector: A Selection of International Statistics, by Susan Saxon-Harrold.

[28] Quoted in *Le Volontariat*, op.cit., pp. 77–78.

[29] *Charity Trends*, op.cit., pp. 95–96.

120

million adults 18 years of age or older. The 45 percent of respondents who volunteered gave an average of 4.7 hours per week. Based on this finding, it is estimated that 80 million adults gave a total of 19.5 billion hours in both formal and informal volunteering in 1987. Formal volunteering involves regular work with an organization; informal volunteering involves helping neighbours or organizations on an *ad hoc* basis, such as babysitting for free or baking cookies for a school fair. Americans who volunteered formally gave 14.9 billion hours. They represented the equivalent of 8.8 million full-time employees.

The most frequently cited reasons respondents gave for starting to volunteer were that: they wanted to do something useful (56 percent), they thought they would enjoy the work (34 percent), a family member or friend would benefit (27 percent), or they volunteered for religious reasons (22 percent).

In 1987, the largest proportion of persons volunteering were between 35 and 44 years of age (54 percent), among females (47 percent), (as has been found in Britain), among whites (47 percent), among persons with household incomes between \$50,000 and \$74,999 (57 percent), and among those who are self-employed part-time.

An unknown number of U.S. volunteers work abroad for religious or secular NGOs. More data are available concerning the U.S. Peace Corps.

The U.S. Peace Corps

The U.S. Peace Corps is the largest national, government-sponsored and financed volunteer body engaged in international assistance work. Over 30 years, more than 125,000 Peace Corps volunteers, men and women, have committed 250,000 volunteer years to service overseas.

In December 1989, more than 6,300 volunteers were serving in 66 host countries around the world, providing technical assistance and training in agriculture, education, health, natural resources conservation, business, skilled trades and other areas. The Peace Corps budget for the fiscal year ending on 30 September 1990 was \$165 million. The President of the U.S. has requested an increase to \$181 million for fiscal year 1991, in order to extend the numbers of volunteers to 10,000[30].

The U.S. Peace Corps was established by President John F. Kennedy in 1961. In 1977, the Peace Corps Act was amended to emphasize the Peace Corps commitment towards programming to meet the basic needs of those living in the poorest areas of the countries in which the Peace Corps operates. It was made an independent agency in 1981[31].

Peace Corps projects are designed to match the skills and community-level

[30] U.S. *Daily Bulletin*, Geneva, EUR210 of 5 Dec. 1989, and EUR506 of 15 June 1990.
[31] Peace Corps Act of 1961, as amended (22 U.S.C., 2501, and Title VI of the International Security and Development Cooperation Act of 1981 (22 U.S.C. 2501–1).

approach of the volunteers with the resources of host-country agencies and other international assistance organizations to help solve specific development problems, often in conjunction with private voluntary organizations.

To fulfil the Peace Corps mandate, men and women of all ages and varied education and experience, when admitted to the Corps, are trained for a 9- to 14-week period in the appropriate local language, the technical skills necessary for their particular job, and the cross-cultural skills needed to adjust to a society with traditions and attitudes different from their own. Volunteers serve for a period of two years, living among the people with whom they work. They are expected to become a part of the community and to demonstrate through their voluntary service that people can be an important impetus for change.

Finding volunteers is not a problem. More than 14,000 applied in 1989 for the 3,200 training slots that were open.

Volunteers receive a living allowance in the local currency to cover housing, food, essentials and a little spending money. When service is completed, volunteers receive a $200 readjustment allowance for every month served. Volunteers receive full health benefits.

Over 50 graduate schools provide scholarships for returned volunteers.

Like other volunteer organizations, U.S. Peace Corps volunteers are recruited mainly from white, middle-class sections. In 1989, the proportion of black volunteers was 6.8 percent. The Peace Corps Director's objective was to enlarge this proportion to 10 percent[32].

The Peace Corps also serves as the sponsor for U.S. citizens who wish to serve in the U.N. Volunteer Programme (UNV)(see Chapter 8), similarly to the sponsorship of French candidates for UNV service by the French equivalent body, the French "Progress Volunteers".

An auxiliary effort within the Peace Corps programme is the Peace Corps Partnership Program, which provides opportunities for schools, civic groups, neighbourhood and youth organizations in the U.S. to meet a specific need of an overseas community by financial sponsorship of the construction of a school, clinic or community facility recommended by a Peace Corps volunteer. Corporate and foundation support is also encouraged to match other private contributions and to advance funds based on pledges[33].

In May 1990, Peace Corps Director Paul Coverdell said in a congressional testimony that his agency will emphasize environmental, small business development and urban development efforts while continuing its traditional programmes in agriculture, health and education[34]. For example, Peace Corps volunteers are develop-

---

[32] U.S. *Daily Bulletin*, Geneva, EUR303 of 30 Aug. 1989. See also U.S. Peace Corps booklet (PC 7004), the *Washington Post*, 25 Apr. 1990, the *New York Times* of 30 Apr. 1990, the U.S. General Accounting Office Report on *Peace Corps – Meeting the Challenges of the 1990s*, Doc. GAO/NSIAD-90-122.

[33] *U.S. Government Manual*, pp. 688–691.

[34] U.S. *Daily Bulletin*, Geneva, EUR211 of 22 May 1990.

ing outreach and care programmes for street children in Costa Rica, Honduras and the Philippines.

Following the 1989 democratization of Eastern European countries, the U.S. Peace Corps sent volunteers, at the request of their government, to Hungary, Poland and Czechoslovakia, mainly as English-language teachers.

To enter or re-enter any country, the Peace Corps must be invited and must be guaranteed security. For instance, the 19 Peace Corps volunteers were withdrawn from Haiti when political violence erupted in December 1987. The Peace Corps kept a small support staff in the country so that the agreement made in 1982 would not lapse. In June 1990, the U.S. Embassy ordered all Peace Corps volunteers in the Philippines (numbering 261) to return to Manilla because of intelligence reports that Communist rebels were planning to kill volunteers. Timothy Swanson, one of the 261, was kidnapped by the rebels on 13 June[35].

As a symbolic symptom and a product of the détente between the U.S. and the USSR, and as evidence of the opening of the Soviet Union to non-governmental initiatives, the formation of the first U.S./Soviet volunteer corps to aid developing countries was announced on 31 May 1990[36].

Called "Operation U.S.A./USSR", the non-profit, privately sponsored development corps will place teams of American and Soviet professionals in developing countries to work on health care, environmental and agriculture programmes. The first team, consisting of two American, two Soviet and two Mexican doctors, will provide primary health care and medical manpower training to the village of Lerma, home to thousands of victims of Mexico's 1985 earthquake.

While the U.S. Peace Corps is financed by the U.S. government, Operation U.S.A./USSR will be financed by U.S. corporations and the Soviet Peace Committee, an organization of "private individuals".

Pros and Cons of National Voluntary Corps

National, government-sponsored, volunteer organizations provide structured openings for motivated, altruistic, idealistic persons who wish to give concrete, individual and personalized assistance to the people of Third World countries, under the flag of their country, rather than under the responsibility of a secular or religious, national or international NGO.

National Peace Corps volunteers benefit from the official support and protection of their government and its diplomatic services. On the other hand, as American, French or Japanese[37] volunteers, they are identified with their country and may be

---

[35] *International Herald Tribune*, 27 June and 2 July 1990.

[36] U.S. *Daily Bulletin*, Geneva, EUR408 of 1 June 1990.

[37] Japan has created a Peace Corps in 1965. 9,000 volunteers have been sent on missions since 1965. In 1990, about 2,000 volunteers were serving in 45 developing countries. The Japanese programme emphasizes technical expertise and recruits men and women up to the age of 40: *International Herald Tribune*, 19 June 1990.

involved more directly than other volunteers in political crises affecting their country and the recipient state.

The deployment of national volunteers is a concrete demonstration of good will and assistance given by the country concerned to relief or development needs of Third World countries. The national flag of the volunteer corps is explicitly or implicitly part of the volunteer's presence and work. The national volunteer corps may promote directly or indirectly the national ideology and culture, as well as the political, industrial and commercial interests of the corps' country. Viewed positively, the U.S. Peace Corps volunteers have been called the "ambassadors of democracy and American goodwill": viewed negatively, some have been accused of working for the CIA. Similarly, French Progress Corps volunteers run the risk of being accused of neo-colonialism, and Japanese Peace Corps volunteers may be consciously or unconsciously associated with Japan's past military conquests. In June 1990, Communist rebels in the Philippines charged that U.S. and Japanese volunteers were secretly assisting the government in counter-insurgency operations. Washington and Tokyo denied the charges[38].

While the vast majority of national Peace Corps volunteers are probably more motivated by altruism and the attraction of an overseas experience than by aggressive patriotism, their official sponsorship by their own government gives them a national "stamp of approval" which associates them closely to their government's official internal and external policies.

The use of even a few national Peace Corps volunteers for overt or covert political, military, commercial or espionage activities is counterproductive: it would taint the image of the whole corps for an extended period and severely restrict the deployment of national volunteers in many countries.

The self-interest of the national Peace Corps is that their volunteers are seen and perceived as totally dedicated to their work and mission in the local community, with the minimum of intervention and interference by their country's authorities.

Voluntarism in France

Voluntarism in France has been historically supported by three main currents.

The first one, since the Middle Age, is represented by the Christian Church's assistance activities in the fields of education (schools), health (hospitals), welfare (orphanages and institutions for the blind). Assistance overseas was carried out by the religious orders and the missions (see Chapter 6).

The second current is that of the solidarity of labourers and workers who created trade guilds, and as from the 11th century, corporations and confraternities, ancestors of modern mutual benefit societies and trade unions. This current was taken over by the 19th century socialism and 20th century communism, and their affiliated trade unions, which promoted the spirit of the solidarity of the "working class".

[38] *International Herald Tribune*, 27 June 1990.

The third current is that of secular "republicanism", based on a commitment to democracy, freedoms, the liberating power of education, the duties of the Welfare State towards all citizens.

Following the decolonization movement of the 1960s, all three currents were influenced by a pro-Third World ideology ("Tiers-Mondisme"): the Christian duty to care for the poor and the socialist and republican demands for equality were integrated into a duty for the rich nations to help the underdeveloped countries, and a responsibility of the citizen of the former colonial power towards the former colonized "subject".

The French Revolution "Declaration of the Rights of Man and of the Citizen" of 1789 and the Constitution of 1848 had proclaimed the freedom of association. The development of voluntarism in France however dates from the 1901 Law of Association, which guarantees the right of association as a public freedom, a fundamental democratic notion.

It is now estimated that in France there are at least 500,000 associations, that almost 50,000 are created each year, with an annual increase of 20 percent between 1977 and 1983, and that on average, one Frenchman in two is a member of an association, whereas one Frenchman in three was a member of an association less than ten years ago. Ninety-five per cent of associations have the simplest status, that of "registered" associations; five per cent have the status of associations recognized as being of "public utility".

It is estimated that associations in France have more than 700,000 paid employees. According to moderate estimates, they have between 2 and 3 million voluntary workers, representing the equivalent of between 100,000 and 150,000 full-time jobs. Their annual budget is assessed at approximately 50,000 million francs[39].

In France, as in other Western countries, most volunteers come from middle and higher levels of the population, managerial, urban and "bourgeois" categories, rather than from rural and workers' categories.

The fields of action of the French associations can be classified in the following categories:

— the medical environment: hospital-related work, visits to patients, management of clinics, nursing schools, kindergartens, first-aid, blood donations etc.
— social services: assistance to the homeless, former convicts, handicapped persons, former prostitutes, old people without financial means, immigrants, refugees etc.
— education and culture: family planning groups, preparation to married life, school cooperatives, sports clubs, summer camps, youth centres and hostels, adult education, cultural, scientific, library, artistic groups.
— political groups, related to political parties.

[39] "Report on Non-Profit Making Associations in the European Community", by N. Fontaine, 1986, Appendix 3.7, paras. 15 and 16, in *International Association Statutes Series*, 1988, Union of International Associations Publ.

— consumers' associations
— ecologists' groups.

France has an active programme of development aid to the Third World.

In 1987, France's net Official Development Assistance (ODA) to developing countries and multilateral agencies was 0.51 percent of its Gross National Product, and in 1989, 0.54 percent, while the average of industrialized countries was around 0.36 percent. In 1987, French bilateral aid represented 71 percent of its total aid, and its multilateral aid 29 percent[40].

In 1988, the French Cooperation Programme sent and financed 7,500 "coopérants" (paid volunteers) to 36 countries: 81 percent were assigned to the former French colonies in Sub-Sahara Africa. Two-third were teachers and professors, the remaining one third included agriculture specialists, veterinarians, engineers, doctors, administrators, computer specialists etc. A few of them were National Service volunteers, who volunteered as "coopérants" in lieu of military service, but for a two-year period instead of the obligatory 12 month military service.

Relief and development assistance outside France is carried out both by governmental and non-governmental agencies.

Among the former, following the example of the American Peace Corps, the French government created in 1963 the "French Association of Progress Volunteers". In 1987, out of ten French volunteers on development assignments, three were Progress Volunteers, i.e. 600 out of 2,100 French volunteers serving overseas wholly or partly financed by official aid agencies. The French Ministry of Cooperation and Development finances entirely the cost of the Progress Volunteers.

More age-conscious than the U.S. Peace Corps, the French Association sets an age range of 21 to 30 to be accepted as a Progress Volunteer. Assignments are for two years, renewable. Employment conditions correspond to those of the standard French "volunteer status": round-trip travel is paid, a subsistence allowance ("to live decently" at the place of assignment), social security coverage, emergency repatriation for health reasons, repatriation indemnity.

French candidates to the U.N. Volunteer Programme have to be sponsored by the French Association of Progress Volunteers.

In the non-governmental category, the medical "No-Border" Movement started in France in 1971 with the creation of "Médecins sans Frontières" (see Chapter 7). The French-initiated "No-border" Movement has, since then, extended to other fields and professions: architects, educators, engineers, veterinarians and others.

In 1989, more than 600 French associations were concerned directly or indirectly with Third World issues. Out of these, 40 were listed as actively calling for volunteers[41].

---

[40] French Ministry of Cooperation and Development, *Le choix de l'Afrique*, Dec. 1988. The ODAs of Norway, the Netherlands, Denmark and Sweden are higher than France's. France's ODA is ahead of the British and U.S. ODAs.

[41] *Petit guide du Volontariat et du Bénévolat*, Commission Coopération Développement, Paris, 1989.

In 1989, the number of French volunteers sent by NGOs to work overseas, mostly in French-speaking African countries, was approximately 3,000.

NGOs may benefit from "co-financing" by the French government for the costs of volunteers, subject to the approval of the validity of the proposed project by a governmental committee. Co-financing by the government is normally granted up to 50 percent of the volunteer's costs, or in some cases up to 70 percent, not to exceed F.Frs 120,000 per volunteer's position[42].

Voluntarism in the U.K.

The U.K. has a long tradition of voluntarism and some of the major humanitarian NGOs were created in Britain. A review of some of the "British Charities", including Oxfam and Save the Children Fund, is contained in Chapter 5.

After World War II, the British Labour government introduced extensive state welfare services in the U.K. Despite these, volunteering remained an important activity, which has been encouraged by the present conservative government. Faithful to its liberal views, the British government is looking to the voluntary sector and to volunteers to take an expanded role in the provision of welfare and other services to the community.

By the end of 1985, there were 154,135 charities. In 1988/1989, the funding of charities by the public sector, corporations and individuals amounted to more than 5,000 million pounds, of which individual donations were estimated at between 3,000 and 4,500 million pounds[43].

Figures on volunteering in 1987[44] report that 44 percent of respondents had given time to at least one of 24 named ways of helping charities in the month prior to interview. The mean overall time given in the month prior to interview was five hours 10 minutes. It was estimated that over 27 million people participated in voluntary work. This estimate is equivalent to 1.3 million people working a full-time 40 hours week.

The 1981 General Household Survey, based on a sample of 23,000 adults, found that women were more likely than men to volunteer through schools, hospitals and churches. Men were more likely than women to serve on committees and less likely to fundraise or give practical help. Volunteers were involved in helping children and teenagers, the disabled and the elderly.

As in other Western countries, volunteering in the U.K. remains closely linked to socio-economic class, material well-being and educational achievement.

The U.K. is the only country to have created a government public service covering the activities of the national volunteer associations. The "Volunteer Centre" was

---

[42] "Opération Volontaires 1989", leaflet, French Ministry of Foreign Affairs and Ministry of Cooperation and Development.

[43] *Charity Trends*, op.cit., pp.3–7.

[44] Ibid. pp. 94–95.

created in 1973 through a government subvention. It is part of the Home Office.

The Centre is a national agency advising on volunteer and community involvement. The Centre "speaks with an independent voice in the world of volunteer action, aiming to foster dispassionate — and sometimes critical — debate on a current practice in volunteering"[45].

Senior Experts

National and international voluntarism appears to draw on characteristics of youth, such as a spirit of adventure and wholehearted enthusiasm, selfless dedication to worthy causes, concern for the less privileged, physical endurance, ability to adjust to different and stressful environments.

In the 1960s, it was realized that young, and not so young, retirees could also contribute usefully to voluntary service: their knowledge, experience and wisdom acquired over many years of business, industrial, technical, educational, administrative or management responsibilities could be tapped for the benefit of their own country and for the benefit of Third World countries. The fact that most of the "seniors" had a retirement pension and did not need additional income made them willing candidates for "unpaid" voluntary service. In fact, many of these willing or reluctant retirees wanted to remain professionally and intellectually active, and were ready to contribute, without financial gain, to worthy causes.

This rich reservoir of intellectual, technical and spiritual potential was revealed relatively recently on account of various factors such as the extension of life expectation, the early retirement of many managers for economic or other reasons, the belief, in some countries, that reducing the retirement age would help solve unemployment.

The U.S. "International Executive Service Corps" was the first to be created in industrialized countries, in 1964. It was followed by the creation of the "Canadian Executive Service Overseas" in 1967, the British "Executive Service Overseas" in 1972, the French "Echanges et consultations techniques internationaux" (ECTI) in 1975, the "Japan Silver Volunteers" in 1977, the Swiss "Senior Expert Corps" in 1979, another French senior group, AGIR, in 1983, and similar bodies in the Netherlands, Australia, the Federal Republic of Germany, Ireland, Belgium and Spain. These national senior services meet every two years to review and compare their activities.

Together, these senior expert services have about 15,000 members. They carried out 2,000 interventions in Third World countries in 1982.

These figures have increased since 1982: in 1987, ECTI alone carried out 1,500 interventions, a third in France itself, and two third overseas[46].

---

[45] The Volunteer Centre, Policy Discussion Doc. 3, 1983.
[46] *Le Volontariat*, op.cit., pp. 121–122, and *ECTI Information*, Bulletin 88–01, Jan. 1988.

Charters for Volunteers

The British Volunteer Centre proposed a "Charter for Volunteers" in 1983: its text is in Table 3.4.

The main purposes of this document appear to be the following:

— to legitimize volunteering as producing social benefit, and as the right of citizens;
— to provide that volunteers are entitled to proper treatment by their organization, including a right to be consulted on major decisions;
— to encourage the government to remove legal obstacles (such as taxation on income support) to voluntarism;
— to recognize the particular domaine and collective interests of both volunteers and paid workers, and their associations, in an attempt to defuse the potential rivalry and conflicts between the two groups.

Table 3.4. The U.K. "Charter for Volunteers: A Proposal"

The Volunteer Centre proposes that this charter should be voluntarily adopted by all organizations that are concerned directly or indirectly with the work of volunteers, and by volunteers themselves. Recognising the wide variation in practices and standards, this represents a statement of aims; for the present only partial adoption may be feasible in some circumstances.

"Volunteers" and "volunteering" generally refer to: work undertaken on behalf of self or others outside the immediate family, not directly in return for wages, undertaken by free choice, not required by the state or its agencies.

1. Volunteering to produce social benefit is legitimately:
   — an expression of humanitarian concern
   — a means by which the individual makes a personal contribution to, and takes part in, the life of the community
   — a means of enhancing the quality of life for the whole of society
   — a means of enabling society to meet its obligations to its members
   — a means of expressing the interests of individuals and groups

It may take place in many different fields, such as social welfare, the arts, sport and political life. To volunteer should be the right of every citizen.

2. The right to volunteer may also be expressed informally between family members, neighbours or members of mutual help groups. It may take place in the framework of a voluntary or statutory agency.
3. Volunteers, while they generally give their time and work without pay, are entitled to consideration and treatment at least as good as that of paid workers in other respects. The organization for which they work should recognize an ethical contract which requires at the minimum proper management, clear expectations, training where it is appropriate, indemnity against reasonable risks, and reimbursement of necessary expenses.
4. All citizens who voluntarily contribute within an organized framework have the right to be consulted on all major decisions that will affect what they do. Existing and planned public policies should be reviewed to ensure that they take into account the needs and interests of volunteers where appropriate, and that as a minimum they do not unintentionally limit the rights of volunteers.
5. Every citizen irrespective of personal means has the right to make that contribution according to per-

sonal talents and capabilities so long as this does not restrict the rights or reasonable expectations of others. No citizen should be prevented from volunteering because of lack of economic resources or other handicap.

6. Volunteering is not the prerogative of the majority or of any racial group in society. All racial groups develop arrangements to support disadvantaged members within their communities and provide volunteers for initiatives which serve all races.

7. Unnecessary obstacles in law, in systems of taxation or income support should be removed where this will enable more citizens to undertake action as volunteers. Where, for reasons of physical, mental, legal or other restriction, individuals do not have the full liberty of other citizens, they should be enabled to give and receive from society as volunteers.

8. Citizens who volunteer have the right to expect that they will not be exploited and that the true social value of their contribution is recognized and respected by the authorities concerned.

9. Both volunteers and paid workers should recognize the particular tasks that each is best able to perform. Each should acknowledge the value of the other's contribution; should support it, and should not attempt to undermine or replace it. In particular, codes of practice should recognize the collective interests of paid workers in trades unions or professional associations vis à vis the collective interests of volunteers.

Source: The Volunteer Centre, Policy Discussion Document 3, 1983.

"Volonteurope", a Committee created to encourage unpaid voluntary action in countries of the European Community, has submitted a "European Charter for Volunteers—A Basic Declaration" in 1986: its text is in Table 3.5.

Similarly to the British Charter, it underlines the value of voluntary service, volunteers' rights, the mutual value of volunteers and paid workers. In addition, it refers to the volunteers' obligations (to be dependable), and to the financial support to be provided by governments.

Both texts are proposals to be adopted by NGOs, governments and by volunteers, in full or in part. They are both useful documents which help clarify the respective roles of volunteers, voluntary organizations, paid workers and governments in relation to voluntary service.

Rather than adopting such a general Charter, a number of NGOs have defined their own, more specific charter: see for instance the Volunteer Charter of the French Red Cross (see p. 118), the MSF Charter (Table 7.1) and the Charter of AMI (Table 7.2), in Chapter 7.

Table 3.5. A European Charter for Volunteers — A Basic Declaration

1. Volunteer work has a value for the community, for:
   — improvement of the quality of society,
   — defending the interests of people and groups which are in a disadvantaged position,
   — and can be a fundamentally democratic way to meet needs and to create
   — opportunities in society.

Volunteer work can be either autonomous or additional to professional service, to renew, enlarge or support it.

Volunteer work is done both by men and by women, in the field of human service, culture and citizens actions.

2. Every citizen has a right to do volunteer work according to his/her capacities.
   This is a right, but not an obligation.
3. The right to do volunteer work does not mean that any volunteer can do all kinds of volunteer work. Organizations can select according to the tasks. The development of a wide range of opportunities, from more to less demanding should be encouraged, so that there is a place for everybody who is interested.
4. Volunteer work should not be the privilege of certain groups in society. This means that no citizen should be excluded from volunteer work because of financial problems (expenses), or social handicaps like being out of work, being old, very young or handicapped or belonging to a minority group. Unnecessary obstacles in law, in systems of taxation, or income should be removed.
5. Volunteers have rights. These rights should be respected and put into operation by the organizations which work with volunteers.

Volunteers have a right to:

— information about the work and the organization
— introduction in the work
— support
— a chance to learn and progress in the work
— a chance to have a say in the work being done if they so wish
— a chance to participate in their organizational structure
— when volunteers are working in a professional setting, they have a right to have their own organizational structure (group or association)
— volunteers have a right to get out of pocket expenses refunded. If the organization is not in a position to do so, this must be discussed and plans made to remedy the situation
— insurance

6. Volunteers have obligations. Volunteering does not mean without commitment. Volunteers should act as agreed, and do as promised; volunteers should be dependable.
7. Citizens who volunteer have a right to expect that they will not be exploited and that the true social value of their contribution will be recognized and respected by the authorities concerned.
8. Both volunteers and paid workers are indispensable. Each should acknowledge the value of the other's contribution, and each should receive equal appreciation in society and by the organizations with which they work. Both volunteers and paid staff should be able to contribute from their own specific positions and possibilities, which include respect for each other's codes of work and interests, and the general interest of the public.
9. Volunteers should be valued and recognized by government — at all levels. This includes the financial support which should make the functioning of volunteer work possible. When establishing advisory councils etc., the government should see that representation of the volunteer field is present.
10. Volunteer work has a function for the future. It is a power for renewal of the present system, shaping, together with others, the society of tomorrow.

Source: Volonteurope, Bussum, Netherlands, 1986.

The European Parliament, by a resolution on voluntary work adopted on 16 December 1983[47], asked the Commission of the European Community

to draw up a "statute for voluntary workers" laying down economic provisions for the reimbursement of expenses and whatever else might prove necessary for the performance of their duties, and providing insurance cover for damage and responsibility.

[47] *Official Journal of the European Communities*, No. C 10/2/289–290.

The resolution also asked the Commission to support innovative and experimental projects than would set an example at European level. The European voluntary work policy should consider:

— financing voluntary work organizations, beginning with work on behalf of elderly people;
— incorporating voluntary work in the European Community programmes to combat poverty;
— providing greater opportunities for the unemployed to do voluntary work;
— establishing an EC forum for voluntary work responsible for the coordination of and research into voluntary work and the exchange of information and experience.

Finally, the Commission was asked

> to consider the possibility, on the basis of Article 118 of the EEC Treaty, of drafting a recommendation, to be agreed with the two sides of industry, aimed at establishing the broad criteria for a set of rules defining the nature and conditions of voluntary work and paid employment, bearing in mind the need to submit this recommendation to examination at local and regional level, a process in which the voluntary workers' organizations must also be involved.

The increasing interest of European policy-makers in voluntarism was also shown by the adoption by the European Parliament, on 16 December 1983, of another resolution recommending the establishment of a "European Voluntary Service Scheme for Young People"[48].

The Scheme was not to be considered an alternative to unemployment, nor a way of camouflaging it, but a permanent feature aimed at creating a greater sense of personal responsibility and at broadening young people's experience. Its proposed activities would extend and raise the quality of existing services, tackle conservation projects which would otherwise be neglected, undertake new projects and result in tangible achievements. The Scheme would be open to young people from all backgrounds and should include opportunities for young people with handicaps.

The Scheme would be extended at a later stage to include voluntary service in developing countries.

International Umbrella Groups

The Coordinating Committee for International Voluntary Service (CCIVS) was the first international body to serve as a liaison centre on voluntarism. It was created in 1948 under the aegis of UNESCO as a permanent Committee initially to coordinate workcamps of the then existing voluntary service organizations, organizations sited mainly in Europe and North America.

CCIVS has, since that time, extended its scope and now has 110 member organi-

[48] Ibid. No. C 10/286–287.

zations in 50 countries, including 12 international or regional organizations with branches in over 100 countries. At present, half of the membership is based in Africa, Asia and Latin America.

In view of its close association with UNESCO (its offices are in the UNESCO building and it has a consultative and associate status (category A) with UNESCO), CCIVS has adopted some of UNESCO's Third World or Socialist-oriented slogans: to fight against the dangers of war, social and racial discrimination, the consequences of neo-colonialism and imperialism, to establish a just international economic and social order. This orientation affects its image in the views of some of the more conservative Western-based voluntary associations, although CCIVS claims to be truly international, non-political and non-denominational.

CCIVS's function is broadly to act as an information and liaison centre on all matters concerning international, both long- and medium-term voluntary service as well as international workcamps. It also acts as a centre for study and research, evaluation and exchange of experiences. It organizes an international conference of voluntary service organizers to meeting every 2 or 3 years in order to evaluate the role of voluntary service and study the perspectives of contributing to national development, to peace and international understanding. The theme of the 1986 conference was "Working together for mutual respect, cooperation and peace". Also in 1986, CCIVS organized another conference on the "Mobilization of rural youth for the promotion of peace, disarmament and development"[49].

In 1962, the International Council of Voluntary Agencies (ICVA) was created in Geneva: it brings together more than 80 member associations engaged in humanitarian or development work. Details on ICVA have been given in Chapter 2 (pages 97–98).

In 1970, another group was founded, in the U.S.A., to promote international cooperation of voluntarism: the International Association for Voluntary Effort (IAVE), with its headquarters in Washington, D.C. IAVE has been admitted to consultative status (category II) with the U.N. Economic and Social Council.

Open to all voluntary associations, in 1988 IAVE's membership included most Western and Latin American associations:

— in North America, associations from the U.S. and Canada
— in Latin America, associations from 7 countries
— in Western Europe, associations from France, Italy, Portugal, Switzerland, the U.K.
— in Asia, associations from Japan, Korea, Singapore, Taiwan
— in the Western Pacific, Australia and New Zealand.

IAVE's action is carried out by its yearly information newsletter, "Learn through International Voluntary Effort" (LIVE), and by its biennial world conferences, also called LIVE.

[49] *News from CCIVS*, UNESCO, Paris, No. 4/86, p. 1.

LIVE 90 took place in Paris in September 1990, on the theme of "volunteers-partners". One Conference group studied partnership with governmental sources, local organizations, businesses, institutions (hospitals, prisons etc.), professional people and interested public. The second group focused on poverty-exclusion-insertion, participation in local life, culture and leisure time, environment and protection of the patrimony[50].

Following the 1970 LIVE Conference in Los Angeles, the "Association pour le Volontariat en Europe" (AVE) was created, in 1972, in Lyons, grouping volunteers' centres of member states of the Council of Europe.

In 1979, the Commission of the European Community, following the creation of AVE, invited two representatives from each of the EC countries to advise it on current volunteer issues. In 1980, "Volonteurope" was created, with a membership limited to associations within the EC. Its secretariat is in the Netherlands.

Volonteurope is a Committee whose purpose is to encourage cooperation on unpaid voluntary action, to facilitate the flow of information and to help promote an increase in the amount and effectiveness of volunteer work (broadly defined) within the countries of the EC. In its work it concentrates on new forms of volunteer work, in particular on increasing people's knowledge and understanding of it and its importance for society. One of its purposes is to encourage the EC to take account of voluntary action when developing and making policy, and actively propose policies and advice on voluntary action to the EC.

Volonteurope sponsored the "European Charter for Volunteers" (see Table 3.5). It organizes conferences, initiates research, publishes conference and research papers, compiles and disseminates documentation on voluntarism. It encourages volunteer exchanges[51].

There is no doubt that voluntarism, practised in the volunteer's home country or abroad, is a healthy and growing "business".

The reason is probably that voluntarism satisfies two very basic and important human needs: to give and to receive.

---

[50] *Le Volontariat*, op.cit., pp. 115–116 and annoucement of LIVE 90.
[51] "Volonteurope: Joint Action"; 2nd Policy Paper, Vol. 26, 1986.

PART II

NEUTRALITY OR POLITICIZATION? DISCRETION OR DISCLOSURE?

Intergovernmental organizations (IGOs) are required by their constitutions and nature not to become involved in individual countries' internal politics nor to take any public position on international issues other than that adopted by their governing bodies.

In contrast with these obligations, the non-governmental organizations' (NGOs) independence from governments' authority gives them, in principle, a total freedom of choice, of action and of expression, with related risks.

An NGO may respect or oppose the government authorities of its own country, as well as their political, economic and other decisions. An international NGO may adopt similar attitudes towards the government authorities of the foreign country which hosts their work.

The access of an NGO to a foreign recipient country is subject to that country's clearance and approval. Entering a country and working on its territory without the required permission may lay the NGO open to legal proceedings, sanctions and possible expulsion.

Siding with armed rebels fighting against the legitimate government of the host country may expose the NGO members to serious physical and legal risks, including detainment and death.

NGOs also have a choice in their public information policy.

An NGO may carry out its particular operational activities as agreed with the recipient country's authorities, and abstain from "speaking out", taking sides and publicly denouncing human rights violations committed or allowed by these authorities.

Alternatively, the NGO may issue, either at its headquarters, or in the recipient country, public critical pronouncements in relation to the recipient country's internal politics, economic and social practices and alleged violations of international humanitarian law and human rights instruments.

Any such public pronouncements may in consequence affect the attitude of the recipient country's government towards the NGO, which may be barred from continuing its work in the country.

The position adopted by an NGO in these matters may result from the organization's statutory mandate, the attitudes and beliefs of its constituency in the donor countries, political, religious or moral considerations, or the personality and attitudes of its leaders.

Some organizations have clear-cut positions: for instance, the neutrality of the Red Cross is one of the Fundamental Principles of the Movement, together with its rule of discretion.

Some of the religious organizations have a tradition of public advocacy in the name of social justice.

Some of the "French Doctors" associations have deliberately allied emergency humanitarian assistance with "mediatization" in the defence of human rights.

Some NGOs may be generally discreet and only occasionally take a public stand.

In the following Chapters, we will review the role and activities of a few selected international humanitarian NGOs, as well as their attitudes and practices in relation to politics and public disclosure of humanitarian and human rights abuses.

The traditional policy of neutrality and impartiality of the Red Cross will be considered in Chapter 4.

We will then review the activities and attitudes of a few British Charities in Chapter 5, of Religious Agencies in Chapter 6 and of Medical Volunteers in Chapter 7.

In Chapter 8, we will consider the role of the U.N. Volunteers Programme in development and humanitarian activities.

THE NEUTRALITY OF THE RED CROSS

Neutrality is one of the Fundamental Principles of the Red Cross, together with the allied principles of impartiality and independence. The Red Cross neutrality is implemented and guaranteed in particular by its policy of discretion, the golden "rule of silence" imposed on all Red Cross employees.

In his controversy with the former Secretary-General of the United Nations, Dag Hammarskjold, over the concept of impartiality of international civil servants, Nikita Khruschev is reported to have once remarked that

> while there are neutral countries, there are no neutral men[1]

In a similar vein, while the neutral status of Switzerland has been recognized legally and politically in international law since 1815, one may wonder about the significance and reality of the "neutrality" of a humanitarian non-governmental organization (NGO) in its international activities.

While the Fundamental Principles apply to all the Red Cross organizations, we will focus on the role and activities of the International Committee of the Red Cross (ICRC) in trying to assess the extent to which the neutrality principle has been respected in the past by the ICRC and the problems and tensions experienced recently by the Movement.

Why the ICRC and not the League of Red Cross and Red Crescent Societies, or the National Societies? Because the ICRC is the guardian, the promoter and the monitor of the Geneva Conventions, and more generally, of international humanitarian law in the Red Cross Movement, the central policy body of the Red Cross. The positions adopted by the ICRC, the decisions to take, or not to take, humanitarian initiatives, are those taken by the ICRC, as a specifically neutral and independent institution and intermediary, a role played only by the ICRC, and not by the operational National Societies, nor by their Federation, the League.

We will first recall the statutory basis of the Red Cross Principles of neutrality, impartiality and independence, and the related obligation of discretion, in other words, the long-standing, traditional "dogma" of the Red Cross.

---

[1] As reported by Walter Lippmann, *New York Herald Tribune*, 17 April 1961.

This dogma has been challenged in internal Red Cross reports, and by public criticisms related to external events.

In 1972, the ICRC and the League asked a Committee to carry out a thorough examination of the Red Cross role in the world. Part of the Committee's Report refers to the ICRC policy on operational information.

The attitude of the ICRC during the Second World War has raised controversies and criticisms. In 1988, the publication of Jean-Claude Favez' book entitled "An Impossible Mission? — The ICRC, deportations and Nazi concentration camps", based on an authorized study of the ICRC archives, showed some of the problems caused by the Red Cross rule of discretion. Arieh Ben-Tov's book on "The ICRC and the Jews in Hungary", also published in 1988, was openly critical of the ICRC's action, or inaction, in that period.

Some ICRC delegates have faced problems of conscience, torn between their sworn obligation of discretion, and their daily, direct exposure to the ill-treatment of prisoners and detainees, torture, and bad faith on the part of some government authorities. A recent collective letter signed by 200 ICRC delegates has challenged the traditional role of the ICRC and warned that it may end as a museum.

The Nigerian Civil War, in 1967–1970, gave an acid test to the ICRC's assertion of neutrality: can a humanitarian organization be deemed neutral when it gives relief assistance to a rebellious and secessionist part of a sovereign state's territory?

The continuing Middle-East conflict, the Iran-Iraq War and the situation in Lebanon made the ICRC go public: do its public denunciations of governments' violations of the Geneva Conventions indicate a change in the ICRC traditional policy of discretion?

The suspension of South Africa from the International Conference of the Red Cross in October 1986 was interpreted as a sign that the Red Cross, like U.N. organizations, was becoming "politicized". Was this judgement correct, or has the Red Cross retained its non-political, independent character?

The final question is whether the ICRC should change its policies and practices, on the basis of past experience, or whether it should remain as it has been, and still is, a "different" organization.

The "Dogma": The Statutory Basis of the Principles of Neutrality and Discretion

Neutrality

The Geneva International Conference of 1863 recommended

> that in time of war the belligerent nations should proclaim the neutrality of ambulances and military hospitals, and that neutrality should likewise be recognized, fully and absolutely, in respect of official medical personnel, voluntary

medical personnel, inhabitants of the country who go to the relief of the wounded, and the wounded themselves[2].

The proclaimed recognition that hospitals, ambulances and personnel, including the victims, were to be treated as "neutral", e.g. not as belligerents engaged in warfare, gave protection to the medical activities of the Red Cross, identified under a uniform distinctive sign and flag.

An essential condition for this recognition was a scrupulous observance of the principle of racial, religious and political neutrality, a principle which enables the Red Cross to recruit its helpers among all races, creeds and parties, without excluding any.

Neutrality applies to the work of the National Societies: they are to develop and organize within their territories, on a neutral basis, "the efforts of charitable persons"[3].

Neutrality is one of the Fundamental Principles of the Red Cross, on the grounds that:

> In order to continue to enjoy the confidence of all, the Red Cross may not take sides in hostilities or engage at any time in controversies of a political, racial, religious or ideological nature[4].

The initial basis of the Red Cross neutrality was to establish its non-military participation in a conflict, and its abstention from choosing one or the other camp, in order to privilege its purely humanitarian role.

The second aspect of the Red Cross neutrality is to refrain from political, racial, religious or ideological controversies. This requires a constant reserve and distance to be maintained between the Red Cross and national and international politics and ideology. The Red Cross commitment is to those who suffer.

As stated by Pictet[5], the ICRC, the very embodiment of neutrality, must observe, with particular strictness, complete ideological neutrality. As the ICRC is nevertheless unceasingly confronted by political events, it must reckon with politics without becoming a part of it.

> It is thanks to the fact that its (the ICRC) members and principal staff members belong to a country whose neutrality is permanent and traditional that the ICRC, in times of war and turmoil, has a solid base for its mission as an intermediary.

---

[2] *International Red Cross Handbook*, 12th Ed., Geneva, July 1983, p. 548.

[3] *Handbook*, op.cit., p. 558: XIVth International Conference of the Red Cross, 1930, Resol. No. XXV.

[4] Preamble of the Statutes of the International Red Cross and Red Crescent Movement, *Compendium of Reference Texts on the International Red Cross and Red Crescent Movement*, Geneva, 1990, p. 12.

[5] Jean Pictet, *The Fundamental Principles of the Red Cross, Commentary*, Henry Dunant Institute, Geneva, 1979—see in particular commentaries on impartiality, neutrality and independence, pp. 37–69.

142

This neutrality, reinforced by ideological neutrality, offers belligerents an added guarantee of its independence[6].

In order to maintain the relations of confidence essential for continuing cooperation with governments and to gain and retain access to the victims, the ICRC generally abstains from making public pronouncements about specific acts committed in violation of law and humanity and attributed to belligerents. If it set itself up as a judge, the ICRC would be abandoning the neutrality it has voluntarily assumed.

Taking sides would antagonize governments, close the doors of prison camps or detention places and prevent the ICRC from fulfilling its protection functions.

The rationale for this position is based on pragmatic considerations of ensuring continued access to victims. The alternative of public denunciations would, in the view of the ICRC, affect its neutral image and decrease its effectiveness.

Neutrality also requires full compliance with international law, and in particular the recognition of the rights and prerogatives of sovereign states.

The Geneva Conventions[7] make it clear that the protection role of the ICRC is subject to the "consent" of the Parties to the conflict, in case of prisoners of war, or to the approval of the Power governing the territories where the delegates will visit places of internment, detention and work, in case of protected civilian persons.

Neutrality requires impartiality, another Fundamental Principle:

It makes no discrimination as to nationality, race, religious beliefs, class or political opinions. It endeavours only to relieve suffering, giving priority to the most urgent cases of distress[8].

Like neutrality, the purpose of impartiality is to assure the Red Cross of the confidence of all parties, which is indispensable to its humanitarian mission. Like neutrality, it requires the Red Cross and its delegates not to take sides, to act without favour or prejudice towards or against anyone.

The Red Cross can be neutral and impartial only if it is independent, if it is free and sovereign in its decisions, acts and words. Its independence is a guarantee of the neutrality of the Red Cross.

The Red Cross independence must be asserted in relation to national and international public authorities and in connection with both national and international politics. The Red Cross must refrain from any involvement in internal or external politics. It must resist all pressures which would tend to infringe on its integrity and independence, be they political, ideological, social, economic or financial.

For the same reasons, the Red Cross cannot associate with any other institution which does not have absolute respect for its moral and material independence. The Red Cross will cooperate with other humanitarian organizations only on the condition that these institutions, in the common work, fully respect Red Cross principles.

[6] Ibid., p. 59.
[7] 1949 Geneva Conventions, Art. 9/III, 126/III, al. 4, 143/IV, al. 5.
[8] *Compendium*, op.cit., p. 12.

In particular, international humanitarian organizations engaged, together with the Red Cross, in assistance to civilian populations in natural or other disaster situations, should also be "impartial"[9].

Discretion

The Fundamental Principle of neutrality requires the Red Cross to refrain from engaging in political and other controversies.

Any such public expression of support for one or another side or position would jeopardize its claimed neutrality and impartiality.

National Societies should be vigilant in the maintenance of such neutrality at all times. They should ensure that their written communications, publicity material, official publications and pronouncements do not contain political opinions or judgements or any other statements which might cast doubt on the political neutrality of the Red Cross[10].

National Societies require their staff and volunteers to abide by the "Clause of Reserve", forbidding them to issue an oral or written statement concerning a Red Cross mission or action, at the local, national or international level, without the prior authority of the relevant Red Cross authority. This obligation is, for instance, included in the "Charter of the French Red Cross Volunteer" (see Chapter 3).

The Collective Labour Convention concluded between the ICRC and its Staff Association (January 1988) includes a "Duty of Discretion" in its article 10. On appointment, all ICRC employees have to sign a "Commitment to Discretion", stating in its Preamble, in part:

> The aim of the ICRC is to assure protection and assistance to the victims of war, civil wars and internal disturbances, as well as to other victims in favour of whom the ICRC is called upon to intervene. In order to be able to achieve its aim in the most efficient way, the ICRC needs, at all times, the confidence of governments and victims.
>
> This confidence relies to a large extent on the neutrality of the ICRC and on the discretion with which it carries out its action and more particularly its commitment according to which its delegates will not divulge what they observe in the country where they work, particularly when visiting places of detention.
>
> In consequence, (ICRC) collaborators must observe an absolute discretion on the ICRC activities of a confidential nature in which they participate or of which they have knowledge . . . [11].

---

[9] *Handbook*, op.cit., pp. 661–662 — XXIst International Conference of the Red Cross, Istambul 1969, Resol. No. XXVI.

[10] *Handbook*, op. cit., pp. 609 – 610—Board of Governors. XXVth Session, Athens 1959, Resol. No. 16.

[11] Our translation from the French.

This "Commitment to Discretion" continues beyond and after the period of ICRC employment.

Before giving a public speech, or before accepting to participate in a radio or television programme, or before submitting a publication or statements to the press related to the activity of the ICRC, ICRC employees or former employees must receive the authorization of the Chief of the Communication Department.

To ensure the protection of war prisoners and other detainees, ICRC delegates visit hospitals, camps, work places, prisons and anywhere else that captives may be held. Whether these visits are carried out under the Geneva Conventions or outside the scope of international humanitarian law (as in the case of "security detainees"), the following criteria are followed:

— delegates must be allowed to see all the prisoners and detainees and be able to talk to them in private, without witnesses;
— they must be given access to all places of detention and be able to make repeated follow-up visits;
— they must be given a list of the people to be visited.

Their purpose is to determine and, if necessary, improve, material and psychological conditions of detention and the treatment of the prisoners or detainees. They are not to examine the reasons of detention, this being outside the competence of the ICRC.

The delegates write confidential reports after each visit. The reports should be drafted objectively and in a constructive spirit. According to the "Model Memorandum" on visits by delegates of the ICRC to places of detention[12], when drafting the reports, local conditions and material difficulties, if any, which the persons in charge of the place of detention may have to face, must be taken into consideration.

The confidential reports are submitted first to the ICRC headquarters, and then sent to the detaining authority. In the case of prisoners of war, the reports are also sent to the government of the prisoners of war's home country. As a rule, the confidential reports are not divulged to other governments or to third parties. The reports are meant to give confidential information to the authority to which they are submitted.

In such matters, as in others, the ICRC acts with the utmost discretion and does not seek any publicity.

In the case of detainees, in any publication issued by the ICRC or the detaining authority, only the names of the places of detention visited and the dates of such visits are mentioned. No comments relating to conditions of detention or to suggestions put forward by the ICRC are made. Any other information regarding the visit may be published only after agreement is reached between the parties.

---

[12] *International Review of the Red Cross*, Jan. Feb. 1988, No. 262, Annex III, pp. 33–34, ICRC, Geneva.

If the government concerned chooses to publish a confidential report, however, it must do so in its entirety and without distortion. Otherwise, the ICRC retains the right to publish the entire report, as it did in the case of Iran[13].

The Transmission of Protests

Under Article 4.1.c) of its Statutes, the role of the ICRC is, in part

to take cognizance of any complaints based on alleged breaches of that (international humanitarian law applicable in armed conflicts) law.

These communications fall into two separate categories: the first includes the numerous *complaints* from National Societies, but principally from governments, families and prisoners etc. concerning the non-application of one or other provision of the Conventions. They mainly relate to the treatment of war prisoners and often to a permanent *de facto* situation. The ICRC can generally remedy the unsatisfactory situations reported to it by appropriate interventions, camp visits etc. The complaints' procedure has not been challenged and is continuing as an appropriate duty of the ICRC.

The second category comprises *protests* that generally relate to serious breaches of the Conventions or of humanitarian principles and concern past events where the ICRC no longer has any hold and cannot verify facts. The only possible procedure is to communicate the protest to the accused party requesting it to investigate and report whether the facts are accurate or, on the contrary, false or distorted. The protests come mainly from National Societies, governments, private persons or bodies, who generally ask that they should be transmitted to the accused party, to all the National Societies, or even laid before public opinion.

In a memorandum of 12 September 1939, at the beginning of the Second World War, the ICRC had determined the attitude it would observe in such situations.

The memorandum first recalled that, during the First World War, the ICRC did not make inquiries into alleged violations. In international conflicts after 1918, the Committee sent complaints received from the Red Cross Society of a belligerent state to the Red Cross Society of the country complained of, asking the latter to formulate a reply. The Committee has always reserved the right to publish or not publish such documents. In one case, the Committee endeavoured to apply Art. 30 of the Geneva Convention by arranging the constitution, with the assent of both Parties in conflict, of an Inquiry Commission. This attempt proved abortive.

The memorandum attached very restrictive conditions to the exercise of this function by the Committee.

The function, in regard to violations of the Conventions or any other action likely to be contested between belligerent parties, which the Committee might assume, should be exercised only insofar as they do not interfere with its posi-

[13] J.D. Armstrong, "The ICRC and Political Prisoners", *International Organization*, Vol. 39, No. 4, Autumn 1985, p. 634.

tive humanitarian work, or render it more difficult. In any case, such functions should not absorb too much of its time and energy, nor, above all, risk compromising its reputation which is indispensable—for impartiality and neutrality.

The Committee would not constitute itself into an Inquiry Commission or an Arbitration Tribunal, nor designate its own members to inquire or arbitrate. It would limit itself to "trying" to find one or more persons qualified to conduct the Inquiry and, if called upon to do so, to pronounce upon points raised by the contending Parties. If a belligerent asked the Committee to make an Inquiry, no communication to the public, by the press or in any other way, would be made or authorized on the subject without the consent of the Committee.

In fact, according to a 1981 ICRC statement, the ICRC had never wished to be proposed as a body responsible for such inquiries, because that would be the first step of a judicial procedure, which does not lie within its purview. Moreover, by assuming that role, the ICRC would find its neutrality called in question by at least one of the two parties, to the detriment of the unquestionably useful humanitarian activities carried out on that party's territory, "for an illusory result".

During the Second World War, the ICRC chiefly received protests concerning the bombardment of hospitals, ambulances, the torpedoing of hospital ships, and air raids on civilian populations.

The ICRC stated its attitude concerning protests at the preliminary Conference of the National Red Cross Societies (Geneva, July-August 1946), wondering whether it should not cease to transmit protests[14].

It stated that the protest procedure had yielded very few positive results. There were no really effective means for dealing with them. The ICRC could not act as a law court or as an arbitrator. It questioned whether protests against a violation of the law of nations really fell within its competence. Its chief duty in time of war was to carry out relief work, and it should not be exposed to the danger of compromising its humanitarian activities by interventions which very seldom yield concrete results.

If the ICRC was to continue this aspect of its activities, its role should be subject to the following conditions: it should be compatible with the Red Cross principles of impartiality and neutrality and should not risk restricting or jeopardizing the "real work" of the ICRC; National Societies and their governments should make appropriate investigations of each protest and give detailed replies. There was no point in delegating such a role to the ICRC unless the accused parties were prepared to play their own parts.

---

[14] See "Mémorandum sur l'activité du CICR en ce qui a trait aux violations du droit international" of 12 September 1939, in *International Review of the Red Cross*, Sept. 1939, No. 249, pp. 766–769, "Action by the ICRC in the event of breaches of international humanitarian law", *International Review of the Red Cross*, March-Apr. 1981, p. 5,–XXth International Conference of the Red Cross, Vienna, Oct. 1965, "Respect of the Geneva Conventions, Transmission of Protests", Doc.Conf. D.4 b/1, Feb. 1965 and Report, 2–9 Sept. 1965, p. 83–84,.

The XVIIth International Conference of the Red Cross (Stockholm, 1948) considered that the ICRC should continue to transmit protests it may receive concerning alleged violations of the Conventions, — it emphasized the duty of National Societies to forward these protests to their governments and recommended that National Societies do all in their power to ensure that their governments make a thorough investigation, the result of which should be communicated without delay to the ICRC.

In 1965, the ICRC reported that, since 1948, the number of protests had significantly increased, because they frequently come from National Societies whose countries are not directly involved. These communications, in the view of the ICRC, are vain and useless; in addition, they are generally ill-received and sometimes irritate the accused party. They never lead to thorough investigations or detailed replies. The situation which the ICRC censured in 1946 had not improved, but on the contrary, it had considerably degenerated.

During the last decade, conflicts have increasingly taken the shape of civil wars or internal disturbances. In such cases, the transmission of protests is often difficult, and even impossible, because the Parties generally refuse to recognize each other and are little disposed to receive communications from political adversaries.

During the debate of the XXth International Conference of the Red Cross (Vienna, 1965), the opinions of members of the International Humanitarian Law Commission which reviewed this item were very divided. Those who supported the proposal that the ICRC should no longer transmit such protests felt that such protests often had aims which were only political. Other members considered that the ICRC should in no way abandon the important and useful role it had played in transmitting protests: the ICRC should not consider itself as a mere letter-box.

The Conference finally approved a resolution "noting" that the ICRC would no longer transmit protests, except in the absence of any other regular channel where there is need of a neutral intermediary between two countries directly concerned[15].

The reason for not transmitting protests was therefore in part not to jeopardize the ICRC's "real work", e.g. its humanitarian activities, an argument which will be used again by the ICRC in relation to its attitude during the Second World War. The other reason is "utilitarian", based on the lack of useful results of the procedure. The possible exemplary effect (with or without concrete results) was not referred to, nor the effect of moral pressure through publicizing protests (or complaints).

Challenges to the Dogma

The Red Cross "dogma" is clear, as well as its rationale. However times change, history proceeds and circumstances may alter, at times, the very basis and assump-

---

[15] The Resolution was adopted by 108 votes in favour, 15 against and 6 abstentions. See Report Conf. D.4 b/1 of February 1965 and Resol. No. XXVII, Vienna 1965, *Handbook*, op.cit., pp. 625–626.

tions on which dogmas are defined.

Since the Red Cross was created, almost 130 years ago, the principles of neutrality and discretion of the ICRC have been challenged, in theory and in practice, on many occasions, by observers, the media, public opinion, other NGOs and by members of the Red Cross and Red Crescent organizations.

It is to the credit of the ICRC and of the League that these organizations decided in 1972 to initiate an examination of the Red Cross role in the world, which included an assessment of the ICRC policy on discretion.

It is to the credit of the ICRC that this institution decided, in 1980, to open its very confidential archives to a Swiss scholar, Mr. Jean-Claude Favez, in order to make an independent assessment of the role of the ICRC in relation to the Jewish holocaust.

These two initiatives are a proof that these organizations are prepared to accept internal and external assessments of their work and attitudes, and to review possible criticisms and proposals. It does not necessarily mean that they will accept the recommendations of these bodies, nor change some of their more revered policies.

The Tansley Report

In 1972, the ICRC and the League of Red Cross Societies decided to initiate a thorough examination of the Red Cross role in the world in order to give thought to its future.

The rapidity of changes in recent years had given rise to concern within the Movement on its own evolution. Had the Red Cross really a mission in the world, today and in the years ahead, and how could it prepare itself to discharge it?

The ICRC and the League assigned this study to a Joint Committee on the Reappraisal of the Role of the Red Cross. The Committee, directed by D.D. Tansley, worked from February 1973 to June 1975.

During that period, members of the research group created by the Joint Committee visited forty-five countries and subjected twenty-three National Societies to a "searching inquiry". They saw the Red Cross in action in war, internal tension and natural disaster. They attended regional and international meetings of the Red Cross. They also sought opinions on the Red Cross from all National Societies, from governments signatories to the Geneva Conventions, from most United Nations agencies, from NGOs, and from many eminent people throughout the world.

The results of this wide and thorough investigation were published in July 1975 in a *Final Report: An Agenda for the Red Cross*, also called *The Tansley Report*. In another document, *The ICRC, the League and the Tansley Report*, submitted to the Twenty-Third International Conference of the Red Cross in Bucharest in 1977, both institutions replied to the main questions raised in the Tansley Report and also attempted a projection into the future with a view to setting forth general guidelines resulting from their deliberations. From this document, the following comments are those related to issues of neutrality and discretion, as raised by the Tansley Report and as replied to by the institutions[16].

Concerning "the Red Cross and Peace", the Tansley Report refers to "direct action", as proposed by some National Societies, consisting mainly in mobilizing public opinion against particular groups or governments whose conduct may constitute a threat to peace. The Report says that such action as the naming of aggressors and injustices will not be viewed as non-political, impartial, neutral and humanitarian: it can only damage and probably destroy the useful protection and assistance activity of the Red Cross. The Movement should therefore recognize and state that certain forms of direct action for peace are simply incompatible with other Red Cross primary roles.

Not surprisingly, the ICRC expressed its agreement with the Report opinion that it would be unwise for the Red Cross to denounce publicly and by name those responsible for aggression and injustice, and that any such declarations would be of worse than dubious value as contributions to peace. The prudence of the Red Cross, with regard to controversies which are alien to it, is based upon "profound wisdom" and must be maintained at all costs, for the life of the Red Cross depends on it.

> By entering the arena of conflicting interests and opinions which divide the world and align peoples against one another, the Red Cross would be rushing headlong towards its own destruction. However slightly it might venture upon this slippery path, it would not be able to stop.

The ICRC also made it clear that the tendencies which appear within the Red Cross in favour of open criticism of governments and parties described as responsible for tensions or conflicts have never been followed by the Movement as a whole.

Concerning the ICRC policy on operational information, the Tansley Report said that the policy of discretion of the ICRC has, in the past, been justified on the grounds of ensuring that the most possible is achieved for the victims.

> While the Red Cross has achieved much on the basis of discretion in the past, the Movement should recognize the danger that discretion is comfortable to both the controlling authority and the Red Cross. Thus it may be continued not because it is necessary but simply because it is comfortable.

The Report added that the ultimate test of Red Cross acceptability is action within the bounds of expectations. If there is a general expectation that the Red Cross should use some types of publicity, then such action should be acceptable even if opposed by a particular party.

In short, the Tansley Report was suggesting that the policy of discretion, which has generally served the interests of the victims, should become more flexible.

[16] *The ICRC, the League and the Report on the Re-Appraisal of the role of the Red Cross*, Reprinted from the International Review of the Red Cross (from March-April 1978 to January-February 1979), Geneva, 1979.

Not unexpectedly, the ICRC disagreed with this suggestion and re-affirmed its traditional position: discretion is a working method that has long since proved its worth and does not indicate a preference for secrecy. In protection activities, discretion is the rule and publicity the exception. The ICRC distinguishes between its information policy in the context of fundamental humanitarian principles or of the Geneva Conventions, and its information policy on activities outside the Conventions.

On the former, in the event of serious violations of fundamental humanitarian principles or of the Geneva Conventions, the ICRC established doctrine does not consider discretion to be an unbreakable rule. Although the ICRC normally refrains from making public statements on acts attributed to belligerents, it does from time to time drop its reserve, provided the following two criteria are met: such publicity must be in the interest of the persons or groups affected or threatened,—ICRC delegates must have been eye-witnesses of the violations alleged.

The ICRC recognized that such cases have been extremely rare in comparison with the number of violations of humanitarian law.

Indeed, in our view, the first condition regarding the "interest of the victims" is essentially a subjective judgement of value which can be applied more or less conservatively.

While maintaining its traditional policy of discretion, the ICRC agreed to "make an effort" to publicize in its Annual Report or through the press such matters as:

— appeals of a general nature addressed to belligerents asking them to respect the Geneva Conventions and fundamental humanitarian principles;
— special approaches to belligerents in grave cases of non-observance of the Conventions witnessed by its delegates;
— request to the parties to obtain the essential facilities which must be granted to the ICRC in conformity with the Geneva Conventions;
— offers of the ICRC's services addressed, in accordance with Article 3 common to the four Geneva Conventions, to the parties to a non-international armed conflict, and the response thereto.

The ICRC's information policy on activities outside the Conventions appears even stricter, as the access to political detainees can only be obtained through discreet negotiations conducted on a purely pragmatic basis.

Consequently, information published by the ICRC about its activities in aid of political detainees is very succinct, and generally comprises only the names of places of detention visited and the date of the visit to each, together with a reference to the conditions under which the visits were made (e.g., interviews without witnesses). These communications contain no details of the delegates' findings, these being transmitted only to the detaining authorities.

However, the ICRC reserves the right to state publicly the limits of its action if a government does not respect the procedure agreed on or attempts to exploit abusively—for the purposes of propaganda, for example—the activities of the ICRC. Moreover, the ICRC may suspend or terminate its protection activities if it is convinced that the presence of its delegates serves as a cover-up for the detaining authorities and that it is not or is no longer possible to continue working in the interests of the victims. Finally, the ICRC may publish a detaining authority's refusal of its services. The ICRC recognized that the discretion it has shown in this area may have been an encouragement to those States which systematically refuse any protection activities by the ICRC. It considers that a refusal in such a case constitutes a denial of the humanitarian mission conferred upon it by the international community, and that community should be informed of the fact.

We will give later in this Chapter a few examples of "public appeals" issued by the ICRC, which have somewhat liberalized its discretion policy.

The Second World War

In 1944, the ICRC received its second Nobel Prize for Peace, while its attitude when confronted with the political and racial persecutions committed by the Third Reich was already being questioned.

During the Second World War, the ICRC had certainly not been inactive: according to an official report by the Swiss authorities[17], during that period, the ICRC had dealt with 7 million prisoners of war and 175,000 civilian internees. 173 delegates made more than 5,000 visits. On 1 September 1939, the ICRC staff consisted of 5O employees: at the end of April 1945, 3,921; the Central Tracing Agency of prisoners of war employed 2,585 of the total staff.

More than 33 million Red Cross packages were sent by the ICRC to prisoners of war. From 12 November 1943 to 8 May 1945, 750,000 packages were sent to deportees in concentration camps. By the end of October 1946, the Central Tracing Agency had made out and filed 39 million index-cards, forwarded 13 million letters and post-cards for prisoners of war, censured, transmitted—and often transcribed —24 million civilian messages.

From 1 September 1939 to the end of 1945, the ICRC expenditures amounted to Sw.F. 45 million, 55 percent of which was donated by Swiss official or non-governmental sources: the ICRC noted that this was equivalent to six hours of the war effort of all the belligerents[18].

Such activities and statistics are not in question. The main accusation against the ICRC during World War II is the silence it has kept in front of public opinion on racial persecutions, deportations and extermination, in spite of many appeals demanding a public protest by the renowned international humanitarian organization against the crimes committed by the Nazi regime.

A first response was given by the ICRC in its 1948 Report.

---

[17] Jean-Claude Favez, *Une mission impossible -Le CICR, les déportations et les camps de concentration nazis*, Payot Lausanne, 1988, pp. 365–366.

[18] *Inter Arma Caritas—The Work of the ICRC during the second World War*, 2nd Ed., Geneva 1973, p. 93.

The Response of the ICRC in 1948

The *Report of the ICRC on its activities during the Second World War (September 1, 1939—June 30, 1947)*, published by the ICRC in May 1948, gives evidence of the extent of its protection and relief work. At the same time, it shows that such activities did not extend to all victims and explains the limitations of its means of action[19].

Under National-Socialism, the Jews had become outcasts, condemned by rigid racial legislation to suffer tyranny, persecution and systematic extermination. The supervision which the ICRC was empowered to exercise under the Geneva Conventions in favour of prisoners of war and civilian internees did not apply to them. The ICRC had received the most insistent appeals on behalf of these victims, but in the absence of any basis in law, its activities depended to a very great extent upon the good will of the belligerent States.

The ICRC had, through the intermediary of the German Red Cross, asked for information concerning civilian deportees "without distinction of race or religion", which was plainly refused in the following terms:

The responsible authorities decline to give any information concerning non-Aryan deportees.

Thus, enquiries as a matter of principle concerning the Jews led to no results, and

continual protests would have been resented by the authorities concerned and might have been detrimental both to the Jews themselves and to the whole field of the Committee's activities.

In consequence, the ICRC, "while avoiding useless protest", did its utmost to help the Jews by practical means, and its delegates abroad were instructed on these lines.

In retrospect, it is difficult to see how the ICRC protests might have made the fate of Jews worse than what it was, and what it came to be. On the other hand, it is likely that the probable irritation of the German authorities caused by ICRC protests might have made its humanitarian assistance to other "legitimate" victims (covered by the Geneva Conventions) more difficult.

According to the 1948 Report, in Germany, the Committee's activities on behalf of the Jews met with almost insuperable difficulties. Camps exclusively reserved for Jews were not open to inspection for humanitarian purposes until the end.

In 1944 and 1945, in Romania and Hungary, the Report says that the ICRC became in truth the "Protecting Power" for the Jews. In Greece, in May 1943, the insistence of the ICRC's delegation to give food parcels to Jews being sent to Germany led to "difficulties" with the German authorities, who, "in their resentment" demanded that one of the delegates should be replaced.

In Hungary, following the replacement in October 1944 of Admiral Horthy's

---

[19] *Report of the ICRC on its activities during the Second World War (September 1, 1939—June 30, 1947)*, Vol. I, General Activities, Geneva, May 1948, No. 1A, pp. 641–657.

government by a more pro-Nazi one, the ICRC, to alleviate the sufferings of the Jewish population, "took action with vigour and authority". The ICRC delegate obtained that the ICRC buildings be granted extraterritoriality and carried out active protection and relief assistance to the Hungarian Jews. When the delegate had to leave, a Hungarian minister paid him the tribute of stating that he had, in a time of historic crisis, succeeded in making the capital a "protectorate of Geneva".

Tribute was also paid by the American Joint Distribution Committee of New York to the humanitarian work of the ICRC in helping the Jewish population in Romania.

Why did the ICRC, on receiving trustworthy information as to grave violations of international humanitarian law or of human rights, not raise public protest of its own initiative?

The same Report gives three reasons why the ICRC did not accept this idea[20]:

— first, every protest is a judgement. No impartial judgement is possible unless the conviction reached is based on exact and certain knowledge of the circumstances. This involves an impartial enquiry, hardly ever feasible in war-time;
— secondly, the indicted party will either keep its own public in ignorance of the protest, or present it in one-sided fashion, whilst the opposing side will be free to use it for purposes of propaganda. In every case, the indicted party will demand to know why similar genuine or alleged breaches by the adversary have not called forth similar protests. Should the ICRC adopt the method of public protest, it would inevitably be forced more and more into taking a definite stand with regard to all kinds of acts of war, and even of political matters. It must also measure all the consequences of this policy, not only as affecting its position in relation to governments, but also its possibilities of humanitarian action, the safeguarding of which is, in the last analysis, its sole concern;
— thirdly, the ICRC's considered view, on the grounds of past experience, is that public protests are not only ineffectual, but are apt to produce a stiffening of the indicted country's attitude with regard to the Committee, even the rupture of relations with it. There would thus be a serious risk of sacrificing concrete relief work on behalf of all war victims to the defence of a legal principle.

In brief, the ICRC has had to give precedence to the practical work of relief, rather than to sit in judgement.

The 1948 internal ICRC Report did not end the controversy nor dispel the criticisms.

In 1980, the ICRC took the courageous and necessary initiative of opening its archives to an eminent Swiss scholar, Jean-Claude Favez, who was then allowed to carry out an entirely independent research study concerning the attitude of the ICRC during the Second World War in relation to the Nazi deportations and concentration camps.

[20] Ibid., p. 21.

An Impossible Mission?

The objective of the ICRC, in proposing this research, was double:

— to establish a complete assessment of what the ICRC knew of the "Final Solution", of what it wanted and what it was able to do in favour of the victims of Nazi persecutions;
— to have a reference text on this question.

Professor Favez' book, "*Une mission impossible? Le CICR, les déportations et les camps de concentration nazis*", published in 1988, gives careful, well-documented and detailed answers to those questions.

What the ICRC Knew of the "Final Solution"?

According to Favez[21], there can be no doubt that the ICRC knew that the concentration camps existed and was aware of the conditions prevailing there. By the ICRC, he meant primarily the delegates in the field—some of whom were eye-witnesses—but also members of the staff at the Geneva headquarters and members of the Committee itself. As for the racial persecution and systematic extermination of certain population groups, the ICRC, like the rest of the international community, acquired information over time and gradually came to realize what was happening.

The pre-World War II Nazi concentration camps hosted mostly German inmates: their existence was not hidden, as they played an educational role in mobilizing all the German population behind the Führer. During the war, the deportation of "terrorists" from occupied territories into the Nazi camps expanded the use of terror: as formulated by the "Night and Fog" decree of 7 December 1941, those who endangered the security of the occupying forces, had to disappear, in order to paralyse, through silence and mystery, the relatives and acquaintances of the disappeared ones, and beyond those, the populations of the occupied territories. The decision of the Nazi authorities to concentrate and deport Jews to East European camps with a view to their extermination, (the "Final Solution"), decision taken at Wannsee on 20 January 1942, was also made under total secrecy.

The actual extermination started in 1941, under secrecy and camouflage measures, in the East European camps.

Information about what was really taking place was therefore not readily available, and it was not verifiable. Some information filtered through some of the German officials, escaped victims, observers and witnesses.

During the Second World War, the Swiss territory was one of the privileged and rare places of contact between the belligerents for all kinds of exchanges, including information.

The ICRC could then benefit from information obtained from some of the intergovernmental organizations established in Geneva, from the many humanitarian

---

[21] Interview of Jean-Claude Favez, *Red Cross, Red Crescent*, Jan.-Apr. 1989, pp. 30–31. Information in this section is mostly based on Chapter 4 of Favez' book.

NGOs, including the Young Men's Christian Association, the Quakers, the World Council of Churches (being created), and such Jewish organizations as the World Jewish Congress, the Jewish Agency for Palestine and the American Jewish Joint Distribution Committee.

The ICRC also received information from the Swiss government, itself informed by its diplomatic channels, as well as from the national and international press. Within the Red Cross Movement, the ICRC exchanged information with the National Societies: some of those were in direct relations with some camps or other detention places. Even the German Red Cross allowed its Chief of External Relations, Walter G. Hartmann, to visit Geneva eighteen times between 1939 and 1945. The ICRC delegates are an important and reliable source of information, in addition to their operational role.

When the war starts, the ICRC knows about concentration camps, anti-Jewish persecutions in Germany and Jewish emigration. When does the ICRC become aware of the extermination process?

In November 1939, an ICRC delegate, Marcel Junod, is sent on mission to Berlin and Warsaw, following a request from Jewish agencies: the anonymous report obtained by Junod refers to the forced deportation of Jews mostly from Poland (one and a half million) and from Bohemia, Moravia, Austria, Western Prussia and Germany, as from October 1939, ordered by Himmler. The deportees can only retain a maximum of DM 300: all their properties are confiscated. Other testimonies on the deportation of Jews from Germany are sent to the ICRC by its delegates in that country in 1940, 1941 and 1942. In February 1942, the ICRC delegate Roland Marti reports to the ICRC the killing of all Russian prisoners and civilians in occupied territories by the SS troops.

In August 1942, Gerhart Riegner advises the World Jewish Congress in New York of the elaboration by the Nazis of a general extermination plan by gasses: he and Paul Guggenheim transmitted this information to three members of the ICRC in August or September. In November, the Vatican acknowledges the extermination of Polish Jews. In November, Carl J. Burckhardt, another member of the Committee confirms to the U.S. Consul in Geneva, Paul C. Squire, that Hitler had given the order in 1941 to make Germany "judenfrei". Mid-November, Marti reports that 60,000 Jews have been liquidated in Latvia.

In 1942–1943, the ICRC is informed of the slaughter of more than 100,000 Jews in Romania and of the deportation of another 140,000.

From the second half of 1943, and especially from the Summer of 1944, the information given to the ICRC from internal and external sources increases in quality and quantity.

In February 1944, the Assistant High Commissioner for Refugees, G. Kullmann, asks Burckhardt if it is true that only 140,000 remain of the 3 million Polish Jews: Burckhardt replies that he has received confidential reports on this subject, reports which were circulated in the League of Nations.

In September 1944, the ICRC delegate Maurice Rossel visits the Kommandantur

156

offices (he is not allowed in the camp itself) of Auschwitz, Oranienburg and Ravensbrück. He reports that, according to unconfirmed rumours, inmates are gassed in groups in very modern "shower rooms". He reports that Auschwitz, an almost entirely Jewish camp, is a "90 percent extermination camp".

Favez does not give a specific date on which the ICRC would have known and acknowledged the reality of the German extermination plan: the ICRC archives examined by him do not clarify this point.

In his recent interview, he says:

> One thing is sure: by 1943, the pursuit of the "final solution" had become only too evident.

What Did the ICRC Want To Do?

In the knowledge of the Nazi persecution, and later of the Nazi extermination of the Jews, what policy was then adopted by the ICRC?

The official position of the ICRC, in 1948, has been recalled above. It may be summarized as follows:

— the Geneva Conventions did not give the ICRC any legitimate protection role concerning the Jews;
— any intervention by the ICRC was subject to the good will of the authorities: the Nazi regime had no intention of allowing any external intervention or interference in the implementation of its racist policies;
— the German Red Cross could not and did not give any assistance in this matter;
— repeated interventions with the German authorities would have been useless
— such repeated interventions would have been resented by the German authorities, and might have prejudiced the "legitimate" protection activities of the ICRC concerning prisoners of war etc. The German authorities might have repudiated the Conventions
— public protests would not be made because:
  — they need to be based on an impartial enquiry, not possible in the circumstances;
  — it would affect the ICRC's relations with governments and politicize the institution
  — they are ineffectual
  — they might sacrifice concrete relief work in the defence of a legal principle.

In the 1938–1939 period, in spite of the efforts of a few members of the ICRC, the Committee exercised the greatest caution concerning the German political detainees, the persecution of Jews in the Reich, and the assistance to persons forced to exile.

Then, and during the War, the Committee focused its perspective, preparations and efforts on the implementation of the Conventions and the protection of the wounded and sick military personnel, and the prisoners of war.

On 16 January 1941, in the ICRC Coordination Commission, President Max Huber notes that

> we cannot take care of political prisoners, because the status of civilian internees, borrowed from the status of prisoners of war, could not be extended to a third category of persons.

The ICRC's instructions to its delegates concerning a possible assistance to the Jewish population were generally cautious and restrictive.

For instance, in February 1943, the ICRC sent the following instructions to its delegate in Romania, Vladimir de Steiger, concerning possible assistance to the Jewish population:

> We request you to proceed with caution and very discreetly. We want to avoid at all costs that the authorities or the public be alerted and assume that the ICRC envisages to undertake a large action in favour of the Jews. Such an assumption would have very unfortunate consequences and would risk to endanger our intention, which is only not to exclude Jews from actions organized by the Joint Commission, within the context of possibilities and with the consent of interested governments, in favour of the civilian populations of the occupied countries[22].

On 20 August 1942, the ICRC delegate in Berlin, Roland Marti writes to the ICRC that ICRC delegates will never be admitted in jails or concentration camps; even if they were, they could not exercise any control. Concerning relief assistance to those detained in those jails or camps, this would have to be clarified with the relevant authorities[23].

On 24 September 1942, the ICRC sends to Marti a note concerning deportees of foreign nationalities detained in Germany. The note is not sent directly to the German Foreign Affairs Ministry: Marti is to discuss it verbally at the Ministry and to decide whether to submit it formally. The note refers to the requests received by the ICRC concerning numerous cases of deportations, for Jewish and non-Jewish persons, hostages etc. The ICRC would like to assure to these persons, in agreement with the detaining Power, the facilities foreseen in their favour, on the one hand by the extension to civilian internees of the 1929 Convention on the treatment of prisoners of war, and on the other hand by the implementation of the articles of the Tokyo draft Convention, which had received the approval in principle of all the delegates of governments and National Societies represented at the XVth International Conference of the Red Cross. During the present conflict, the German Government had informed the ICRC that it would be prepared, under conditions of reciprocity, to apply these articles.

---

[22] Favez, op.cit., pp. 126 and 284. Our translation from the French.
[23] Ibid., pp. 133–134.

The questions to be asked of the German Ministry of Foreign Affairs were:

— Could the ICRC receive individual information on the present domicile of persons arrested, jailed or deported abroad, in order to inform their families and others?
— Could these persons be allowed to send news to their family, possibly through the use of printed forms?
— Could the families and the National Societies be authorized to send them packages?
— Could ICRC delegates be authorized to visit them?

As Marti's discussions with the German authorities make no progress, the ICRC decides to attempt a relief action, rather than to try to obtain protection rights, by sending new instructions to Marti and a personal letter from the ICRC President, Max Huber, to the German Ministry of Foreign Affairs. On 15 February, the Ministry gives a restrictive reply: Germany refuses the principle of sending relief to deported persons, depending on their category. No access can be given to persons accused of serious crimes against the Reich (these include the "Night and Fog"). Deported persons guilty of less serious crimes may receive books and clothes, but not food, provided that the packages are sent by their relatives, do not contain messages and follow regulations. Finally, foreign "Schutzhäftlinge" may receive an unlimited number of packages: however, they need to be sent to identified names and addresses...

On 14 October 1942, a proposal for a public appeal was presented to the meeting of the ICRC as

Appeal in favour of the application of the essential principles of *jus gentium*, relating to the conduct of hostilities"

The proposed appeal recalled the wish of the ICRC to alleviate the ills of the war generally, of its own initiative or in implementation of its mandates. It recalled the appeal concerning the protection of the civilian population against air bombings issued by the ICRC on 12 March and 12 May 1940, the protests of all kinds received in Geneva, and similar communications from National Societies. From everywhere, the ICRC is therefore asked to intervene, but it can do so only on the basis of two fundamental principles: to maintain its absolute neutrality, and its concern for the most effective assistance to the war victims. Still, the accomplishment of its practical tasks does not exempt the ICRC from expressing its concerns regarding the air war and the economic war.

After reviewing the numerous categories of civilian victims and types of persecution, the appeal referred to the plight of the Jews as follows:

But, beside the civilian internees, certain categories of civilians of various nationalities, are, for reasons related to the war situation, deprived of their freedom, deported or taken as hostages, and they may even for this reason suffer attacks on their lives for acts which they often have not committed.

The proposed appeal then asked the belligerent Powers to give to such civilians the same protection and guarantees as those provided to war prisoners and civilian internees: protection of life and health, prompt notification of their place of internment or detention, facilities of correspondence, under certain conditions, with their families, to receive relief packages and to be visited by representatives of a Protecting Power or of the ICRC, in accordance with the Tokyo draft Convention.

The text did not condemn any country in particular: it was not addressed directly to Germany. The Jews were not mentioned by name.

Under the influence of the Swiss Government, the ICRC members rejected the proposed public appeal, which was to have been sent to all States party to the Geneva Conventions. On the other hand, they agreed that the Committee should intervene directly with specific States, in certain serious cases[24].

According to Gerhart Riegner, of the World Jewish Congress, quoted by Ben-Tov[25], it was possible that the Swiss government was against the proposed appeal for two reasons connected with its "extraordinary caution" in anything concerning the Jews in relation to Germany. One was that Germany was at the height of its military might and Switzerland' was afraid of a German invasion, and the second was connected with the commercial relations between the two countries, since Swiss industry worked mainly for Germany.

In his book, *The Terrible Secret*[26], Walter Laqueur said that the intervention of Philip Etter, a former Swiss Foreign Minister, prevailed in the meeting of 14 October 1942: he argued successfully against the draft statement, which in his view could be interpreted as a violation of impartiality.

During the meeting Carl J. Burckhardt said that he doubted that the appeal could be considered as a courageous act. It was more advisable to intervene directly and discreetly with the concerned governments.

On 17 December 1942, a statement approved by the Allied Governments condemned publicly and with the utmost energy the "beastly methods of extermination" of the European Jews by the German authorities. The statement referred to the oft-repeated threat by Hitler to exterminate the Jews of Europe. From all the occupied regions, Jews were deported towards the East in frightful conditions. Poland had been made into the principal National Socialist slaughterhouse. The sick and the weak were fated to die of cold or hunger or to be murdered in mass, deliberately. Hundreds of thousands of innocent men, women and children had already been the victims of these cruel methods[27].

What Was the ICRC Able To Do?

In 1935, the ICRC obtained permission from the Gestapo to visit four camps, Lichtenburg, Esterwegen, Oranienburg and Dachau, the model camp. The dele-

---

[24] Ibid., pp. 158–164.

[25] Arieh Ben-Tov, *Facing the Holocaust in Budapest—The ICRC and the Jews in Hungary, 1943–1945*, Henry Dunant Institute, Geneva, Martinus Nijhoff Pub., 1988, p. 137.

[26] Quoted by Ben-Tov, p. 137.

[27] Favez, op.cit., p. 162.

gate's report was not submitted to the Germans, nor published in the International Review of the Red Cross, nor noted in the ICRC Report to the International Conference of the Red Cross, but safely deposited in the ICRC's safe. This extreme discretion had been negotiated with the Germans[28].

Two other delegates visit the Dachau camp on 19 August 1938, together with two SS Officers. Their report reflects their very good impression of the conditions of housing, hygiene, treatment, food and work of the detainees. The ICRC decided not to make a public communication on this visit.

In September 1938, the ICRC was asked by Protestant priests to intervene in favour of Pastor Martin Niemöller. The Committee decided not to intervene, as such a move would be badly received by the German authorities, and as the state of health of Pastor Niemöller had improved[29].

In the Summer of 1940, two ICRC delegates were authorized to visit the 212 Dutch civilian detainees in the Buchenwald concentration camp. Their observations refer to good material and hygiene conditions, but also to an "iron" discipline and the quasi-terror of the detainees[30].

In 1941, the German Red Cross refuses to process any more ICRC requests to locate individuals in camps.

During the Nazi era, the German Red Cross was placed under strict control of the National Socialist State and it adopted racial policies and practices which excluded the Jews from membership and assistance. These clear violations of the Principles of neutrality and independence were not censured by the ICRC, which did not withdraw the recognition of the German Red Cross as a National Society. Its President, Max Huber, preferred a "flexible" interpretation of the Principles to the risk of breaking up of the universal Red Cross Movement[31].

Until June 1944, no other ICRC mission was allowed to a concentration camp, nor *a fortiori*, to a camp of extermination.

As we have seen, the ICRC was not allowed to exercise any protection role with regard to the persecuted Jews. Its delegates tried, sometimes with a degree of success, to save victims of racial persecution and to provide some relief assistance. Starting in 1943, the ICRC initiates two relief programmes: one by the dispatch of food parcels to concentration camps, and the other through assistance addressed to Jews in the satellites or allied countries of Nazi Germany.

Favez' Conclusion

In the conclusion to his book[32], Favez first confirms that the apparent lack of interest and impotence of the ICRC concerning the detainees of concentration camps, political prisoners and those persecuted on racial grounds is explained by the inflexible refusal of the Nazis and the limits of the Geneva Conventions.

[28] Ibid., pp. 60–61.
[29] Ibid., pp. 67–69.
[30] Ibid., p. 90.
[31] Ibid., pp. 41–44.
[32] Ibid., Chap. 9.

He adds that the ICRC did not want to accuse the German Reich in the fear that the fate of detainees could become worse, and also in order to protect its neutrality.

> After having given in to the Bosheviks in the 1920s, in 1931 to Mussolini, it (the ICRC) yielded to the conditions of Nazi Germany, even when those resulted in negating the universality of the Red Cross, with, for example, the exclusion of the Jews from the German Red Cross.

Favez says that the ICRC did not take the supreme risk of throwing in favour of the victims all the weight of its moral authority: the ICRC should have spoken. The importance accorded by the ICRC to its credibility led it paradoxically to a loss of credibility, and therefore of authority within the Red Cross Movement and in the world in general.

He concluded:

> In the use of international law, the ICRC, confronted with juridically unnamed victims who turned to it, often sought not the means to act, but on the contrary a justification for not acting, so as not to disturb the conventional missions on which, in its eyes, its very existence stood.

The ICRC gave its own viewpoint at the end of Favez' book[33]. It acknowledged that the institution had not tried at the time to gather systematically all the information which was received on the persecutions of civilians, and in particular, of Jews: this could have led it to re-examine its objectives and its priorities. The book shows that the ICRC had not sufficiently perceived the exceptional character of the drama and had not adapted its priorities as a consequence. This deficiency was probably the consequence of the overwhelming responsibilities of the ICRC in relation to other groups of victims, in particular the prisoners of war, as well as the hustle and bustle of daily tasks of a humanitarian institution confronted with the consequences of "total war".

Concerning the aborted 1942 appeal, the ICRC still considers that such an appeal would not have had any effect, independently from the risk of jeopardizing the possibilities of assistance to the millions of prisoners of war for whom the Committee had a direct responsibility.

While the ICRC could have been more active concerning the Third Reich's satellites, the ICRC continues to think that the fate of the Jews in the German territory and in occupied Poland was hopeless.

The ICRC's reply to Favez seems to focus on the protection of the statutory mandate of the ICRC and on the lack of usefulness of any public appeal. It does not address the main question which Favez has answered: The ICRC was not prepared at the time to take the public risk of changing its objectives and priorities by taking the initiative to denounce publicly the persecutions and the final extermination of the Jews and other victims in the Nazi concentration camps.

---

[33] Ibid., pp. 376–379.

Ben-Tov's Book

Arieh Ben-Tov, in his study on *Facing the Holocaust in Budapest—The ICRC and the Jews in Hungary, 1943–1945*[34], is very critical of the ICRC and of its alleged excessive concern for, and alignment with, the Swiss government's international policies during World War II.

Ben-Tov has concluded from his study that Max Huber, President of the ICRC from 1928 to 1944, and from 1945 to 1947, an eminent international jurist, was more concerned with Switzerland's interests than with the interests of the victims that the ICRC was supposed to help and protect.

In his biography of Max Huber, Peter Vogelsanger stated:

> That the position and activity of the ICRC were firmly linked to Swiss neutrality was, for Max Huber, a truth that brooked no argument. Swiss neutrality had been a prerequisite for the creation and development of the Red Cross ideal, and conversely the existence of a functioning Red Cross, above all the branch represented in the ICRC, had been an essential factor in the maintenance and recognition of Swiss neutrality in the world at large.

If true, this allegation is particularly serious: while the ICRC can legitimately benefit from having been created and being staffed by neutral Swiss citizens, from being hosted in neutral Switzerland, from being financed to a large extent by the neutral Swiss government, the utilization by Switzerland of the activities of the ICRC to support and maintain its own neutrality appears abusive.

Ben-Tov believes that, during the Second World War, the ICRC headquarters adopted

> the dominance of the political stance ... with the principle of neutrality in first place and the human being, no matter how great his suffering, in second place. The standpoint of strict neutrality had its origin in Swiss government policy and its agreements with Germany, and it was determined by the particular relations between the Swiss government and the ICRC.

Concerning Hungary, according to Ben-Tov, it was only in October 1943, despite the urging of Jewish organizations, that the ICRC's first permanent delegate, Jean de Bavier, was sent to Budapest. The instructions he received from the ICRC in Geneva "limited his freedom of action" and he was "disheartened by the lack of vigour" in those instructions.

On 27 March 1944, de Bavier suggested in a telegram that Huber should go and see Hitler with a view to improving the plight of the Jews in Hungary. The ICRC did not follow up on this suggestion: for Ben-Tov, this was "one of its greatest failures" in that period. For Ben-Tov, the "extreme reticence" displayed by the ICRC during the crucial months of its presence in Hungary was a denial of one of the tenets of its statutes, which states that the ICRC is free to take any initiative which is compatible with its traditional role.

---

[34] Ben-Tov, op.cit., pp. 131–137 and 385–389, in particular.

A Difficult Assessment

Favez' research has established that, during World War II, the ICRC acted with extreme caution concerning the treatment of political prisoners, including the persecution and extermination of the Jews, in its relations with the German authorities and in its instructions to its delegates.

This extreme caution was manifest in the "non-appeal" of 1942, even though the proposed appeal was to be addressed to all countries, and not only to Germany, and even though it did not mention the Jews by name.

The ICRC caution was justified by a strict legalistic adherence to the letter of the existing Conventions, and by a cost-benefit argument: any public support for the Jews, or even repeated, non-public appeals to the Germans in order to obtain access to the victims would in any case have been futile and without benefit to the Jews; such initiatives would have only antagonized the German authorities and thus prejudiced the ICRC's legitimate and accepted protection and relief assistance work for the millions of prisoners of war and other protected persons.

Indeed, the Nazis tried to keep their "Final Solution" as a closely guarded secret. They had no intention of changing their racialist policies, to stop the deportation and extermination of the Jews, to "humanize" in any way their barbaric methods. Under no circumstances would they have allowed any witness to enter the concentration camps, to talk to the surviving inmates, even under the strictest rules of discretion. The Nazis had no possible interest in allowing Red Cross delegates to be even silent witnesses to their mass crimes: there was no possible reciprocity between the Nazi "treatment" of the Jews and other victims in concentration and extermination camps, and the case of German prisoners of war in allied prisoners' camps. The few visits of ICRC delegates to concentration camps in 1935, 1938 and 1940, and their contacts with camp leadership were mostly a mockery of the tragedy, a mockery which was not always unnoticed by some delegates.

In a 1988 statement, Moreillon[35] said that the Nazi zones of influence should be divided into two:

> On the Eastern Front and in Germany, in view of the determination—as it is known today—with which the Nazis pursued their policy of systematic annihilation of the Jews and considering the constant rejection by the Nazis of any gesture in favour of Jewish individuals, the ICRC even now doubts that it would have been able to exert any decisive influence on the fate of these people in Poland, in the occupied territories of the USSR or in the territory of the Third Reich.

> In other countries however, if the International Committee had evaluated sooner and better its activities in the other territories under the Axis influence, and pursued them earlier and more resolutely, if it had given greater encouragement to its delegates in the field, if might well have been effective. This is true in particular for Romania and Hungary, where its delegates still managed to save more Jews than elsewhere in the war.

[35] *The Independent*, 3 Sept. 1988.

Most external observers believe that the ICRC's caution was strongly influenced by the Swiss Government, anxious to protect its neutrality and to avoid any public move which might provoke the ire of the German authorities: Switzerland, a small democratic "island" in the midst of the huge "ocean" of Nazified Europe was then under the constant threat of a German invasion[36]. The prudence and legalistic approach of some of the ICRC leaders, in close "symbiosis" with Swiss authorities, was another factor in some of the cautious decisions (or non-decisions) taken.

Favez also attributes to the ICRC's elitist amateurism and its small staff its inability to analyze and properly assess the information received and to review its priorities. The ICRC was content to carry on with its usual activities such as tracing missing persons and sending parcels, without making any real effort to find new solutions to new problems. The ICRC, like the rest of Switzerland, had an entirely obsolete outlook[37].

It has been argued that the perspective of the ICRC concerning the "Final Solution" was not different from that of the Allied Governments, which were even better informed than the ICRC. The realization that the Jews might be totally exterminated did not change their strategy and tactics in order to care for this particular group of victims: all their efforts concentrated on winning the war. Victory was the only way to stop the slaughter. This argument has its limits: the ICRC was not fighting a war, and the objectives of a humanitarian organization are not those of belligerents.

More appropriately, the ICRC itself, in its reply to Favez' book[38], wondered whether the Committee should not have been more insistent with the allied and neutral governments, so that they would have accorded to the rescue of the Jews a more important place in their concerns and objectives.

This belated suggestion of limited and indirect intervention is rather typical of the ICRC's past and present response to the criticisms addressed to its attitude during World War II. It still rejects the option of a public appeal, on utilitarian grounds, and only notes the few successes of discreet action, even though these remained out of all proportion with the tragic dimension of the extermination.

One wonders, with retrospective wisdom, and once the Allies' victory was safely assured, whether this tragic dimension would not have justified an extraordinary, risky, public response, in giving a voice to the helpless victims: perhaps the humanitarian risk should have prevailed over "reasonable" political, legal and practical considerations.

---

[36] German threats of intervention ("S Plan" or "Aktion Schweiz") were particularly serious in March 1943 and in the Spring of 1944: see Ch. Rousseau, *Droit international public*, Sirey, Paris, 1953, p. 149.

[37] *Red Cross, Red Crescent*, Geneva, Jan. Apr. 1989, p. 31.

[38] Favez, op. cit., p. 378.

The Delegates' Problems of Conscience

In August 1988, about twenty senior ICRC staff members, by-passing the hierarchy, wrote directly to the Committee and its President, Cornelio Sommaruga. The letter said, in summary, that the institution was going through a crisis of identity and that highly qualified colleagues were leaving. The ICRC could not be only the guarantor of the great humanitarian principles. "We must promote them actively", otherwise "we will be stifled by the venerable and ancient tradition" of the institution. The ICRC may end as an academy or a museum.

In March 1989, the twenty became 200: they included middle-level managers or chiefs of delegations. The reformists advised the Committee in a collective letter that the internal climate was worsening, in Geneva and in the field, that resignations were continuing. They deplored the weaknesses of the collegial Direction, its

> patent lack of creativity and moral authority which had installed a climate of mistrust and insecurity.

They considered that the ICRC did not show enough courage in relation to governments.

The ICRC tried to keep the collective letter secret, but it was revealed by a Swiss-German television programme.

The ICRC's reaction was in part to de-dramatize the crisis. The President found positive that the staff wanted to bring improvements to the work of the ICRC, but found some of the criticisms unfair. He said that the ICRC's effectiveness concerning the victims cannot be challenged.

In August 1989, the ICRC appointed a Director General, Mr. Guy Deluz, in order to reinforce the existing administrative structure of the ICRC. Concretely, the President continued to chair the ICRC Assembly, the Executive Board and the Committee itself.

This internal protest was probably caused, in part, by a feeling that other humanitarian NGOs are more open than the ICRC and dare challenge publicly some governments' abuses in the domain of human rights. The publication of Favez' book in 1988 and its critical assessment of the role of the ICRC during World War II may also have been an element in the delegates' decision to question openly their leadership and some of the long-standing tenets of the Red Cross work.

Besides the decision to create a Director's post, the delegates' protest did not result in any fundamental re-assessment of the ICRC's role, principles, policies and practices[39].

This collective written protest had been preceded, a decade before, by the rebellion of an individual delegate, for reasons of conscience, against the policy of discretion of the ICRC.

---

[39] *24 Heures*, Lausanne, 18 Aug. 1989—*Tribune de Genève* and *Journal de Genève*, 25 Aug. 1989 and *Le Monde*, 26 Aug. 1989.

Vichniac[40] relates the case of the rebellious delegate, Andreas Balmer.

On 19 April 1979, Balmer is sent on his first ICRC mission as a delegate to Zaire, where he will stay about 7 months. His assignment was for him a terrible shock: he visited prisons built for a maximum of 800 prisoners, filled with 2,000 persons. The detainees were dying of hunger, some were selling water to others.

From 21 December 1979 to 20 April 1980, Balmer is sent on a second mission. He participates in the major relief operations on the Thai border, giving assistance to the survivors of the Khmer Rouge genocide. Balmer recognizes the value of the ICRC's work: need assessment, the transportation and distribution of relief goods and materials are well-defined tasks.

Balmer's third mission raises critical problems of conscience for him. Sent to El Salvador from 18 July 1980 to 1 February 1981, he sees what the Western media have already publicized: violence and arbitrary action on the part of the police and the army. During his visits to prisons as an ICRC delegate, he sees and listens to the victims and measures the limits of the assistance provided to them by the ICRC. For him, the ICRC cannot remain mute: in the circumstances under which the people of El Salvador have to live, humanitarian assistance is somewhat "paradoxical, if not absurd". Should the ICRC maintain, or insist upon, its obligation of discretion? Is not the ICRC assurance of discretion promised to governments a form of collusion, as it covers criminal acts? Is not the presence of ICRC delegates in the prisons an alibi for some governments?

In conscience, Balmer then gave an affirmative answer to these questions.

He wrote a manuscript on what he had seen. He felt that he did not violate his obligation of discretion, because what he wrote had already been publicized in the media. His "novel", first called "Salvador Requiem", then "L'heure du cuivre" (The copper hour), in order not to refer precisely to that country, does not mention the ICRC, but an "international organization" whose employees are all Swiss citizens...

Although a few ICRC colleagues had told him informally that the Committee would not authorize the publication of his novel, Balmer gave his manuscript to a publisher in Zürich on 17 December 1981. On 2 February 1982, he was sent by the ICRC again to El Salvador, after having signed, again, the oath of discretion.

Balmer's book was published in German on 22 July 1982. He gave an interview to the Washington Post and to the Salvadoran newspaper "Diario de Hoy".

Called back to Geneva, Balmer is dismissed for "just cause" on 27 July 1982 and ordered to stop all and any publication concerning any ICRC assignment. The publisher is also warned by the ICRC against the publication of Balmer's book.

The ICRC then submits a petition to the Tribunals of Fribourg and Zürich, requesting that:

---

[40] Isabelle Vichniak, *Croix-Rouge—Les stratèges de la bonne conscience*, A. Moreau Publ., Paris, 1988, pp. 111–119.

— all copies of the book be seized
— Balmer be forbidden to promote his book and to pursue the marketing of his copyright
— Balmer be forbidden to communicate any information on his missions as an ICRC delegate, in view of his obligation of discretion.

In its petition, the ICRC recalled that the fundamental criterion of all its action is the interest of the victims whom it seeks to protect and assist. This activity is particularly difficult to carry out in countries such as El Salvador, because in situations of internal conflict or civil war, states have no obligations to accept the ICRC offers of services nor the presence of its delegates. Furthermore, Balmer, in taking sides, imperils the victims of other countries where the ICRC intervenes in a similar way. If the ICRC did not pursue this matter, it could not impose discretion and neutrality to its other delegates. In order to obtain and retain the confidence of all parties, the ICRC and its staff must therefore abstain from taking part in political controversies, not only in their action, but also in their words and written texts.

The Tribunals ruled in favour of the ICRC's position and accepted its claims.

In 1984, Balmer's book was published in French in Lausanne and the ICRC finally decided to withdraw its complaint.

Many ICRC delegates have lived through the same dramas and may understand the problems of conscience of Balmer. Those few who have published their memoirs did so with the approval of the ICRC.

Balmer's story is exemplary as it seems to be the only known case of an open, public rebellion of an ICRC delegate against the Red Cross rule of silence.

This individual rebellion brought to the fore some of the political, moral and tactical issues hidden behind the rule: it had no effect on the ICRC's policy.

The Influence of External Events on the "Dogma"

Since the end of World War II, regional or civil wars and international issues such as the South African policy of apartheid, have severely tested some of the principles and policies of the ICRC. A few examples follow.

The Nigerian Civil War and the ICRC's Neutrality

The assistance provided by the ICRC to both sides during the Biafra conflict (1967-1970) went through several crises as the impartiality and neutrality of the ICRC was being questioned by one party, the Federal Government.

The relief assistance provided by the ICRC, or other humanitarian NGOs, to a secessionist region, is likely to be considered by the central government as a support to the rebels, and not as an impartial, neutral, purely humanitarian gesture.

168

According to Forsythe[41], elements of Western opinion pressured the ICRC to pursue policies of assistance without regard to the wishes of Lagos: Western opinion believed the Ibos in the eastern region to be threatened by genocide, either directly by conscious policy of the Federal Government or indirectly from the governmental blockade.

During the first year of the war, the ICRC maintained a neutral image with both fighting parties. It had access to both leaders, Gowen and Ojukwu. During this early period, Biafra asked that ICRC assistance not be flown into Biafra directly from Nigeria. The ICRC avoided a major controversy over this symbolic issue by flying food and medicine into Biafra on a small scale from another territory, with a "fly at your own risk" agreement negotiated with Lagos.

On 27 May 1969, Ambassador August Lindt, ICRC General Commissioner for West Africa and two of his collaborators were detained by the Lagos Airport authorities.

On 5 June, an aircraft carrying food supplies to Biafra, which had been put at the disposal of the ICRC by the Swedish Red Cross, was shot down by a Nigerian fighter, costing the lives of the four members of the crew. On 6 June, ICRC personnel working at Lagos Airport received orders to withdraw within three days.

On 8 June, the Federal Military Government warned all countries against the violation of its air space; it had changed its attitude with regard to its toleration hitherto in allowing the ICRC to carry out night flights at its own risk and peril.

The ICRC was then faced with a choice. It could either remain assertive, flaunt the Nigerian policy, and possibly jeopardize its future role in armed conflicts,—or it could suspend flights, thus reducing its relief activities and seek a new negotiated arrangement.

On 11 June, the ICRC decided to discontinue airlift operations and stepped up negotiations with both belligerents, but to no avail.

On 14 June, the Federal Military Government declared Ambassador Lindt "persona non grata" and on 30 June, the Government announced that, in future, the ICRC would no longer be in charge of the coordination of relief action: this was to be assumed by the Nigerian National Commission for Rehabilitation.

In the words of Forsythe[42],

At that point the ICRC ceased its flirtation with being a revolutionary humanitarian actor and reverted to its more traditional style of acting only with the consent of the parties involved in the conflict.

[41] David P. Forsythe, *Humanitarian Politics—The ICRC*, The Johns Hopkins University Press, 1977, p. 46.

[42] David P. Forsythe, "Humanitarian Mediation by the ICRC", in *International Mediation in Theory and Practice*, S. Touval and I. W. Zartman Ed., Conflict Management Studies, SAIS, Westview Press, 1985, No. 6, p. 244. See also the ICRC *Annual Report 1969*, pp. 6–18, and Laurie S. Wiseberg, "Humanitarian Intervention: Lessons from the Nigerian Civil War", in *Human Rights Journal*, A. Pedone, Vol. VII–1, 1974, pp. 61–98.

The Biafra civil war was at the origin of an initially "revolutionary" humanitarian actor, "Médecins Sans Frontières", at the initiative of a rebellious French Red Cross doctor, Bernard Kouchner, who challenged the ICRC rule of discretion (see Chapter 7).

Israel and Arab Countries

During the 1973 war in the Middle East, the ICRC launched a series of public appeals to the parties, reminding them of their obligations under the Fourth Convention to protect and assist civilians. When Israel shelled Damascus, the ICRC made public appeals not only for all parties to respect the 1949 Convention, but even that the parties should respect the draft Protocol Additional to the Conventions, which would offer more extensive civilian protection but was not yet approved and binding. When Israel refused to adhere to that appeal, the ICRC publicized this refusal. The ICRC also offered to create a commission of inquiry to investigate all alleged violations of the Geneva Conventions in that war[43].

Thus, in contrast with its non-appeal of 1942, the ICRC did "go public" in 1973, in circumstances which had of course no similarity with those of the Second World War. Still, it showed a new, more open and more assertive attitude on the part of the ICRC in relation to States.

In 1989, the ICRC issued strong public protests concerning the "unrestrained" use of firearms by Israeli Armed Forces in the occupied territories and the expulsions of residents from the West Bank and the Gaza Strip to Lebanon.

On 13 April, the ICRC issued a strong public protest, after Israeli Armed Forces in the occupied territories shot dead several people and wounded some thirty others during an incident in the West Bank village of Nahalin, near Bethlehem.

The statement deplored the tragic humanitarian consequences of the incident and firmly protested against the indiscriminate and unrestrained use of arms by the troops.

On 29 June 1989, Israel expelled eight residents from the West Bank and the Gaza Strip to Lebanon, who arrived at the IRCR office in Ksara (Lebanon) on 30 June. The ICRC, in a press release, advised that these new expulsions were in violation of Article 49 of the Fourth Geneva Convention, which stipulates that individual or mass forcible transfers from occupied territories are prohibited, regardless of their motive.

The ICRC had notified Israel in the past of its disapproval whenever residents had been expelled from the occupied territories, because of the serious humanitarian consequences such expulsions entail. On 30 June, the ICRC expressed its disappointment and spoke out firmly against these latest expulsions[44].

---

[43] Forsythe, *Humanitarian Politics*, op.cit., pp. 174–175. See the ICRC *Annual Report 1973*, pp. 10–11, and *Annual Report 1974*, pp. 18–19.

[44] *ICRC Bulletin*, No. 160, May 1989, and ICRC Press Release No. 89/7.

Iran-Iraq: The Public Appeal

On 9 May 1983, the ICRC issued another public appeal to all the States party to the Geneva Conventions.

The ICRC had been unable to obtain the cessation of grave breaches of international humanitarian law, witnessed by ICRC delegates, repeatedly committed by both belligerent countries.

These included summary executions of captured soldiers, the abandonment of enemy wounded on the battlefield, the indiscriminate bombardment of towns and villages and the treatment of prisoners of war[45].

In its appeal, the ICRC referred to Article 1 of the Conventions, which places States under the obligation not only to respect but also to "ensure respect" for the Conventions, and urged that every means provided for to ensure respect for international humanitarian law should be put into effect, in particular the designation of protecting powers to represent the belligerents' interests in the enemy country.

In 1984, the ICRC continued its public pressure on both countries. On 13 February, it made a second appeal to all the States party to the Geneva Conventions. In this appeal, it pointed out that some 50,000 Iraqi prisoners benefitted from no protection in Iran since the suspension of the ICRC visits on 27 July 1983. It also stated that a large number of Iranian prisoners had regularly been concealed during visits to Iraq by the ICRC. It also pointed out that the Iraqi bombardment of Iranian civilian zones constituted a violation of the customary law of war.

On 7 March, after a medical survey, conducted in Iran,the ICRC reiterated publicly that the use on the battlefield of substances (chemical weapons) prohibited by the international law of war was incompatible with humanitarian principles.

On 7 June, the ICRC issued a press release on the bombing of Iraqi and Iranian cities.

A third appeal to the States party to the Geneva Conventions was issued on 23 November 1984, stating that the ICRC was no longer able alone to provide protection for the roughly 50,000 Iraqi prisoners of war[46].

Withdrawal from Lebanon

In December 1988, the ICRC withdrew its 17 delegates from Lebanon, after receiving death threats against them, just four days after Peter Winkler, the ICRC delegate kidnapped in Southern Lebanon, was released (see Chapter 9).

This was the first time that the ICRC had left a war-torn country under such circumstances.

[45] ICRC *Annual Report 1983*, pp. 56–57.

[46] ICRC *Annual Report 1984*, pp. 60–61, *International Herald Tribune*, 16 Feb. 1984, *Le Monde*, 17 Feb. and 14 March 1984, *La Suisse*, 8 March 1984.

In a public statement, the ICRC described the threats as "intolerable". While it always accepted the risks inherent in conflict situations, the ICRC said that it could not put up with a threat that negates the "very essence of its humanitarian mission".

The leaders of Lebanon's two governments both urged the ICRC to reverse its decision.

The ICRC had been present in Lebanon for over twenty years, working in favour of victims on all sides. In many areas, particularly in the South, the ICRC was often the only organization able to provide protection and assistance.

The ICRC decided to resume its activities in Lebanon in February 1989. This decision followed assurances on the future safety of the ICRC staff given during intensive contacts with the various "groups" present in Lebanon and several States connected with the Lebanese crisis.

During its seven-week absence, the ICRC maintained its administrative and operational infrastructure in Lebanon through its local staff. It also continued to support the activities of the Lebanese Red Cross by providing medical and relief supplies for distribution to the hospitals and civilians most in need of assistance.

In spite of the "assurances" mentioned above, two ICRC delegates were kidnapped in Sidon (Southern Lebanon) on 6 October 1989: the symbolic withdrawal of the ICRC did not obtain the desired results in the anarchy of Lebanon. The two delegates were finally released on 8 and 13 August 1990[47].

The Suspension of South Africa: The Politicization of the Red Cross?

On 25 October 1986, after a point of order raised by the Kenyan Government's delegation on behalf of the African Group at the Twenty-Fifth International Conference of the Red Cross, the Conference agreed, by an open vote and a simple majority

> that the representatives of the Government of South Africa be suspended from participating in the Twenty-Fifth International Conference of the Red Cross[48].

The vote was a protest against South Africa's official policy of apartheid.

This was the first time that a government's delegation had been excluded from a Red Cross Conference in the organization's history.

In response to this expulsion, the South African Government ordered the 16 delegates of the ICRC to leave the country "as quickly as possible", thus justifying the fears of Western countries that the expulsion of South Africa would in fact "punish" the victims of apartheid.

---

[47] *ICRC Bulletins*, No. 156, 158, 166, of Jan., March and Nov. 1989.

[48] The vote was adopted by 159 votes for, 25 against and 8 abstentions, including that of the League. 47 National Societies, four States and the ICRC took no part in the vote because they considered that the suspension was contrary to the Statutes of the International Red Cross and the Rules of Procedures of the Conference: ICRC *Annual Report 1986*, p. 97.

This unprecedented decision of the supreme body of the Red Cross Movement was also interpreted in Western circles as a disturbing symptom of the politicization of the Red Cross, following the trend observed in several of the U.N. specialized agencies, through the "automatic majority" of Third World countries, supported (in the U.N.) by the Socialist countries. It raised concern that the Red Cross Principles of universality, impartiality and neutrality had been compromised publicly, and that the expulsion of a government's delegation could be considered as a precedent for the expulsion of other "pariah" states[49].

Finally, there was the risk that this majority decision would create a durable division between the Western governments which had opposed it, and their public opinions, and the other governments.

Moreillon[50], has listed and commented upon the main arguments used by those "for" and "against" the final decision. Some of these arguments are summarized hereunder.

1. Arguments for the Suspension

— Apartheid is a crime against humanity, an institutionalized and openly declared violation of the Red Cross Fundamental Principle of humanity;
— South Africa is barred from all other international organizations;
— the Conference is competent to take such a decision, in particular because the South African representative represents only a minority of the population of this country;
— the question goes beyond law: it involves fundamental ethical principles and touches on a historic symbol of all forms of discrimination;
— no precedent is created as the case of South Africa is unique: no other state sets up racial discrimination as a principle of government;
— the principle of universality remains intact, as only the government's delegation of South Africa is suspended, only from the International Conference, while its National Society may continue its work;
— the loss of universality is the fault of South Africa, not of the Conference;
— it is not a political question and the principles of neutrality and impartiality cannot be invoked, nor those Articles of the Statutes which forbid the Conference to deal with political questions;
— it does involve the credibility of the Conference in the eyes of the majority of countries and of the peoples of the world;
— the decision moves in the direction that history is moving;
— it is no more than a time-limited suspension, which may be lifted when the South African Government renounces apartheid;

[49] *International Herald Tribune*, 27 Oct., 1–2 Nov. 1986, *Le Monde*, 28 Oct. 1986.

[50] Jacques Moreillon, "Suspension of the Government Delegation of the Republic of South Africa at the Twenty-Fifth International Conference of the Red Cross, Geneva 1986—Different perceptions of the same event", in *International Review of the Red Cross*, Mar.-Apr. 1987, 27th Year, No. 257, pp. 133–151.

— the non-suspension of South Africa would have obliged many delegations, Africans and others, to withdraw from the meeting.

2. *Arguments Against the Suspension*

— the subject of the discussion is not apartheid, which is opposed by all participants to the Conference. The question is whether the Conference can challenge the presence of any State party to the Geneva Conventions, or dispute the representative character of the government of that State. Do we want South Africa *not* to be bound by the Geneva Conventions and the obligations they entail? Created to act in time of war, the Red Cross finds its true prestige in time of war and in the simultaneous presence within it of all friends and enemies. Preventing the participation of one considered as a hostile antagonist runs counter to the very spirit and purpose of the Red Cross;
— the Statutes of the International Red Cross do not provide for the possibility of suspending a State or challenging the representativity of its government;
— this suspension creates a dangerous precedent;
— the suspension can only harm the victims, those whom the Red Cross,—and in particular the ICRC—must at all times be capable of protecting;
— the suspension violates the principle of universality and denies the entitlement of a State which has signed the Conventions to take part in the work of the Movement's supreme body;
— the suspension violates the principle of neutrality, and in particular, abstention from politics;
— the politicization in this case may lead towards a general politicization which would divest the Red Cross of its specific characteristics, and hence its efficacity in humanitarian action;
— the Red Cross must remain the ultimate place for dialogue. The Red Cross is fundamentally different from other international organizations such as the United Nations and there is no need or obligation to align the Red Cross with other international organizations;
— the Red Cross exists to help and not to condemn. It must be able to help victims everywhere, which implies moderation in its criticisms. The United Nations and human rights organizations can legitimately condemn, not the Red Cross;
— through this suspension, the Red Cross Movement compromises its image as a neutral and non-political institution and also loses credibility, particularly among hundreds of thousands of volunteers who have adhered to it precisely because of its concrete, non-political, purely humanitarian, neutral and non-discriminatory action;
— some of those who demand the suspension of South Africa may themselves be responsible for grave violations of human rights and humanitarian law. Is not a double standard being applied?
— elementary rules of procedure were ignored, insofar as the representative of South Africa was not allowed to present its defence and a "public" vote was imposed, when the vote should have been secret.

174

In our view, the African and Third World initiative in favour of the suspension of South Africa was "political" or "politicized" insofar as it introduced an international political and human rights issue concerning a government's internal policies and its related representativity in the debates of the International Conference of the Red Cross. This initiative went counter to Article 11.4 of the Statutes of the International Red Cross and Red Crescent Movement, which requires that

> none of the speakers at any time engages in controversies of a political, racial, religious or ideological nature.

Under Article 9, the members of the International Conference "shall be" the delegates from the National Societies, from the International Committee, from the League and from the States parties to the Geneva Conventions.

There are no provisions in the Statutes and Rules of Procedure of the Movement to "suspend" the participation of a State party to the Geneva Conventions.

The African and Third World initiative was essentially meant as a public international political and moral censure of the South African Government for its apartheid policies and as a pressure intended to influence this government into changing these policies. The pro-suspension governments were using the International Conference of the Red Cross as another international forum, similar to the U.N. General Assembly or the governing bodies of U.N. specialized agencies, to legitimize and publicize their views. They were not particularly concerned about the legal aspects of their initiative nor about its consequences for the "different" humanitarian Red Cross Movement and its neutrality.

Moreillon has reported that the press in Third World countries usually treated the suspension of South Africa as a mere item of information, with little comment: the few newspapers which gave comments expressed their approval of the suspension.

This contrasted with the extent of news coverage and comments in the press of Western countries. In virtually all press reports the decision was criticized and the politicization of the Movement was denounced. The refusal of a secret ballot and denial of the floor to the South African representative were regarded as violations of fundamental democratic rights and as an infringement of the National Societies' independence.

In the Western countries, National Societies are directly dependent on public opinion for their support in general, and more particularly financially. This support is largely based on the conviction that "Red Cross" = "neutrality" = "non-political" = "pure humanitarianism", an image seriously undermined in public opinion by the Conference.

In his 1987 commentary, Moreillon said that by holding the International Conference in Geneva for the first time since 1925, the Movement rediscovered the "other" Geneva, that of the U.N. European headquarters. In other words,

> the humanitarian Geneva met the Geneva of great debates and political passions, and perhaps the Movement's rallying to an international community already

mobilized and politically unanimous on the struggle against apartheid was then all too inevitable... it can be hoped that the spirit of humanitarian Geneva will in time prevail in the wake of that eminently political decision[51].

Four Years after the Suspension: An Assessment

In itself, the suspension of South Africa from the International Conference of the Red Cross was a symbolic, limited gesture: it was a time-limited suspension, not an expulsion, — it was addressed to the Government's delegation, not to the South African National Society, — it concerned only the Conference, which normally meets every four years, — it had no effect on South Africa's acceptance of the Geneva Conventions.

During and after the crisis, the ICRC and the League attempted to restore the neutral and independent image of the Red Cross.

The South African request of 28 October 1986 to the ICRC to withdraw its delegation from the country by 30 November, in response to the suspension, was promptly revoked. Following a series of representations made by the ICRC, the South African authorities reconsidered their decision on 26 November 1986, but imposed restrictions on the number of ICRC delegates authorized to operate in the country (5 delegates at the beginning of 1987 as against 20 stationed there the previous year)[52].

Politically, the lifting of the "state of emergency" by President F.W. de Klerk in June 1990, the release of political prisoners, the gradual repeal of apartheid laws and the expectation that an agreement may be concluded in 1991 between the South African Government and the African National Congress, all these measures tend to defuse the "South African" question[53].

Whether this progressive liberalization will prevent a repetition of the 1986 conflict at the next International Conference of the Red Cross, scheduled for 1991, remains to be seen.

In 1986, in his closing address to the Conference, the President of the ICRC stated:

...however troubled our hours together may have been, they cannot possibly keep us divided and lead us to resignation, for we do not have the right to doubt either the importance of our mission or the strength of the Red Cross and Red Crescent ideal[54].

It now appears that the Movement has overcome most of the negative consequences of the serious crisis of 1986 and that it has succeeded in keeping its "difference" as a non-political humanitarian movement.

---

[51] Ibid., p. 151.

[52] ICRC *Annual Report 1986*, p. 13, and *Annual Report 1987*, p. 15.

[53] *Newsweek*, June 18, 1990, p. 28.

[54] Moreillon, "Suspension", op.cit., p. 136.

Concluding Remarks

The ICRC is not a "human rights" organization, like Amnesty International or the International Commission of Jurists. It has a different mandate, as promoter of international humanitarian law, as monitor of the Geneva Conventions, with explicit protection duties, and as one of the many operational actors in international relief assistance.

Its quasi-intergovernmental role in relation to the elaboration, conclusion and implementation of international humanitarian agreements by governments restricts its freedom of expression and action. The ICRC believes that operating only through States, and only with the consent of States, is the most realistic way of protecting and assisting the victims.

The ICRC generally does not seek confrontation with States, on the basis that some humanitarian benefit can be obtained for the victims, even if the governments promote, directly or indirectly, human rights violations.

For van Boven[55], the ICRC faces a moral dilemma, insofar as gross and systematic violations of human rights affecting the life and the physical integrity of large numbers of human beings are often the result of government policies and practices involving torture, disappearances and arbitrary and summary executions. There is thus a moral contradiction in the work of the ICRC:

> in order to be able to carry out its humanitarian mission on behalf of the victims, the ICRC has, in some instances, to secure the cooperation of authorities which cannot be considered as legitimate partners in the quest for justice and humanity.

This moral contradiction was crudely exposed during World War II and the silence of the ICRC condemned.

Perhaps as a repentance for its attitude during that period, the ICRC changed its policy of absolute confidentiality and discretion with its public appeals to the parties to the 1973 War in the Middle East. This was followed during the Iran/Iraq War by the public appeals to all the States party to the Geneva Conventions in 1983 and 1984, the 1988 public statement about the intolerable threat to its delegates in Lebanon, and the 1989 public protests addressed to Israel.

While the ICRC still requires its delegates to observe total discretion concerning their ICRC missions, it seems that the institution has become more open and outspoken with regard to flagrant and repeated violations of the Geneva Conventions or of the law of the war.

Through its public statements and appeals, the ICRC attempts to draw the parties' attention to the legal issues, to their freely-accepted obligations under the Geneva Conventions, in order to entice them to respond, and to mobilize diplomatic and media pressure on them.

---

[55] Theo C. van Boven, "Some reflections on the principle of neutrality", in *Studies and Essays on International Humanitarian Law and Red Cross Principles in honour of Jean Pictet*, ICRC, Nijhoff, Geneva, 1984, p. 647.

Cynics may say that it is easier to criticize publicly Iran, Iraq or Israel in recent years, than Nazi Germany in the 1940s. While it is true that the stakes and risks are not comparable, the evolution of the ICRC in this domain is undeniable and commendable.

On the other hand, there are limits to issuing public appeals: they should be exceptional, they should be reserved to very grave, documented and repeated cases of violations of the Geneva Conventions and of the law of the war. They should not show any bias or imbalance, so that the ICRC does not lose its image of neutrality, impartiality, is able to maintain its role of neutral intermediary and to retain access to victims.

In June 1990, the ICRC received a public tribute for its assistance work for prisoners, authorized only under conditions of discretion.

Nelson Mandela, the Deputy President of the African National Congress (ANC), had been released from detention in South Africa in February 1990 after 27 years. He was visited regularly by ICRC delegates while in detention.

During his visit to the ICRC in Geneva, Mandela expressed his gratitude to the ICRC and praised its "professional and efficient" work. He also thanked the institution on behalf of all past and present ANC detainees, and said that only a prisoner can understand how beneficial and essential the visits were[56].

While the ICRC, with its unique characteristics and its own international mandate, will continue its essential humanitarian work, under its traditional Fundamental Principles, it will need to remain alert and responsive to international political, socio-economic and ideological changes, as well as to the "competition" of other humanitarian NGOs. Its new acceptance of public appeals is a sign that it now realizes that an excessive discretion may be misinterpreted and counterproductive, and that symbolic declarations, even without immediate, obvious usefulness, may in fact be more effective and important for the future of the Red Cross than diplomatic reserve.

Pictet wrote in 1979[57] that

One cannot be at one and the same time the champion of justice and charity. One must choose, and the ICRC has long since chosen to be a defender of charity.

This may be true, but one cannot divorce the defence of human rights from humanitarian concerns: one of the Red Cross purposes, under the Fundamental Principle of humanity is "to ensure respect for the human being".

[56] *ICRC Bulletin*, July 1990, No. 174.
[57] *The Fundamental Principles of the Red Cross*, op.cit., p. 60.

CHAPTER 5

BRITISH CHARITIES

Voluntary service is a strong British tradition. The nineteenth century "charity organizations" arose from the urge of individuals and informal groups to help combat suffering and social injustice. Compassion for the orphan, the waif, the stray, the blind or destitute produced many of the British humanitarian or human rights non-governmental organizations (NGOs). Voluntary individual and group initiatives opened the way for later social welfare schemes and services assumed by government departments. No doubt the initial hardships brought to the workers and their families by the industrial revolution together with the prevailing philosophy of laissez-faire offered a large field of opportunities for charitable persons and organizations.

The British tradition expresses itself by the gift of one's own time to work, essentially without monetary compensation, for worthy causes,—the gift of money on the part of individuals, groups and corporations to support such causes, and to support voluntary organizations which promote them,—a sense of civic solidarity with those less endowed with wealth, health, intellectual capacities or professional potential.

This tradition is based in part on a Christian obligation to "help thy neighbour", —a moral duty of the rich to the poor, or of those able to help those in need,—a Protestant, puritan, belief that the individual should take the initiative to change and improve society, rather than leaving it to the government.

The influence of British citizens in the leadership of international NGOs, and in the leadership of international umbrella NGOs, in research studies and practical experiments of development and relief assistance, are evident to the outside observer.

How to illustrate this basic national root of humanitarianism fairly is an almost impossible task. How to choose among the hundreds of national and international associations which were born, in the 19th and the present century, in Britain is, again, unfair and arbitrary.

Charities in the U.K. are estimated to number around 185,000. The voluntary sector as a whole is thought to employ the equivalent of between 140,000 and 200,000 people full-time in its work.

British Charities are

non-profit seeking, non-governmental organizations established for the public benefit

and are assured of taxation privileges, applying to both the organizations and their donors.

Charitable causes include the causes of medicine and health, care for the young and the elderly, the advancement of education, religion, and international aid[1].

Following a review of a British human rights organization born in the 19th century, this Chapter is limited to a review of the creation, objectives and activities of three British humanitarian NGOs with a view to assessing whether their role is limited to direct, practical assistance, or whether they have decided to take political sides and publicly preach social justice and human rights to unwilling governments.

The Anti-Slavery Society for the Protection of Human Rights, created in London in 1839, claims to be the world's oldest human rights organization, in some ways a predecessor to Amnesty International, another British-based human rights NGO. Still active in the 1990s, the Society has shown that a small NGO can exert an international influence well beyond the country of its birth, and far beyond its limited resources. As a human rights organization, the Society has adopted a strong public advocacy role against contemporary slavery and for the rights of indigenous people.

Also born in the 19th century, the Salvation Army, considered old-fashioned in some quarters because of its military structure and uniforms, has maintained its objectives and commitments and has proved its continuing ability to help the poor: it is a truly international Christian movement which allies in its programmes evangelization, social work in industrialized countries, medical assistance and education in the Third World, and emergency relief assistance.

Its religious determination to remain politically neutral and to be free of any ideology caused the Salvation Army to resign from the more activist World Council of Churches in 1981.

Another "impartial", but a non-religious organisation, Save the Children Fund, was created in 1913 by an inspired young English woman, Eglantyne Jebb, out of her concern for the suffering of children. The British association has now flowered into an International Alliance of national branches working on relief and development projects, but mainly concerned with children. E. Jebb has remained famous for drafting the first "Charter of the Rights of the Child" in 1923, which was at the origin of a U.N. Convention.

Oxfam was created during World War II by a group of concerned individuals, as a small fund-raising committee to relieve famine and send supplies to those in need. It is now the number one British Charity with extensive international activities:

---

[1] *Meeting People's Needs in Britain*, Display Europhil, Yalding, Kent, 1990, pp. 13–14.

besides its development and relief work, it gives public support to sensitive international political causes, in particular in the field of international public health.

The Anti-Slavery Society for the Protection of Human Rights

The Anti-Slavery Society, the world's oldest international human rights NGO, is the only one devoted exclusively to combating modern forms of slavery[2].

The Society, based in London, was founded in 1839 as the "British and Foreign Anti-Slavery Society", five years after the emancipation of slaves in British colonies. In 1840, it organized the First Anti-Slavery Convention in London.

Between 1840 and 1890, the Society promoted international campaigns for the abolition of slavery: the slave trade was outlawed in British India and Ceylon, the territories of Sweden, France, Denmark and Brazil. In 1867, the slave trade over the Atlantic was finally abolished, due to American and British cooperation.

In 1909, the Society merged with the Aborigines' Protection Society, which was campaigning for the rights of indigenous people.

In 1926, the League of Nations adopted the Convention on the Abolition of Slavery and the Slave Trade. Between 1933 and 1939, the League's Standing Committee of Experts on Slavery monitored the implementation of the Convention with some success.

In 1948, the U.N. General Assembly adopted the Universal Declaration of Human Rights. Its Article 4 states that

No one shall be held in slavery or servitude; slavery and the slave trade shall be prohibited in all their forms.

In 1948, the Society was granted consultative status with the U.N. Economic and Social Council, Category II.

In 1956, the U.N. adopted the Supplementary Convention on the Abolition of Slavery, the Slave Trade, and Institutions and Practices similar to Slavery.

On 25 August 1975, after 18 years of continuous pressure led by the Society, the U.N. appointed a Working Group on Slavery (now the Working Group on Contemporary Slavery). This was the first international body since 1933 appointed specifically to examine ways of eradicating slavery.

The Society has a general objective, the promotion of human rights, in accordance with the 1948 Universal Declaration of Human Rights, and two more specific aims:

— the elimination of all forms of slavery,
— the representation and defence of indigenous peoples.

---

[2] Information on the Anti-Slavery Society is based on the organization's documents, including its Annual Report 1987–1988, *The Reporter*, 1988, *Anti-Slavery Newsletter*, 1/1989.

Slavery still exists: the number of slaves in the world today is estimated at 200 million. The Society concentrates on the most cruel and common forms of slavery. These are:

— chattel slavery (the total ownership of one person by another) which still occurs in parts of Northern Africa;
— debt bondage or bonded labour (the pledging of labour for an unspecified time to pay off a debt), which is entrenched in South and South-East Asia, parts of South America, and also occurs in Western countries;
— child labour: the exploitation of children under 18 or of their labour by adults throughout the world.

The Society has also campaigned against the oppression of women in servile forms of marriage, and female circumcision.

The Society recalls that indigenous people have suffered dispossession, enslavement and massacre at the hand of invaders throughout history. The threats today comes from "development": flooding of land through hydro-electric schemes, deforestation and the consequent damage to agriculture, government-backed forced settlement programmes or "squatting" by landless peasant farmers. Indigenous survivors, some 200 million worldwide, live in dependent poverty, with their livelihood, their purpose and their hope destroyed.

The Society works to ensure that indigenous people are part of the development process, and not victims of profiteering or alien government.

The Society recognizes that governments are the sole agencies capable of enforcing international conventions and respect for human rights in their territories. Their cooperation must first be sought. Where governments are unwilling to take effective action, or are themselves the perpetrators of abuse, the Society takes the issue to the public and to the United Nations.

Like other human rights NGOs, the Society publicizes human rights violations in various countries, in an effort to "shame" governments into compliance with international conventions and to entice them to humanize their laws and practices.

As a registered charity in the U.K., the Society is financially supported by subscriptions and donations, and by grants for research from foundations and trusts. There were 1,143 subscribers at 31 March 1988. In January 1989, the Society only employed three full-time persons, two half-time secretaries and two temporary volunteers.

The Salvation Army

The Salvation Army is an integral part of the Christian Church, although distinctive in its organization and practice. It has two closely linked objectives. The basic one is to evangelize: its founder, William Booth, wanted to see people saved from sin, and to that end, created a new and distinctive denomination, the "Christian

Mission", as it was known until 1878. Its second, very concrete, objective was to promote the social betterment of the poor. The evangelical and the social work are two activities

> of the one and same salvation which is concerned with the total redemption of man... one does not preach the Gospel to a man who is cold and hungry: he must first be clad and fed[3].

Most religious or Church-related NGOs distinguish their relief assistance and development activities from evangelization. The Salvation Army is an exception: the propagation of its Christian beliefs is an integral part of its social action.

Created in 1865 in London, the movement is now at work in 90 countries, where it continues to "fight sin and evil" in the lives of men through God's message of love and peace, and to relieve poverty, and fulfil other charitable enterprises.

An "Army without guns", the organization has continued to use certain military features such as uniforms, flags and ranks to inspire and regulate its fight in a spiritual warfare.

Today, its officers bear the ranks of lieutenant, captain, major, lieutenant-colonel, colonel or commissioner. The General is elected by the Salvation Army's High Council.

The Salvation Army spread from the U.K. to the U.S.A., Australia, France, New Zealand, Canada and India between 1879 and 1882.

In 1866, William Booth opened a soup kitchen, and in 1888 his first hostel for "down and outs". That same year, 23 years before the British Government opened its first employment exchange, the Salvation Army's labour bureau started operations. Within seven years, 69,000 men had found work.

A French "salvationist", Charles Péan, was instrumental in obtaining the closing by the French Government of the notorious convict settlement in Devil's Island, French Guiana.

Currently, the Salvation Army has over 14,000 evangelical centres worldwide, as well as a wide range of social, medical, educational and community services. Its programmes—designed to minister to the whole man, physically, emotionally and spiritually—include, among other facilities:

— 71 alcoholics' homes
— 26 homes for women, 18 maternity homes
— 263 food distribution centres
— 634 hostels for homeless people and transient workers
— 13 institutes for the blind, 14 leagues for deaf and dumb, 27 homes and institutes for the handicapped
— 130 dispensaries and clinics

[3] Cyril Barnes, *Army without Guns*, The Salvation Army, 1986, p. 6,—*The Salvation Army, Report, 1988–1989,*—see also Salvation Army leaflets Ref. S1, S5, S7, S9, S13,S14, S26, S27, S28, S33, S54.

— 8 teacher-training schools, 985 kindergarten and primary schools, 105 secondary and high schools, 29 domestic and trade schools etc.

Every year, recipients of emergency, disaster or general relief number over 2 million.

Assistance to the Third World has developed mainly in two areas: medical assistance and education.

In Asia, India is the oldest "mission" country of the Salvation Army. In 1882, the Salvation Army set up relief centres to assist victims of famine, epidemics and floods and opened schools at all levels. A medical service was opened at Nagercoil in 1896. The purely evangelical work was developing simultaneously. Nowadays, more than 2,000 officers, almost all Indians, helped by many employees, run some 1,500 evangelization centres, 1,500 schools—from elementary schools to higher level institutes—and a hundred various social institutions: farms, children's homes, centres for handicapped persons, for the blind, orphanages, convalescence homes, dispensaries and a number of hospitals, leprosy centres and maternity hospitals. Similar work is carried out in Sri Lanka, Indonesia, Burma, Hong Kong, Taiwan, Singapore, Malaysia, the Philippines, Pakistan and Bangladesh.

In Africa, the Movement was first established in most English-speaking, former British colonies. Over the last fifty years, it spread to the Congo, Zaire, Angola and Mozambique. Responsible officers are all African.

The Salvation Army also operates in Central and South America.

The Salvation Army takes part in emergency relief assistance. During the cyclone which devastated Bangladesh in 1970, emergency relief teams were sent to the country. Later, in Dacca, the Salvation Army opened food distribution centres for children, a home for blind children, dispensaries, a maternity hospital, centres of rehabilitation through work, mobile clinics.

Following the earthquake which killed 6,000 people in Southern Italy in November 1980, the Salvation Army sent relief teams from the U.K., Switzerland and France.

At the request of the Government of Pakistan, the Salvation Army runs camps for Afghan refugees.

The worldwide evangelical and social enterprises of the Salvation Army are carried out by 18,930 full-time officers and cadets, 65,141 paid employees and one and a half million voluntary unpaid members (salvationists)[4]. Each member is a committed believer to the Christian faith, and each one accepts to lead a disciplined and compassionate life of high moral standards, including abstinence from alcohol and tobacco.

Expenditures of the Salvation Army for the year ended on 31 March 1988 amounted to 46,6 million pounds[5].

[4] Raymond Delcourt, *L'Armée du Salut*, PUF, Paris, 1989, pp. 79–80, 89–92. *The Salvation Army. Report, 1988–1989.*

[5] *Charity Trends*, 12th Ed., Charities Aid Foundation, Tonbridge, 1989, p. 101.

The Salvation Army and Politics

The Salvation Army claims to be politically neutral. Its position is based on the following religious grounds, according to a former Chief of the French Salvation Army[6].

The Church of Jesus Christ should be free of any allegiance, any ideology, and thus be open and welcoming to all. The Salvation Army's vocation is to announce the good news of Christian salvation to all, without any exceptions. Taking sides would raise barriers, and therefore separate, divide and create confrontations. The evangelical message is a message of reconciliation and peace. The Salvation Army's respect for different opinions and options allows people of diverse political opinions to coexist within its community, without creating any conflict. In view of the extreme diversity of countries where the Salvation Army is present and working, its only possible attitude is one of great tolerance.

There is an incompatibility between a political commitment and the mission entrusted by The Lord to His Church. The evil forces against which Christians must fight have invaded the structures of society only because they are rooted in man's heart.

The Salvation Army denounces the deep cause of conflicts, of antagonisms, of divisions and of all human turpitudes, and proposes the only remedy and the only possible liberation: salvation in Jesus Christ.

For the Salvation Army, there is no real and lasting social revolution without conversion to the Gospel. For the Christians, the absolute priority must be given to the proclamation of the liberating Gospel.

The Salvation Army's strongly asserted and maintained political neutrality caused its resignation from the World Council of Churches (WCC) in 1981.

The Salvation Army was among the 146 WCC founding members in 1948. It had participated in the Assemblies of Edinburgh in 1910 and Stockholm in 1925. It played an active role in the WCC until it suspended its membership in 1978, following the announcement of a $85,000 grant from the WCC Programme to Combat Racism Special Fund to the Patriotic Front in Zimbabwe.

WCC and Army officials met in December 1978 and June 1981 to discuss the issues. The Army's position was summarized in Army General Arnold Brown's letter of 31 July 1981[7]. Its position was based on the Salvation Army's internationality which implies diversity of views concerning the relationship between the Army and the WCC.

> There are unquestionably aspects of the WCC's activity which demand our full support, e.g. the Commission on Evangelism, the Commission on Faith and Order, CICARWS, and CMC ... Our gravamen has to do with the issuance by

---

[6] Delcourt, op.cit., p. 93–104. Mr. Delcourt was Chief of the Salvation Army, France, from 1972 to 1980.

[7] WCC Doc. EPS No. 23 of 27 Aug. 1981 and 24 of 3 Sept. 1981.

the WCC of statements, the developing of policies and the carrying out of actions which we regard as political, and which, as such, endanger the non-political nature of the Army, the preservation of which is basic to the Movement's effectiveness in a number of countries. Refusal to identify with political factions, as distinct from deep social concern for the needy people of all lands regardless of creed, colour or political persuasion, has been the essence of the Army's life and endeavour from its very beginnings. Indeed, we see clearly that any such political identification would inevitably cut us off from large numbers of those very people we seek to succour. The Salvation Army's foundation belief is that the only real hope for the transformation of society lies in personal salvation through faith in the redemptive grace of Christ.

More precisely, although unsaid in this letter, the Army could not accept the WCC's support to liberation movements using violence in order to reach their objectives. The WCC was also accused of bias, in supporting only movements of marxist ideology and fighting only against white racism,—and not against abuses in Socialist Eastern Europe.

The reply from the WCC Central Committee disagreed with the Army's view of WCC policies and actions. Rather, it said, WCC actions stem from a conviction that the gospel affects all aspects of life. It also noted that under the WCC Constitution and operating procedures the expression of various gifts and emphasis is ensured, the theological basis of membership has remained unchanged and no WCC member body is bound by council decisions.

The Committee also referred to a second area of WCC-Army disagreement, which surfaced following a decision by the 1975 WCC Assembly in Nairobi to foster full eucharistic fellowship. The Committee reiterated earlier assurances that the eucharistic fellowship emphasis does not exclude non-sacramental movements like the Army as WCC members.

The WCC offered to maintain cooperative international relationships with the Army, hoping for continued Army ecumenical involvements on local, national, and regional levels, and assured the Army of WCC understanding if the Army reapplied for membership.

In the meantime, the Army moved from full membership in the WCC to "fraternal status" under the provision in the WCC Constitution (section VI.1, and section XII of the Rules).

The Army had chosen the "liberating Gospel" and rejected the "Liberation Theology". More will be said on the latter, and more generally on the WCC in Chapter 6.

The Save the Children Fund (SCF)

The story of "The Save the Children Fund" shows the creation of an NGO by an inspired, charitable and effective individual in one country, which later developed into a major international movement, the "International Save the Children Alliance".

Save the Children was born British and is now multinational. A non-religious organization, it deals with both relief and development with an orientation on children, like UNICEF at the intergovernmental level.

It is politically neutral and impartial in general, even though the Swedish SCF has recently engaged in political advocacy in addition to the more traditional assistance and development work.

Save the Children's founder, Eglantyne Jebb, has remained famous for drafting the first Charter of the "Rights of the Child" in 1923, which evolved into the International Convention on the Rights of the Child, adopted in November 1989 by the U.N. General Assembly.

The Creation of Save the Children Fund

The Red Cross Movement found its origin in the personal experience of a young Swiss citizen, Henry Dunant, horrified by the suffering and lack of care of wounded soldiers at the Battle of Solferino in 1859.

In 1913, Eglantyne Jebb, a young English woman of 37 years of age and an Oxford history graduate who wrote poetry, came to the Balkans to administer help and supplies on behalf of the Macedonian Relief Fund. Jebb's distress at the finding that so many children were abandoned and suffering was at the origin of the creation of Save the Children Fund (SCF)[8].

Born in 1876, Jebb came from a well-to-do, cultured and socially conscious family. She first taught in an elementary school, where her experience with children from poor homes in Marlborough showed her the urgency for reform and change of outlook in social administration. She learned the importance of the "scientific approach" to social problems which was later to become the guiding principle of SCF. She joined a Charity Society and undertook and published a social survey of Cambridge. In her book, she stressed that charity should not be a gift from the authorities or anyone else, but rather help between neighbours, each contributing according to his ability. She felt keenly the "one-ness" of the whole human race.

During World War I, conscious of the sufferings of civilians, Jebb, her sister and her friends tried to awaken the public conscience and making ordinary men and women aware of the situation.

It was from the periodical reports sent to them by friends in the International Red Cross that Jebb first learned how the people of Vienna were starving to death, and that children of six

[8] The information on Save the Children Fund is based in part on Kathleen Freeman's book *If Any Man Build—The History of Save the Children Fund*, Hodder and Stoughton, London, SCF, 1965,—on an interview with a SCF official in London in August 1989 and on SCF documentation.

were so thin and small that they looked like babies of two.

In spite of the widely-held opinion that the fate of ex-enemies was no concern of the British people, the sisters managed to get a "Fight the Famine Council" formed early in 1919 to stir the Government to action by protesting against one of the chief causes of famine, the Allied blockade.

On 19 May 1919, a new organization was created, the "Save the Children Fund", a sub-Committee of the Council, as a special relief fund. In its first year, the Fund raised more than 400,000 pounds, in the knowledge that money would be instantly translated into tins of milk, hospital supplies and clothing to help children throughout famine and war-stricken areas.

The Fund later separated from the "Fight the Famine Council", which preferred to attack the political and economic injustices of the blockade at government level, thus keeping the Fund protected from politics.

Jebb was forty-three when she founded the Fund, and for the next nine years it became her whole life. Her gifts for building the SCF movement were based on her abilities to communicate her own values and ideals to others as well as her real humility.

She was not a sentimentalist but a practical humanitarian. An Anglican, she and her organization received the full support of Pope Benedict XV: he begged her to ensure that organizations to save the children were formed in every country and that the relief was administered regardless of race, colour or creed.

On 6 January 1920, Jebb created the "Save the Children International Union" in Geneva: national SCF groups were set up in the 1920s in Switzerland, France, Sweden, in other European countries and in Commonwealth countries.

When Jebb died in Geneva on 17 December 1928, worn out from illness, tributes poured in from all over Europe.

Past Activities of the British "Save the Children Fund"

The British Fund first embarked on a programme of feeding starving children in Europe. Its method was to work through existing organizations with similar aims. In cooperation with the Society of Friends and the Vienna Relief Fund, 150,000 pounds were made available to feed 30,000 Austrian children under six daily. Relief took the form of milk for infants and food for expectant mothers.

The SCF also gave large grants for the administration of relief in other countries, such as Czechoslovakia and the Baltic States, under the supervision of an SCF team of doctors.

One of Jebb's more revolutionary ideas was that "the new charity must be scientific", in the sense that it should apply the methods successfully applied by business: if a voluntary society is worthy to be entrusted with large sums of money to meet an increasingly wide set of commitments, it must employ methods at least as efficient as those of its commercial counterparts. To help increase funds, she employed a publicity officer, a former newspaper reporter, whose policy was to adapt to the needs of philanthropy methods which had hitherto been reserved for the publicizing of "patent medicines". The business of charity "discovered" by the French humanitarian NGOs in the 1970s[9] had already been practised by SCF since the 1920s. Voluntary agencies had to become professional in their organization and work methods.

In two years, the new methods raised over one million pounds for the SCF's work and gave it a great national and international status.

In an effort to fight the Russian famine of August 1921, SCF sent its own teams which, in a remarkable example of international cooperation, acted as agents to administer relief for 14 different national member organizations of the Save the Children International Union, in the Province of Saratov. Over 120 million children's meals were served, in addition to over twice that number of adult rations on behalf of the Russian Famine Relief Fund, which was administered by F. Nansen. The SCF set up hundreds of feeding centres, run by British, Russian-speaking, experienced workers.

The Fund initiated various programmes to assist refugees: — feeding programmes, provision of clothing, protection against epidemics, — the Sponsorship Scheme, by means of which individuals, or a group of people, or an institution (such as a school) "adopt" a child or group, sending money, letters and presents. Another pioneer scheme of the Fund was the building of a model village for Armenian refugees in Bulgaria in 1926, followed by the building of two more villages in Albania.

Jebb helped in setting up work schools in the poorer districts of Budapest: the first one opened in 1920. Girls from very poor homes were given training in crafts, given good meals and paid according to the quality of their work.

During the Spanish Civil War, the Fund looked after many children who were in holiday camps when fighting broke out: they were brought to safety in France until they could be reunited with their families.

All the initial activities of the Fund, relief, resettlement of refugees, child welfare, medical help and education, are still carried out by the present-day SCF.

Commonwealth members have been partners in all overseas projects undertaken by the SCF, either by financial or material help, or by sending volunteers to join SCF in the field.

Towards the end of World War II, teams of SCF volunteers, following the liberating armies, helped in France and the Netherlands, and then in Germany itself to care for orphans and for the children of displaced persons, unwilling immigrants from other countries. Feeding centres, nurseries and clubs were established. The Austrian Government, with the British and Canadian SCFs, set up a permanent rehabilitation centre for crippled children at Hermagor. In Greece, SCF workers opened hospitals and clinics, feeding centres and welfare clinics; they also distributed clothes.

[9] Bernard Kouchner, *Charité Business*, Le Pré aux Clercs, Paris, 1986.

The 1950s and 1960s were years of expansion in the Fund's work overseas. Disaster relief was (and still is) a frequent need, and these years saw SCF providing food and shelter in Korea, helping the victims of the Agadir earthquake, caring for injured and orphan children in Vietnam and for Tibetan refugees fleeing to India.

In the Middle East, in 1948, SCF's work began with emergency relief to Arab refugees after the creation of the State of Israel. The Fund provided medical help, started clinics and feeding centres and trained young Arab people as orderlies to help with medical treatment. In Jordan, in 1962, the SCF, with support from the country's Government and the Oxford Committee for Famine Relief (Oxfam), carried out an all-winter distribution of food and clothing to more than 10,000 starving Bedouin children.

Following the earthquake at Agadir, in 1960, the SCF took on a new role, in addition to its prompt relief work: it laid 5,000 cement floors in place of the earthen floors, a cause of tuberculosis; it also provided work for the unemployed. With the French "Ligue de Protection de l'Enfance", the SCF ran a supplementary school-feeding scheme for over 6,000 children.

Alongside this emergency work, and often leading on from it, SCF's long-term work was developing. Teaching nutrition and hygiene became a major part of SCF's mother and child health programmes in the Third World. Training local staff became an essential part of SCF's aim of handing over its projects to the country itself.

In the 1970s, SCF became more involved in helping families to provide for their children's basic needs through schemes enabling villages to construct their own water supply, or create a vegetable garden.

The Present "Save the Children—UK"

Save the Children is the U.K.'s largest international voluntary agency concerned with child health and welfare. Although it is best known as a disaster relief organization, it attempts to turn emergency relief into long-term programmes.

SCF's strategy is to work with the poorest people in the poorest parts of the world. The emphasis is on health, nutrition, education and social programmes in some 50 countries.

As major policy-makers and coordinators of services for children are governments, the main thrust of SCF programmes is on strengthening child-related government services. These range from support for village health workers' schemes to advice on establishing a national nursing council. The welfare programme has expanded in the areas of community-based rehabilitation for disabled children and care for street children and young victims of conflicts. SCF/U.K.'s contribution to the fight against AIDS has focused on research, training and public education.

An important part of the organization's work is in sustaining public awareness and support for long-term development.

Work overseas is normally undertaken on the basis of a signed partnership agreement with governments and ministerial departments, sometimes leading to eventual handover of a project to the government. SCF ensures that the cost per head is reasonable and can be afforded by the government concerned.

Training and technical assistance are key components of the majority of SCF programmes and the skills gained by local staff in primary health techniques are of a world recognized standard[10].

Wherever possible, local staff are employed and the number of expatriates is limited to those who have medical, administrative or other expertise not available locally.

In Nepal, for instance, SCF helps to recruit and train volunteer health workers and runs basic and refresher training courses in all aspects of health care for local staff and staff employed by the government or other organizations. Student doctors and nurses from a state university learn community medicine at one of the Fund's projects.

In Mozambique, an SCF epidemiologist is contributing to planning, management and evaluation of the national immunization programme against children's diseases: measles, poliomyelitis, diphtheria, tetanus, tuberculosis and whooping cough, under the WHO/UNICEF Expanded Programme of Immunization. In Uganda, an SCF team of four persons is working with local counterparts to train Ministry of Health staff, middle management and refrigeration technicians.

An SCF nutrition field worker programme, set up after Ethiopia's famine in the mid-seventies, played a key part in raising the alarm in the 1980s. Rural field workers, trained by SCF, weigh and measure children regularly to assess their nutritional status, and collect information about crop conditions, market prices and the availability of food. Monthly reports enable government and relief agencies to plan ahead and to target aid so that it can be directed to the localities most in need[11].

SCF/U.K. has major programmes in some thirty countries worldwide. In most countries, there is a Field Director who is in charge of the administration of SCF work in that country. A total of about 2,000 local and 140 expatriate staff are employed in SCF projects overseas. In another 20 countries, SCF supports the work of government and other local organizations whose programmes are in accordance with the Fund's aims.

For instance, in Ethiopia, the SCF Field Director is maintaining contacts with government departments and other agencies working in the country. Early in 1989, there were 250 SCF workers in Ethiopia, including 13 expatriates. The total SCF expenditure in the country in 1988/1989 was almost 7 million pounds.

In India, the Government encourages its own educated people and backs indigenous NGOs with funding. It ensures that no non-essential expatriates work in NGO projects, a philosophy shared by SCF.

[10] SCF *Information Sheet 8*, July 1988.
[11] SCF *Development Matters*, Doc. OSL/89.

SCF/U.K. thus employs few expatriate staff overseas: it gives full priority to the employment of nationals, in line with the Fund's aim to encourage self-sufficiency and independence.

The few expatriate staff must be qualified and experienced professionals, including health staff (doctors, nurses, health visitors), nutritionists, social workers, management, transport/engineering staff.

Expatriate staff are recruited on fixed-term contracts of up to two years' duration. Famine and refugee programmes often require short-term assistance staff who are normally recruited on 3 or 6 month contracts. All expatriate staff are salaried and are paid in line with appropriate U.K.-based salary scales. The Fund also provides air fares, in-country expenses, insurance etc.[12].

The total expenditures of SCF/U.K. were, in 1987/1988, 41,6 million pounds and 41,9 million in 1989/1990[13]. As an average over five years, 88.7 percent was spent on operations, 9 percent on fundraising and publicity, and 2.3 percent on general administration.

SCF/U.K. has adopted a policy on long-term field work, according to which two-thirds of expenditures goes towards overseas projects, and one-third is used in the U.K.

Also in 1987/1988, most of the income came from voluntary private contributions and donations, and the sales of products. Contributions from government sources and intergovernmental organizations amounted to 29 percent. Corporate fundraising contributed to 3 percent of the income[14].

SCF/U.K. is in consultative status (Category II) with the U.N. Economic and Social Council and has a similar status with WHO.

WHO appreciates SCF's partnership. SCF actively supports WHO technical policies and is an important advocate for primary health care. There are frequent contacts between SCF and WHO on emergency relief, nutrition and child health in general. The Fund provides technical, material and financial support to WHO/national immunization programmes in 13 countries. The Fund is an influential member of the U.K./NGO AIDS Consortium for the Third World, having itself taken an early role in responding to AIDS in Uganda. The Fund supports the WHO Global strategy for the control and prevention of AIDS and promotes this with other NGOs.

The International Save the Children Alliance (ISCA)

As mentioned above,it was largely in response to the wishes of Pope Benedict XV that the Save the Children Movement should spread to all countries, that Jebb put

[12] SCF *Information Sheet 4* and *11* of July 1988, SCF *Country Report India*, Aug. 1988 and *Ethiopia*, March 1989.

[13] *International Save the Children Alliance, Annual Reports, 1988, 1989.*

[14] *Save the Children Review 1987–1988.*

forward the idea of an international organization to link the various national bodies with the same aims as the SCF, so that they could work on a world wide scale more effectively.

On 6 January 1920, Jebb founded the "Save the Children International Union" in Geneva, with the International Committee of the Red Cross, the Save the Children Fund (U.K.) and a Swiss Committee as members. The Swedish Rädda Barnen and the French "Comité de secours aux enfants" joined the Union, followed by organizations in South Africa, Australia, Canada, Ireland, Germany, the Netherlands, Italy and Turkey.

After World War I, the Union instituted relief action, with the emergency distribution of foods. It later set up homes, clinics and hospitals, and supplied qualified social workers to help in planning and establishing national child welfare councils. It introduced the system of "sponsorships", now applied by many organizations in different regions, and established the central clearing station for information known as the International Child Welfare Bureau, originally placed under the authority of the League of Nations[15].

In 1944, the Union amalgamated with the International Association for the Promotion of Child Welfare to form the "International Union for Child Welfare" (IUCW).

The new Union was a federation of national and international organizations, both voluntary and statutory, pledged to make known throughout the world the principles of the Declaration of the Rights of the Child: to relieve children in case of distress, to raise the standards of child welfare and to contribute to the physical, moral and spiritual development of the child. The Union had consultative status with the Economic and Social Council of the U.N. and a similar status with UNESCO, FAO and WHO. The Union was disbanded on 15 April 1986, allegedly for reasons of internal financial management.

The "International Save the Children Alliance" (ISCA) was formed partly as a consequence of a joint response to the 1976 earthquake in Guatemala by several Save the Children organizations. It was formally registered in Denmark in 1979. The founders were the British, American, Danish, Norwegian and Canadian Save the Children organizations. It now has 22 members. In 1988, the General Assembly of the Alliance decided to relocate the office of the Alliance from Denmark to Geneva, with a sub-office in New York.

The purposes of the Alliance are to represent the Save the Children Movement internationally, to coordinate activities of common interest, to offer members mutual support and to protect the logo and name. The full membership of the Alliance meets annually to exchange views on policy matters and other information related to members' field operations, fundraising and other matters. The Alliance secretariat has represented its members' interests in U.N. and NGO fora on issues such as refugee children, children in armed conflict, sexually-exploited children, street and homeless children. It has assisted in the preparation of the U.N.

---

[15] K. Freeman, op.cit., pp. 150–151.

Convention on the Rights of the Child, promoted its adoption and will monitor its implementation[16].

A few recent examples of current programmes of members of the Alliance in 1988-1989 follow[17].

In the field of health, SCF Malawi has a nutrition intervention programme in Blantyre which is aimed at 5,000 children and 2,000 women. In Burkina-Faso, the Dutch member of the Alliance started an immunization programme, which is now being integrated into the primary health care programme of three provinces. It also supports a primary health care project in rural Mexico. Save the Children Egypt has established physiotherapy clinics for the deaf and blind; its Centres of Integrated Services for Families and Children comprise a day nursery, day care facilities, a children's club and a club for elderly citizens. SCF/Egypt also runs workshops in family planning, literacy training and productive workshops for young women.

Red Barnet, the Danish Save the Children group, has established a leprosy project in the Amazon region of Peru. The Dominican Republic Foundation set up a major Child Survival Programme, to reduce morbidity and mortality in mothers and children. In collaboration with the U.S. member and the UNHCR, SCF Malawi has implemented a food security programme for Mozambican refugees. SCF/Mauritius joined other members in mobilizing support for flood victims in Bangladesh and the Sudan, as well as providing funds for emergency relief and long-term development in these countries.

The mandate of the Swedish group, Rädda Barnen, is to defend the rights of the child worldwide. It combines development cooperation and education with advocacy. Its development programme concentrates on the right to health and on the protection of children in difficult circumstances, such as refugee children, children in armed conflict, and other marginalized groups such as street children.

While the SCF Movement is non-political and non-sectarian, its Swedish branch is known to be more activist and outspoken in sensitive political human rights issues than other national branches, and than the Alliance itself.

For instance, in May 1990, the Swedish group published a report accusing Israel of major human rights violations against children during the 30 months of the Arab uprising in the occupied territories, including its responsibility in the deaths of more than 150 children. The report supported arguments by some Israelis and human rights groups that the Israeli army had used excessive force against protesting youths in violation of its own regulations.

The Israeli Government spokesman said in response that SCF was an organization that had shown itself in the past to be biased against Israel[18].

---

[16] *ISCA, Annual Report, 1989, Save the Children Information Sheet 6.* An interview was also held with the ISCA representative in Geneva on 17 Jan. 1990.

[17] *ISCA, Annual Report, 1989.*

[18] *International Herald Tribune,* 17 May 1990.

A Charter for Children

In 1923, Jebb drafted, near Geneva, her "Charter of the Rights of the Child", known as the "Declaration of Geneva" (see Table 5.1).

It declared that men and women of all nations accept as their duty an obligation of assistance and protection of the child, while the child will be brought up in the consciousness that its talents will be devoted to the service of its fellow men.

In drafting this Declaration, Jebb wanted to give a focus, a unifying principle to a growing interest in international child welfare. In substance, her rationale was that children are the most important part of mankind, as they are the nations of tomorrow.

If they are allowed to grow up stunted or neglected or strangers to moral values, or are ignored in their misery by the more fortunate, they will inevitably grow up to hate and destroy, and tomorrow's world can only end up in disaster, politically and economically[19].

Table 5.1. The Declaration of Geneva

By the present Declaration of the Rights of the Child, commonly known as the Declaration of Geneva, men and women of all nations, recognizing that Mankind owes to the Child the best that it has to give, declare and accept it as their duty to meet this obligation in all respects:

I. THE CHILD must be protected beyond and above all considerations of race, nationality or creed.
II. THE CHILD must be cared for with due respect for the family as an entity.
III. THE CHILD must be given the means requisite for its normal development, materially, morally and spiritually.
IV. THE CHILD that is hungry must be fed, the child that is sick must be nursed, the child that is physically or mentally handicapped must be helped, the maladjusted child must be re-educated, the orphan and the waif must be sheltered and succoured.
V. THE CHILD must be the first to receive relief in times of distress.
VI. THE CHILD must enjoy the full benefits provided by social welfare and social security schemes, must receive a training which will enable it, at the right time, to earn a livelihood, and must be protected against every form of exploitation.
VII. THE CHILD must be brought up in the consciousness that its talents must be devoted to the service of its fellow men.

Source: If Any Man Build, the History of Save the Children Fund, Kathleen Freeman, Hodder and Stoughton, London, 1965, Appendix A, p. 147–148. Declaration drafted in 1923 by Eglantyne Jebb (1876–1928). Revised in 1948.

The International Save the Children Union adopted the Declaration and agreed to sponsor it internationally. In 1924, the Declaration was adopted by the League of Nations: it became the "Charter of Child Welfare of the League of Nations".

At its Fifteenth Assembly in 1934, the League of Nations reaffirmed the Declaration.

[19] K. Freeman, op.cit., p. 41.

In April 1946, the Social, Humanitarian and Cultural (Third) Committee of the U.N. General Assembly approved a resolution which asserted that

> the welfare of children, physically, mentally and spiritually, must be the first concern of every nation, having particular regard to the ravages of two world wars. The terms of the Declaration should be as binding on the peoples of the world today as they were in 1924[20].

On 20 November 1959, the U.N. proclaimed its own Declaration of the Rights of the Child (Resol. 1386(XIV)). It recognized implicitly the work of the International Union and of its founder in part of its Preamble, which reads:

> ...the child, by reason of his physical and mental immaturity, needs special safeguards and care, including appropriate legal protection ... the need for such special safeguards has been stated in the Geneva Declaration of the Rights of the Child in 1924, and recognized in the Universal Declaration of Human Rights and in the statutes of specialized agencies and international organizations concerned with the welfare of children ...

In 1979, the International Year of the Child, Poland initiated a proposal for the drafting of a Convention on the Rights of the Child, which would complement the 1959 U.N. Declaration by holding governments legally accountable for meeting the obligations that make the rights meaningful. Many governments, U.N. agencies and a network of some 50 NGOs serviced by "Defence for Children International" assisted in drafting the Convention and in promoting its adoption.

UNICEF related in its 1989 Annual Report that about 100 million children live abandoned by their families, many of them condemned to spending their lives on the streets engaged in hard labour, or eking out a living from various forms of petty crime or prostitution. Of the 13 million child deaths that occur every year, more than a quarter are the result of preventable diseases,—about 45 percent of children under 5 in developing countries are living in absolute poverty: this amounts to some 155 million children,—child abuse plagues many countries,—an estimated 120 million children between the ages of 6 and 11 do not attend school,—drug abuse and the AIDS virus are taking an increasing toll on children.

The Convention on the Rights of the Child was adopted on 20 November 1989 by the U.N. General Assembly (Resol. 44/25) without a vote.

The Convention rests on three building blocks:

— Provision—the right to possess, receive or have access to certain things or services: for instance, a name, a nationality, health care, education, rest and play, care for the disabled and orphaned children;

— Protection—the right to be shielded from harmful acts and practices: for example, separation from parents, commercial or sexual exploitation, physical and mental abuse, engagement in warfare;

---

[20] Quoted by K. Freeman, p. 148, from Edward Fuller's book, *The Rights of the Child*.

— Participation—the child's right to be heard on decisions affecting his life. As capacities evolve, the child should have increasing opportunities to take part in activities of society, as preparation for responsible adulthood.

The Convention includes a modicum of monitoring. The countries that accept the Convention as binding must ensure that their national legislation meet its standards, —they must file and publicize regular progress reports on compliance,—a committee of ten experts elected by the countries that ratify the Convention will review the national reports, ask for more information as needed, and inform the U.N. General Assembly every two years on the status of compliance,—once the Convention standards are built into national laws, governments can require their observance by private institutions and individuals,—equally, the private sector can invoke the laws to ensure the compliance of state agencies.

In January 1990, sixty countries signed the Convention. On 2 September 1990, the Convention came into force: 31 states had ratified the Convention and 103 had signed it[21].

Following the lead of an inspired visionary, Eglantyne Jebb, with the active support of national and international NGOs, the protection of children has now become an international concern, giving children internationally recognized rights and requiring governments to respect their obligations towards them.

Oxfam

Oxfam is another organization born out of the concern of individuals and informal groups for the human suffering and famine caused by a war,—in this case, World War II.

A Historical Review

In September 1942, a group of people met at the Friends (Quakers) Meeting House in Oxford to discuss reports of starvation among the civilian population in enemy-occupied Europe. They formed the "Oxford Committee for Famine Relief": their purpose was to give immediate help through raising funds and supplies, and finding ways and means on how to get the aid to those in need[22].

The Committee was responding to an appeal from the Greek Red Cross to help starving Greek children. 3,200 pounds were raised and sent via the Greek Red Cross Society, and later another 13,000 pounds.

[21] *NGO Bulletin*, U.N./Geneva Doc. INF/NGO/89/31 of 21 Nov. 1989 and U.N. *Press Release* SG/SM/1126, HR/2651 of 30 Aug. 1990.

[22] This historical review is based in part on *A brief history of Oxfam*, Oxfam Information Department, updated Sept. 1989, and Elizabeth Stamp's chapter on "Oxfam and Development", in *Pressure Groups in the Global System*, Peter Willetts Ed., Pinter, London, 1982, pp. 84–104.

In 1944, the British Ministry of Economic Warfare refused to allow the lifting of the Allied naval blockade to send supplies to Greece. A petition with more than 8,000 signatures failed to change the decision. However, the notion was established, or rather, revived, that meeting human needs should override political and military considerations. Meantime, further funds were raised and sent to the Greek Red Cross.

At the end of the War, many people in Europe were hungry and homeless, and many were refugees. The Oxford Committee collected clothes and money and sent them to agencies working on the spot. This way of working, through local groups, rather than running its own programmes, has been Oxfam's main method of operation ever since.

In 1948, the first big national appeal raised 96,692 pounds worth of clothing and goods. The first permanent shop opened in Broad Street, Oxford.

As the situation in Europe improved, the Committee wondered if its task was completed. A strong body of opinion within the group felt that, having fulfilled its initial purpose of aiding war-torn Europe, the organization should close down. Then the State of Israel was created, and many Palestinians became refugees and needed help. The Committee decided that its work could not end. In 1949, a new aim was defined:

> The relief of suffering arising out of war or any other cause in any part of the world.

A permanent Gift Shop manager was appointed at the end of 1949, and in 1950, the Committee obtained the services of a Quaker advertising man who initiated national charity press advertising. Oxfam was thus following the "scientific approach" to charity fundraising and management pioneered by Eglantyne Jebb for Save the Children Fund in the 1920s.

The 1950s were the "clothing years" when Oxfam collected and sent overseas more clothing and supplies than money. In 1949–1950, Oxfam's income was over 1 million pounds, and for the first time, cash income exceeded the value of donated clothing.

The staff had expanded to include regional organizers recruited for World Refugee Year. They collected money and clothing in particular areas of the U.K., and encouraged the formation of local groups. Much of Oxfam's work concerned refugees. Some resulted from man-made disasters: the Korean War, 1950–1953, the Hungarian uprising of 1956, the Algerian War, 1954–1962. 1959–1960 was declared World Refugee Year, and Oxfam contributed over 755,000 pounds to the world-wide effort to resettle displaced persons.

Oxfam also responded to natural disasters. These included drought in Bihar (1951) and an earthquake in the greek Ionian Islands (1953). Severe flooding hit the East coast of England in 1953, and Oxfam helped with clothing and relief. Ever since, Oxfam has made occasional grants to emergencies in the U.K.

In the 1960s, Oxfam became a development agency, while retaining its role in disaster assistance. It supported the Freedom from Hunger Campaign launched by the U.N. in 1960 to improve agriculture and food production in poor countries. Newly independent countries needed long-term development aid: Oxfam decided to help by attacking the causes of hunger, poverty and disease.

An overseas aid officer was appointed in 1958, and in the 1960s, Field Directors were appointed with responsibility for a particular geographic area. This was linked to the expansion of Oxfam's overseas programmes. Longer-term relief and welfare projects required closer assessment and monitoring, involving on-the-spot discussion and contacts. Field Directors were appointed for Eastern and Southern Africa, and countries in Asia and Latin America.

By the end of the 1960s, there were 11 Field Directors around the world.

According to Stamp[23], the Field Directors play a key role in Oxfam's overseas programmes. No project is supported unless a Field Director has visited and investigated the project. Field Directors monitor the implementation of projects and they may also seek out possible projects for funding.

According to an OECD report[24], the functions of Field Directors include the identification of smaller especially deprived groups in areas of the country not assisted by other agencies. Once small community groups are identified, the experience of Field Directors is that they can realistically absorb only quite small amounts of funds. It may look questionable from a purely cost-effective standpoint for a Field Director to travel several thousands of miles yearly searching for tiny projects. For the OECD report,

> the answer lies with the "philosophy" of the agency, which seeks opportunities for providing grants as catalytic inputs to processes which it sees as being the responsibility of local groups. In fact, grants from Oxfam frequently figure among lists of early donors to groups which later became significant NGOs within developing countries.

Oxfam chose from the start not to implement projects itself but fund small local initiatives, averaging about 1.000 pounds each in the early 1980s, although it provides on occasion sizable amounts for emergencies and development.

For instance, Oxfam has provided support to a Roman Catholic Mission in Dubbo, Ethiopia, since 1976. The Mission's work started in the late 1950s with a school and a church, and in 1960, a small clinic. Since 1984, Oxfam grants have provided food supplies, salary for a water team, support for agriculture and women's programmes, health projects etc.

Oxfam supports a local Indian Association for Leprosy Education, Rehabilitation and Treatment (ALERT) in Bombay. Between 1981 and 1984, Oxfam contributed 94,368 pounds: this included grants for office and clinic furnishings, drugs, transport and educational supplies as well as salaries[25].

[23] E. Stamp, op.cit., p. 87.

[24] Organization for Economic Cooperation and Development (OECD) Report on *Voluntary Aid for Development -The role of NGOs*, Paris, 1988, pp. 22–23.

[25] *Oxfam Projects—Sidamo 99, Ethiopia*, 20 March 1989, and *Maharashtra 86, India*, Dec. 1988.

By the end of 1987, Oxfam's field offices numbered 35, covering about 70 countries. With prolonged experience and familiarity with local communities and groups, Field Directors progressively acquire an expertise in community development which enables them to identify and stimulate promising initiatives.

For instance, the discernment of Oxfam in devoting a high share of its health aid to primary health care from the early 1970s has been ascribed in part to the experience and active stance of its Field Directors.

Project applications are reviewed by Oxfam "Field Committees" in London, composed of experts in different fields. These Committees are responsible for making grants and for the development of overseas policy.

In 1961/1962, Oxfam was helping over 400 projects in more than 50 countries, mostly in Asia, Africa and the Middle East. Ten years later, the number had doubled and included more than 150 projects in Latin America and the Caribbean. By then, the majority of projects were longer-term. Family planning support has been included since 1965.

Oxfam continued to help in disasters, such as the ex-Belgian Congo decolonization crisis in 1960 and following years, and the Nigeria/Biafra civil war in 1967–1970: both caused famine and refugees.

In 1965, the Oxford Committee for Famine Relief became "Oxfam".

In order to help long-term schemes, fund-raising in the U.K was strengthened. By 1965, twenty Regional Organisers helped coordinate the activities of over 400 Oxfam groups. Gift shops, selling goods donated by the public, were 200 by 1970. Oxfam's trading company "Oxfam Activities" was founded in 1965 to handle goods like Christmas cards and tea towels. It also imports handicrafts from developing countries. Income increased from 1 million pounds in 1959/1960 to 3 1/4 million pounds by the end of the 1960s.

In 1974, Oxfam's Council of Management agreed that up to 5 percent of the income could be spent on educating people in the U.K. about the causes of world poverty.

Oxfam continued to help in disasters: the vast Bengal refugee crisis during the Bangladesh war of independence; the "hidden" famine in Ethiopia in 1973; the Guatemalan earthquake of 1976 when Oxfam made grants of over one million pounds for the first time; the Indian cyclone of 1977; the Burmese refugee problem in Bangladesh in 1978 and the Vietnamese Boat People in 1979. The late 1970s and early 1980s saw the influx of refugees into Sudan and Somalia; the Karamoja famine in Uganda which followed the overthrow of Idi Amin and the suffering and hardship in Lebanon in 1982/1983.

As a result of experience gained in disasters, technology devised by Oxfam in association with other specialists has produced an emergency sanitation unit, a water supply kit, well drilling and water testing kits, and selective feeding procedures which have all been tested and are ready for use in other emergencies.

A major event in Oxfam's history came in 1979 when the organization was involved in alerting the world to the situation in Cambodia following the ousting of

Pol Pot. Oxfam moved quickly to provide rehabilitation assistance. A consortium of 31 voluntary agencies was formed to mount a joint aid effort: in the two years of its existence, assistance worth over 20 million pounds was sent. With the immediate rehabilitation programme completed and the consortium disbanded, Oxfam moved into the longer-term development phase and appointed a Field Director based in Phnom Penh.

By 1987, nearly 235 million pounds had been sent to projects overseas in the 45 years of Oxfam's existence. The network of shops reached more than 800, and there were some 21 area offices in the U.K. and Ireland. 2,400 overseas projects received support in 77 different countries in 1986–1987. Oxfam had 33 field offices with increasing numbers of locally recruited staff. Most projects are run by local people rather than by expatriates, with funds being invested in people—paying training costs and salaries for key workers—rather than for capital items.

However, Oxfam still recruits a limited number of expatriate volunteers. In recent years, like other emergency relief NGOs, Oxfam has maintained a disaster register of "volunteers"—medical and technical personnel who can go overseas at short notice on short-term disaster assignments. Since the early 1980s, Oxfam has been recruiting longer-term specialist staff to work overseas under UNHCR auspices, notably with the boat people refugees in Malaysia, and with refugees in Somalia. Similarly with the World Food Programme in Uganda, Oxfam has provided logistics staff to help with the movement of supplies to drought-stricken Karamoja. This reflects the fact that an NGO like Oxfam can recruit personnel for service overseas more cheaply and speedily than a U.N. organization can. Oxfam has also recruited doctors to go out to Zimbabwe to reopen mission hospitals after independence. As noted by Stamp[26], to a limited extent, Oxfam has gone "operational" with more than a hundred personnel working overseas in 1980.

Oxfam Now

Oxfam is the number one British Charity in terms of voluntary income (approximately 41 million pounds in 1988) and total expenditures (approximately 48.5 million pounds in 1988), leaving the Salvation Army, Save the Children, Christian Aid and the British Red Cross Society well behind[27].

Oxfam, said its present Director, Frank Judd, is a team:

Approximately 25,000 volunteers serving in more than 770 shops, others working in Oxfam offices, several hundred thousand individual subscribers, more than 40,000 supporters who, by deeds of covenant, guarantee an income of 5 million pounds per year, a growing number of people developing their understanding of Third World problems through "Oxfam 2000" (a campaigning

[26] E. Stamp, op.cit., p. 98.
[27] *Charity Trends*, op.cit., pp. 100–101.

network) and "Hungry for Change" groups: all this, supported by a dedicated staff, is the key to Oxfam's strength[28].

Besides its volunteers, Oxfam employs about 800 paid staff in the U.K., and 130 abroad.

Oxfam is a secular organization, although it was initially closely associated with the Quakers: its first Director, Sir Leslie Kirkley, was a Quaker. It is a non-specialist agency: it is not an organization specialized in medical work, or in child welfare only: it deals with most aspects of relief and development assistance. It is essentially non-operational, although it has Field Directors in 34 developing countries. It is not committed to any single political ideology, although it has taken political positions on a number of occasions. It is not tied to any rigid constitution. Its flexibility and openness have enabled Oxfam to be involved in a wide range of initiatives in more than 80 countries, over more than 40 years.

Oxfam's main objective is

to relieve poverty, distress and suffering in any part of the world and in connection therewith to educate the public concerning the nature, cause and effects of poverty.

Oxfam provides people in the U.K. as well as overseas with the opportunity of playing a small part in a much larger struggle to eliminate poverty and to help mankind develop in a spirit of love, brotherhood and solidarity[29].

Oxfam's main priority is long-term development—helping small groups and organizations to create and sustain their own opportunities for change and improvement in their living and working conditions.

Oxfam projects are aimed at two targets. They are designed

— for the poorest to *have more*, particularly in terms of food and health, and control of a fair share of the world's resources, and
— for the poorest to *be more* in terms of confidence and ability to manage their own future, and their status in society at large.

Oxfam exists to serve people, not to promote a set of ideas. Compassion, the humanitarian impulse, must be tempered with realism and not degenerate into mere sentimentality.

Oxfam prefers to work through local voluntary agencies: field staff are encouraged to find, stimulate and help indigenous organizations, locally organized community development and adult literacy groups.

In the health field, Oxfam gives priority to a preventive approach while accepting that basic curative services are an essential part of any health system. Within

---

[28] *Ways you can help Oxfam as a volunteer—Help*, Oxfam Publ., May 1988.
[29] *Oxfam in Action*, Doc. OX476, and *Oxfam Report and Accounts for the year ended 30th April 1988*.

the primary health care concept, special emphasis is given to the problems of leprosy and the disabled[30].

Oxfam's Politics

In contrast with Save the Children's generally neutral attitude in international politics, some of Oxfam's positions, projects, publications and public pronouncements have shown that the organization often "takes sides".

An observer[31] noted that NGOs do not have to represent national interests but can be active champions of the oppressed and directly engage in the political dimensions of development, such as consciousness-raising and empowerment at the project level, and development education and advocacy at the institutional level:

> Oxfam most closely approximated this ideal as its politically explicit community outreach program had as high a priority as its overseas development work. Because Oxfam does not have an ongoing field presence, it can work in controversial situations more easily without threats of reprisal or deportation. Oxfam keeps its distance from governments and identifies strongly with popular movements for social change.

A few examples of criticisms or disobedience against governments' authorities follow.

During the Biafra Civil War in 1967–1970, Oxfam and Christian Aid implicitly criticized Britain's seemingly unreserved support of the Lagos Government. Telegrams were sent to the British Prime Minister, M.P.s lobbied, press statements issued, and the public urged to bring pressure on the politicians themselves.

Lissner revealed that it was an Oxfam field officer in the drought-stricken province of Wollo who leaked the news to the world press, via The Guardian, that the Ethiopian Government was deliberately covering up the deaths of thousands of people by starvation in the Tigre and Wollo provinces in the Spring and Summer of 1973[32].

Oxfam's financial support of the Union of Palestinian Medical Relief Committees cannot be considered purely "neutral" by the Israeli authorities. The Union is a network of volunteer doctors, nurses and health workers who give their free time to provide both curative medical care and health education to villages

---

[30] *Oxfam Handbook Section Booklet 1 — Oxfam Overseas Programme — Objectives and Strategies,* 1980, and *Oxfam and Health.*

[31] Warren A. Van Wicklin III, "Private Voluntary Organizations as Agents of Alternative Development Strategies: Existing Constraints and Future Possibilities", Paper presented to the 31st Annual Convention of the International Studies Association, Washington D.C., April 10–14, 1990, p. 15.

[32] Jorgen Lissner, *The Politics of Altruism — A Study of the Political Behaviour of Voluntary Development Agencies,* LWF, Geneva, 1977, pp. 214, 220.

throughout the West Bank and Gaza. The uprising ("intifada") in the Occupied Territories has placed extra demands on the Committees. The Oxfam Review for 1987–1988 justifies Oxfam intervention by stating that

> Throughout the Occupied Territories many Palestinians suffer from poor health as the services provided by the Israeli military authorities and by the U.N. are rudimentary and inadequate.

As shown above, Oxfam was instrumental in alerting the world to the situation in Cambodia following the Pol Pot's overthrow in 1979, and in providing short- and long-term assistance to the Vietnam-supported Government. In January 1989, delegations from all parts of the U.K. travelled to London in support of Oxfam's Cambodia campaign, to meet officials at a number of Embassies and at the Foreign and Commonwealth Offices. At each of the Embassies, which included China, Vietnam, the U.S.A., the U.S.S.R., Indonesia and France, the delegations urged the importance of international action to safeguard Cambodia's future (e.g. to prevent the return to power of the Khmer Rouge forces)[33].

In November 1989, the Director of Oxfam urged the U.N. to try to stop refugee food aid being channelled to Chinese-backed Khmer Rouge guerrillas fighting to recapture power in Cambodia. Frank Judd said that the U.N. was supplying refugee camps which were controlled by the Khmer Rouge and that these supplies were being used for the supply of food to the fighting Khmer Rouge.

Also in November, 85 IGOs and NGOs asked the Secretary-General of the U.N. to declare vacant the seat of Cambodia: a symbolic request which was not in the power of the Secretary-General to accede to[34].

Some of Oxfam's publications address overtly or indirectly international politics and politically sensitive international development issues.

The authors of "The Poverty of Diplomacy — Kampuchea and the Outside World", and "Punishing the Poor — The International Isolation of Kampuchea" call for the international community to work for an end to the isolation of a people who have already suffered too much, after the destructive regime of the Khmer Rouge.

Other publications focus on "Conflict and Poverty in Southern Africa" and the apartheid rule in South Africa and Namibia. Oxfam has advocated sanctions against South Africa. The Sandinista's Nicaragua and its major social advances are the subject of three Oxfam books.

Third World development problems and the responsibility of the wealthier nations for the poverty of the underdeveloped countries are brought out in the publication "For Richer For Poorer — Western Connections with World Hunger": the book investigates how the debt crisis and economic policies of the world's wealthier nations are creating mounting poverty in the Third World.

---

[33] *Oxfam News*, Spring 1989.
[34] *International Herald Tribune*, 13 Nov. 1989, *Le Monde*, 17 Nov. 1989.

Oxfam has had a particularly activist, pro-Third World, stance in Third World public health issues.

Oxfam helped to launch the International Baby Food Action Network (IBFAN) to campaign for governments and WHO to encourage breast feeding and to regulate commercial promotion of milk substitutes. It thus opposed powerful multinationals (including Nestlé) and the U.S.A, which was the only country to vote against the WHO Code of Marketing for Breast-milk Substitutes at the World Health Assembly in May 1981[35].

Following research in Asia, Latin America and the Middle East, Oxfam found that unethical promotion of drugs withdrawn or restricted in the North, and of unnecessary, overpriced multivitamins and tonics, together with inconsistent standards of information, and the inertia of the medical profession and of governments, were

facets of a massive exploitation of vulnerable people everywhere.

Oxfam's research was published in 1982 as "Bitter Pills—Medicines and the Third World Poor" in which the Oxfam author calls for greater international control of pharmaceutical sales and promotion.

Oxfam then started the "Rational Health Campaign", aimed at a reform of attitudes and practices concerning the use and supply of medicines. It offered a "ready-made solution": the WHO's Essential Drugs Concept. This Concept demonstrated that by prioritising drugs to match real health needs, and through careful purchasing of off-patent generic drugs, even very poor countries could afford to meet their requirements more safely and effectively than before. It proposed a model list of about 220 drugs sufficient to meet priority needs, and identified 30 or 40 drugs for use in primary health care.

Oxfam recalled that the Essential Drugs Concept challenged a multi million pound industry, and caused an international furore when first implemented in the private sector in Bangladesh in 1982.

Oxfam justified its involvement in the Essential Drugs issue by saying that, as a U.K. based organization, it could contribute to change, since the U.K. is a major drug-producing and exporting nation. Five years after the launching of the Rational Health Campaign, Oxfam concluded that the conduct of a controversial and specialized campaign had not harmed Oxfam's good name: rather the reverse was true.

Oxfam is also active in the sensitive and also controversial area of birth control and family planning. The organization found, like WHO, that simply handing out contraceptives or performing sterilizations do not achieve lasting success. The most effective family planning services are those provided in the context of general mother and child health programmes. For example, Oxfam gave a 3,500 pounds

[35] See "International Health and Transnational Business: Conflict or Cooperation?", by Steven Leonard (Y. Beigbeder's pseudonym) in International Review of Administrative Sciences, 3/1983, pp. 259–268.

grant to the Family Planning Association of Pakistan to launch an education campaign on family planning and its practice. Oxfam funded in 1986 a family planning
clinic for men in Nairobi, to offer advice and contraceptive supplies to men[36].

Besides the social and cultural obstacles to such campaigns, birth control and
family planning programmes have been criticized or condemned by religious
groups and by such governments as the U.S.A., insofar as such programmes
included abortion.

Oxfam Finances in 1988

Oxfam raised 52 million pounds in the year ended on 30 April 1988. This was an
increase of 24 percent over the previous year.

Approximately two-fifth of its income was provided by the sales of donated
goods from Oxfam's more than 800 shops, less expenses, and trading profits from
Oxfam Activities Ltd. About one third of the total income was produced by
covenants, legacies, campaigns, appeals and other donations.

Less than 10 percent (4,9 million pounds) was provided by the British
Government through the Overseas Development Administration. This proportion
reflects Oxfam's policy of restricting the share of national public sector funding in
its annual budget to less than 10 percent, to maintain its autonomy[37].

The European Economic Community's contribution amounted to almost 3
million pounds. Both the British Government and the European Community contributed to Oxfam's overseas aid through their co-funding schemes. Selected projects are financed on a pound-for pound basis.

Expenditures on fundraising and administration constituted 16 percent of total
income. 63 percent of 1988 overseas funds were allocated to Africa. Total overseas
funds were allocated to:

— agriculture projects   – 8 percent
— health projects   – 15 percent
— social development, education, income generation   – 32 percent
— emergencies   – 45 percent[38]

Oxfam's Relations with Other Organizations

Oxfam has had consultative status, category II, with the U.N. Economic and Social
Council since the mid-sixties. Its most extensive contacts with U.N. organizations,
such as UNRWA, UNHCR, FAO, WHO and UNICEF, have been at the grassroot
level. The Oxfam Field Directors establish close working relationships with UNDP

[36] *Oxfam Project—Birth Control and Family Planning: Some Oxfam-supported projects*, 26 May
1987.
[37] *OECD Report*, op.cit., p. 31.
[38] *Oxfam Report and Accounts for the year ended 30 April 1988* and *Oxfam Review, 1987 –1988.*

Resident Representatives and representatives of other IGOs at country or regional level. Oxfam also works closely in the field with other NGOs: for instance, it is closely associated with Save the Children in Mozambique.

Oxfam is a member of the International Council of Voluntary Agencies in Geneva, and of the Liaison Committee of Development NGOs to the European Community in Brussels. Oxfam is a member of the Licross/Volags Steering Committee for Disasters created in 1972 (see Chapter 2).

In 1982, Oxfam joined other organizations in setting up the Independent Group on British Aid, a group of development experts who analyze the British Government's aid programme and produce recommendations.

The Disasters Emergency Committee

The Committee was set up in 1963 to provide British aid agencies with a channel of cooperation for emergency relief overseas after large-scale disasters. The Committee met after major disasters, shared information, discussed their planned response and, where appropriate, undertook joint action. It also served to coordinate fundraising efforts of the charities so as to avoid competition and provide a focus for the public's response. To that end, arrangements were made with the broadcasting authorities for the making of television appeals and with the banks and the Post Office for the receipt of donations.

The Committee itself is not a registered charity, but it is recognized by the Charity Commissioners as the operative agency through which the charities jointly launch television appeals to the public over the national networks following a major disaster overseas. It remains an informal body used by its members as a focus for coordination and consultation on disasters and related issues.

The full members of the Committee are: The British Red Cross Society, the Catholic Fund for Overseas Development, Christian Aid, Oxfam and the Save the Children Fund. The Foreign and Commonwealth Office, the London office of the UNHCR and the British Refugee Council are observer members. Since its establishment in 1974, the Disaster Unit of the Ministry of Overseas Development (now the Overseas Development Administration (ODA) within the Foreign Office) has also been represented and works closely with the Committee. On a number of occasions the Government has channelled aid through the Committee or assisted by arranging air freight and allowing member agencies to fill the space with relief supplies as part of a joint effort. The ODA pays a grant towards the running costs of the Committee's Secretariat, which is located at the Headquarters of the British Red Cross Society and staffed by Red Cross personnel.

Following television and radio appeals, as funds become available, each member charity is generally allocated an equal share of the appeal proceeds, depending on the extent of each agency's involvement in the affected country[39].

---

[39] *Information Note on the Disasters Emergency Committee*, April 1987.

CHAPTER 6

RELIGIOUS AGENCIES

If the main purpose of the Christian church is to create "a fellowship of believers whose members assemble together for common worship"[1] and if some Christians have long contended that they are only "pilgrims and strangers" on this earth, the extension of church activities from the purely religious evangelism and worship into assistance and development was not self-evident. Still many Christians, since the origins of Christianity, have made it their duty, and sometimes their main activity, following the "Great Healer", to provide charitable assistance to the poor and the sick.

Relief, education and health care (for the latter, see Chapter 7) outside of Europe and North America were originally carried out by the religious orders, and later by the mission societies. Then specific denominational or interdenominational, national or international, Christian organizations were set up for religious and assistance purposes.

The Society of Friends, founded in the 17th century, carries out relief assistance in addition to its advocacy for peace and human rights.

The activities of the Salvation Army, a separate Christian Church created in 1865, have been reviewed in Chapter 5 as a British-born Charity.

The modern Roman Catholic pioneers were Caritas, Germany founded in 1897, followed by Caritas, Switzerland (1901) and others, which now form Caritas Internationalis, created in 1951.

On the Protestant side, the General Evangelical Lutheran Conference set up in 1869 and the International Missionary Council, created in 1921, were the forerunners of the present Lutheran World Federation and the World Council of Churches, created respectively in 1947 and 1948.

The two World Wars created an impetus for an increase in the activities of church-related aid societies, as did the First Development Decade, in view of the dramatic needs for relief and refugee assistance.

---

[1] Quoted by George H.T. Kimble in *Tropical Africa*, Vol. 2, Twentieth Century Fund, New York, 1960, p. 202.

210

Among others, World Vision International was established in 1950 as an Christian inter-denominational, international, humanitarian organization.

As noted in an OECD report[2], the churches were innovators, in the late 1960s in promoting the concept of "partners" in developing countries. Their first partners were the national churches overseas, which in many countries were re-shaped following independence, implying changes in relationships with sister churches in the industrialized countries. Churches were the originators, and, by the virtue of the universality of their constituencies, powerful vehicles of many of the values shared today by a large section of the NGO community. For example, the encyclical letters *Pacem in Terris* (1963) and *Populorum Progressio* (1967) of Popes John XXIII and Paul VI established the principle that human beings are the agents and goals of development and enunciated principles of self-reliance and international solidarity. These documents listed the "legitimate aspirations" of populations in developing and newly independent countries: freedom from poverty, greater assurance of finding their sustenance, health, stable employment, more responsibility, freedom from all oppression, more education, and, in newly independent countries, autonomous growth and dignity, both economic and social, in addition to the political freedom represented by independence. They also underlined the "scandal of crying inequalities" in the sharing of goods and of power. In 1958, the World Council of Churches recommended for the first time the target of 1 percent of industrial countries' national income for financial transfers to developing countries, a target which was later to be adopted by the United Nations (General Assembly Resolution 2626 (XXV), para. 44) and to evolve into the more specific target of 0.7 percent for official development assistance. Protestant churches were invited by the World Council of Churches from 1968 onwards to devote a share of their resources (later specified at 2 percent) to development aid—over and above their aid for developing countries' churches themselves. Sharing was instituted "not as a remedy but as a form of education". In 1981, for example, 416 of the 1,160 parishes of the Dutch Reformed Church devoted 2 percent of their resources to development aid. The vast majority of the church-related NGOs distinguish their religious from their relief or developmental activities, and exclude proselytising from the latter.

However, church-related voluntary agencies have characteristics which distinguish them from secular agencies.

A U.S. Lutheran spokesman has asserted that voluntary religious agencies exist "for reasons which go beyond those of human compassion or enlightened self-interest...the primary thrust of the programme of a voluntary relief agency is that of giving specific witness...to the faith of its constituents"[3].

The Department of World Service of the Lutheran World Federation said in 1963:

[2] *Voluntary aid for development—The role of NGOs*, OECD, Paris, 1988, pp. 19–20.
[3] Testimony of Dr. Paul C. Empie on behalf of the U.S. Lutheran World Relief before the U.S. Senate Foreign Relations Committee in Jorgen Lissner, *The politics of altruism—A study of the political behaviour of voluntary development agencies*, Lutheran World Federation, Geneva, 1977, p. 264.

That which distinguishes from secular welfare organizations more than anything else surely is the *personal witness* of those who are working in the fellowship of our service in *a spirit of Christian dedication* and with *a deep sense of vocation*.

... when measured against the vastness of governmental and intergovernmental assistance schemes, the contribution Christian services agencies can make seems to fade almost into insignificance. It is the more important, therefore, that that which quantitatively is relatively small contains *a quality of motivation and effectiveness* that reflects the *selflessness and devotion* of a love inspired by Him who said of Himself that "He did not come to be served but to serve".

In 1989, the report of an International Development Consultation organized under the auspices of the Lutheran World Federation added:

If anything distinguishes development work done by Churches from similar efforts carried out by other agencies, it should be the attitude toward the people involved—a "servanthood approach" in addition to the technical and professional qualifications that must be of the same standard as others[4].

As appropriately noted by Lissner[5], critics are prompt to ask what right any church-related agency has to assume that individual Christians working in secular organizations do not display such qualities? One may add that it may be difficult to weigh the relative quality of motivation and effectiveness among Christian and non-Christian volunteers, all being devoted to humanitarian goals.

Representatives of church-related agencies frequently emphasize that their major advantage over governmental and secular agencies is the existence of churches, priests and pastors in virtually every corner of the world. Thus church agencies have direct access to a world-wide network of helpers "on the spot" who can be mobilized quickly at little or no extra cost. This is clearly an important practical advantage in emergency situations as well as in long-term projects.

On the other hand, this practical difference between church-related and secular agencies does not seem to express itself through any major difference in their values or operational objectives.

This Chapter will review some of the major international Christian groups, the Quakers, Caritas Internationalis and the Catholic Relief Services, the World Council of Churches, the Lutheran World Federation and World Vision International.

They all employ national and international volunteers in their assistance and development work. The type of assistance given by the volunteers is of course coloured by the image, policies and actual practices of the sponsoring organization. We will try to identify the characteristics of each of these organizations and assess whether, like some other NGOs, they are, or want to appear, politically neutral, or whether their Christian faith leads them to take position.

---

[4] *Lutheran World Information*, Geneva, No. 41/89.
[5] Lissner, op.cit., pp. 110–111.

As an introduction, we will recall the origin and activities of the Order of Malta, which has successfully evolved from the medieval role of a military/religious/hospital care body to that of a modern international relief organization.

The Order of Malta

The Order was founded before the taking of Jerusalem in 1099 by the armies of the First Crusade. It began as a monastic community, dedicated to St. John the Baptist, which administered a hospice-infirmary for pilgrims to the Holy Land. Under the Blessed Gerard (+1120), it became an independent organization to give religious and hospital care to Christian pilgrims and crusaders in Jerusalem. In 1113, Pope Paschal II approved the confraternity of the Hospital of St. John.

In 1126, military and chivalry duties were added to these functions and in 1130, Pope Innocent II approved its flag, the white octagonal cross (the Maltese cross). The insularity of the Order made it create a powerful fleet from the 13th to the 17th century. The military character of the Order ceased in 1798.

It is officially named the Sovereign Military Hospitaller Order of St. John of Jerusalem, of Rhodes and of Malta, in short the Order of Malta.

The Order is composed of Knights and Dames under the authority of an elected Grand Master: his appointment is subject to the approval of the Pope. The Order is internationally recognized as sovereign and independent of any civil power.

The Order maintains diplomatic relations, through accredited representatives, with the Holy See on which, in its double nature, it depends as religious order, but of which, as a sovereign Order of Knighthood, it is independent. It also exchanges diplomatic representatives with six European, 19 South American, 3 Asian and 20 African countries. It maintains delegations in Belgium, France, the Federal Republic of Germany, Monaco and Switzerland and in the following international organizations: the U.N. in Vienna, UNHCR, UNESCO, WHO, FAO, IOM, ICRC, the Council of Europe and the European Economic Community Commission. Its sovereign, religious and international character allows the Order to be active in most countries of the world.

While never abandoning its aim of the defence of Christendom,

the Order is dedicated to charitable assistance, particularly for those stricken by natural disasters or by war[6].

Through its national associations, the Order operates 200 hospitals, dispensaries and nursery schools. It provides medicaments, food and financial help to refugees.

In general, the Order's activities fall into three categories: leprosy control, care and research, and spiritual assistance to leper patients, — emergency assistance related to natural catastrophes (earthquakes, floods, volcano eruptions), or due to

---

[6] 1988 Annuaire of the Order of Malta—Historical Survey, pp. XVII–XXIII.

man-made conflicts (the 1956 Hungarian revolt, the Vietnam War, Biafra, Northern Ireland, hostages),—permanent assistance to the sick and the wounded, first-aid courses, courses for civil protection, training of stretcher bearers, first-aid stations on highways, home assistance to paralysed patients or patients with respiratory handicaps, blood collection and shipment of medicaments.

The Order has now approximately 10,000 knights and more than one million associate members (volunteers), including about half a million in France alone.

Members of the French association created in 1927 the "Oeuvres Hospitalières Françaises de l'Ordre de Malte "(OHFOM). Its budget amounted to approximately F. Francs 40 million in 1987, financed by donations of members, public donations, the sale of stamps and medals. In addition to the "regular budget", F. Francs 150 million worth of medicaments were dispatched from France to such countries as Lebanon, Poland, Burkina-Faso and Senegal. The shipments were sent through the Order's embassies or through the national Caritas organizations[7].

The OHFOM has activities in France (medical care and research, assistance to handicapped persons, health care courses, shipment of medicaments) and in 47 other countries in Europe, Africa, the Near East, Asia, the Pacific, Central and South America and the Caribbean.

In October 1989, the Knights returned to Malta, the island which they ruled for 268 years until Napoleon I forced them into exile in 1798[8].

The Order pursues its humanitarian mission on both the legal and charitable planes. At the legal humanitarian level, the Order participates in the International Conference of the Red Cross.

The Final Act of the 1929 Geneva Diplomatic Conference contained a recommendation in the following terms: "In view of a request by the Sovereign and Military Order of...Malta the Conference considers that the provisions laid down by the Geneva Convention governing the position of Aid Societies with armies in the field are applicable to the national organizations of this Order". As noted by Macalister-Smith[9], the importance of this provision lay in its extension to the Order of the articles establishing respect and protection for medical units and their materials, transports and personnel.

The Order has provided ambulance corps in every European war since 1864. In World War II, the Order enjoyed a position of neutrality and operated ambulance aircraft, relief trains and hospital ships.

The Order respects the same principle of impartiality as the Red Cross and plays a useful international humanitarian operational role. However, the Order does not have the mandate entrusted to the ICRC in relation to international humanitarian law. Its religious, denominational character and its less universal presence place it

---

[7] *L'Ordre souverain de Malte—Dieu est amour*", No. 109, Nov. 1988.

[8] *International Herald Tribune*, 19 Oct. 1989.

[9] Peter Macalister-Smith, *International Humanitarian Assistance—Disaster Relief Actions in International Law and Organizations*, Martinus Nijhoff, 1985, p. 123.

in a different and more limited category of international humanitarian organization, in parallel to, but outside the mainstream Red Cross Movement.

The role and activities of other Roman Catholic organizations are described later in this Chapter.

The Quakers

The "Religious Society of Friends", as a branch of the universal Christian church, provides humanitarian assistance, like other Christian denominations, besides purely religious and other advocacy activities. It pursues a policy of unobtrusive international humanitarianism based on strict principles of neutrality and impartiality.

The Society of Friends was founded by George Fox following a spiritual discovery in 1647 in England. Its world membership now totals approximately 240,000, with Friends in 56 countries.

The essential feature of the Society is that it is a non-hierarchical worshipping community, without priests or pastors.

In 1937, Friends established the "Friends World Committee for Consultation" (FWCC), the international body created to facilitate communication between the independent groups of Friends. FWCC has been granted consultative status with the U.N. Economic and Social Council (Category II). Its goals are

> to facilitate loving understanding of diversities among Friends while we discover together, with God's help, our common spiritual ground,—to facilitate full consideration of our Quaker witness in response to today's issues of peace and social justice[10].

The Quakers' Advocacy

Friends have consistently maintained their testimony against war, first enunciated in a declaration issued in 1661. This testimony has led them to refuse military service and to develop alternative forms of service in wartime, both for their own members and for others who share their pacifist convictions.

For instance, the American Friends Service Committee was founded in 1917 to provide conscientious objectors with an opportunity to aid civilian victims during World War I.

With this long history of opposition to war, Friends are keen supporters of international peace-keeping institutions, such as the League of Nations and the U.N.

---

[10] Friends World Committee for Consultation *Booklet* and *The People called Quakers*, by Duncan Wood.

The Friends militate for peace and disarmament, for the abolition of the death penalty (like Amnesty International). The influential Quaker United Nations Office in Geneva (QUNO) participates in various U.N. bodies' meetings, such as the U.N. Commission on Human Rights, its Sub-Commission on Prevention of Discrimination and Protection of Minorities, the Committee against Torture, Disarmament sessions.

QUNO has been instrumental in including an article (Art. 38) in the 1989 U.N. Convention on the Rights of the Child to restrict the recruitment and participation in armed conflicts of children under 15. QUNO has served as a resource to an international network of academics, journalists and activists concerned with promoting the Chemical Weapons Convention.

Humanitarian Work

Friends have undertaken extensive relief and rehabilitation programmes during World War II, — to Palestinian Arab refugees, prior to the establishment of UNRWA, — in Algeria, after the end of hostilities[11].

The Friends have established permanent organs for the administration of relief and other forms of service, notably the American Friends Service Committee (AFSC) in the United States, and the Friends Service Council (FSC) in London which were jointly awarded the Nobel Peace Prize in 1947. The Friends Service Council was incorporated with the Friends Peace and International Relations Committee to form the present Quaker Peace and Service (QPS) in 1978.

The aims of QPS are

to enable committed people, young and old, to contribute in a practical way to reducing both the causes and results of violence, suffering and mutual misunderstanding; to promote human rights and a more equitable sharing of the world's resources; to respond to human need, from a war-battered child to a perplexed statesman; to work closely with like-minded organizations and thereby to increase public awareness of particular problems.

Friends have collaborated closely and continuously with UNHCR in the solution of refugee problems in Europe, Asia, Africa and Latin America.

Assistance and development is mainly carried out by national staff, assisted, if need be, by international "coordinators", representatives or specialists. Funds may also be provided by the Quaker organizations as well as supplies.

For instance, Friends from the U.K. and the U.S.A. have been working in the Horn of Africa in order to assist Ethiopian refugees. In 1982, a joint agreement

---

[11] *The background to Quaker work at the U.N.*, Duncan Wood, 1987. See also the *Annual Report—Quaker Peace and Service 1989*.

between AFSC, QPS and the Somali government resulted in the setting up of two projects: one at Darye Macaane camp for Ethiopian refugees, coordinated by QPS, and one for which AFSC was responsible, Springs Development Project in the North-East. The latter was concerned with the development of community water resources.

Two expatriate QPS workers started work in 1982 in Darye Macaane to assist refugees in developing skills to reduce their dependence on food aid. They provided training in elementary horticulture. They worked through their local staff who were trained in community development methods. Unlike most expatriates, the QPS workers, like U.S. Peace Corps or U.N. volunteers, lived in a hut within the camp, adopting a simple life-style and living in close proximity to the problems faced by the refugees.

In April 1988, the Southern African International Affairs Quaker Representative helped arrange a visit to Zimbabwe by nine development workers from South African church groups. The visit helped the participants gain a sense of what they were fighting for, not only against, of how others had struggled for change, and problems they could expect in a post-Apartheid South Africa[12].

In October 1988, AFSC sent a Canadian physiotherapist to work with the Union of Palestinian Medical Relief Committees in the West Bank.

Also in 1988, an AFSC Health Training Programme was initiated in the Philippines. The two programme staff are a Philippino couple.

Material and financial assistance has been provided by the Friends in response to natural disasters. For instance, in 1988: AFSC purchased and shipped 380 tons of Thai rice to a province in Laos for distribution to farmers, whose rice harvest had been reduced by the drought. Following the flooding in Bangladesh, $2,500 were sent to an integrated rural development group that grew out of Quaker work in the 1970s. After the destruction caused by hurricanes Gilbert and Joan in the Caribbean in September and October 1988, AFSC joined with Oxfam-America to send a cargo flight to Nicaragua containing 50,000 pounds of relief supplies and reconstruction tools. Prosthetic supplies were sent to help re-supply several regional physical rehabilitation centres in Southern Vietnam. Two large shipments of clothing and school supplies went to refugees in the Gaza Strip.

In the development field, the Friends established in 1967 Hlakweni in Zimbabwe as a centre offering training in a broad variety of agricultural, rural and domestic skills to local people. The Centre receives annual grants from QPS and from other agencies. The permanent staff are all Zimbabwean: QPS and other agencies send international workers there as required.

In 1961, AFSC sent young volunteers to work in developing countries in the VISA programme, a forerunner to the U.S. Peace Corps Programme.

However, the Friends are not a major recruitment agency for international volunteers. True to the "self-reliance" principle they train and employ nationals to run

---

[12] American Friends Service Committee *International Program Bulletin, Highlights for 1988.*

their projects. Only a few expatriates either initiate projects, monitor them or decide on financial or material aid.

The Quakers' advocacy for peace and their concern for human rights are carried out, like other NGOs, by public appeals and publications, oral and written statements in international meetings and by their pragmatic relief and development work. Their influence and advocacy are mostly applied at the international level. When the Quakers have a clear position, on such areas as disarmament, human rights, refugees and the sharing of world resources, they intervene during debates at the U.N. and inform member states of their concern.

In the AFSC Annual Report for 1987, the agency's Chairman said of his organization that it is not a peace agency, or a relief agency, or a human rights agency:

> it is all of them together, for we believe God calls us to cultivate the whole vineyard.

However, as witnesses for Christ, the Friends do not feel that their field assistance to victims of natural or man-made disasters has to be accompanied by public denunciations of human rights abuses in countries where they work. They wish to maintain their reputation of an impartial, effective humanitarian organization of a religious nature.

Other Roman Catholic Organizations

The international humanitarian umbrella organization of the Roman Catholic Church is "Caritas Internationalis". One of its major national member organizations is "Catholic Relief Services" (CRS), a U.S. NGO with large international programmes. A description of their mandates and activities will show that these, and most other Catholic charities, focus more on Christian service than on politics[13].

Caritas Internationalis

Founded in 1950, Caritas Internationalis (the "International Confederation of Catholic Organizations for Charitable and Social Action) is an international confederation of 120 autonomous national member organizations, directed by its statutes "to spread charity and social justice in the world". It is based in the Vatican.

The root idea of the organization originated in 1947 when the future Pope Paul VI, then Substitute Secretary of State, wanted to ensure a Catholic presence in the field of relief and social welfare. Caritas Internationalis' aim was to provide coordination, information and representation of all the charitable and social welfare efforts of the Church everywhere.

---

[13] B. Holzer and F. Lenoir, *Les risques de la solidarité*, Ed. Fayard, Paris, 1989.

The members of Caritas Internationalis are the national Catholic organizations which have been mandated by their respective Episcopal Conferences to help, develop and sustain the Church's engagement in social service and charitable activities. Each national Caritas is independent and its programme differs according to local needs and conditions.

National organizations pre-existed Caritas Internationalis. Caritas Germany was founded in 1897,—Polish Caritas was founded in 1900 "to serve the poor and the disabled of society, the orphaned, the aged and the blind"[14],—Swiss Caritas was founded in 1901, the Catholic Charities USA in 1910, and Caritas Holland in 1924. By 1957, there were 36 member organizations, and 118 by 1983[15].

Caritas Internationalis is a member of the Conference of International Catholic Organizations and of the Pontifical Council. It has consultative status with the U.N. Economic and Social Council (Category II), UNESCO, FAO, ILO, UNICEF, the Council of Europe, the Organization for African Unity. Caritas Internationalis works closely with the Red Cross, the UNHCR and many other NGOs. In 1980, Caritas Internationalis accepted an invitation to join the "Licross/Volags" Joint Steering Committee for Disasters, which ensures working coordination between the main non-governmental relief organizations based in Geneva. The Committee was formed by the Catholic Relief Services, the Lutheran World Federation, the World Council of Churches, Oxfam and the League of Red Cross and Red Crescent Societies in 1972[16].

The Christian mission of Caritas Internationalis is expressed in the Gospel Beatitudes: Caritas works

> among the powerless, the refugees, the marginals, the hungry, the exiles, the homeless, fostering human promotion and providing the solidarity needed to nourish that hope which alone will enable our less fortunate brothers and sisters to take personal charge of their own lives and destiny and thus achieve that liberty which is their inalienable right as children of God.

As Caritas Internationalis is essentially a representative and coordinating network, only its members can effectively work towards this ideal of Christian clarity and justice.

As an example, Caritas Internationalis launched a reconstruction programme following the Armenian earthquake. The re-building of lodgings was carried out with technical advice from experts of Caritas Germany,—a maternity unit was re-built with the assistance of Caritas Italy,—the funding came from Caritas France ("Secours Catholique"). Also in 1989, Caritas France gave financial help to various African Caritas (Djibouti, Ghana, Madagascar, Malawi) and to Romanian refugees in Hungary[17].

---

[14] Eileen Egan, *Catholic Relief Services—The Beginning Years*, CRS, New York, 1988, p. 156.

[15] Caritas Internationalis leaflet *What it is, What it does*.

[16] Macalister-Smith, op.cit., p. 145.

[17] *Messages du Secours Catholique*, Paris, July-Aug. 1989, No. 417.

Catholic Relief Services (CRS)

CRS was founded in 1943 by the Catholic Bishops of the U.S. to assist the poor and disadvantaged outside the U.S.A. It is the largest private relief agency in the U.S. and one of the largest in the world.

The fundamental motivating force in all CRS activities is the Gospel of Jesus Christ as it pertains to the alleviation of human suffering, the development of people and the fostering of charity and justice in the world. The policies and programmes of the agency reflect and express the teaching of the Catholic Church. At the same time, CRS assists persons on the basis of need, not creed, race or nationality.

CRS fulfils its mission in the following ways:

— by responding to victims of natural and man-made disasters;
— by providing assistance to the poor to alleviate their immediate needs;
— by supporting self-help programmes which involve people and communities in their own development;
— by helping those it serves to restore and preserve their dignity and to realize their potential;
— by collaborating with religious and non-sectarian persons and groups of good will in programmes and projects which contribute to a more equitable society;
— and, by helping to educate the people of the U.S. to fulfil their moral responsibilities in alleviating human suffering, removing its causes, and promoting social justice[18].

CRS is in consultative status with the U.N. Economic and Social Council (Category II).

CRS Finances and Staffing

In 1988, CRS revenues amounted to $288 million, of which:

— 44% was "Food for Peace" given to CRS as authorized by the U.S. Congress for humanitarian purposes,
— 21% represented ocean freight reimbursed by the U.S. government for overseas freight expenses, primarily for the Food for Peace programme,
— 10% was cash grants from the U.S. government for emergency relief and the support of development projects,
— 6% donated by the European Community, U.N. organizations and other governments,
— 19% as private support in cash and material donated by individuals and groups in the U.S.A.

---

[18] Information on CRS is based on its *Annual Reports*, *Spectrum*, CRS quarterly publication, Egan, op.cit., and an interview with the CRS Senior Director, Eurasia, in Geneva on 7 August 1989. He also represents Caritas Internationalis in Geneva.

4/5th of the CRS 1988 budget was therefore financed by government and intergovernmental sources (74% in 1987) which tends to emphasize the governmental, rather than the non-governmental, nature of the organization. One might ask whether CRS is part of the relief arm of the U.S. government, or is it a genuine, independent NGO?

In February 1964, a Lutheran World Federation spokesman, at a hearing of the U.S. House of Representatives, expressed the fear that "voluntary agencies, and especially religious agencies, were becoming instruments of governments". He suggested that the proportion of receipts from government sources should be limited to 50%. In 1962, CRS had taken 82% of its resources from the government, and LWF only 47%. The LWF attack was also addressed against the alleged excessive zeal of Catholic organizations, whose "overriding religious motivations and objectives encompass their humanitarian activities"[19].

While ecumenism has somewhat defused this inter-religious strife, NGOs financial dependence on one government's funds is not healthy. It is in their own interest to try to enlarge the proportion of private donations as well as support from international organizations, which cannot apply the same type of pressure on an NGO as a national government on a national NGO.

In 1988, CRS spent $297 million, the balance over income being taken from prior years' funds. Of these expenditures:

— 62% consisted of development assistance, including nutrition programmes, rural development,water and agricultural projects and community promotion,
— 21% on disaster and emergency relief,
— 7% on general assistance to the aged, ill, orphans and indigents,
— 4% on refugee relief and resettlement,
— 4% on administration,
— and 2% on fund-raising and awareness.

In 1990, an audit carried out by the U.S. accounting firm Price Waterhouse revealed serious financial control problems in the delivery of USAID programme in India, the biggest food relief programme. This programme is sub-contracted to CRS.

The audit showed evidence that some bishops, priests and nuns in India's Roman Catholic Church could have "misused" from $3 to $4 million of U.S. food donations in 1987–1988.

Although CRS disputed the audit's findings, it admitted weak financial management control and initiated changes.

This episode confirms the absolute need for "charities" to apply effective management methods to their programme and financial operations, including permanent monitoring and control. The consequence of faulty management made public is a temporary or permanent loss of image, which may affect the attitude of the present

---

[19] Lissner, op.cit., p. 266.

and potential private and public donors towards this and other NGOs[20].

CRS employs 170 staff members at its Baltimore headquarters and 10 at its Geneva office. 800 are local resident staff in 42 countries, while assistance is addressed directly to local project holders in 26 other countries.

Expatriate volunteers (interns) are limited in numbers (a maximum of 30 at any time) and in tenure (6 month appointments). They receive a stipend.

Past CRS Activities

The CRS (then called War Relief Services) was created on 15 January 1943. Its first project was to respond to the needs of Polish refugees who had been deported by the USSR to Siberia and Asiatic Russia, following the Hitler-Stalin Pact of 1939. Upon pressure of the Allied Powers after the German attack in June 1941, the deportees were "amnestied" and left free. 250,000 were helped by CRS in Iran, India, the Middle East, East Africa, Palestine and Mexico, as temporary or permanent refugees.

Between 1946 and 1948, food, medicaments, blankets and clothing were collected in the U.S.A. and shipped to Poland itself. Over 134,000 people were fed at Caritas' run centres in 1948, and care given to 166,700 children through CRS assistance.

CRS was forced to close its work in Poland by the authorities at the end of 1949, as well as in Czechoslovakia and Hungary. In July 1948, the Romanian government had prohibited all foreign religious interventions on its territory.

When France was liberated, the thousands of Sisters of Charity of St. Vincent de Paul assisted CRS in the distribution of aid to war victims.

In June 1944, CRS conducted a nationwide collection of clothing for war victims in over fifteen thousand U.S. Catholic parishes to be given to displaced and homeless Italians. Food, medicines and vitamins were also provided. From emergency aid, the Italian programme expanded into development, and in 1956, into disaster aid, in response to the river Po's floods, and in 1980, following an earthquake in South Italy.

In 1946, the founding father of CRS, Patrick A. O'Boyle, faced up to the U.S. Secretary of State to prevent the forced closing of Displaced Persons (DPs) camps of Eastern European refugees.

The Western Allies, particularly the U.K. and the U.S. wanted to rid themselves of the DPs problem at the earliest opportunity. UNRRA had been established in 1943 to concern itself with relief, rehabilitation and resettlement of certain groups of DPs. Neither at the Yalta Conference nor in the UNRRA Agreement were there any provisions for people to exercise free choice regarding repatriation or to claim the right of asylum.

After having forcibly and secretly repatriated Soviet citizens and war prisoners

---

[20] *International Herald Tribune*, 26–27 May 1990.

to Soviet authorities in 1946, in accordance with the Yalta Agreements, the Western Allies were left with over 1,5 million Eastern Europeans who also refused repatriation in Soviet-held areas.

According to Eileen Egan[21], a secret UNRRA order, No. 199, indicated that the withdrawal of support from the refugees would in effect force them to return to their homelands.

Following pressure from CRS, the State Department informed the agency that the decision to close the DP camps had been reversed, as well as another UNRRA order to close camp schools.

As from 1946, the CRS- sponsored "Works of Peace" linked Catholic women in the USA to the needs of overseas refugees, the hungry, homeless and displaced, in such countries as Haiti, Kenya and El Salvador. This programme began with emergency relief projects in the wake of war. Towards the end of the 1950s, the programme broadened its scope to include training, development and health programmes for women in the developing world (Egypt, Uganda, Philippines, Korea, Brazil, India).

The second Director of CRS, Edward E. Swanstrom, made an important intervention at the Second Vatican Council which resulted in ensuring coordination of Catholic aid and development agencies through Caritas Internationalis. It was stressed that Catholic charitable support should be part of an overall national development, related to the Catholic Church in the country but integrated on a ecumenical basis with other aid efforts[22].

Current CRS Programmes

CRS has been in India since 1951. The mainstay of its $37 million annual programme is a variety of food projects. Under the "Food for Work" scheme, people are paid in foodstuff for their labour on community projects such as road-building and well-digging. Additionally, lessons in vocational training and adult literacy were given[23].

Emergency relief was provided to Mozambique in 1987: clothing, quilts, medicines, soap, farm supplies, waterwells and pumps for an amount of $100,000. Longer-term development assistance, in cooperation with the Catholic Church in Mozambique, will follow, in the areas of food production and teaching income-generating skills.

In Pakistan, CRS provides funds to a non-profit organization, the Behbud Association, in order to establish a vocational training centre for women, giving courses in tailoring, nutrition and secretarial skills[24].

In 1977, in Thailand, CRS has worked with the Catholic Organization for Emergency Relief and Refugees (COERR), the official body of the Catholic

---

[21] Egan, op.cit., pp. 108, 153–154, 158, 162, 180, 210–217.

[22] Egan, op.cit., p. 288.

[23] CRS *Spectrum*, Fall 1987.

[24] *Spectrum*, Summer 1987.

Bishop's Conference of Thailand. CRS provides financial and management assistance to COERR. The organization's work in the refugees' camps encompasses medical and dental services, food and nutrition education, vocational training and agricultural projects. It also provides emergency assistance during natural disasters. It promotes skills building and food production in the camps.

In 1988, following major floods, CRS channelled emergency assistance through Caritas, Bangladesh, the local development organization CRS helped establish in the 1970s. The staff of Caritas, Bangladesh, aided by 1,000 local volunteers, guided boats to deliver dry food rations, clothing and medicines and to rescue people who were stranded on roofs. It also distributed winter vegetable seeds.

In such emergencies, CRS responds first by filling the immediate needs: temporary shelter, food, clothing and medical care. Later, CRS supplies materials and seeds for the people to start re-building their homes and replanting their fields[25].

CRS has been in Ethiopia since the late 50s. During the 1984-1986 emergency and through the end of 1987, CRS fed up to 2 million people a month, dug wells, distributed seeds, planted trees, trained 400 community health workers for 6 to 12 months each. CRS worked in partnership with the Lutheran World Federation in Ethiopia[26].

The Politics of CRS

CRS is a Christian, denominational organization which works mainly through and with the Catholic Churches and the national Caritas. However, it asserts that it assists persons on the basis of need, not creed, race or nationality. It also affirms that it does not mix evangelization with relief and development work.

CRS representatives also claim that the agency is non-political. Any political statement or position would be taken and expressed by the U.S. Catholic Church, not by CRS.

CRS does not agree with the public denunciations of human rights violations in some countries voiced by some humanitarian organizations, such as one of the "French Doctors" associations, "Médecins du Monde". It believes that any such public stand would endanger the relief operations by arousing the hostility of the host government, at the risk of having to stop all humanitarian activities.

When faced with human rights violations, CRS may consult with the local organizations and Church on the reality of the charges and on the advisability of a reaction. It may also discuss the problem discreetly with the government authorities.

CRS believes that denouncing human rights violations is a responsibility of such organizations as "Amnesty International", not of relief agencies, whose role is different and who have operational responsibilities. This would not prevent an organization like CRS from sending information on local problems in the human rights domain to other interested bodies.

[25] *1988 Annual Report*, CRS, pp. 4, 19.
[26] *Spectrum*, Winter 1988.

In spite of this official position of political neutrality, or abstinence, a relief organization cannot avoid, in all circumstances, having to take sides.

Defending the Eastern European DPs in 1946 and helping them not to be forcibly repatriated to their Soviet-controlled countries of origin, could be interpreted as an anti-Soviet or anti-Communist stance. Feeding the Cambodian refugees, displaced by the Pol Pot regime, was not a neutral act of assistance[27].

The development activities of the Asia Partnership for Human Development (APHD) have been criticized by the Pacific Christian Anti-Communism Crusade. APHD groups development agencies of the Catholic episcopal conferences of 20 countries, and the Federation of Asian Bishops' Conferences. In particular, the allegation that Australian church and overseas aid had been channelled to Communist insurgents in the Philippines was denied in 1989 by the Australian Catholic Bishops Conference.

In countries torn by civil war and violently opposed ideologies, can a relief agency run projects to "conscientize and organize the poor for self-reliance and social amelioration as well as to promote human rights" without been seen as partisan?[28].

Like the World Council of Churches and the Lutheran World Federation, CRS believes in social justice, human rights and economic justice for all. In some countries, these terms have a revolutionary connotation, as they challenge the social and economic *status quo* and privileges. CRS defines social justice as

> that area of justice which focuses on the societal/structural level. It aims at transforming those structures which contribute to oppression and marginality and at establishing or maintaining and supporting those which enhance human dignity[29].

CRS promotes justice and the development of peoples through support to community initiatives in agriculture, cooperative formation, small industries, clean water, leadership training, health and child care.

While "justice" is a broad, general objective, CRS real work is in assistance to operational, grass-roots activities, rather than the more radical and vocal advocacy of some of its non-Catholic partners.

The world-wide Catholic network, its centuries-old structures and traditions, its religious, moral, economic and civic responsibilities, its traditional respect for the established government and the diplomatic caution of the Vatican may explain the differences between the generally restrained positions taken by the Catholic agencies and the more vocal positions taken by the reformist, individualistic Protestant groups.

---

[27] Egan, op.cit., pp. 263–264.

[28] *The Manila Chronicle*, 17 July 1989.

[29] *Teaching towards global understanding and action*, CRS, undated.

The World Council of Churches (WCC)

The WCC is an international ecumenical organization which promotes cooperation between 307 churches of various Christian denominations, excluding the Roman Catholic. This "fellowship of churches" involves encounter, theological study, witness and service. Among the latter, WCC's principal international relief activities are conducted through its Commission on Inter-Church Aid, Refugee and World Service (CICARWS). The WCC Christian Medical Commission also assists the churches in promoting community-based primary health care.

CICARWS initiates and coordinates the recruitment of thousands of national and international staff and volunteers providing humanitarian and development assistance to Third World churches and populations.

The WCC's basic motivation in providing this assistance is a religious conviction, the Christian spirit to bear witness and help those in need, but not the missionary, proselyting urge of past times.

The WCC's Christian conviction goes beyond purely ecumenical efforts to unify the Church, theological research and assistance. It has led the Council to take public position on sensitive international political and economic issues and to provide financial or material assistance to controversial "liberation movements".

A Short History

On 23 August 1948, delegates from 147 churches, gathered in Amsterdam, approved a resolution creating the WCC.

The origin of the ecumenical movement may be traced to the evangelization movement linked to the 18th- and 19th-century revivals in Europe and North America. Confessional rivalry among mission-sending churches convinced many missionaries that division among Christians was a scandal[30].

Following a World Missionary Conference in Edinburgh in 1910, the drive towards unity started to take organizational shape. The Christian "unity" was however limited, at the Conference, to Protestant mission societies, mostly from North America and the U.K.

Three related movements were founded in the 1920s. The "International Missionary Council" (1921) brought together foreign missionary societies and national Christian Councils for study and common action on Christian witness. The "Life and Work Movement" (1925) explored Christian responsibility in the face of burning issues facing society. And the "Faith and Order Movement" (1927) confronted thorny controversies and differences over doctrine and authority which spawn or strengthen church divisions. These movements lay behind the decision in

---

[30] For a history of the WCC by the WCC, see *One World*, No. 138, Aug.Sept. 1988, *And so set up signs...The WCC first 40 years.*

1937 to form a WCC, though its actual formation was delayed for 11 years by World War II.

At the Amsterdam founding Assembly, 146 churches joined, again mostly from Europe and North America. Since 1948, the Council has become more of a world body: Asian, African, Latin American, Pacific and Caribbean churches have joined the WCC. 430 churches are now members of the Council, including Anglicans, Baptists, Disciples of Christ, Eastern and Oriental Orthodox, Friends, Lutherans, Methodists, Moravians, Old Catholics Reformed, Pentecostal bodies and "Independent" churches in Africa and Asia. The Council cooperates with the Roman Catholic Church, although that Church is not a member of the WCC. The Salvation Army, a founding member of the WCC, resigned in 1981 (see Chapter 5). It has now "fraternal status" with the WCC.

The WCC maintains a staff of about 300 people at its headquarters in Geneva.

Some of the early concerns of the ecumenical movement remain on the agenda today. The association of the missionary expansion with colonialism was later reflected in the dependent situation of churches in former colonies. In reaction, this, and its Christian convictions, led the WCC to adopt anti-colonialist and anti-racist policies and to stress partnership between churches, rather than assistance from the rich to the poor.

The First Assembly in Amsterdam met in a Cold War climate and had to face internal conflictual pressures. Taking an independent, "non-aligned" position, the Assembly rejected the assumption that capitalism and communism were the only two choices available. It rejected war in principle as "contrary to the will of God". It stated that every kind of tyranny and imperialism calls for opposition and struggle to secure human rights and basic liberties, mainly in terms of religious freedom. It thus set human rights and religious freedom well above the citizens' duty of loyalty to the state.

By taking these and later positions, the WCC has not escaped harsh criticisms from conservative circles, charging that ecumenical bodies support radical, revolutionary and often violent Marxist causes with money given by sincere members of Christian churches. On the Socialist side of the political spectrum, Pravda and Izvestia attacked the Council for its stand on human rights at the Nairobi Assembly in 1975. The Beijing's "People's Daily" labelled the Council's strategy as an "American Imperialist Missionary Enterprise". The WCC was attacked from all sides in the tangle of Middle Eastern politics. The South African government has tried to discredit the WCC as a whole.

The General Secretary

The first General Secretary of the WCC was W.A. Visser't Hooft, from the Netherlands, a charismatic leader who served the Council until 1966. It was said that, without his combination of gifts, the WCC might never have existed. He was succeeded by Eugene Carson Blake, an American Presbyterian, who promoted the internationalization of the WCC staff. Because of his opposition to the U.S.-led Vietnam War, he was placed on President Richard Nixon's infamous "enemies' list". Blake finished his term in 1972.

Philip Potter, a native of the West Indian island of Dominica, and a Methodist, was the Council' third General Secretary from 1972 to 1984. Potter had ardently espoused "liberation theology", which finds scriptural justification for those who rebel, even violently, against oppressive social and political systems.

Liberation theology is a school of Roman Catholic thought that emerged in Latin America in the late 1960s. It teaches that a primary duty of the church must be to promote social and economic justice. In the beginning, most prominent liberation theologians were overtly Marxist in their beliefs. They saw that the capitalist system had not caused Latin America to develop out of its dependence and poverty. Development had benefited only foreign business interests and the wealthy elites in Central and South America, not the poor majority. For that reason, they believed, revolutionary struggle to overthrow the capitalist system was the only way the suffering people of Latin America could improve their lot. Twenty years later, liberation theologians retain anticapitalism as one of their themes, but increasingly reject armed revolution as the way to change things.

While liberation theology had many advocates in Third World churches, it has been criticized by conservatives in the U.S. and in Europe as a code phrase for Christian support of Marxist revolutionary movements. Under Potter's twelve year stewardship, the WCC endorsed Palestinian rights and opposed U.S. policy in Central America. The WCC had been only mildly critical of the Soviet intervention in Afghanistan and almost mute about religious and human rights violations in the Eastern bloc. To these charges, the Council had replied that churches in Eastern European countries would be harmed if such attacks were made[31].

In 1984, Emilio Castro, a Methodist minister from Uruguay, was elected to the post of General Secretary by the 158-member Central Committee. On his appointment, Castro was seen as a "bridge-builder between those who want to emphasize the role of the church in the world and those who favour the evangelical approach"[32].

Without underestimating the potential or real influence of the General Secretary on the WCC's positions and programmes, it should be recalled that the important policy decisions and general orientation are taken by the Council's governing bodies (Assembly, Central and Executive Committees), and not by the General Secretary.

---

[31] *One World*, pp. 47, 57. See also *Liberation Theology at the Crossroads — Democracy or Revolution?*, by Paul E. Sigmund, Oxford University Press, 1989.

[32] Statement of Willem Visser't Hooft, first WCC General Secretary, in *Time*, 23 July 1984. See also *The New York Times*, 13 July 1984 and *Le Monde*, 18 July 1984.

The Finances of the WCC

In 1988, the Council received Swiss Francs 38.5 million and spent 39.1 million. The shortfall was covered from reserves and fund balances in the budget.

In addition, the Council received about $55 million in 1988 for emergency relief and development activities around the world. It is estimated that the funds channelled ecumenically through the Council represent 6 to 10 percent of the global sharing between and among the churches in the Council.

The Council budget is financed mainly by donations from member churches and their agencies, and to a smaller extent by sales of publications, services to other organizations and investment income. About 10 percent of the budget is financed by governments for non-theological activities.

The financial position of the Council will probably be affected negatively by the declining membership of the churches in Europe and North America. On the other hand, with the liberalizing movement in Eastern Europe, member churches in that region may be able, in the future, to contribute to the Council budget proportionately to their size[33].

The Council's Programme to Combat Racism (PCR)

PCR was set up by the Central Committee in 1969 and became a permanent part of the WCC structure in 1974. PCR was an effort to go beyond exhortation to action, with the understanding that the victims of racism must undertake their own liberation, with outsiders playing only a supportive role. PCR's mandate stipulated that "white racism is the most dangerous form of racism today". The emphasis was placed on combating institutional racism, which is entrenched in social, economic and political power structures. Finally it was recognized that racism could be overcome only by redistributing power from the powerful to the powerless. The Special Fund of PCR made annual grants of money to organizations of the racially oppressed and groups supporting victims of racism. These grants are made for humanitarian activities (such as education, legal defence and refugee work) without control of the manner in which they are spent. Disagreement arose when grants went to organizations engaged in armed struggle against the racist South African government.

This policy marked a new approach in the history of church aid, and it stirred up considerable debate and controversy in many church circles in the early 1970s. The WCC was in effect saying that the churches could no longer keep their involvement in the racial conflicts of Southern Africa depoliticized, and that an exclusive reliance on "neutral" and "detached" forms of humanitarian assistance does not serve the long-term interests of the victims. A number of church leaders charged

---

[33] *One World*, No. 147, July 1989, "WCC Finances in 1989".

that PCR was political, as its aid enabled the liberation movements to transfer some of their scarce resources from civilian to military needs.

As related in Chapter 5, the Salvation Army suspended its WCC membership in 1978, following the announcement of a grant of $85,000 to the Patriotic Front of Zimbabwe from the PCR special fund. In 1981, the Salvation Army resigned from the WCC, in part to preserve its non-political nature, and in part for reasons of religious practice[34].

In spite of these controversies, through the clear stand of PCR on the conflicts in Southern Africa and the long record of assistance by the WCC aid section (CICARWS) to Southern Sudanese refugees in neighbouring countries, the Council commanded sufficient respect and confidence with both the Khartoum government and the Southern Sudan Liberation Movement to be accepted as an intermediary in peace negotiations in 1972. Thus, "taking sides" made the WCC and its regional counterpart, the All-African Conference of Churches contribute significantly to bringing about the 1972 peace settlement of the civil war in Sudan (unfortunately shortlived)[35].

A negative result of the WCC's PCR is that all representatives of the WCC have been denied entry into the Republic of South Africa since the early 1970s, thus preventing any direct WCC assistance to the "victims".

Social Justice: A Christian Duty of Political Intervention

WCC statements stress the "basic Christian imperative to participate in the struggle for human dignity and social justice"[36]. Christians will discern what is just and unjust, human and inhuman in the complexities of political and economic change "in continual dialogue with biblical resources, the mind of the church through history and today and the best insights of social scientific analysis".

For the WCC, politics is an inescapable reality and involvement in it is a Christian duty. To be non-political in the sense of doing nothing is tacitly to support things as they are and to do so irresponsibly without thinking about it.

More precisely:

— the churches should be prepared to assist and support the victims of political decisions and to intervene where possible with government authorities on their behalf.
— in situations where human rights of people are systematically and continuously being violated, the political action of the churches should go beyond assistance

---

[34] Lissner, op.cit., pp. 234–235, 257–261. See also WCC Doc. EPS No. 23, 27 Aug. 1981 and No. 24, 3 Sept. 1981.

[35] Lissner, op. cit., p. 286.

[36] For this, and following quotations, see *The role of the WCC in International Affairs*, WCC, 1986.

and efforts to rescue the victims: it must address the root causes and structural origins of such violations of human rights.

— ...all churches are called upon to bear witness to the truth...persons in political life should be reminded of their proper tasks and responsibilities.

The various forms of WCC action include:

— monitoring, analysis and interpretation of major political developments.
— sending delegations to churches in critical situations and discussions with governments.
— teams to study and report on particular situations. Reports are shared with churches, selected governments and IGOs.
— confidential representations to governments, sometimes through one or more member churches, which may have special influence on a government.
— representations to IGOs. "Good offices" of U.N. officials and diplomatic channels are sometimes used. Information is shared also with leading NGOs with whom joint actions are sometimes undertaken.
— support for action groups, many of them church-related, engaged in the struggle for human rights, for the rights of workers and peasants, for peace and disarmament and in the struggle against racism.
— efforts for peaceful resolution of conflicts.
— public statements addressed primarily, but not only, to churches.

Clearly, the WCC has adopted an activist and interventionist role in political and human rights issues which sets it aside from the "neutral" NGOs.

Relief and Development Assistance

After World War II, the WCC set up a centralized refugee service which operated under an agreement with UNRRA, in Germany, Austria, Italy, Poland, Czechoslovakia and Hungary. From stocks furnished by Councils of churches, the WCC supplied and distributed food, clothing and medicines.

In December 1951, the WCC obtained money for emergency aid to help survivors of a typhoon that destroyed a Philippine refugee camp for Russians who had fled from China. The WCC successfully resettled some of the refugees in church-supported institutions in a dozen countries.

After this operation, channelling ecumenical aid to victims of disasters—natural or human-caused—became a regular element of interchurch aid in the WCC.

The Third Assembly in New Delhi, in 1961, stated that WCC interchurch aid should strengthen churches "in their service to the world around them (diakonia) and provide facilities by which the churches may serve men and women in acute human need everywhere". The churches were encouraged to participate in "nation-building". The idea of a diakonia was extended beyond "charitable" relief and service to programmes of social advancement.

A 1970 consultation in Montreux, Switzerland, said that development should aim at three interrelated objectives: justice, self-reliance and economic growth.

In 1984, the WCC joined with three other Christian organizations to form the Churches' Drought Action in Africa (CDAA) which sought funds to address both short-term and longer range food needs in two dozen African countries, suffering from famine. By March 1986, the organizations involved had received more than $500 million. The WCC response, as usual, focused more on enabling others to provide assistance than on setting up a relief operation of its own. CDAA commissioned a team of 52 Africans from various countries, churches and professional backgrounds, to study the causes of the famine. Their report said that the 1984 famine was more the result of poverty and underdevelopment than of drought. It also identified the root causes of poverty and underdevelopment as political and economic systems that oppress and exploit people.

The Commission on Inter-Church Aid, Refugee and World Service (CICARWS)

This Commission of the WCC assists churches in providing aid. Each year, $600 to 800 million worth of cash and material aid are channelled through the WCC network to programmes for human welfare and development in more than 80 countries. 90% is bilateral aid, from church to church with WCC coordination,—and 10% is handled directly by the WCC. The WCC role is larger when there is no member national church in the country (for instance, in Cambodia), or when the national church is not equipped to handle the aid. The aid is given in response to needs indicated by the local churches. The WCC plays an important role in providing information and advocacy, requesting the resources needed from church and other agencies, and seeing to their distribution.

There are from 5,000 to 6,000 staff and volunteers employed by national churches each year, either within their own country, or on an international basis. Employment conditions vary, depending on the churches' history, practice and ability to pay. Only a score or two are employed annually, directly by the Council as international coordinators or advisers, but CICARWS often coordinates the sharing of expatriates between churches[37].

According to a June 1986 report of CICARWS ("Secretariat for Personnel"), Western Europe and North America continued to be a source for skilled persons to be sent to places of need. For instance, Canadian personnel went to serve in Ethiopia, Lebanon and Sudan. Less expatriate personnel were sent to Asia, as many Asian countries have a surplus of locally available, well-trained technical and managerial personnel, and also in view of increasingly stringent visa regulations. Expatriate personnel continued to be needed in Africa for refugee and emergency/disaster needs, in such countries as Ethiopia and Sudan. For example, in

---

[37] Based on an interview with a WCC official in Geneva on 27 July 1989.

the eight countries of the Sahel region, CICARWS has sent, for more than a decade, a team of six persons, whose abilities as agronomists, social workers and development communicators have helped village communities in building up their skills and self-reliance for survival and development under inhospitable geographical and climatic conditions.

However, the report stressed that the human resource programmes for the churches cannot be based solely on the sharing of expatriate personnel. Churches should be assisted in developing their identity, and increase their capacity for self-reliance. Greater attention will be needed in the placement of expatriate personnel, increasing inter-cultural sensitivities, greater mutuality in the development of goal-oriented job descriptions by both the sending and the receiving bodies, and greater clarity with regard to responsibilities, obligations and expectations of the expatriate personnel themselves. South-south exchanges should also be encouraged, in spite of the financial constraints for arranging such processes between materially poor communities.

In a policy paper approved by CICARWS in June 1987, an ecumenical human resource programme was adopted.

The paper recalled the developmental priorities of the Third World in the 1960s and the early 1970s, and the promotion of the concept of economic development transfer of capital, equipment and know-how, as promoted by U.N. agencies. These priorities and concept were reflected in the way churches conducted their joint programmes for service and development. In addition to financial aid, ecumenical personnel and teams moved between churches and countries on the basis of sharing skills and technology.

However the limitations of this approach became apparent:

1) The sharing of people tended to be in one direction, North-South.
2) Social change and development are based more on local struggle for social justice, human rights and equality than on mere transfer of capital, equipment and know-how.

CICARWS was asked "to promote global diakonia through awareness-building and networking", emphasizing the prophetic diakonia with the vision of a new society, recognizing that this will be realized in its fullness only by the churches having the ability to establish "close dialogue with people of other faiths, secular groups and popular movements"[38].

The main recommendations related to improving the sharing of personnel, learning by facilitating exchanges, networks and visitation, education and training. The movement of personnel between countries in the South should be strengthened, while recognizing and coordinating the current North-South personnel programmes.

---

[38] *An ecumenical human resources programme*, WCC/CICARWS, Policy Paper as approved by the Commission in its meeting at Chavannes, Switzerland, June 1987.

In this sense, CICARWS has established an exchange between Latin American and Southern African women involved in working with victims of torture and repression.

The West German ecumenical body "Service Overseas" ("Dienste in Uebersee") has agreed to voluntarily restrict the number of German volunteers to be sent abroad and to support South-South movements.

The Commission also invites people from the South for short high-impact visits in Europe on such common world issues as poverty, hunger, unemployment, racial and social intolerance etc.

A Personnel Exchange Fund has been authorized at a level of $150,000[39].

Individual exchanges are encouraged of persons engaged in such programmes as social and economic development of communities, community health, agriculture and rural development, urban programmes, social justice and human rights, peoples' movements engaged in liberation and reconciliation initiatives.

Education and training has included leadership development programmes. For instance, CICARWS has assisted the Christian Councils of Burma, Philippines and Zimbabwe with such programmes, in association with the Association of the Churches' Development Services in West Germany (AG-KED). The common elements of these programmes is (1) that their target groups are "ordinary" people (church members, women, youth, teachers etc.), (2) that they encourage people to develop their capacity to analyze social issues and problems, and to look beyond symptoms, at the root causes, (3) and that they assist them in discovering their own abilities as individuals.

In 1988, the Commission collaborated with the Lutheran World Federation in running a ten-day workshop for Africa in Harare, Zimbabwe on Human Resource Management. Similar workshops will be run at the national and sub-national levels in Africa, in cooperation with existing management training organizations.

Trends in 1989

In 1989, the WCC maintained its political activism for social justice, anti-racism and support for liberation movements.

The Council announced grants to 59 groups worth a total of $635,000 from its Special Fund to Combat Racism. While the amounts granted were relatively small, the selected groups and the grant criteria could not but raise questions among conservative churches and observers. The bulk of the money ($352,000) went to groups fighting white minority rule in South Africa and Namibia. Other recipients included groups defending the rights of aborigines in Australia and New Zealand, indigenous people in Costa Rica and Canada etc.[40]. Grant criteria specify that the

[39] WCC/CICARWS Meeting in Salvador, Bahia, Brazil, Oct. 4–8, 1988, Doc. No. 10 on *Human resources programme-Some key issues for consideration.*
[40] WCC *Ecumenical Press Service*, EPS 89.09.73, 21–30 Sept. 1989.

money is for "humanitarian activities" of organizations with purposes "not . . . in conflict with the general purposes of the WCC". Grants are "without control of the manner in which they are spent"[41].

At its October 1989 meeting in Madras, the WCC Commission of PCR, in a discussion of appropriate ways of affirming the identity, culture and sovereignty of indigenous people, stated that it was "painfully aware of the complicity of the churches in their suffering, the suppression of their cultures, denial of their rights, and abuse of their traditional spirituality"[42].

Also in October 1989, a WCC group denounced the evidence of discrimination and racial oppression of minorities in Japan. The group called upon the Government of Japan to recognize the cultural diversity of that nation so that the society could be enriched by the culture of all the Japanese[43].

A WCC sponsored "Pacific Ecumenical Roundtable" held in October 1989 in Geneva noted the nuclear activities, such as testing of bombs and dumping of wastes in the Pacific region,—island economies "vastly affected and dominated by outside forces" and "continuing struggles for self-determination" in such places as Palau (now a Trust Territory of the U.S.) and New Caledonia (now an overseas territory of France)[44].

In an oral intervention to the 41st Session of the U.N. Sub-Commission on Prevention of Discrimination and Protection of Minorities, the Council representative denounced the anti-communist hysteria in the Philippines, involving not only the military, but also some foreign religious groups. As a case in point, a member church of the WCC, the United Church of Christ in the Philippines (UCCP) was listed in November 1987 as a "Red Front", or communist-infiltrated group. Since then, church members have been victims of harassment, arrest and murder.

The Council representative recalled its long-held position that insurgency and rebellion in many parts of the world are rooted in unjust social, political and economic structures, and not in the infiltration of societies by particular ideological forces[45].

Upholding "social justice" implies taking sides in a country's internal politics. Financing liberation movements, for humanitarian purposes, but without control of the expenditures, means taking sides against the established order.

The open, avowed "partiality" of the WCC for the poor and the afflicted affects the spirit and the scope of its humanitarian work: its volunteers and representatives are "crusaders" at the same time as relief workers. The Council does not pretend to be neutral in humanitarian and human rights issues.

---

[41] WCC EPS 89.09.73.
[42] WCC EPS 89.11.02, 1–10 Nov. 1989.
[43] WCC *Ecutext* in EPS, 22–31 Oct. 1989.
[44] WCC EPS 89.11.10, 1–10 Nov. 1989.
[45] WCC EPS 89.09.81, 21–30 Sept. 1989.

The Lutheran World Federation (LWF)

The LWF is not a member of the World Council of Churches, but most of its members are. Its headquarters is lodged in the same Geneva building as that of the Council. In spite of their apparent similarity of purposes and symbiotic common residence, the LWF has its own objectives, programmes and characteristics[46]. What the WCC and LWF have in common is Christian belief and witness. What differentiates them is that the WCC is interdenominational, while the LWF is by definition denominational. Most LWF member churches contribute funds and personnel to both WCC and LWF.

History

The LWF was founded in 1947 at a constituting Assembly in Lund, Sweden, by 47 Lutheran Churches from six continents.

A forerunner to the LWF was the General Evangelical Lutheran Conference in 1869: it originated in Germany and gradually involved Lutheran churches in Scandinavia, Eastern and Western Europe and North America.

In 1918, the National Lutheran Council was created in the U.S.A. After World War I, it provided material assistance for the churches in Europe and ensured the continuation of mission work in areas (former German colonies) where German mission societies could no longer operate.

The first Lutheran World Convention took place in 1923 in Eisenach, Germany: 144 delegates from 22 countries took part. The Convention did not develop beyond a loosely knit organization of European and North American churches.

Impetus for a Federation grew after a quarter of the world's Lutherans, those in Germany and Eastern Europe, were directly affected by World War II. Australian, North and South American, South African and Swedish Lutherans responded to the needs through relief work, refugee resettlement and reconstruction programmes. During the war, Lutheran missionaries were forced out of many mission fields. By working together, Lutherans were able to meet the needs of these "orphaned" missions.

Additionally, the formation of the World Council of Churches in 1948 necessitated inter-Lutheran cooperation in the ecumenical movement.

---

[46] Information is based on LWF documentation including a *Fact Sheet*, the LWF/World Service *Staff Letter* of 10 Aug. 1988, containing a five year report, 1984–1989. An interview was also arranged with an official of the LWF/WS on 31 Aug. 1989.

Mandate, Structure and Budget of the LWF

The LWF is a free association of 105 member churches, representing 54.9 million persons,—93% of the world Lutherans. The Federation has no power to legislate for the member churches nor to limit their autonomy. It acts as the churches' agent in matters assigned to it.

Besides its religious and ecumenical functions, the LWF "shall help Lutheran churches and groups, as a sharing community, to serve human need and to promote social and economic justice and human rights"[47].

This part of its mandate is carried out by the LWF Department of World Service, under the direction of the Commission on World Service, which reports annually to the 29-member Executive Committee. The supreme body is the Assembly of member churches' representatives, which normally meets every six years.

Some 120 employees work at the Geneva headquarters, under the direction of a General Secretary. In 1989, 5,420 employees worked in the 20 LWF World Service field offices, implementing various relief, refugee and development programmes.

The LWF budget, including material aid, amounted to $101 million in 1988, and $104 million in 1989. For the latter, three fourth of the total go to some 700 projects and programmes in 70 countries. About one third of the budget goes to Africa, one third is used globally and one fifth goes to Asia. 9 percent of the 1989 budget was spent on administration, 38 percent on service programmes and emergencies, 26 percent consisted of donated commodities. Financial (about 60 million) and material (from 20 to 40 million) aid comes from all member churches, with local resources in recipient countries usually complementing grants that come mostly from church-related and other agencies in the Federal Republic of Germany, the Nordic countries and North America.

The LWF World Service (LWF/WS)

As shown in Table 6–1, the Commission on World Service assists member churches in the general field of Christian service (diakonia) in two directions:

a) social service and development, including emergency relief, rehabilitation, service to refugees.
b) fostering Christian social responsibility with special efforts to address the root causes of social and economic injustice.

While the first mission is within the traditional field of relief work, the second has political implications which will be taken up below.

---

[47] LWF *Constitution*, Art. III 1. and 2.

Partnership with Member Churches

Member churches have the basic responsibility for diaconic tasks. The Federation World Service usually assists only on request of a member church when the local resources are insufficient to meet the needs, whether of an emergency or of a longer-term developmental nature. This assistance will be phased out as soon as possible. Thus local or national self-reliance is emphasized. Member churches and World Service want to avoid any misperception that a giver-receiver relationship exists which manifests dependency.

In the same vein, LWF/WS does not want to be seen as a characteristic organization of benevolent expatriates assisting the indigenous. While the LWF is an international organization, only a modest number of its staff is expatriate and contributes occasionally to field relief and development activities.

In 1989, 5,420 national staff were serving LWF/WS in 25 nations of Asia, Africa and Latin America. International staff were recruited only when no indigenous personnel with the required skills and expertise were available. They never exceeded, since 1984, 2% of the total staff. Efforts are being made to enhance the development of national staff through training and the conferring of additional responsibilities. 19 employees from developing nations, including three field representatives (Angola, Botswana and Mozambique) are included in the 104 international staff from 22 countries currently employed by LWF/WS.

Table 6.1. Terms of reference for the Commission on World Service Lutheran World Federation (Extracts)

The specific assignment of the Commission on World Service is:

To assist the member churches of the LWF in the fulfilment of their individual and corporate responsibilities in the general field of Christian service, (including) a) social service and development, such as relief, rehabilitation, service to refugees and other related concerns; and b) the fostering of Christian social responsibility with special efforts to address the root causes of social and economic injustice.

In pursuance of its assignment and within the limits of its resources, the Commission is authorized to:

1. Encourage LWF member churches and their related agencies to provide services for the alleviation of human need in their respective countries and to support them in such endeavours.
2. Support, in cooperation with the other Commissions and units of the LWF, the LWF member churches when they seek to identify and foster awareness of issues related to social and economic injustice and when they act to change practices and patterns which prevent the just sharing of the world's resources and the realization of human dignity and freedom.
3. Furnish coordinative services for LWF member churches and their related agencies with respect to international service and development programs and provide them with information and facilities for the channelling of resources and the assignment of personnel.
4. Conduct, administer, support and participate in service, development and resettlement services and programs with particular reference to emergency situations, areas of endemic need and refugees...These services shall be global in scope and for the benefit of people in need irrespective of race, sex, creed, nationality or political conviction.

Source: LWF *Document: Basic Information*

Under the terms of a youth internship scheme, a number of young people have also participated in LWF/WS field programmes in Asia and Africa.

National and international staff of LWF/WS working in the field are subject to the same security hazards as other relief workers.

In 1987, a locally employed Sudanese staff member, together with his wife and child, lost their lives when the aircraft they were travelling in was shot down near Malakal, Upper Nile Province of the Sudan. In January 1988, several members of the international staff team in Kampala were shot at by bandits and some wounded. One month later, two Ugandan LWF/WS field workers in the West Nile programme lost their lives in an ambush. In September 1988, while carrying out his work, a member of LWF/WS international field staff in the Tete Province of Mozambique was injured by the explosion of a land mine and lost the sight of one eye. In January 1989, attacks were made against national workers of the Lutheran Church in El Salvador and a bomb exploded in the church office in San Salvador[48].

Emergency Assistance

On a selective basis, the LWF/WS has responded to natural emergencies, such as floods and cyclones in India and Bangladesh, earthquakes in Central and Latin America, as well as man-made disasters, civil strifes and wars.

The LWF/WS emergency desk participates in the League of Red Cross/Voluntary Agencies Steering Committee meetings, held every month in Geneva to coordinate emergency action. In the field, emergency coordinating groups are often formed among NGOs on a nation-wide basis to prevent an overlapping of activities.

LWF/WS initiated a coordinated ecumenical group to respond to the drought which affected 22 African nations. In February/March 1984, the Churches' Drought Action on Africa (CDAA) was founded. Its members were the LWF, WCC, Caritas Internationalis, CRS and "International Cooperation for Socio-Economic Development" (CIDSE)[49]. Between 1984 and 1988, the ecumenical partners raised over $600 million in cash and kind for this programme. Emergency programmes were also carried out by LWF/WS in Botswana, Ethiopia, Mozambique, Zambia and Zimbabwe, to be followed by long-term development programmes.

Also in 1984, LWF, CRS and local churches in Ethiopia founded the Joint Relief Partnership (JRP), a coordinating body. The U.S. government and the European Community channelled large quantities of food aid through the JRP. JRP members divided among themselves geographic responsibility for coordinating food transportation and distribution. During the peak period of the emergency in 1985, the JRP was feeding about 1.1 million Ethiopians daily.

As another example of joint action, in November 1988, the LWF and WCC

---

[48] LWF *Kit*, 10 Aug. 1989, para. 156.
[49] CIDSE and Caritas Internationalis are both international networks in the Catholic Church. Caritas deals with interchurch aid, while CIDSE deals with the participation of churches in development.

started daily relief flights from Nairobi to Sudan carrying food, fuel, medical supplies, tools, seeds and other emergency goods, because of the famine in Sudan. Because of the civil war between the Sudanese government and the Sudan People's Liberation Army in the South, food convoys were unable to get through, making airlifts the only alternative[50].

Refugees

In 1964, the LWF was the first international NGO invited by Tanzania and the UNHCR to take responsibility for a whole-nation refugee programme[51].

The Federation has a dual approach towards refugee assistance. It offers practical humanitarian assistance and also tries to understand why refugees have become refugees and, if feasible, takes corrective action.

The LWF/WS has identified common elements to its refugee programmes:

— concern for refugee self-sufficiency by providing education and training, and promoting self-help schemes.
— a link between refugee assistance and development, including national and regional development goals.
— concern for the needs of the refugees' national hosts: eligible nationals should also benefit from LWF/WS assistance, in order to assure equality of treatment between refugees and their hosts. This will help alleviate the refugee burden borne by Third World countries, which have the largest numbers of refugees but can least afford their presence.
— concern for the special needs of refugee women and children, who form an estimated 80 percent of the world's refugee population and are among its most vulnerable categories.
— concern for displaced persons who live under refugee-like conditions but are not protected by the international refugee system. LWF/WS considers that this lack of protection for those who have not been able to leave their country is a critical weakness in the international refugee response apparatus.
— concern for the environment and for the needs of "environmental refugees", i.e. people who have been left with no choice but to abandon areas becoming unfit for human living. As they move, these refugees compete with local populations for scarce food, water and land, thus accelerating the environmental damage.

Finally, LWF/WS activities are in support of voluntary repatriation, the best solution for refugees.

In the 20 field programmes operated by LWF/WS in 25 countries, refugees and other displaced persons are among those most often receiving assistance. Such programmes have been carried out in several African countries (Angola, Botswana, Ethiopia, Malawi, Mauritania, Mozambique, Swaziland, Tanzania, Uganda, Zambia

---

[50] LWF *Lutheran World Information*, Nov. 1989, No. 11.
[51] Lissner, op.cit., p. 66.

and Zimbabwe), in Jordan and the West Bank, in Latin America (El Salvador, Peru), in Haiti and the Caribbean, in Asia (Bangladesh, India, Kampuchea, Nepal).

The LWF/WS Office for Resettlement has assisted Lutheran Churches as they counselled and resettled uprooted people-refugees, migrants, asylum seekers, undocumented persons and unaccompanied minors. The Office provided assistance related to travel loans, family reunification, counselling services to approximately 6,000 individuals from 1984 to 1989. The Office also facilitated coordination between the UNHCR, the IOM, the ICRC and the church agencies.

During the past five years, some 7,500 refugees and migrants were resettled annually from Indochina, East Europe, Ethiopia, Afghanistan and the Near East, to the U.S., Canada and Australia with the assistance of Lutheran churches and social services agencies in the receiving countries.

In June/July 1989, the LWF cooperated with UNHCR and the WCC to assist in the repatriation of about 40,000 Namibians who had fled repression since the 1970s. The UNHCR ensured their safe return to Namibia by chartering some 350 flights. Once back, their resettlement fell on the Council of Churches in Namibia and the Repatriation, Resettlement and Reconstruction Committee (RRR) the body set up to carry out this vast operation.

International ecumenical cooperation with the RRR programme was channelled through the WCC Commission on Inter-Church Aid, Refugee and World Service.

The LWF, under the umbrella of the RRR Committee, was the executing agency for this programme, which included the setting up of reception centres, lodging facilities, the delivery of food rations for 10 months. UNHCR obtained cash donations of $31 million and $4,5 million worth of food from the World Food Programme[52].

Coordination

The LWF/WS cooperates closely with Christian Councils and with the WCC, on policy and operational matters related to emergencies, refugees and development assistance. LWF/WS also cooperates with Caritas Internationalis and the League of Red Cross Societies. LWF/WS works with the UNHCR as an operational partner in most of its African field programmes.

LWF/WS is a founding and active member of the 65 member International Council of Voluntary Agencies (ICVA) in Geneva. ICVA is a NGO forum for all matters pertaining to refugees, migration and development questions. It is also a group through which the U.N. system can be addressed on matters of common interest.

In 1988, the LWF signed its first contract with the World Bank for the development of a rural school programme in Tanzania.

---

[52] WCC *One World*, Aug. Sept. 1989, pp. 4–6.

A Struggle for Justice, Liberation and Peace

The LWF is not only a federation of churches, a public witness to Jesus Christ and a relief agency. It is also mandated to foster "Christian social responsibility with special efforts to address the root causes of social and economic injustice".

This additional mandate leads the Federation to take political positions, insofar as the roots of social and economic injustice are often found in government policies and practices.

A LWF/WCC international consultation held in Geneva in September 1988, concluded that, as Christians, the participants should struggle towards the restoration of fullness of life through "...empowering people to take action for their rights...and bring about fundamental structural changes in unjust societies..."

They recognized that there is a "grossly unjust distribution of resources between the North and the South and within the countries. Development must have a bias towards redressing (equalizing) the balance and empower people to challenge their governments to provide their legitimate rights, e.g. health, education, etc....We should...include support groups who struggle for justice, liberation and peace, bring about fundamental structural changes in unjust societies".

Linked to this strong platform in favour of Third World international claims for a New International Economic Order, but also for internal social and economic reform (or revolution?) within countries, the Federation promotes the defence of human rights as a legitimate part of its LWF/WS activities.

In particular, the churches have long understood that human rights violations are the fundamental cause of the refugee problem[53].

Taking position against Portuguese colonialism, the LWF and its related agencies in Western Europe and North America invested millions of dollars over a ten year period in the 1960s in Mozambiquan and Angolan refugees settlement in Tanzania and Zambia[54].

In 1970, the LWF General Assembly at Evian adopted a resolution on human rights calling for, among other things, church assistance to people struggling "against oppression" and to "areas liberated from colonial rule".

In implementation of this resolution, the LWF/WS provided a large-scale material relief programme to FRELIMO-controlled areas of Northern Mozambique and MPLA-controlled areas of Eastern Angola. The Commission on World Service pointed out "that the working with the social welfare and other related departments of the liberation movements, as the relevant authorities in control of the area in which the needy people live, is naturally limited to the purposes of the humanitarian programme, as required for the channelling of relief supplies, the carrying out of the specific projects and access to the area for observing proper implementation, and does not imply support for the organizations *per se*". In fact, it is difficult to

---

[53] LWF *Kit*, pp. 18–19, and *Lutheran World Information*, Nov. 1989, No. 11.
[54] Lissner, op.cit., p. 285.

deny that this form of open cooperation with FRELIMO and MPLA "rebels" really implied support for and recognition of these organizations *per se*[55].

At the national level of donor countries, the Lutheran World Relief, the overseas aid and development agency for North American Lutheran churches, protested in February 1976 against a new State Department policy, which may use food aid as a weapon against countries opposing U.S. policies. Dr. Paul C. Empie, President of Lutheran World Relief, stated that such a policy would "hold human lives hostage, penalizing hungry people for the actions of their government"[56]. A similar dilemma occurred in the 1980s in relation to aid for Ethiopia, insofar as assistance to its population reinforces the legitimacy of the government.

In September 1989, taking some distance with SWAPO, the General Secretary of the LWF said that the Federation was "shocked and dismayed" by reports of torture and killing of prisoners by SWAPO personnel: "There are points at which our interests coincide, that is for the liberation of oppressed people, but there are also points at which we are not identical, that is in ways and means to achieve liberation".

Intervening in the "domestic affairs" of South Africa, the LWF called, in November 1989, on the country's authorities to hold formal meetings with leaders of the liberation movement. The Federation supported the abolition of apartheid and the recognition of the rights of all people to universal suffrage. It recommended to the South African President Frederick W. de Klerk to declare a moratorium on capital punishment, to release immediately all political detainees, including Nelson Mandela, lift the state of emergency, and lift restrictions and bans against individuals and organizations.

Also in November 1989, the LWF urged its member churches, national committees and related agencies to express objection to the proposed new legislation of the government of President Alfredo Cristiani in El Salvador. The new laws would treat persons engaged in peaceful political protest as terrorists, with punishment from ten to twenty years in prison. It would also be a punishable crime for local human rights groups to be in contact with international organizations such as the U.N.(!), Amnesty International, or the ICRC.

Bishop Medardo Gomez of the Lutheran Salvadoran Synod described the eventual adoption of this legislation as a "historical sin of great dimensions", leading to "the emergence of fascist laws" in the legal system of El Salvador[57].

The bishops of Lutheran churches in the German Democratic Republic took a public pro-reform stand during the October/November 1989 demonstrations. They protested against the use of violence against the demonstrators. They called unanimously for a "renewal of state and society in the truth". This required a public and

---

[55] Lissner, op.cit., pp. 235–237.
[56] Lissner, op.cit., p. 221.
[57] *Lutheran World Information*, Nov. 1989.

open discussion of the circumstances in the land, a free press, secret elections, the right of freedom to travel. In the example of Dr. Martin Luther King, they called on parishioners and citizens to hold to the principle of non-violence[58]. Protestant ministers said that the Lutheran Church's position had been influenced by the "liberation theology" of the Latin America church. As noted by an observer[59], with the virtual collapse of the East German Communist Party, the leading moral authority in the region was once again what it had been for much of the time since the Reformation, the Lutheran Church. While the Church's support for democracy was evident, it claimed that it had no political programme of its own and wanted to play a role independent from the state and from political parties.

More generally, the Director of the LWF/WS in Geneva said in November 1989 that the LWF World Service should intensify its advocacy efforts as a way of working in a more preventive manner. "Activities in defence of human rights are a legitimate part of this advocacy work".

During the second International Development Consultation organized in Ethiopia in October 1989 by LWF/WS, the point was made that "all churches should be ready to challenge governments on difficult issues[60].

Politics and Field Work

In spite of its recurrent political interventions, in its field work, the LWF is reputed to generally give priority to its humanitarian work, in precedence to social justice or human rights appeals. The Federation members are guests in Third World host countries, by invitation or agreement with government authorities. They work with and through the National Church and LWF does not want to take openly a stand which might create problems between the National Church and the government, unless there is full agreement between the National Church and LWF on a specific issue. Human rights problems might be referred discreetly to the National Church for any possible action with the government, or reported, also discreetly, to Amnesty International or the International Commission of Jurists.

In its field work, the LWF believes in education and patience, self-reliance, partnership,—and discretion.

The apparent contradiction between a neutral, discreet LWF in its field activities as a relief worker, and a partisan, interventionist LWF as an international Christian Federation of Churches, does not seem to have caused any major difficulties with its member churches, nor with recipient states' authorities.

---

[58] *Lutheran World Information*, 41/89.
[59] *International Herald Tribune*, 8 Dec. 1989.
[60] *Lutheran World Information*, Nov. 1989 and 41/89.

World Vision International (WVI)

World Vision International (WVI) is a non-profit, Christian interdenominational humanitarian organization established in 1950 to carry out the international ministry of nationally-based World Vision organizations in Australia, Canada, U.K./Ireland, Finland, Germany/Austria/Switzerland, Hong-Kong, Singapore, Netherlands, New Zealand, Southern Africa and the U.S.[61].

WVI is headquartered in Monrovia, California, U.S.A. The Organization is controlled by an International Board of Directors, meeting twice a year, which appoints the senior officers of WVI, approves plans and budgets, and determines international policy. The Board comprises 18 members from twelve support and field countries. The present Chairman is Roberta Hestenes (U.S.), Graeme Irvine (Australia) is the international President.

WVI's programmes include in part relief assistance and care projects, and in part religious (Christian) and evangelistic projects. However, as the organization's approach in practice is an integrated one, this distinction is not a clear division of activities.

In the first category, WVI assists needy children through orphanage, school and family,—aid programmes by feeding, clothing, nursing, healing and spiritual ministries. Funding of this work is mainly through a sponsorship programme which links a donor or groups with a specific child.

Sponsorship of a child is part of a wider programme to try to improve lives in a Third World community. Once the community has identified its own needs and a plan of action has been created, specific projects are initiated such as immunization, school supplies, clean water, sanitation, health care, skills training and nutrition classes. Some projects include agricultural training, irrigation, marketing cooperatives, interest-free loans or the construction of roads, bridges and schools.

Community members decide which children are selected. The number of children sponsored depends on the funding required to accomplish the goals of the project. Each of the children chosen is assigned a sponsor from Canada, Britain, Japan or other support countries. All of the community's children receive benefits. Sponsored children differ in that they have a personal relationship (normally through correspondence) with a sponsor. Approximately half of WVI programmes are funded through sponsorship.

In its programmes, WVI attempts to develop community self-reliance, by helping families and individuals to produce adequate food, earn income and create a community life resulting in long-term survival and growth.

WVI has a role in emergency aid and relief. It provides food, medical aid and housing programmes for people suffering as a result of wars or natural disasters. In emergency aid, WVI attempts to think developmentally by encouraging maximum

---

[61] See *Understanding Who We Are—World Vision International*, and *Audited Financial Statements and Other Financial Information*, WVI, Sept. 30, 1989,—*Childview*, WV Canada, May-June and July-Aug. 1990. Information was also given by a WVI official in Geneva, in an interview on 6 Aug. 1990.

participation,—being sensitive to local culture and relationships,—working when possible through national partners,—looking towards long-term solutions,—minimizing dependency,—and helping build the skills, confidence and resourcefulness needed by the affected people to restore and improve their quality of life. Approximately one third of WVI's work is relief and rehabilitation.

The majority of WVI funds are distributed to its offices located in various countries. These offices then distribute the funds for the charitable purposes intended.

On the religious side, WVI seeks to support, encourage and strengthen Christian leaders through pastors' conferences, consultations, training programmes and educational opportunities. These activities include both clergy and lay people.

As a Christian organization, WVI's approach is holistic: it refuses to set the spiritual against the physical, or the personal against the social. The aim is to transform the whole person in all of his relationships. WVI's approach is also ecumenical: it welcomes partnership with all Christian churches and, by board policy, it is opposed to proselytism or coercion of any kind.

World Vision International and the Church

WVI does not have a structural affiliation with any church, or interchurch body, such as the World Council of Churches.

In field countries, the working relationship is formed mostly at the community level, sometimes with a local church or a group of local churches, sometimes with a community committee on which the churches are represented, and sometimes with a project committee of individual Christians.

In support countries, WVI's donors are members of most churches. WVI avoids a competitive spirit: its policy is to be a unifying influence rather than a divisive influence within the church as a whole.

However, the origin of WVI and its major constituencies represent mainly members of Protestant churches. The Roman Catholic Church has its own charity organizations and was likely, at least in the past, to view WVI as a religious and charitable competitor, more than as a partner.

WVI and Governments

In principle, WVI has a "good citizen", loyalist attitude towards governments, but maintains some distance, a "detachment", from governmental politics and policies. As it works within countries representing a wide diversity of political and ideological systems, WVI respects the authority of the governments of those countries and maintains appropriate protocol and working arrangements with each. At the same time, WVI avoids identification with the particular economic, political or social position of any government, whether an industrialized or Third World country.

In field countries, WVI attempts to work in a manner parallel with or supplementary to national development programmes. Generally, WVI does not fund government programmes or assign funds to government agencies.

WVI may accept funding from the humanitarian aid departments of governments provided there is compatibility of objectives between WVI and such departments in any given project.

Excluding gifts-in-kind, cash funds received from several governments generally average about 5 percent of WVI total funds. Gifts-in-kind (mainly grain or other food) from government sources are utilized from time to time in emergency relief.

WVI and Politics

The current President of WVI, Graeme Irvine, has said that

> World Vision does not have a political agenda. We do have a Christian and humanitarian agenda, which inevitably has political consequences[62].

During its forty years' life, it seems that WVI evolved slowly from a neutral, non-political position to a more vocal advocacy stance, from pure, bland charity to a concern for social and economic justice.

The first response of the WVI to human needs has been primarily social welfare in nature, concentrating on child care and relief. Increasingly, the organization's ministry of development drove it, in the 1980s, to deal with issues of justice. This evolution was not easy, in view of the worldwide spectrum of political, economic and theological perspectives represented in the WVI partnership.

In 1987, WVI approved a policy paper on the issue of justice. It said that, as a worldwide partnership, WVI must increasingly respond to situations of injustice. It acknowledged God's special concern for the powerless and therefore WVI' obligation to facilitate the empowerment of both urban and rural poor.

> Commitment to such an obligation means that we need to consider how to defend the oppressed and work for their redemption and self-determination, even when this creates tension with structures of power.

At the same time, activism must be tempered by wisdom and prudence. As stated by the Chairman of World Vision/New Zealand, John Rymer

> there is not much point in attacking a government if your work there is cut off[63].

WVI's position and pronouncements about Cambodia and Israel have been particularly unequivocal, as expressed in the World Vision "Together" Quarterly of July-September 1990.

Concerning the Palestinian "human tragedy", it said:

---

[62] *Together*, a Journal of WVI, No. 27, July-Sept. 1990.

[63] Ibid., p. 6.

Those who are living in the occupied territories have endured 40 years of oppression. In the last twenty years they have been subjected to a pervasive, systematic and brutal denial of human rights by the Israeli occupation forces.

WVI could not become part of the silence that has treated the Palestinian tragedy "with indifference" for more than 40 years. It decided to tell the Palestinians' story, not as a call to be anti-Israel: in the end, as a call for salvaging Israel's own integrity and honour as a people.

The U.N. General Assembly Resolution of November 1989 to maintain the Khmer Rouge-dominated Coalition Government for Democratic Kampuchea as the U.N.-recognized Government was sharply criticized by WVI's President: he regarded this decision as shameful and outrageous, a "monstrous injustice". It imposed Pol Pot and his "murderous Khmer Rouge" once again on the Cambodian people, and it continued Cambodia's isolation from the mainstream of development aid which they desperately needed. The country was denied access to the international resources of the UNDP, WHO and nearly all bilateral aid. He called this Resolution "an international crime" in moral terms.

The reasons why Graeme Irvine decided to make public statements in Australia concerning the situation in Cambodia were that

— WVI had a background of knowledge and commitment, having worked in the country for 20 years and having earned the "right to speak",
— the cause was just and urgent,
— wide consultation was possible within the WVI partnership, with WVI staff in Cambodia, with diplomats in Geneva and Southeast Asia, and with Cambodian cabinet ministers,
— Australia provided an exceptional platform for advocacy and the possibility of influencing Australian policy.

WVI's call to the international community was to:

— exclude the Khmer Rouge from participation in the future of Cambodia,
— bring the Khmer Rouge leadership to trial in the International Court of Justice for their crimes against humanity,
— withdraw recognition and remove from the Cambodian seat at the U.N. General Assembly the Coalition Government,
— cease all military aid to all parties involved in the conflict,
— remove aid and trade embargoes against Cambodia and reconstruction and development aid,
— press for internationally monitored elections in the country.

Staffing and Budget

As of 1 August 1990, WVI had a total of 5,563 permanent employees worldwide, including 165 in its international offices in Los Angeles and Geneva. In addition,

67 specialists in such areas as health care, agriculture, etc., were employed on limited term assignments, mainly in emergency situations.

The total number of volunteers working with WVI was estimated at several thousands. WVI's policy is not to employ volunteers in front line positions, but volunteers' assistance is considered essential to the effective work of the organization.

It is WVI policy that all of its staff are Christians, so that they will identify with and carry out the objectives of the organization without conflict of conscience.

WVI staff worldwide reflect the international character of the organization. National staff are employed in priority in field locations.

In emergency situations, international teams of short-term contract staff are frequently recruited for specialized management or technical work.

Total WVI expenditures amounted to $162.6 million in 1988 and $191.6 million in 1989. In 1989, approximately 90 percent were spent on programme services. Total relief expenditures amounted to $28.6 million[64].

WVI's integrity was attacked in an article published in a British weekly, followed by a television programme aired in London in March 1990. WV of Britain has since instituted legal proceedings against the TV film producers.

One allegation was that more than half of the money raised for Third World relief by WV goes on overheads, administration, marketing and "lavish expenses for its top officials".

The reply of WV of Britain was: in 1989, the organization spent 7 percent of its income on administration, 15 percent on investment on fund-raising, 8 percent on development education in Britain and 70 percent on overseas programmes.

Another allegation was that some of the money given to WV for Third World aid was sent on to "Missions' Advanced Research and Communications Centre", or MARC.MARC is a separate, independent charity, which provides evangelical research, training and publishing for the churches.

This was also refuted: WV of Britain only gave to MARC less that half of one percent of its income.

Such public attacks against charities are not infrequent: they may be caused by, or contribute to, compassion fatigue. Some may be mischievous and sensationalist, playing on the fears of the donor that his money may not be used directly, effectively and mainly to assist the victims, but may be wasted on excessive administrative overheads, or useless projects or supplies, diverted to unpublished other projects, or that the assistance may not be delivered to those in need when and where they need it.

On the other hand, charities' records and activities should be reliable and transparent: they should be open to inquiries and audits. The NGOs' indirect expenses should be kept to a minimum. They should ensure that their "real" activities reflect and implement their announced objectives and programmes.

As recently stated by Save the Children Fund (U.K.), it is imperative that chari-

---

[64] *Audited Financial Statements*, op.cit.

ties have the most scrupulous systems of management and accountability. Support for charities remains essential in enabling public concern to be translated into effective action[65].

Cooperation with Other Agencies

WVI is in consultative status, Category II, with the U.N. Economic and Social Council and has similar status with UNICEF, UNHCR, the World Food Programme and WHO.

WVI is a member of the International Council of Voluntary Agencies in Geneva, and a member of the Geneva Monthly Meeting of International Agencies on Disaster Information, a sub-Committee of the Licross/Volags Steering Committee for Disasters (see Chapter 2).

A Summary

Like other humanitarian NGOs, the religious agencies provide relief assistance, emergency aid and assist refugees. They also believe that relief work should be linked with and followed by, development assistance. They also encourage local and national self-reliance in Third World countries, limit expatriate service from North countries and encourage the employment and training of local volunteers and employees.

Church-related agencies are ecumenical in their operational assistance: in the field, they often work together with agencies of different denominations, as well as with non-religious NGOs and with IGOs.

Coordination is also effected centrally. In Geneva, CRS, the American Friends Service Committee, the LWF, the WCC and other religious agencies[66] are members of the International Council of Voluntary Agencies, created in 1962. Caritas Internationalis is an observer. As mentioned above, the Licross/Volags Joint Steering Committee for disasters was formed in 1972 by CRS, the LWF, the WCC and Oxfam, together with the League of Red Cross Societies. Caritas Internationalis joined the Committee in 1980.

The organizations reviewed in this Chapter are all international umbrella organizations, which have their own policies and programmes, but work essentially through national churches or other religious organizations. Their humanitarian

[65] *Today*, July 1990, "The Charitable Realities", by Mags Law, pp. 36–38.

[66] For instance, the "Adventist Development and Relief Agency, International", U.S.A., "All Africa Conference of Churches", Kenya, "Baptist World Alliance Relief Program", U.S.A .S.A., "Jesuit Refugee Service", Italy, "Islamic African Relief Agency", Sudan, among others. See ICVA *Annual Report—1987–1988*.

functions are in part operational, but mostly in the nature of policy guidelines, fund-raising, coordination, distribution of funds, supplies and equipment, providing or assisting in providing international or national volunteer personnel. In particular, neither the WCC nor the LWF are "super-churches": they both exist to serve their member churches.

The international religious agencies' Christianity affects and colours their humanitarian work. While most of them have separated evangelization and relief assistance, their work through and with churches and religious organizations differentiates them from secular agencies. It gives them a spiritual, human and material network which supports and strengthens their work and gives it more continuity. Their main focus is to work and care for the individual.

Their Christian conviction implies the fostering of charity and justice. This dual mission is not an exclusive preserve of Christians: non-believers may have similar goals. In fact, the Church's conservative traditions in many countries, its close association with ruling governments and elites, have initially placed the Christian social reformers in a category of rebels, if not revolutionaries. The "liberation theology" was, and still is, a scandal to a number of church groups.

While all Christian churches believe in social justice, it appears that the WCC and its member churches have gone further than other Christian denominations in taking public positions in favour of politically, economically or socially "oppressed" groups and in the support of human rights.

Catholic organizations also believe in social justice, but they tend, generally, to separate more clearly their relief work from advocacy. Similarly, the Quakers advocate for peace, disarmament and human rights in U.N. bodies, but carry out their relief work in a discreet and impartial manner.

Similarly, secular agencies have adopted either the neutrality of the Red Cross (most British Charities, for instance), while others consider that their humanitarian role demands that they bear witness to injustice and human rights violations (like the "French Doctors").

Commitment to social justice and public advocacy have their risks and their costs. Governments may expel those volunteers whose agencies take adverse political positions. For those agencies, the religious and/or moral duty to testify overrides other considerations.

In a seminar organized in 1987 by the Geneva Centre for Applied Studies in International Negotiations[67], the participants agreed that the activities of Church organizations transcend every political system, and their interests cover every level of international life—human rights, disarmament, development assistance, international finance, diplomacy and conflict resolution, to which we can add humanitarian assistance. Through their worldwide network, they monitor closely the activities of governments and multilateral institutions. At the same time, they are themselves

---

[67] Centre for Applied Studies in International Negotiations, "Church Organizations Involvement in International Affairs", Geneva, Oct. 5–6th, 1987, *Report of the Seminar*, by John Zarocostas.

actors within the international system. Church NGOs are a constructive and powerful group seeking positive change. Church organizations have been instrumental in raising to the global level issues such as racism and the protection of human rights. They have taken the lead in suggesting the integration of social values and business ethics in the corporate sector.

One cannot but agree with the conclusion of the seminar that the involvement of Church (and more generally, religious) organizations is now an integral part of the international system and that their contribution is seen as invaluable, in particular by the poor and oppressed of the world who have neither political nor economic power.

CHAPTER 7

MEDICAL VOLUNTEERS

Medical assistance to the sick and the poor was considered by the Christians as a religious obligation and was originally carried out under the direction of the Church by religious orders.

International medical assistance was also initiated under religious auspices. As related above (Chapter 6), the order of St. John (now Malta) began in the 11th century as a monastic community which administered a hospice-infirmary for pilgrims to the Holy Land. However, as the religious Order had to assume military functions for the protection of the sick, the pilgrims and the Christian territories which the Crusaders had won back from the Moslims, the Order's medical duties seemed to be addressed only, or mostly to the care of the Christians. Nowadays, the Order of Malta continues its charitable work which is, in part, of a medical nature: campaigns against leprosy, emergency assistance, supply of medicaments, vaccinations, creation of and subsidies to hospitals and dispensaries etc.

Late colonization (in the 19th and the first half of the twentieth centuries) also had health concerns and programmes. Colonial administrations usually set up health services initially for the European military and civilian groups, and later, for the local populations.

The conquering soldiers were at times preceded or followed by Christian missionaries who, like explorers and surveyors, often assumed medical duties. For instance, in Africa, many bush missions, in addition to evangelical functions, ran schools, medical centres and other community services. Qualified medical missionaries accompanied traditional Christian missions in Asia, Africa and Latin America as early as the 18th century, but mostly in the 19th and 20th centuries.

The first generation of secular international medical volunteers was initiated by the Red Cross movement since its creation in 1863. Although Red Cross bodies are not medical NGOs as such, they employ doctors and paramedical staff. Some of the ICRC' delegates are doctors, and many national and international doctors, nurses and other health personnel participate in disaster relief programmes under the auspices of the League of Red Cross and Red Crescent Societies, in order to provide first-aid, medical and nursing care. ICRC, WHO and the University of Geneva organize annually an international training course for doctors and health workers on health emergencies in large populations. The Red Cross movement is the only world-wide humanitarian NGO network.

The French medical volunteers "no borders" movement started in the nineteen sixties in reaction against some of the principles and rules of conduct of the Red Cross, its alleged strict legalism and excessive respect for governments' approval. Outside the "no borders" movement, other medical voluntary aid organizations have been created since the nineteen fifties.

This Chapter will first review the role of medical missionaries, then the impact of the French "no borders" movement, then the activities of some of the other, more traditional, international medical groups.

Medical Missionaries

In early Christianity, the sick and poor were cared for in the homes of the Christian bishops. Later, their homes became hospitals, and orders of deacons and dea-conesses assumed these tasks. In the fifth century, Christian hospitals developed, specialized for the sick, the helpless poor, the aged and the pilgrims. In the ninth century, religious orders took over this work of charity: Benedictine monasteries became centres where medicine was studied and practiced.

At the time of the Crusades, additional orders spring up, such as the Alexians, the Antonines, the Beguines, the Hospitallers, the Order of St. John of Jerusalem and the Teutonic Orders. The Teutonic Knights vowed themselves to care for the sick and to build hospitals wherever their order was established. French Jesuits introduced some Western medical and anatomical concepts to the Chinese Emperor's court in Beijing in the 17th and 18th centuries[1].

Protestant Medical Missionaries

Prior to the 20th century, Protestants were the only ones who made a concerted effort to organize medical missions.

The first Protestant medical missionaries are deemed to have been Danish and German doctors who went to India in the 18th century, but died quickly of tropical diseases. In 1793, Dr. John Thomas of England and non-medical missionaries brought Protestant missions to India. The first American medical missionary was Dr. John Snedder, who went to Ceylon in 1819 and later to India. The first woman doctor from the West to go to India was Dr. Clara Swain, under the auspices of the

---

[1] "The Medical Mission Sisters", by Sister M. Regis Polcino, in *Transactions and Studies of the College of Physicians of Philadelphia*, Vol. 35, No. 1, July 1987, and "French Jesuits and the 'Manchu Anatomy—how China missed the Vesalian Revolution", by T. Kue-Hing Young, *CMA Journal*, Sept. 21, 1974, Vol. III, pp. 565–568.

Board of Missions of the Methodist Church. She was a pioneer in medical education of Christian missions in India. She opened a hospital at Bareilly in 1874.

In 1850, there were no more than fifteen medical missionaries in all the non-Christian world. In 1895, they were 359.

In the second half of the 19th century, the philosophy of missions was: the overseas missionary enterprise is strictly a preaching enterprise. Only ministers are responsible for this function. Doctors are needed to look after the health of the ministers, missionaries and their families, but nothing more. Such doctors are auxiliaries, but not full-fledged missionaries. Evangelism was first: doctors, in the early days, served largely in a supportive capacity.

It was progressively realized and accepted that:

— the mission of preaching and healing harmonizes with the example of Christ,
— medical work serves as a helpful introduction to Christianity,
— physical help aids the reception of the spiritual message,
— medical work attracts a daily audience,
— it gives women opportunities to serve,
— it supports the preacher,
— it is an opportunity for manifesting Christian love.

In 1897, the American Board of Commissioners for Foreign Missions decided that henceforth the medical personnel should have the status of "missionary", not "assistant missionary" as had been the case for 87 years.

The modern Christian doctrine refers to the "wholeness of man". In the words of Phyllis Garlick[2],

We try to minister to man's physical, intellectual and social needs—and always with the spiritual as the apex of this broad pyramid. Medical work, undertaken in this spirit, is just as truly a part of the great commission which came from the Great Physician himself, as preaching. He said, 'Go heal'.

The scientific advances and medical discoveries since the second half of the 19th century (Joseph L. Lister, Robert Koch, G. A. Hansen and Louis Pasteur among others) and the progress of travel and communications influenced and developed the missionary as well as the secular medical work in the Third World.

As an example, the British "Mission to Lepers in India" (since 1966, the "Leprosy Mission") has played a significant role, since 1875, in all the major advances in the treatment of sufferers from leprosy. Currently, the Mission is responsible for the treatment of about 240,000 sufferers from leprosy in 30 countries, and assists in the leprosy programmes of about 90 Protestant missionary bodies[3].

---

[2] The information in this section is mainly based on the following book by Dodd, Edward M., *The gift of the Healer*, Friendship Press, New York, 1964.

[3] "The Leprosy Mission—A Century of Service", by S. G. Browne, *Leprosy Review*, 1974, 45, pp. 166–169.

The following statistics show the extent of medical missionary work at various periods.

In the late 1930s, at the height of the Dutch colonisation in the East Indies, there were thirty mission hospitals, 70 sub-hospitals, 237 polyclinics and seven leprosaria. These were staffed by 90 medical doctors (61 European, 29 Indonesian), 124 European nurses, 2,279 Indonesian nurses.

In 1904, there were 476 mission hospitals of all Christian denominations around the world. In 1948, they totalled 1,142:

Africa	277
Asia	702
Indonesia and South Pacific	118
Latin America	45

In 1959, statistics on Protestant Medical Missions in 80 countries confirmed the trend towards more national doctors (1,307) and national nurses (5,937) and less expatriate missionary doctors (883) and nurses (1,415). The proportion was inverse 50 years before. The number of schools of nursing also showed the education effort of missions. One-and-a-half million in-patients were being treated annually in the 700 mission hospitals, and nearly 8 million outpatients. A million more was cared for in outlying dispensaries.

Roman Catholic Medical Missions

The lay Roman Catholic medical mission movement started after World War I. Its pioneers and promoters were two Scottish Protestant converts, Dr. Agnes McLaren and Dr. Margaret Lamont, who had been active in Protestant medical mission work early in the 20th century in India, Egypt, China and South Africa.

Catholic Medical Missions Institutes or Boards were created in Germany, Holland, France and the U.S.A between 1918 and 1924. In 1925, the U.S.-based Society of Catholic Medical Missionaries was set up at the initiative of Mother Anna Dengel. The Society Sisters were qualified doctors and nurses for women and children in mission lands. They responded to a need in Catholic missions for organized, systematic medical care by professionally trained medical sisters. In 1948, the hospitals of the Society had cared for nearly 10,000 in-patients, while 122,783 patients had visited its various dispensaries. Missions had been established in India, Ghana and in the U.S.A. In 1947, Dutch sisters started a mission in Indonesia. The Society's General Administration was transferred to Rome in 1957, giving it pontifical status. By 1967, the Society's missions had extended to 13 Third World countries. In that year, the sisters cared for over 650,000 patients in their hospitals.

In 1926, in Belgium, the Medical Foundation of the University of Louvain was founded for the recruitment of doctors for the Belgian Congo and for the setting up of medical centres for training indigenous personnel[4].

---

[4] Sister M. Regis Polcino, op.cit.

The development of medical and nursing education and public health efforts in the Third World has lessened the need for sending expatriate health personnel to a number of those countries. However, religious missions, like other NGOs, can still assist in initiating or strengthening the education and training of nationals in the health professions. There is also a recurring need for complementary medical aid in emergencies.

In some countries, nationalism and increased government interest in and control of health programmes have also decreased the scope for imported foreign assistance within a reduced private sector.

Religious missions have suffered from the Communist take-over of some countries. In Communist China, foreign missionaries were ordered out or imprisoned, all mission hospitals and other medical institutions were taken over by the government, all Christian institutions as such were closed out. The current evolution in a number of Socialist countries may however open new prospects for mission work.

Whatever the obstacles, restrictions or socio-economic or political changes, the Churches believe that the Christian ministry of healing will still be needed. Medical missionaries were the first to introduce Western medicine into many tropical countries. They have made, and can still make, a distinctive contribution to health care in developing countries.

The "French Doctors"

Since the late 1960s, several French associations of medical doctors have been created to give emergency medical assistance in developing countries, in war or other natural catastrophe situations. In contrast with the policies of many other volunteer organizations, they advocate the "right and duty to interfere" and publicize violations of human rights. Should humanitarian non-governmental organizations be discreet and neutral and only give assistance, or should they also denounce human rights violations?

The rise to political power of humanitarians in the French socialist government has recently triggered a few official initiatives: a proposed U.N. resolution to give international recognition to a "humanitarian right of intervention" and a medical/military intervention in Lebanon: both generous initiatives have backfired (see Chapter 11).

Should humanitarianism be government business, or is it better carried out by volunteer organizations?

France and Human Rights

Among much controversy, France celebrated in 1989 the 200th anniversary of her Revolution. While differences of political and historical opinions focused on the Terror, the guillotine, the beheading of King and Queen, there was general agreement that 1789 symbolized, for many peoples of the world, the advent of human rights, the rights of the people, freedom and democracy. Even though the French "Declaration of the Rights of Man and of the Citizen" was preceded, two years earlier, by the American Declaration, and in spite of the later killings, wars and Napoleonic dictatorship, the French Revolution remains as a landmark of the birth of modern democracy, nurtured by the French philosophers of the 18th century.

The French jurist René Cassin contributed to the drafting of the Universal Declaration of Human Rights and other eminent French jurists have actively participated in the creation and work of human rights bodies in the U.N. and in the Council of Europe. In the eighties, French governments showed their concern for human rights and humanitarian issues by appointing a Junior Minister for Human Rights (Claude Malhuret, in the Chirac government) and a Secretary of State for Humanitarian Affairs (Bernard Kouchner, in the Rocard government). Both incumbents had played a key role in the creation of the French medical associations.

In 1990, France has selected and trained about 30 diplomats to be assigned to French embassies as "humanitarian attachés", in order to reinforce the humanitarian component of its diplomacy and to be able to adjust it to situations of natural disasters.

The "humanitarian diplomats" will have a role of evaluation and information in case of a natural disaster or political crisis. They will define the action best adapted to such situations,—monitor questions requiring a "constant humanitarian vigilance", such as refugees and displaced populations, endemic and epidemic diseases, street children,—serve as a contact and liaison focal point for French NGOs concerned with medical emergencies, rural development, environment,—prepare and organize the ways and means by which France could react in case of disaster or crisis, and, after the emergency phase, follow-up on on-going programmes[5].

French Colonization

The French colonial administration set up and manned hospitals and dispensaries. French military doctors played an important role in the prevention and control of communicable diseases, particularly in Africa. The French-sponsored "Organization for Coordination and Cooperation in the Control of the Major Endemic Diseases" continued its work after decolonization. A few independent French doctors ran hospitals and clinics in the hospitals, like Dr. Albert Schweitzer and his famous hospital in Gabon.

Decolonization left the French with a bitter taste, and for some of them, a sense of guilt. The French students' "revolution" of 1968 challenged the political, social and ethical status quo. Some medical students and doctors wondered whether their only objective was to establish themselves in a comfortable, bourgeois, life in a big

---

[5] *Le Monde*, 19 May 1990.

city, with a valuable specialization. Some doctors wanted to help those most in need, in the Third World, and joined Red Cross teams in conflict areas.

Bernard Kouchner, the founder of "Médecins Sans Frontières" (MSF) and "Médecins du Monde" (MDM), said that he went to Biafra in 1968 because he had not been in Guernica, in Auschwitz, in Babi-Yar, in Oradour-sur-Glane, nor in Sétif. "In Biafra, we were going to exorcise the nightmares of the great slaughters of mankind, against which one had not done enough" (5).

Biafra is the starting point of the French Doctors' epic.

Biafra

The Nigerian Civil War generated extreme passion and partisanship in and outside the conflict area. From May 1968 to January 1970, the war produced a "humanitarian crisis" in North America and Western Europe. Its main focus was starvation, in epidemic proportions, in the blockaded secessionist area of the country. Biafra was claiming the right to national self-determination. Biafra alleged that the Federal Military Government was perpetrating genocide on the Biafran people through the slaughter of civilians by federal ground troops, the indiscriminate bombing of civilian targets and the blockage and the consequent starvation in the East.

The International Committee of the Red Cross (ICRC) had been able to arrange one relief flight to the enclave in November 1967. Although further efforts to obtain a relief agreement proved futile, in April 1968, the Nigerians were forced to turn to ICRC for aid: ICRC was called in to coordinate the relief programme and to make international appeals for assistance. ICRC accepted the coordination task with a condition: that it be permitted to minister to the needs on both sides of the front, in Biafra as well as in Nigeria.

Non-governmental actors, including Caritas Internationalis, Catholic Relief Services, the World Council of Churches, CARE and others, continued to spearhead relief efforts and organized illicit airlifts. After a Red Cross plane had been shot down by a Nigerian Mig, and the ICRC declared *persona non grata* and expelled from Nigeria, ICRC stopped the night flights and tried to obtain a daytime agreement. According to Wiseberg[6], ICRC feared that, because its neutrality and political independence were being called into question, its legitimacy was being undermined. From the perspective of organization survival, it appeared strategic to withdraw from Nigerian relief—its coordinating mandate was revoked by Nigeria at this time—so as to protect its legitimacy to act in future situations.

The French Red Cross organized a minor airlift from Libreville, Gabon, to Biafra, with the support of the French Government. France was supporting the

---

[6] Bettati, Mario et Kouchner, Bernard, *Le devoir d'ingérence*, Ed. Denoel, Paris, pp. 17–18. On Biafra, see Wiseberg, Laurie S., "Humanitarian Intervention: Lessons from the Nigerian Civil War", *Revue des Droits de l'Homme*, Ed. Pedone, Paris.

Biafrans and was providing them with arms. There was then no effort to distinguish between French humanitarian and French political/military support for Biafra.

Although the relief agencies and churches were in principle motivated by pure humanitarian concerns, by generating relief for the starving Biafrans, they seemed to identify with and generate support for Biafra. Furthermore, relief operations had political consequences.

The nine young French Red Cross doctors sent to Biafra in November 1968 were shocked by the suffering of the wounded, the brutality of the federal forces and frustrated by ICRC's caution and statutory silence, its need for negotiating with the established government, its adherence to the "technicalities" of international law.

Their hospital, several times bombed by Nigerian Migs, was receiving up to 800 patients a day. Coming close to the hospital, the Nigerian troops had sworn that they would kill the Red Cross doctors, considered as mercenaries. Still, the ICRC asked the doctors to stay in the hospital. They accepted, on the condition that a press conference be held in Geneva, so that international public opinion would focus on the hospital. They did not want the sick and the doctors to be killed in silence and submission.

One of the French Red Cross doctors, Bernard Kouchner, was designated by his colleagues to speak on their behalf of human rights and the respect of the Geneva Conventions. He was not allowed to speak in public, presumably by the ICRC headquarters[7].

This incident was at the origin of the "Doctors without borders" concept: to give medical care to those in need, but at the same time, to break the law of silence, of submission to government authorities, which prevented Red Cross doctors from bearing witness to what they saw.

Birth of the Medical "No Borders" Movement

On 21 December 1971, "Médecins Sans Frontières" (MSF) was born and its' Charter adopted (see Table 1). Ironically, MSF took as its emblem a white cross against a red background, the inverse of the Red Cross flag, itself the reverse of the Swiss flag. A French Tribunal ordered in October 1989 that MSF should change its emblem, as it was too similar to the Swiss flag, and as both MSF and Switzerland work in the humanitarian field[8].

Following an earthquake in Nicaragua in 1972, MSF sent three teams of doctors and surgeons, and ten tons of food and medicaments. In 1974, 25 MSF doctors are sent to Honduras, to help with health problems caused by a typhoon. In 1975, MSF

---

[7] Billot, Florence, *Le mouvement sans frontières—quelle communication pour quel avenir?*, unpublished paper, 1989.

[8] *Le Monde*, 20 Oct. 1989.

intervenes in Lebanon. In 1976, 100 MSF doctors assist refugee camps in Thailand: food assistance, vaccinations, sanitation.

Table 7.1. Charter of "Médecins Sans Frontières"

"Médecins Sans Frontières" is a private organization with an international scope with French status. The organization brings together doctors and members of the health corps exclusively, who, on becoming members agree on their honour to obey the following principles:

1. MSF offers its aid to all victims of natural disasters, mass accidents and belligerent conflicts regardless of race, politics, religion or creed.
2. Working in the strictest neutrality and completely independently, refraining from all unwarrantable interference in the interior affairs of states, governments and parties of the territories they are called to serve in, for its help MSF, in the name of its international scope, calls for full and complete freedom in exercising its medical functions.
3. MSF will not accept or submit to any allegiance to or influence of whatever power, political force, ideology or religion there may be.
4. MSF will respect professional secrets and abstain from judging or publicly expressing opinions— favourable or otherwise—on events, forces and leaders who have accepted their collaboration.
5. Anonymous and unpaid, volunteers are to expect no personal or collective remuneration for their services. They are aware of the risks and hazards of the operations they may carry out and will make no claims for themselves or their beneficiaries for compensation other than what the organization is capable of furnishing them.

Source: MSF Document (in English)

In spite of its success, after only a few years, MSF was torn between two factions, a typically French phenomenon.

Kouchner, supported by a minority, felt that MSF should remain a light and mobile body, non-bureaucratic and keep to specific, newsworthy, missions. MSF should not engage in "classical" relief operations, such as refugee work, well assumed by the "classical" organizations (Red Cross, U.N. High Commissioner for Refugees (UNHCR).

The majority group criticized the Kouchner clan for organizing "testimony" missions (to denounce human rights violations), such as visiting jails in Uruguay, a job better done by the Red Cross delegates or Amnesty International. The excessive interest in media publicity, the "star system" of some MSF leaders, was also criticized, as well as ineffective *ad hoc* one-time operations.

In 1979, the "Boat for Vietnam" operation, launched by Kouchner with the support of the Parisian intelligentsia (including Raymond Aron and Jean-Paul Sartre, re-united at last...) caused the scission. The operation was labelled by its opponents as a typical public relations project, lacking continuity and follow-up. Its supporters extolled its dual achievements: a medical role (2,500 hospitalizations, 400 surgical interventions, hundreds of vaccinations), and a world-wide testimony for the promotion of human rights.

MSF then gave birth to two other groups: "Aide Médicale Internationale"

(AMI), founded in November 1979, and "Médecins du Monde" (MDM), founded in February 1980.

While the three groups are separate, they have common characteristics. They are all non-governmental associations of medical and paramedical professionals. They are French, although independent MSF associations have been set up since 1980 in Belgium, Luxembourg, Netherlands, Spain and Switzerland. AMI groups have been set up in the Netherlands and in the U.K. Their work is mainly international, although MSF and MDM have a few projects in France itself. They all use volunteers for temporary missions, although remunerations vary according to the employing organization. They all need publicity for fund-raising, as most of their resources are financed by individual subscribers. With some variations, they do not accept the Red Cross rule of discretion. They are prepared to cross borders without governments' permission.

What are the characteristics of the three organizations?

Médecins Sans Frontières

The new MSF/France (following the 1979–1980 scission) has become a professional, structured, technical and specialized relief organization It is the major private medical assistance organization in the world[9].

MSF has 110 permanent staff in its impressive, steamboat-like, building in Paris. The cost of the building (34 million French francs) has been paid from business firms' subsidies. Its 1988 budget was 144 million French francs, 22% of which was spent for fund-raising and information. 70% of its resources came from individual or firms' subsidies and donations. The UNHCR and the European Communities (Emergency Aid Fund of the Commission) subsidized 28% of its budget (the remaining 2% accrued from interests).

Since its creation, 4,600 volunteers have been sent on more than 100 missions. They are currently present in 30 countries. Most of the volunteers are sent on 3 to 6 months missions. 40% are doctors, 40% nurses, 20% administrators and logistics specialists. Out of 800 recruits a year, there are usually no more than ten failures and ten medical evacuations.

Doctors and coordinators receive a 4,400 francs stipend a month, paid in France, nurses, other paramedical staff and logistics specialists, 3,400 French francs. Travel and local living expenses are paid by MSF in addition to the stipend. Selection is based on the candidates' professional and linguistic qualifications, their experience and their motivation. The "contract" is based on mutual trust, rather than on an investigation of the individual applicant's credentials and personality.

MSF considers that the era of devoted amateurs is over. MSF wants to create a

---

[9] Information from MSF publications and an interview with a MSF official in Paris on 22 June 1989. See also *1989 Annual Report*, MSF/Switzerland.

professional corps of health professionals in humanitarian assistance: 20 to 30 such professionals are created by MSF each year. MSF has set up the International Centre for Medical Research and Epidemiology in Paris to train doctors, nurses and logistics experts in epidemiology, emergency planning, sanitation, nutrition and public health.

The work of MSF volunteers extends to four types of situation.

In armed conflicts, MSF priorities are medical/surgical treatment,transport and distribution of medicaments and setting up of emergency surgery units. For example, MSF has worked with Christians, Druzes, Palestinians and Shiites in Lebanon since 1975. Since 1980, more than 300 doctors and nurses have served in Afghanistan, each for 6 month periods. They entered the country illegally.

In refugee camps, with the support of UNHCR, MSF has changed its focus from curative to preventive health work: organizing dispensaries, inoculation campaigns, water treatment and waste disposal, training of local staff.

Following natural disasters, MSF can send promptly medical and paramedical teams, with specialized equipment and supplies.

MSF provides technical assistance to countries, such as vaccination campaigns under the WHO/UNICEF Expanded Programme of Immunization in South Yemen and Mauritania.

Logistics are a strength of MSF. Pre-assembled kits allow teams to be fully equipped and to operate in isolated areas at short notice.

MSF has produced a "Diagnostic and Treatment Manual—Clinical Guidelines for Doctors and Nurses in Rural Hospitals, Dispensaries and Refugee Camps" which has been approved by WHO.

Since 1987, MSF has added to its international activities a "Mission Solidarité France": MSF provides in Paris and in the provinces a free-of-charge medical and social individual assistance to the "new poor", the "Fourth World" in industrialized countries.

Since 1980, MSF groups have been created in Belgium, the Netherlands,in Switzerland, in Luxembourg and in Spain. Following the same principles as MSF/France, the groups have carried out a number of operations either separately or jointly. MSF/Belgium has intervened in Chad, Mali, Ethiopia, Zaire, Lebanon, Sudan, Mozambique, Nicaragua, Peru. The Dutch section has operated in Somalia, Sudan, Uganda, Colombia and Surinam. In 1989, the Swiss section was responsible for:

— the restoration of a health care system accessible to all in a war-torn region of Uganda,
— at the request of the UNHCR, an emergency programme including medical, nutritional and sanitary aspects (quality of water, environmental hygiene) related to the arrival of forty thousand Sudanese refugees in Uganda,
— also at the request of UNHCR, the organization of medical care in a Chadian refugee camp in Poli-Faro in Cameroon,

— participation in setting up a public health infrastructure in North Cameroon, where new human settlements followed the creation of an artificial lake,
— survey of the impact of bilharziasis around the lake,
— training health care staff and setting up dispensaries and village pharmacies in deprived regions of Guatemala.

In 1988, the national MSF groups have created a "European Intervention Unit" of MSF. The Unit intervened in 1988 in Sudan, Rwanda, Burundi, Bangladesh and Central America. MSF/France would like to create a supranational European structure of MSF: a European MSF with representation of all national units and a President changing every six months. Fearing a French domination, the other national groups have resisted the proposed union, while retaining a loosely connected operational coordination. Each national group has its own characteristics, making integration difficult: MSF/France, faithful to its founders' objectives, believes in a humanitarian right of intervention. MSF/Belgium is more diplomatic in dealing with governments, while MSF/Switzerland (like the Red Cross organizations) stresses its neutrality.

In 1989, the European Intervention Unit carried out operations in Soviet Armenia and in Romania. MSF/Switzerland was associated with MSF/Netherlands for a mission in Uganda, and with MSF/Belgium for a mission in Guatemala.

The European network and activities of MSF groups in 1989 is shown in Table 7.2.

Table 7.2. The European Network of MSF in 1989

	Belgium	Spain	France	Netherlands	Switzerland	Luxembourg
No. of countries of interventions	21	3	27	11	5	5
No. of current missions	45	10	80	20	10	5
No. of volunteers sent	350	25	750	115	50	10
No. of available volunteers	600	200	2000	250	150	40
No. of permanent staff at hq.	45	10	80	25	5	1

Source: MSF/Switzerland, "Qui êtes-vous?".

Is MSF Neutral?

Some of the interventions of MSF represent an interference in countries' domestic affairs, as demonstrated by the Biafra and later episodes.

In 1984–1985, MSF/France found that the Western aid to Ethiopia was used in part to deport massively some of its rural population out of areas held by rebels into areas controlled by the government. Refusing to be an alibi, MSF publicly denounced this policy and was then expelled from Ethiopia by President Mengistu Haile Mariam. French medical teams then returned surreptitiously[10].

In Honduras since 1980, MSF wanted to remain neutral in the Salvador Civil War. Together with other NGOs (Caritas Internationalis, Catholic Relief Services and others), MSF was involved, under UNHCR supervision in assisting Salvadoran and Guatemalan refugees. The Salvadoran refugee camps served as sanctuaries to the guerrilla of the "Frente Farabundo Marti" of National Liberation (FMLN). According to "Le Monde" (16 November 1988), the camps provided forcibly recruited guerrilleros, medicaments and uniforms to the rebels in collusion with the other UNHCR-sponsored NGOs. MSF felt that providing medicaments and training health assistants reinforced objectively the guerrillas and thus went beyond its strictly neutral medical responsibilities. When MSF decided to withdraw from the Salvadoran refugee camps, and, to re-establish the balance, from Honduras camps of Nicaraguan refugees, the guerrilla radio denounced the "MSF mercenaries in the service of U.S. imperialism". UNHCR supported MSF: "It was impossible to find a body as competent as MSF" and "No serious organization could accept most of the refugees' demands"[11].

In June 1989, MSF mobilized a team of ten persons, logistics specialists, surgeons, anesthesiologists and nurses, and 23 tons of equipment and medicaments to give medical aid to the wounded of Tian-an-men in Peiping. The proposed operation, which cost 2.4 million French francs, collapsed against the refusal of the Chinese authorities to cooperate. The Chinese Red Cross Society had politely declined any medical or humanitarian assistance in a letter to the ICRC. Two tons of medicaments and 2,000 blood units sent by the Hong Kong Medical Association had also been kept at the Peiping airport[12].

In 1988 and 1989, MSF sent four non-official missions to the USSR to assist Soviet citizens who had been hospitalized against their will and declared mentally sick. The condition of 150 persons was assessed by MSF teams consisting of at least a psychiatrist and a translator. MSF then publicly denounced the continuing psychiatric abuses in the USSR and took position against the reintegration of the Soviet Association of Psychiatry in the World Psychiatry Association, from which it had been excluded in 1983[13].

How neutral can a NGO be? How should MSF react in cases of massive exactions, or when human rights are not respected in particular areas? Should the continuation of its relief work prevail over public denunciations? In spite of its iconoclastic origin, it seems that MSF realizes that its main role is that of a medical relief organization and that its humanitarian concern should override other considerations. In a meeting in Toulouse in June 1989, representatives of the six national

---

[10] *Time*, 9 Jan. 1989.

[11] U.N. Doc. A/AC.96/708 (Part IV), p. 14: UNHCR Activities financed by voluntary funds: Report for 1987–1988 and proposed programmes and budget for 1989, and *Le Monde*, 16 Nov. 1988.

[12] *Libération*, Paris, 17–18 June 1989.

[13] *Le Monde*, 23 Sept. 1989.

MSF groups agreed that MSF should not become the "medical section of Amnesty International"[14].

Médecins du Monde (MDM)

The position of MDM is less ambiguous and its objectives more ambitious. It is a medical humanitarian *and* a human rights organization, also based in Paris[15].

MDM is faithful to its founder's (Bernard Kouchner's) philosophy: "we do not tend to bodies, but to human beings, the defence of their fundamental rights cannot, for us, be dissociated from the act of healing...helping, caring, feeding, everywhere, yes, but we do not want to be the hostages of dictators, who tolerate us at the price of our silence"[16].

MDM teams are medico-journalistic. The group's motto is "to care, to train, to bear witness".

MDM budget is about half that of MSF, but it is growing: 49 million French francs in 1987, 60 in 1988. In 1988, 74 per cent of its resources came from private donations, 26 percent from subventions from the French government or IGOs, such as the European Economic Community or UNHCR. 57 percent of its expenditures were allocated to Third World missions, 6 percent to assistance in France, 18 percent for administrative costs. About 600 volunteers were sent on 30 missions in 45 countries. Volunteers also worked in 22 assistance centres in France, providing free medical care and medicaments to those who are not covered by the French Social Security. Volunteers for the Third World receive the same remuneration as MSF volunteers.

In addition to medical and paramedical volunteers, MDM employs nutritionists, architects, agronomists, to assist in supplementary feeding, building or rehabilitation of dispensaries or refugees camps, social or agricultural reorganization. Journalists and other intellectuals have joined the association to bear witness to war, famine or human rights situations. MDM has created regional groups in the French provinces, who assume responsibility for specific missions.

In 1989, MDM had teams in Nicaragua and Mali (anesthesist nurses' training and provision of equipment), Peru (30,000 doses of yellow fever vaccine), Afghanistan (159 doctors, surgeons, nurses, English instructors, agronomists, journalists, veterinarians).

On 10 December 1988, 72 hours after the Armenian earthquake, an MDM charter plane containing volunteers (six surgeons, five anesthesists, four nurses, logistics specialists and interpreters) and twelve tons of medico-surgical material,

[14] *Libération*, 3–4 June 1989.

[15] Information based on MDM publications, including its periodical *Les Nouvelles—MDM*, and an interview with a MDM official in Paris on 11 Oct. 1989.

[16] Kouchner, Bernard, *Charité Business*, Ed. Le pré aux Clercs, Paris, 1986, our translation from the French.

clothes, food and medicaments, landed at the Erevan airport. For the first time, a humanitarian NGO was authorized to send a mission to the USSR. MDM was soon followed by MSF and other Western NGOs from the UK, Federal Republic of Germany and Italy. Following the emergency phase, MDM gave medical and technical support to the reconstitution and improvement of medical structures: maternity hospital, polyclinics, dispensaries, blood transfusion centre, rural hospitals. By March 1989, MDM missions had cost 20 million francs, of which the European Communities had contributed 19 million[17].

Besides these "technical" humanitarian operations, MDM is vocally political in denouncing dictatorships of the right, of the left and in the Third World.

Since 1985, MDM has been working in Chile, initially without government approval, but with the support of the Catholic Church and of the National College of Doctors, which allowed MDM doctors to register with the Chilean Medical Order. MDM doctors entered Chile with tourist visas and gave medical care in slums ("poblaciones"), of Santiago, Concepcion and San Antonio. Following ICRC practice, MDM doctors have visited jails and given medicaments to prisoners. With the progress of democracy in Chile, MDM declared its association officially, thus legalizing its action. It tries to protect Chilean doctors with whom it works. MDM condemned the liberal economic and social policies followed by the Pinochet regime, its violations of human rights and promoted the "right" to medical care[18].

MDM, as well as MSF, assistance to the Afghan rebels was a challenge to the Soviet-supported Afghan government. MDM has condemned the megalomania of Nicolas Ceaucescu, which has caused an increase in child mortality, a decrease in life expectancy and the deterioration of the medical and hospital organization in Romania. Following a Belgian initiative, MDM, other NGOs and personalities have created in 1989 the "Romanian Village Operation": each of the 13,000 Romanian villages earmarked for destruction would be adopted by so many municipalities in Europe[19].

MDM supports democracy, human rights and freedom of expression also in Third World countries. In its periodical, MDM adopted the cause of Maître Ali Yaya Abdennour, persecuted in Algeria for having created the Algerian League of Human Rights in 1985 and for defending political prisoners[20].

MDM supports the association "Reporters sans frontières", based in Montpellier, France. The association has no medical mandate: it reports on violations of freedom of information in various countries and defends journalists in trouble with their government. MDM has supported the association's far-fetched plan to place a boat with radio broadcasting facilities near the China coastline in order to give the Chinese censure-free news[21].

---

[17] *Les Nouvelles—MDM*, No. 13, Apr. 1989.
[18] *Le Devoir d'ingérence*, op.cit., pp. 95–97.
[19] *Les Nouvelles—MDM*, Apr. 1989.
[20] *Les Nouvelles—MDM*, Jan. 1989.
[21] *Le Monde*, 10 Oct. 1989.

One wonders whether a medical NGO should so diversify its action, at the risk of jeopardizing its field medical work and of gaining the unwanted reputation of a "gadfly" NGO.

Whatever the weight of this criticism, MDM, more than MSF, is clearly not a "neutral" medical assistance organization. Far from the Red Cross neutrality and discretion, MDM takes sides and testifies loudly, even outside its medical domaine.

Aide Médicale Internationale (AMI)

The smallest of the three French groups, AMI does not want to grow and become bureaucratic. It is faithful to one of the motives at the origin of the "French Doctors" movement: a reaction against the alleged bureaucracy and legalism of the Red Cross system.

AMI's four permanent staff members receive visitors warmly in an austere two-room locale, provided rent-free by the Mairie of Paris. AMI believes in unpaid voluntary work, which demonstrates the volunteers' real dedication and solidarity[22].

According to its Charter (see Table 7.3), AMI gives priority assistance to peoples in regions where other medical humanitarian organizations do not go. AMI's volunteers may have to cross borders illegally in order to fulfil their duty to assist persons in danger: "The universal right to give care, as well as that of being cared for, knows no borders".

AMI does not consider that to bear witness to human rights violations is the main objective of its missions: human rights missions are more within the domaine of Amnesty International. AMI resists any "star system" which has been created by some human rights activists.

AMI has worked in Afghanistan, in Indian villages of Colombia, in Erythrea, in the Karen and Karenni rebel minorities in Burma, in the Kurdistan in war against Iran, in the Tigré, in Surinam[23].

AMI's priority is to train local health personnel and make them fully autonomous. After two or three years' studies, AMI-trained nurses and health assistants are provided with basic medicaments and locally available medical equipment which will be renewed by AMI. AMI also follows up with its "students" work.

The selection of the "students" is subject to clear-cut criteria:—they must be adapted and receptive to the types of training offered: health assistants, future doctors or specialists,—they must be available,—they must volunteer,—they must be mobile,—they must be recognized and liked by their community, they must gain its confidence.

---

[22] Information based on AMI publications and an interview with AMI officials on 23 June 1989.

[23] Simonnet Julie, "Le Jansénisme humanitaire de l'AMI", *Documentation française*, No. 148, Feb. 1989.

Table 7.3. Chapter of "Aide Médicale Internationale"

AMI is a non-profit, humanitarian association. Its members, who are principally health personnel, declare their acceptance of the following principles:

1. AMI brings relief to all the peoples, victims of natural catastrophes, conflicts or wars, without political, ideological, religious or racial discrimination. This relief, motivated by emergency or quasi-emergency situations, is given priority in regions where other medical humanitarian organizations do not go.

2. AMI members on mission respond to a duty of assistance to persons in danger. They may be required to assume the responsibility, by necessity and not by choice, to cross, in a clandestine way states' borders in order to practise their medical work. They affirm that the universal right to care, as well as that to be cared for, knows no borders.

3. AMI's permanent concern is the effectiveness of its medical work and its continuity. It is conscious of the need to constantly adjust its action in order to respect the traditional cultural, social and religious equilibrium of the social communities where it works. It gives priority to the training of local health assistants.

4. An AMI member may have to bear witness to a violation of human rights. However, to bear witness cannot be the main purpose of a mission and cannot give cause to any personal profit.

5. AMI members are volunteers. They consider that their voluntarism is the guarantee of their dynamism, the independence of their action, the brotherhood which unites them. They work for the Third World, they do not live off the Third World.

6. AMI is financed essentially by private donations. AMI uses these donations with a scrupulous respect for the generosity of the donors, particularly in limiting to the strict minimum its administrative expenses and in directing its expenditures to its medical action.

Source: AMI Document (translated by the author from French)

AMI's budget for 1988 was 2,4 million francs, 71 percent of which was spent on missions. 75 percent of the revenues were private donations. Subventions are received from the French Ministry of Cooperation and from the European Communities' Emergency Aid Fund, but only to finance "open" (not clandestine) missions. Subsidies in kind are received from Air France, the French railways, the French Army Health Services and laboratories. The AMI volunteers do not receive any stipend: only their travel and local expenses are paid by AMI. By reducing its salaries, travel and equipment expenditures, AMI is able to send from 100 to 150 volunteers each year on missions. A volunteer's mission lasts four months on average.

An AMI group was created in the U.K. in 1986 and one in the Netherlands in 1987.

Usually discreet, AMI denounced the excesses of the assistance provided to Armenia (funds, medicaments, clothing etc.) — and the inadmissible "racket" imposed on NGOs trying to assist populations in South Sudan.

AMI has remained the most faithful to the original "spirit of Biafra", the spirit of rebellion, austerity, dedication, forbidden missions beyond borders, what it calls the "humanitarian ethic".

The Risks Taken by Volunteers "Without Borders"

International medical volunteers working in war-torn areas may be wounded or killed. Those crossing borders illegally may be arrested and condemned to long detention, or shot as mercenaries or spies.

In 1981, four of the five MSF hospitals in the Afghan Hazarajat region were bombed by Soviet planes, one was totally destroyed. In Turkey, a MSF doctor and nurse who were trying to reach a hospital in the Iranian Kurdistan in war, were arrested. Accused of "smuggling of medicaments" and "separatist propaganda", they were released after eight months in jail.

In 1982, the MSF hospital in East Chad was bombed by Libyan planes. In Honduras, death threats were painted at night on houses where MSF teams lived and assisted Salvadoran refugees and an MSF plane was set on fire. An AMI hospital, although covered with a red cross, in the Panjshir valley of Afghanistan, was bombed by Soviet planes. Pamphlets dropped by helicopters described two female doctors as the "French whores of the rebel chiefs".

In 1983, the Ambassador of Angola in Paris stated that MSF members working in rebel-held areas would be considered as "mercenaries in white frocks" and treated as such if captured.

In 1984, a Belgian doctor and a nurse working for MSF were detained for more than two months in Chad by the Libya-supported GUNT troops. Their release followed long negotiations between the GUNT and Libya on the one hand, MSF and the Belgian government on the other.

In 1986, in South Africa, two MDM doctors were jailed and beaten during forty-eight hours because they wanted to give care to wounded black demonstrators. A MDM hospital, situated in the Iraqi Kurdistan, where 25 patients were hospitalized and where four French doctors were working, was bombed on 7 October by mortars.

In 1987, in Somalia, a MSF medical team of ten persons was kidnapped by a group of armed rebels and taken to Ethiopia. The group was released two weeks later. In Sri Lanka, the Indian Army made death and other threats against a MSF surgical team[24].

The Augoyard "cause célèbre" is typical of the risks taken by volunteers who work in rebel-held areas.

During his second illegal mission in Afghanistan for AMI, Dr. Philippe Augoyard (French) was arrested by Soviet troops on 16 January 1983. He was accused of spying and illegal entry. He was forced to confess publicly his "crimes" at his trial. On 13 March, he was condemned in Kabul to eight years' jail for having entered Afghanistan illegally and for "having collaborated with counter-revolutionary elements". No French consular authority had been allowed to contact him during his detention, the French Embassy in Kabul had not been notified of his trial

---

[24] Internal document of MSF.

which took place in front of thousands of persons, but without the assistance of a lawyer.

Following diplomatic pressure from the French government, a press campaign and the intervention of the French Communist Party leader, the Soviet authorities allowed the Afghan government to release Dr. Augoyard in June.

MSF acknowledged his liberation as a victory of public opinion, but re-affirmed its "imprescriptible right to give care to those who need it urgently"[25].

Even after the withdrawal of the Soviet forces from Afghanistan, in August 1989, the Afghan government forces attacked a medical convoy of the French association "Handicap International", killing fifteen mujahedeens and a 24 year-old prosthesis specialist, Vincent Gernigon. A medical physiotherapist, Dr. Xavier Lemire had also been arrested. Handicap International was sent to Afghanistan under U.N. auspices to train Afghans in making prosthesis appliances. On 14 September, Lemire was released following formal requests from President Mitterand and U.N. Secretary-General Perez de Cuellar.

On 26 April 1990, a group of Afghans broke into a clinic run by MSF in rebel-held territory within Afghanistan. They beat and burned Frédéric Gallard, a 27-year old logistics specialist, until his face was virtually unrecognizable. They then killed him with a bullet through his head. This incident, other acts of violence and threats appeared to be part of a campaign by extremist elements in the mujahedeen resistance to drive the foreigners, including the foreign relief workers, out of the country[26].

U.N. officials and soldiers, Red Cross delegates and volunteers from other NGOs also risk their life, their freedom, their health. However, U.N. employees and Red Cross delegates enter countries only with the agreement of the government authorities concerned. U.N. employees are legally protected by the U.N. Convention on Privileges and Immunities and Red Cross delegates are generally covered by written agreements with governments. Doctors "without borders" are or are not recognized by governments as NGO members but do not benefit from any special privileges or immunities, except for the protection accorded to medical personnel by the Geneva Conventions and Additional Protocols under certain conditions (see Chapter 10). When they take the risk to enter borders illegally to work in rebel areas, their only *post facto* protection is that of their own country's authorities.

In countries like Lebanon, where the central government is unable to maintain peace and order, members of all types of organizations, IGOs or NGOs, are in a risk situation. The disappearance of Alec Collett, a British journalist and UNRWA staff member, alleged to have been executed in April 1986, the killing of William Richard Higgins, UNTSO Observer, announced in July 1989, the abduction of two

---

[25] *Le Monde*, 15 March and 5–6 June 1983.
[26] *Le Dauphiné Libéré* and *Le Monde*, 19 Aug. 1989, *Le Monde*, 16 Sept. 1989 and *Newsweek* of 30 July 1990.

ICRC delegates in October 1989, the disappearance of two West Germans, members of a humanitarian NGO, ASME-Humanitas since 16 May 1989, the abduction of Jan Cools, from the Norwegian Aid Committee from May to June 1989, are some recent examples. In Sudan, an MSF plane was shot down on 21 December 1989: all four passengers were killed, the pilot, two MSF volunteers and one Sudanese employee of the U.N. World Food Programme. According to humanitarian agencies, the attack was instigated by the Sudanese forces with the purpose of making those agencies stop their assistance in South Sudan and leave the country. Forty MSF volunteers were then giving humanitarian assistance in Sudan[27].

The French Doctors' Motivation

In the absence of reliable data, one can only surmise why doctors, nurses and other specialists volunteer for a mission "without borders". Originally, some wanted to continue the work of former colonial health officers. Some serve out of a sense of moral mission or obligation to care for the poor and the sick of the Third World. Some feel responsible for the "sins" of French colonization, for the failures of decolonization and want to make up for the damage done. Some seek adventure and do not fear physical risk. Some want to leave medical routine and bourgeois life behind, at least for a while. Some want to run away from marital or other personal problems. Some believe in prevention and public health, while their practice in Europe will be mainly curative and, often, highly specialized. Some become professionals in emergency voluntary medicine. Some reject the "yuppie" ideology, the "get rich" objective. Their motivation may be political—Kouchner was a young communist student—, or religious, like that of Max Récamier, another MSF founder. Leftists and Christians, faced with the reality of suffering and dying, like Henry Dunant at Solférino, felt that their duty was to act, care and bear witness.

A Right of Humanitarian Intervention?

All non-governmental medical associations contribute to the health care of the poor, the sick and the wounded. The specificity of the "French Doctors" is to care for populations without excessive concern for governments and borders. They affirm that victims have a right to be cared for, and that medical personnel therefore have an imperative duty to give assistance, wherever the victims are, as fast as possible. Emergency justifies all means of action.

The proclaimed "right and duty" to intervene wherever care is urgently needed

---

[27] *Le Monde*, 2 Aug. 1989, *International Herald Tribune*, 16 June 1989, *Tribune de Genève*, 19 Oct. 1989, *Le Monde*, 28–29 Jan. 1990.

is a direct attack against the international law and international relations principle of the sovereignty of states. Such a right and obligation can at the most constitute a moral recommendation, in the present state of international relations. This issue will be reviewed in more detail in Chapter 11.

Another problem raised by the "non-border" organizations is that of bearing public testimony. Should a humanitarian NGO denounce publicly the bad deeds of a government, at the risk of being expelled from the country and therefore to stop its assistance? Is the medical duty to care for all, which requires the organization to be and appear neutral, compatible with taking sides, judging, condemning?

The Red Cross answer is "no", the answer of some organizations in the "no borders" movement is "yes": for the latter, the defence of human rights is intricately linked with humanitarian work,—for the former, doctors cannot sacrifice their humanitarian duties to the defence of human rights.

Some medical groups react via the media, as giving testimony is part of their engagement. Others, like the Belgian and the Dutch MSF, prefer to react to human rights violations by a quiet, step-by-step, "humanitarian diplomacy" according to the following sequence[28]:

— first, the NGO initiates discussions and correspondence with the local authorities, then, if necessary, with the national authorities;
— if both local and national authorities refuse the offered dialogue or if they exercise pressure, the NGO takes its protest to embassies and to offices of IGOs in the capital of the country where the violations took place;
— at the same time, a confidential report is sent to such organizations as Amnesty International and to the United Nations Human Rights Commission; to institutional or private sponsors; and, since MSF was created in Europe, to European governments, the European Parliament and the European Court of Human Rights;
— finally, a news item may appear in the media: the name of the humanitarian NGO will normally not be mentioned, unless some of its members have been the victims of the abuses.

The drawback of this gradualist, quiet diplomacy is its slowness and its possible ineffectiveness.

On the other hand, immediate publicity may induce the local or national authorities into taking appropriate measures,—or it may trigger a violent, hostile, nationalistic reaction: the authorities may deny and reject all accusations, expel the organization deemed responsible for the publication, or at least withdraw their support to the organization's activities.

---

[28] *Assisting the Victims of Armed Conflict and Other Disasters*, F. Kalshoven, Ed., Nijhoff, 1989, "Humanitarian Diplomacy, The Essence of Humanitarian Assistance", by R. Moreels, pp. 51–52.

Other Medical NGOs

Other organizations, outside the "no-borders" movement contribute supplies and medical personnel to peoples in need.

The African Medical and Research Foundation (AMREF)

AMREF was founded in 1957 by the late Michael Wood, a British surgeon, as an independent non-profit organization. Its aim is to assist the East African governments in improving the health of their people, particularly in rural areas. Headquartered in Nairobi, Kenya, it attempts to identify health needs and it develops, implements, and evaluates methods and programmes to meet those needs through service, training and research. It runs projects in Kenya, Tanzania, Uganda, Somalia and the Southern Sudan with activities in primary health care, preventive medicine, training, consultancy, medical and surgical care.

Its current programmes include:

— primary health care and the training of community health workers through continuing education, teacher training and correspondence courses
— development, printing and distribution of training manuals, medical journals and health education materials
— health project development, planning and evaluation
— medical research into the control of hydatid disease, malaria and sleeping sickness
— ground mobile health services for nomadic pastoralists
— medical radio communication using over 100 two-way radio stations
— airborne support for remote health facilities, including surgical, medical and public health services.

In its 1988 diversified programme, AMREF has helped the Kenya Ministry of Health to plan district primary health care programmes, including traditional birth attendant training. The AMREF Disaster Response Unit has helped in the Kano floods in the Kisumu District. Its team of doctors, public health officers and nurses flew to Khartoum, following the flood disaster, and was initially involved in the emergency supply of drugs and insecticide spraying. AMREF has participated in the Nairobi Area Study looking at cost, efficiency, policies and management of the Health Services in the capital. In Tanzania, AMREF has been involved in various training activities, from village health worker training to management training. In Uganda, AMREF's Tsetse Trapping Project recorded a 95% reduction in the number of flies and a 90% decrease in sleeping sickness in the seven-month period during which 1,750 traps were used. AMREF held a post-basic training course for middle-level health workers (clinical officers, medical assistants, public health officers, public health nurses) from East African countries[29].

[29] AMREF *Annual Report*, 1988, *AMREF News*, January-March 1989 and *AMREF in Action*, 1989.

In 1989, AMREF was involved in two major emergency interventions. These were the KSh 20 million Emergency Rehabilitation Project, funded by the Government of the Federal Republic of Germany, and participation in the U.N. "Operation Lifeline Sudan" programme.

In the former programme, AMREF fed more than 3000 children in the Maridi/Yambio and Tambura areas. A total of 60 tons of specially mixed food was flown into the areas in collaboration with the Lutheran World Federation, which made air cargo space available. In addition to the food supplies, AMREF helped to build more than 1500 pit latrines in Yei and Juba.

For "Operation Lifeline Sudan", AMREF's Disaster Response Unit, at UNICEF's request, helped to rehabilitate Kapoeta Hospital in Eastern Equatoria. This hospital had been damaged in the war and looted, leaving the buildings with no equipment. Initially, AMREF helped to repair the hospital and provided temporary water and electricity systems. Then, with assistance from AMREF-Germany, equipment such as beds, theatre tables, benches, other stores and drugs were brought in.

With basic services functioning, AMREF has begun a training programme for the largely untrained volunteer hospital attendants and laboratory technologists. The curriculum developed for Kapoeta will, according to UNICEF, be used throughout the whole of the southern Sudan.

AMREF is well-known for its "Flying Doctors" Society. The Flying Doctors have flown millions of kilometres, treated hundreds of thousands of patients, performed countless operations and emergency evacuations. Called by AMREF radio control centre in Nairobi, the doctor flies alone, or with a nurse or surgeon to isolated mission hospitals in remote and often hazardous regions.

AMREF has a productive collaboration with WHO, particularly on training national staff in the writing and editing of health learning materials suitable for local needs. AMREF also collaborates in the research and behavioral components of WHO-sponsored AIDS programmes and participates in National AIDS Committees in Kenya, Uganda and Tanzania.

AMREF keeps a low profile in contentious political or other issues, perhaps in part because of its establishment in Kenya.Its Director-General, Christopher Wood, recognizes that AMREF's acceptance in the countries where it works, and its opportunities to contribute to development, depend on avoiding narrow geographical, religious or political affiliations: "This does not mean that we are "neutral" in controversial issues, but we must adhere to our motto "It's people that matter", we must work towards the goal of our new Five-Year Strategic Plan—Assistance in the achievement of sustainable, equitable improvement in health and well-being for selected target populations in Africa".

AMREF's expenditures amounted to KSh 246,352,000 in 1988 and KSh 277,101,000 in 1989. AMREF receives subventions from intergovernmental organizations, including the European Economic Community, the International Bank for Reconstruction and Development, UNICEF, UNDP, UNFPA, WHO,—national aid agencies such as the Canadian and the Swedish International Development Agencies, other NGOs (Oxfam, Save the Children Fund) and private sector busi-

276

ness firms. AMREF's "National Offices" in the Netherlands, the U.S.A., the U.K., the Federal Republic of Germany, Italy, Canada, Sweden, Denmark and France help with fundraising, liaise with governments, recruit staff and circulate information about its work. AMREF has country offices in Tanzania and Uganda.

AMREF has consultative status (roster) with the U.N. Economic and Social Council, UNICEF and WHO[30].

Medical Aid for Palestinians

This British organization was formed in 1972 and reorganized after the Israeli invasion of Lebanon. It has sent more than 70 doctors and nurses, and many tons of medical supplies in recent years to Palestinian refugee camps in Beirut and southern Lebanon. Its annual budget is about $450,000, most of it raised from private donations[31].

German Groups

The "Cap Anamur" Committee, named after the name of a freighter chartered by the group, has rescued approximately 9,500 Vietnamese boat people between 1979 and 1982. Between 1985 and 1987, three more missions took place in cooperation with the French Médecins du Monde, in which a further 2,500 boat people were rescued from the perils of piracy and shipwreck.

In 1980, the Cap Anamur Committee declared that it was willing to provide humanitarian and development aid to people inside Vietnam. In 1981, the Committee responded to an appeal from the Vietnamese Roman Catholic bishops by offering 3,000 tons of rice for the victims of a flood disaster in Thanh Hoa. Between 1988 and 1990, more than $1.2 million has been spent on the rehabilitation of two hospitals in the North of the country. Two German doctors were also sent to the hospitals. A project is now being discussed to help, in Vietnam, the growing number of boat people who have returned voluntarily to their homeland. Having brought 6,500 of the 9,500 boat people who have been resettled in Germany, the Committee also feels a special responsibility for Vietnamese living in Germany.

The Cap Anamur Committee has also sent some 900 doctors and nurses to African countries.

The German "Afghanistan Committee", organized in 1984, offers relief and medical assistance to Afghans inside their country and in refugee camps in Pakistan. The Committee has 20 doctors and 80 paramedical staff in the field, providing medical care for 175,000 people (31).

[30] AMREF Annual Report, 1988, p. 1.
[31] *Time*, 9 January 1989, and *Refugees*, Nov. 1990.

Christian Medical Commission (CMC)

CMC is one of five commissions of the World Council of Churches. It works through worldwide church-related medical/health organizations, including 24 national coordinating agencies. It coordinates church-related medical programmes at country and regional levels, — directs hospital-centred church medical work towards community-based health programmes. CMC collaborates with WHO through a WHO/CMC Standing Committee. Its collaboration includes various activities related to promotion of mental health, AIDS prevention and control, guinea worm eradication, development of health learning materials, health of the elderly, and alcohol and drug use. CMC supports the WHO principles of "Health for All" through primary health care[32].

Medicus Mundi Internationalis (MMI)

Founded in 1964 in the Federal Republic of Germany, MMI, an international organization for cooperation in health care, has now its executive secretariat in the Netherlands. As an international NGO, it claims to be independent from any political or religious affiliation.

Its aims are to promote health, particularly in developing countries, promote partnership and respect of different cultures, integrate health work within the overall development process with the goal of community self-reliance and actively support the WHO policy of primary health care.

MMI serves as a permanent recruitment service for trained medical and paramedical personnel for health work in developing countries. It also provides support to local health officers through scholarships, leadership training programmes, — financial, material and logistical support to health projects, support to local NGOs. As a member of the WHO-NGO Group on Primary Health Care, it takes part in research carried out on behalf of WHO, particularly on malaria, essential drugs and nutrition. MMI actively promotes WHO policies and programmes among its constituent organizations and their staff working at health services delivery level.

MMI has national branches in Belgium, France, the Federal Republic of Germany, Italy, the Netherlands, Spain, Switzerland and has affiliated organizations in the U.S.A., Algeria, Austria, Ireland and South Korea.

MMI has consultative status (roster) with the U.N. Economic and Social Council and with WHO.

MMI employs 60 staff members and has a yearly budget of approximately DM.200,000[33].

---

[32] WHO Doc. EB83/NGO/WP.1, 5 Dec. 1988.
[33] Internal WHO document.

278

How Effective Are These Groups?

A final question is the effectiveness of the various international medical groups, French and others. WHO's general answer is that, in view of the limited resources available, public health prevention, health education and training should prevail over curative work, as the public health structures and measures will have a far greater impact than sending a doctor, a surgeon or a nurse for a few weeks in a dispensary.

Clearly, the work of WHO at policy and government level is essential: the adoption and implementation of sensible public health policies, the strengthening of the public health structure, health education, the training of health personnel, immunization campaigns, epidemiological work, the orientation and stimulation of medical research are in the proper domain of a global intergovernmental health organization.

The IGO responsibilities do not exclude the grass-roots efforts of the medical NGOs. Among these, the action of the 1,500 doctors and other volunteers sent each year by MSF, MDM and AMI to treat the sick and the wounded in more than 40 countries responds to immediate individual and group needs, which would not be satisfied otherwise. The voluntary action also represents a concrete gesture of international solidarity. IGOs and NGOs play a complementary role in international health care, as they do in international relief and development work.

The medical volunteer associations, like other NGOs in other fields, are influenced by the responsible IGOs' policy decisions or recommendations, such as the "Health for All by the Year 2,000" and the primary health care concept for WHO and UNICEF. The action of most of the non-governmental health groups has expanded from purely emergency medical and nursing care to health planning, health education and training of local health staff. MSF trains its volunteers in international health (nutrition, sanitation, vaccinations, epidemiology) and some of its doctors have obtained a U.S. Master's in Public Health. MSF participates in the WHO/UNICEF Expanded Programme of Immunization. MDM has development programmes which include health and social assistance, medical training and nutrition campaigns. AMI's priority is to train local health assistants.

A MSF poster states that its doctors have two billion patients in their waiting room. All helpers are welcome!

CHAPTER 8

THE UNITED NATIONS VOLUNTEERS PROGRAMME (UNV)

> The UNV *is* the United Nations to thousands of people around the world, in schools, in laboratories, in refugee camps[1].

In previous Chapters, we have focused mainly on humanitarian non-governmental organizations (NGOs).

We now turn to a body which is a part of the United Nations intergovernmental "family" of organizations and still retains the specificity and spirit of an international voluntary service. The UNV is the only volunteer programme in the United Nations, and the only volunteer programme managed by an IGO.

The UNV is not a humanitarian organization as such: it was created with the purpose of assisting the U.N. development programmes in the Third World. In the 1980s, it was entrusted with emergency relief missions in addition to its development activities. Its evolution was thus different from that of many humanitarian NGOs which started with pure charity and short-term emergency work, and later saw the need to engage in mid- or long-term development programmes.

The UNV has common characteristics with other volunteer programmes, such as national (government) volunteer programmes. Its creation has been inspired by the creation and overall success of the U.S. Peace Corps (see Chapter 3) and other national or NGO volunteer schemes.

While the UNV has much smaller staff and financial resources than the U.S. Peace Corps and several other humanitarian volunteer NGOs, it has the mandate and the ambition to be regarded by governments, IGOs and NGOs as the "custodian" of the concept of voluntarism for development and to serve as a global focal point for all voluntary agencies. However, the major NGOs, with far longer experience in voluntary work than UNV, do not readily accept these claims.

We will review first the creation of the UNV in the 1970s and its slow and

---

[1] Comment by the U.S. delegate to the 37th Meeting of the UNDP Governing Council on 23 June 1990, in Geneva.

difficult beginnings, followed by an unexpected growth in development and relief assistance activities.

The UNV was instrumental in the adoption of two important Declarations on international voluntarism, the Sana'a and the Maseru Declarations, in 1982 and 1986.

An assessment of the programme's effectiveness was carried out in 1987–1988: its outcome was generally positive.

After a review of the requirements for employment in the UNV programme, we will summarize the main employment conditions of UNVs.

Finally, we will attempt to identify some of the characteristics of the unique UNV programme, its differences and similarities with other volunteer programmes, and future trends[2].

The Origin of the Programme

In 1961, the Economic and Social Council of the U.N. recognized that voluntary technical personnel can play an important role in the economic and social development of developing countries, that their use in international groups can assist in the promotion of peaceful relations among nations and that they may provide additional supporting assistance[3].

The Council approved the use of voluntary technical personnel in the technical assistance activities of the U.N. and invited the specialized agencies to make use of such personnel. It set out the principles governing the use and assignment of voluntary technical personnel: volunteers were not to be assigned to the headquarters of a U.N. organization, the receiving country had to approve the assignment of a volunteer, volunteers were considered as international civil servants (see Table 8.1).

In 1986, an Ad Hoc Inter-Agency Meeting on the Use of Volunteers in Field Projects of the U.N. System recommended that the U.N. and U.N. agencies evolve a framework which would lead to a harmonization of practices for the use of volunteers in U.N. field projects and eventually to a volunteer instrument "identifiable as a corps of volunteers".

On 13 June 1968, the Shah of Iran proposed in a speech at Harvard University the creation of a "legion" of volunteers in the service of mankind:

> Since Imperial Roman times, many legions have been formed for the purpose of military conquest. Let us, for once, create an international legion for the purpose of gaining victory in the fight against the real enemies of humanity: that is, against poverty, hunger and social injustice in any form[4].

---

[2] Information on the UNV programme has been based on UNV documentation and interviews with UNV officials in Geneva in September and October 1990.

[3] Resol. 849(XXXII) of 4 August 1961.

[4] U.N. *Official Records*, U.N. General Assembly, 25th Session, 2nd Committee, 1918th plenary meeting, 7 Dec. 1970, p. 7.

Table 8.1.   U.N. Economic and Social Council Principles governing the use and assignment of volunteer technical personnel

1. The services of volunteers shall be utilized only in connection with programmes and projects certified as eligible for the assignment of volunteer personnel by the executing agencies. Volunteers shall not be placed at the Headquarters of the United Nations or its related agencies in any established posts.
2. No volunteers shall be sent to a country without prior approval of the receiving country, and any such volunteer may remain only with the permission of such country.
3. The final decision for the assignment of volunteers to specific programmes and projects shall rest with the executing agency and the recipient country.
4. Volunteer personnel shall be required to take a United Nations oath of office and be subject to the appropriate staff rules and regulations of the executing agency. They will be subject to the authority of the executive head of the executing agency and his representatives in the field.
5. The acceptance of a volunteer will confer upon him the legal status of an international civil servant and both offering and receiving countries shall undertake to respect this status.
6. The Government providing volunteer personnel shall be responsible for all identifiable costs as maintenance allowances, insurance, costs of transportation to the place of assignment (as appropriate via the headquarters of the executing agencies).

Source Annex to Resolution 849 (XXXII) of the Economic and Social Council, dated 4 August 1961.

On 20 December 1968, the U.N. General Assembly, in resolution 2460(XXIII) on "Human Resources for Development", requested the Economic and Social Council to study the feasibility of creating an international corps of volunteers for development.

In May 1969, the U.N. Secretary-General defined a volunteer as a person who gives his services without remuneration.

He may be a youth, someone in middle age, or a person recently retired from salaried employment. He is usually strongly motivated to donate his energies, his skills, his time for the accomplishment of tasks in whose purpose he believes[5].

In July 1969, the Economic and Social Council further refined the concept and mandate of a future U.N. corps of volunteers: it should consist of persons recruited on as wide a geographical basis as possible,—where possible, the composition of teams should be on a multinational basis,—no volunteer would be sent to a country without the explicit request or approval of the receiving country[6].

The features which came to be the hallmarks of the UNV were thus established before the programme was initiated: volunteer motivation, technical competence, development orientation, approval by the host country and universality.

During the General Assembly 25th Commemorative Session in New York in 1970, a group of delegates felt it was time to introduce a resolution to the General Assembly, in order to finally create the UNV programme. They sincerely believed

---

[5] See Doc. UNV II/1986/BP/3/E of 27 Oct. 1986, p. 3 and U.N. Doc. E/4663, Secretary-General's Note to the Economic and Social Council of May 1969.

[6] Resol. 1444(XLVII).

that by introducing such a "noble and humanitarian" idea, the programme could bring people, and particularly the young generation from developed and developing countries, closer together, and, by doing so, gradually remove the artificial barriers that separated them, thus contributing to greater understanding and peace.

A few countries wanted an independent programme, free from the bureaucratic practices of the U.N. system: this aim was not reached. Others, mostly from the developing countries, wanted the programme strictly linked with the development activities of the U.N., in full respect of their national sovereignty: they made sure that the volunteers would not be sent to countries without the specific request and approval of host governments.

Socialist countries and Malaysia said that the UNV scheme should not be allowed to become a "convenient umbrella" for the endeavours of a few countries, the refuge of bilateral programmes of some member states. The representative from Ukraine said that

the sad and well-known case of the U.S. Peace Corps was a warning which could not be neglected.

He also alleged that the new programme would inevitably swell the administrative machinery of the organization and its "unproductive" administrative expenditure.

Some representatives said that the UNVs should not displace or even compete with local labour, nor compete with local volunteers. They should not compete with, but rather supplement, national associate experts.

The Chilean representative said that the emphasis of the programme should be on sending young volunteers from developing countries to other developing countries, and not from developed countries to the Third World: this suggestion has been fulfilled by the UNV programme to a large extent[7].

Giving a limited satisfaction to those who wanted the UNV programme to be independent, it was decided that the programme Coordinator would be appointed by the U.N. Secretary-General in consultation with the UNDP Administrator, and not the other way around. However, the programme was placed within UNDP, the Coordinator was to be administratively subordinate to the UNDP Administrator, and the programme was to be administered within the rules and regulations of the United Nations and of the UNDP.

A Special Voluntary Fund was envisaged to provide the necessary financial backing, at the initiative of industrialized countries, and in particular the Scandinavian group, benefitting from the experience and advice of their voluntary agencies.

On 7 December 1970, the U.N. General Assembly decided to establish "an international group of volunteers" called U.N. volunteers and designated the UNDP Administrator as the Administrator of the UNVs[8].

[7] *Official Records*, U.N. General Assembly, 25th Session, 2nd Committee, 1318th, 1319th, 1321st meetings, 21, 22, 23 Oct. 1970.
[8] Resol. 2659(XXV).

The resolution set three principles to guide the future operations of the new programme:

1. The programme should emphasize technical competence and skills.
2. It should adhere to the principle of universality in the recruitment and assignment of volunteers.
3. Its activities should be guided by the needs of recipient countries.

Governments, international NGOs and individuals were invited·to contribute to a special voluntary fund in support of the programme.

The First Years: 1971–1977

During these years, the programme's viability and survival were often in question.

The programme began operations in January 1971. Against a target of 200 serving volunteers set by the U.N. General Assembly, only 88 were in service by the end of 1972 and UNV activities were limited to 14 countries of assignment and to 25 countries of recruitment. In 1975, there still were only 250 volunteers in service.

Why was this programme beginning so slowly?

One internal reason was the basic difficulty of starting a completely new programme within the multinational and bureaucratic U.N. world, in a field (voluntarism) completely new to the UNDP.

The financial support promised and expected from many donors was not forthcoming at the rate expected or desired, thus jeopardizing the financial, staffing and logistical support needed for its sound establishment and growth.

The programme's linkage with UNDP, and through its funding, with the projects of the U.N. specialized agencies, caused delays and an initial lack of enthusiasm and confidence on the part of the donors, the industrialized countries.

The U.N. specialized agencies' historical and continued reluctance to see their technical assistance and cooperation programmes placed under UNDP supervision, as well as the administrative complexities of the financing, recruitment, placement and supervision of UNVs did not facilitate their acceptance of the new programme.

Recipient governments and U.N. agencies were also, initially, reluctant to include UNVs in their projects for reasons of costs and competence: they could obtain the services of qualified associate experts without costs to the UNDP country allocations, while the costs of the allegedly less qualified UNVs were charged against these allocations (except in the least developed countries).

But the main problems lay within UNDP itself, both at its New York headquarters and in the field.

According to the first UNV Coordinator, Assad K. Sadry[9], the atmosphere pre-

---

[9] Doc. DP/UNV/CM/1988/OSA/6/E, Consultative Meeting on Voluntary Service and Development, Geneva, 20–22 Apr. 1988, pp. 27–29.

vailing at the UNDP in those days was one of putting many obstacles in the way of the implementation of the new programme. One senior UNDP officer said

> This baby was conceived without our knowledge and thrown into our laps for adoption: we have enough problems of our own.

The third Coordinator, Hikmat Nabulsi, said that the UNDP resident representatives, not the host (recipient) countries, were the major hurdles. Volunteers evoked, in the 1970s, the image of a young man with a beard, guitar in hand, spreading good will in the countryside. Governments of developing countries did not want to host these unpredictable young foreigners: they had their own young people. The UNDP resident representatives had their own notions of volunteers and of the headaches they thought volunteers would cause[10].

In 1972, considerable time and efforts were wasted in the transfer of the UNV headquarters from New York to Geneva.

Although fears had been expressed about the non-cooperation of national volunteer agencies, the Federal Republic of Germany and the Danish Volunteer Services provided the programme with two of their best staff, who gave valuable help.

Between 1971 and 1974, the programme served merely as a channel for assigning volunteers. During that period, the recruitment of UNVs was delegated to the International Secretariat for Volunteer Service and the Coordinating Committee for International Voluntary Service. The programme's main activity consisted then in coordinating the assignment of volunteers to projects carried out by U.N. specialized and executing agencies.

In June 1974, the new Coordinator, John Gordon, decided that the programme would assume responsibility for the recruitment of volunteers. The programme then established a network of working relationships with government institutions and bilateral volunteer-sending agencies in industrialized and developing countries.

Between 1974 and 1977, the pattern of supply of volunteers shifted: the preponderance of UNVs from 18 industrialized countries gradually gave way first to an even share of supply and then to a larger proportional representation from developing countries.

By 1976, the General Assembly added two new mandates to the UNV programme, giving it support through this expression of confidence.

By resolution 31/131 of 16 December 1976, the General Assembly designated UNV as a "major operational unit" of the U.N. for the execution of youth programmes, especially pilot projects to increase the participation of youth in development activities. Under this mandate, UNV offers support for such activities as providing advisory services on national youth policies, training youth leaders, stimulating youth employment and establishing youth documentation and information centres. UNV also assists in creating and strengthening domestic (indigenous) voluntary services for young people.

---

[10] *UNVNews*, No. 46-E, Sept. 1988.

By resolution 31/166 of 21 December 1976, UNV was requested to implement a programme to give support to government and NGO domestic development service (DDS) organizations. These organizations promote self-reliant economic and social development at the grass-roots level through participatory initiatives. Under this mandate, UNV provides to such organizations a range of services which include short-term consultancies, on-the-job training abroad, intercountry exchange of DDS field workers as UNV-DDS volunteers, organization of workshops, and mobilization of bilateral donor funding for small-scale projects.

While the image of UNV was strengthened as an organization serving as an instrument for mobilizing and channelling young people for development work under voluntary conditions, UNV's future continued to be one of uncertainty: it had not yet consolidated its presence in the developing countries, nor obtained the full confidence of the donor countries.

The Years of Growth: 1977–1981

When Hikmat Nabulsi was appointed as third UNV Coordinator, in 1977, the Secretary-General of the U.N., Kurt Waldheim, told him that the General Assembly might wish to review, if not bury, this organization that did not seem to have given the results expected after seven years of existence.

In 1977, the UNDP Governing Council urged the Coordinator to expand the programme to its full potential. New targets were set by the UNV management: 400 volunteers in the field by 1978 and 500 by 1979: the latter target had been set by the Governing Council to be achieved in 1976. 863 volunteers were in the field in 1980. The Council reset the target at 1,000, to be achieved by 1983; it was reached in November 1981.

In 1978, all recruitment and programming operations, including the activities of the New York Liaison Office, were consolidated in Geneva.

In 1979, the first team of DDS field workers was assigned to Asia. The basic element in the DDS programme is that the skills, knowledge and experience for starting self-reliant development are largely to be found already within the developing countries. Field workers are recruited by UNV from grass-roots groups in developing countries. They are then assigned to similar groups in other countries in the same region. The DDS field worker plays a dual role:—as an animator at the local level, helping to create conditions whereby people are encouraged to embark on their own efforts and self-promotion,—as a facilitator for establishing connections horizontally (to other comparable local groups and organizations), as well as vertically (to district, provincial, national authorities, bilateral aid organizations, to national NGOs and coordinating bodies)[11].

---

[11] *UNV and Domestic Development Services*, A success story at the grassroots in Asia and Africa—undated.

In 1980, the UNDP Governing Council commended the increasing role UNV was playing in technical cooperation activities of developing countries. The title of UNV "Coordinator" was changed to "Executive Coordinator"[12].

By the middle of its tenth anniversary year, UNV reached for the first time the level of 1,000 volunteers serving in the field: the General Assembly had set this target to be achieved not later than the end of 1983. This increase reflected the rising demand for the services of UNVs, as well as the expansion in 1976 of the programme's mandate by the General Assembly.

The Substantive New Programme of Action adopted by the U.N. Conference on Least Developed Countries in 1981 stated that full consideration be given to the use of middle-level experts such as U.N. and national volunteers, and volunteers from NGOs. Similarly, the Zimbabwe Conference on Reconstruction and Development held in Harare in April 1981, in which UNV participated, identified considerable needs for middle-level operational expertise[13].

The number of countries receiving UNVs increased from 87 in December 1980 to 91 by the end of 1981. By then, 460 volunteers were serving in 31 least developed countries, underscoring the special relevance of UNV to the particular needs of this group of countries.

In 1981, 3,300 new applications were received , half of which were found qualified for inclusion in the UNV roster, which included more than 2,000 names at the end of 1981.

The relative participation of industrialized countries nationals continued to decline. By December 1981, only 22 percent of the serving volunteers were from 22 industrialized countries.

In 1982 and in 1986, UNV organized two important international conferences during which Declarations on International Voluntarism and Development Cooperation were adopted.

The Sana'a Declaration—1982

This Declaration was adopted by the participants to the UNV High-Level Symposium on International Voluntary Service and Development Cooperation held in Sana'a, Yemen Arab Republic, from 7 to 13 March 1982[14].

The Symposium was the first meeting to bring together under U.N. auspices government officials, representatives of bilateral volunteer-sending organizations and NGOs and representatives of U.N. organizations and specialized agencies, to discuss the concept of international voluntary service and to examine new direc-

---

[12] *UNV Newsletter*, No. 43-E, Oct.-Dec. 1987.

[13] Doc. DP/1982/6/Add.1, Annex, 11 May 1982.

[14] Doc. UNV/SYM/REP/2, *International Volunteer Service and Cooperation*, Report on the UNV High-Level Symposium, Sana'a, Yemen Arab Republic, 7–13 March 1982.

tions for its implementation and growth. Representatives from Australian Volunteers Abroad, the Danish Voluntary Service, the British Volunteer Service Overseas, the Agency for Personal Service Overseas in Ireland, Japan Overseas Cooperation Volunteers, the then Organization of Netherlands Volunteers, the U.S. Peace Corps and from similar Belgian, German (Federal Republic of Germany), Finnish and Swedish governmental or non-governmental bodies, participated in the Symposium. 24 developing countries were represented, as well as 17 U.N. bodies, including the World Bank and four regional IGOs.

The main points of the Sana'a Declaration are summarized hereunder:

1. International voluntary service is an important vehicle for promoting solidarity among nations in pursuance of global objectives of economic and social development and international cooperation.
2. The UNV programme serves effectively and innovatively the cause of self-reliance among developing countries.
3. UNV should convene at least once a year consultative meetings of participating organizations from industrialized and developing countries,—as well as periodic intergovernmental meetings.
4. UNV should develop its documentation service on international voluntarism and increase its "high quality" publications and other information materials, to increase awareness of the UNV programme.
5. UNVs provide operational expertise at the middle and technical levels. Their dedication makes them especially effective for work in remote and difficult regions. They are "cost-effective". There is a vast and largely unfilled need for middle-level operational expertise to support economic and social development activities in developing countries. The requirements for middle-level technicians were estimated in the Report of the Secretary-General of the U.N. Conference on the Least Developed Countries, held in Paris in September 1981, to be in the order of 20,000 per year throughout the 1980s. It was therefore recommended to increase the number of UNVs.
6. There was still insufficient utilization of the UNV programme in international technical cooperation: in other words, UNDP and the specialized agencies should include more volunteers in their projects. UNV should have more flexible lengths of assignment (and not insist on a minimum of two years).
7. The basis of participation in the UNV programme should be widened: more volunteers should be recruited from the industrialized countries, more "senior" (retired) professionals, more women should be recruited in the programme.
8. UNV Domestic Development Service (DDS) for Self-Reliance should be extended from Asia to other developing countries regions.
9. Better briefing and debriefing of UNVs should be arranged.
10. Additional funds should be given to the UNV Special Voluntary Fund and staffing levels revised in line with the size of the operations.

The Declaration praised this "young and dynamic" organization which, in successfully completing its first decade, had truly reflected the letter and spirit of the mandate entrusted to it by the General Assembly. The achievements of the programme and of its Coordinator were thus publicly recognized and the programme's further growth encouraged.

The recommendations contained in the Sana'a Declaration were approved in June 1982 by the Governing Council of the UNDP, which requested the UNV Executive Coordinator to take appropriate follow-up action. The Council also expressed concern about the deteriorating financial situation of the Special Voluntary Fund and appealed for contributions[15].

In 1985, the Council gave a wholehearted endorsement of the UNV programme.

It noted that the relevance and advantages of the programme had now been fully recognized by the developing countries. It urged governments and U.N. organizations to increase the utilization of UNV contributions, where appropriate, in meeting the crucial qualified manpower requirements in the execution of development programmes and projects. It also noted the programme's achievements in participatory development through its DDS activities, aimed at helping the least advantaged communities to participate more actively in their own development[16].

The Maseru Declaration—1986

Four years after the Sana'a Symposium, the "Second UNV High-Level Intergovernmental Meeting on International Voluntarism and Development" was held in Maseru, Lesotho. The Meeting was to examine the impact of voluntary service on development activities, to take stock of the UNV programme's progress during the past years and to make recommendations concerning the programme's future development.

From 16 to 21 November 1986, some 200 participants—representing fifty developing countries' governments, volunteer-sending organizations, U.N. organizations and NGOs—from all five continents, took part in the Meeting.

The Meeting adopted the "Maseru Declaration", which confirmed the participants' conviction that voluntarism is one of the most effective instruments of development today[17].

A consensus was reached on the following principles:

— International voluntarism is an appropriate and complementary source of technical and professional manpower to be used by countries striving for social and economic development.

— UNV and other international volunteer-sending organizations have maintained

---

[15] Decision 82/21 of 18 June 1982.

[16] Decision 85/22, 28 June 1985.

[17] Doc. UNV II/1986/REP/1/E, 2nd High-level Intergovernmental Meeting on International Volunteerism and Development, Maseru, Lesotho, 16–21 Nov. 1986.

high standards of professionalism and have demonstrated commitment to the ideals and goals of international development.

— Young people everywhere have special needs. They possess immense capabilities with which to contribute to national development. New and imaginative programmes are needed to assist them in assuming their rightful role in nation building.

— NGOs and domestic development services are potent instruments of development, especially in local communities. Support for NGOs and DDS organizations is a necessity, and more effective ways to strengthen them must be found.

With regard to UNV, some of the recommendations in a plan of action follow:

— The UNV programme should be expanded according to realistic targets. A total of 2,500 UNVs should be serving by 1989.

— Additional financial resources should be provided urgently to the UNV Special Voluntary Fund by the international community.

— The resources of the UNV headquarters should be increased in personnel and facilities.

— UNV should continue to convene every three years intergovernmental meetings similar to those in Sana'a and Maseru.

— UNV should continue to hold annual consultative meetings with other volunteer-sending organizations, to review common practices and general issues, to be incorporated into a code of standards for international volunteer service.

— UNV, as custodian of the concept of voluntarism for development should create greater awareness of this concept. It should examine the usefulness of a reverse flow of volunteers for development from South to North.

— The proven capacity of UNV to assist in emergency situations should be institutionalized. UNV should include on its roster the names of candidates selected for their ability to respond on short notice to the requirements of emergency situations. This capability should be made known to governments and to international organizations involved in emergency situations.

— To absorb the underutilized technically qualified personnel of some developing countries, UNV should assist governments in establishing national corps of technically qualified volunteers who could be integrated into national development efforts. These volunteers could thus fill posts now occupied by expatriates and international volunteers. The volunteer ethic, which implies sacrifice and modest remuneration, must be reconciled with the need for such national volunteers to receive an adequate allowance commensurate with those of international volunteers.

During the debates, UNV was encouraged to provide extended training and cultural orientation programmes for newly-appointed volunteers, prior to their assignment, along the lines of bilateral volunteer organizations. For example, the U.S. Peace Corps provides systematically to new volunteers an 8 to 14 week orientation programme which includes language tuition, technical and cross-cultural skills training.

Many speakers called for the increased use of UNVs for emergency and humanitarian assistance.

A number of participants said that UNV must be open to the introduction of new forms of international voluntarism, including short-term assignments, assistance in the return of expatriate national competence, etc.

The misconception that UNVs can be seen as competitors to traditional experts was corrected: UNVs are not substitutes for experts, but are an alternative and complementary source and form of technical assistance competence.

Evaluation of the UNV Programme—1987–1988

The UNDP Governing Council asked the Administrator in 1986 and in 1987 (Decisions 86/43 and 87/36) to undertake a review of the UNV programme. The report[18] was generally supportive of the programme:

> The evaluation team felt that the U.N. Volunteer programme has great merit in both concept and implementation. U.N. volunteers respond to a need for additional operational expertise in developing countries unable to meet these needs with national expertise. Volunteers are perceived as being very cost effective, and as being able to function efficiently and effectively under often difficult circumstances. Their dedication and competence are well recognized and much appreciated by U.N. and host country officials alike. The potential for expansion to the programme is considerable, and there appears to be great interest in such an expansion among using agencies, field staff, and host governments. The recent very rapid expansion has, however, resulted in the surfacing of a number of management issues which need to be addressed and resolved before any further major expansion.

Some of the major findings of the team were critical:

— Imbalance in the nationality distribution of volunteers (85 percent of volunteers from developing countries), raising concerns about the universality of the programme;
— UNVs regarded within the U.N. system as "cheap labour";
— Inadequate use of UNVs in development projects;
— Too much decision-making centralized in UNV/Geneva;
— Little attention paid to human needs of volunteers etc.

Among the major recommendations, some concerned the role and mandate of the programme.

[18] Doc.CEO/BPPE/UNDP, No. 6011h, Nov. 1987.

The monopoly of the UNV programme on volunteers for use in U.N. agency projects should be eliminated, while still retaining its coordinating role. The Administrator[19] recognized that the intent of this proposal was to ensure more involvement of volunteers from industrialized countries. However, the word "monopoly" was misleading and, furthermore, he did not feel that he could relinquish his responsibilities in this respect, entrusted to him in compliance with several U.N. General Assembly resolutions.

The team's report questioned whether the UNV programme was in fact a "volunteer" programme and whether it was useful for UNVs to be called "volunteers". This challenge was based on the assumptions that the term "volunteer" understated the high professional calibre of UNV, and that most UNVs (those from developing countries) might be attracted to UNV service more for financial than for altruistic reasons. The Administrator rejected the second argument and decided to add the professional title of the UNV after the word "volunteer": for instance, UNV Epidemiologist, UNV River Engineer, UNV Data Processor.

The team report proposed that the respective roles of the UNV headquarters in Geneva and that of the UNDP resident representatives should be clarified: UNV/Geneva should be responsible for recruitment, placement, promulgation of policies and regulations, and monitoring, while the resident representative would be responsible for the actual implementation of the programme at field level. The latter's role in programming for volunteer participation in country projects would also be strengthened. The Administrator did not feel that any change was necessary in this respect. On the other hand, he agreed with the recommendation that the title of "UNV programme assistant" be changed to "UNV programme officer". He did not agree that these posts should be changed from volunteer positions into regular staff posts in view of the costs involved.

The Administrator rejected the report's proposal that the DDS and youth programmes be merged into the overall UNV programme, with all volunteers receiving the same emoluments, as not realistic. This proposal ignored the fact that UNV DDS personnel are not regular UNV specialists, but participatory development field workers whose conditions of service are designed to harmonize with those of co-workers in the rural settings where they are assigned.

Concerning the national origin of the UNVs, the Administrator agreed with the report's recommendations that there was a need to achieve a wider geographic representation and that the number of women should be increased. In particular, the report had emphasized the importance of a better representation of volunteers from industrialized countries, because it would ensure true universality, it would build a constituency for the programme among donor countries, it would enhance the credibility of the programme and it would provide an opportunity for such individuals to participate in the activities of an international organization.

Other proposals related to recruitment procedures and employment conditions,

---

[19] Doc. DP/1988/46/Add.1, 23 March 1988.

such as the need for flexibility in determining the duration of assignments and various financial questions.

While the UNDP Administrator (counselled by the UNV Executive Coordinator) accepted only part of the report's recommendations, and while more open criticisms of the team's work and conclusions were published in the UNVNews of June 1988, the UNDP Governing Council only took note of the "useful review" of the UNV programme (Decision 88/38), and took note "with appreciation" of the Administrator's response to it. It also noted with satisfaction the increasing practice of the U.N. system to consider the use of volunteers in the project preparation phase.

In 1987, as part of the review exercise, all UNDP resident representatives were asked to assess UNVs activities in their respective countries of assignment, in consultation with the host government. The views received were frank and sometimes critical. They were diverse, considering the political, economic, social and cultural differences of the countries concerned and the complexity and variety of UNV assistance to these countries.

Among the eleven replies selected and published in UNV News[20], a few extracts follow:

> UNV has been found useful in Bhutan mainly as a means of filling manpower gaps and so allowing the start-up of projects/programmes earlier than would otherwise have been the case. Increasingly, emphasis has been placed on the technical assistance aspect of UNV assignments, i.e., the transfer of skills and knowledge to Bhutanese counterparts as they become available. If UNV selection and briefing is well done, the volunteers play an important, appreciated and cost-effective role in the implementation of a wide variety of development programmes.

Positive results had been achieved by UNVs in Botswana: 80 UNVs had completed two or more years in the country during the period 1973 to mid-1987. The UNV input had considerably enhanced the scope of the UNDP programme in the country. It had been a major vehicle to develop collaboration with NGOs and the private sector.

The Government of Laos had expressed on numerous occasions—both formally and informally—its very positive view of the role that can be and was being played by UNVs in the development programme of the country. The Government saw clearly the practical advantage of having cost-effective technicians in the field who can train and support its lower- to middle-level technical manpower. This was particularly relevant in Laos, in view of its recent history and its loss of many technically qualified people. The results of the work of the majority of the UNVs have been quite positive, some even outstanding.

In Liberia, on the whole, the Government found the UNV programme highly

---

[20] "Viewpoints from the field" in *UNVNews*, No. 45-E, June 1988.

valuable and had, accordingly, taken adequate advantage of it under all four UNDP country programmes.

The Governments of Western Samoa, Cook Islands, Niue and Tokelau were pleased with the results obtained from the use of UNV services. The utilization of the UNV programme was extensive and growing. In 1982, there were 10 UNVs in Samoa and 15 in Cook Islands. In 1987, there were 36 and 23 volunteers serving, respectively, in these two countries, with an additional 26 for Samoa and 4 for Cook Islands currently under recruitment. UNVs are older, more experienced and more qualified than volunteers from the U.S. Peace Corps or from the Japan Overseas Cooperation service, and as a result, more respected by governments.

In Uganda, both the Government and UNDP officials were satisfied with the performance of the volunteers. The UNV programme had proved to be an effective institution for providing middle and operational level expertise needed for the various developmental activities:

> It is our view that UNVs, on an average, are more professionally qualified and experienced now than they were 10–15 years back. UNVs are increasingly taking on more senior responsibilities.

In the Yemen Arab Republic, the Government viewed the UNV programme as a valuable source of technical assistance due to its cost-effectiveness and its great potential in skills, experience and professionalism. It had been often noted that UNVs are quickly operational, less demanding in support services and more adaptive to difficult, harsh and isolated working conditions than other technical assistance staff. The increasing demand for UNVs by the Government in almost all sectors of the economy was a clear manifestation that the UNVs render satisfactory services to ministries, departments and projects to which they are assigned.

In Papua New Guinea (PNG), a review of the assessments given by the UNVs' supervisors indicated, not surprisingly, both good and bad experiences. When UNVs have not done well, the cause was either poor project design, non-involvement by supervisors in developing the job description, job duties imprecise or modified after the arrival of the UNV, wrong selection, or language deficiencies. However, there was little doubt that UNVs have contributed to PNG's development efforts, most particularly at the mid-levels of provincial governments.

The picture in Ethiopia was more mixed. The Land Use Planning Department in the Ministry of Agriculture found that all UNVs were not of equal standing. Their recruitment took too long, sometimes even taking a year to a year and a half, thus not being able to fulfil the immediate needs of projects. This Department favoured a greatly increased use of "national experts"[21] in their projects, in preference to a significant expansion of the use of UNVs. On the other hand, UNVs have usefully

[21] National experts are employed by U.N. organizations without acquiring the status of international civil servants. They are paid on the basis of local salary rates. See Yves Beigbeder, *Threats to the international civil service—Past pressures and new trends*, Pinter, London, 1988, pp. 160–163.

contributed to the improvement of the transport sector within the Relief and Rehabilitation Commission.

The UNDP resident representative in Addis Ababa felt that, although the results achieved by UNVs had been mixed, the management of the UNV programme appeared to have failed to capitalize on some of its successes. In the case of the provision of UNV teachers to Kotebe College of Teacher Education, for instance, all of the volunteers had served and left without even one replacement for existing posts and no filling of new posts. Reasons were: the insensitivity of the UNV management to the needs and requirements of the Ethiopian College, the under-qualification of most UNV candidates, the failure of qualified candidates to show up, etc.

A New Executive Coordinator

On 1 November 1988, Brenda McSweeney replaced Hikmat Nabulsi as Executive Coordinator. She had been with the UNDP since 1972 and had served in Burkina Faso, at the UNDP headquarters in New York and, as resident representative in Jamaica. She has brought a different management style to the UNV, which needed a good administrator to consolidate and further develop the growth obtained by her ebullient predecessor.

Called "Mr. Volunteer", H. Nabulsi left his mark on the programme during his leadership from 1977 to 1988, as an unorthodox leader and a hard taskmaster, totally dedicated to his mission. In the words of his chiefs or associates, Nabulsi trod on toes and offended many; he was idiosyncratic, controversial, always unpredictable. On the other hand, he inspired passion, affection and deep loyalty. None could deny his hard work and commitment to the goals of the programme. He had a dream of a rapidly expanding UNV programme, a dream that he helped realize. For another associate, the Coordinator was the super-salesman of volunteers, the dedicated, the infuriating, the untiring, the cold-blooded, warm-hearted, indefatigable, exasperating, incomparable Hikmat Nabulsi[22].

During the 37th Meeting of the UNDP Governing Council in 1990, a session was devoted to the UNV programme on 13 June.

Over 40 delegations intervened and overwhelmingly supported the work of the programme. 16 delegations commented positively on the comparative value of UNVs as long-term expatriate technical cooperation personnel. The delegate of the Federal Republic of Germany said:

> In the long run, volunteer specialists could and should eventually become the main modality for fielding long-term expatriate professionals by the U.N. system of operational activities.

---

[22] Paul Thyness, UNDP, and G. Arthur Brown, Associate Administrator, UNDP, in *UNVNews*, No. 46-E, Sept. 1988, pp. 2 and 15.

Many delegates saw scope for an important role for UNV in providing personnel to boost national execution of development programmes. As the Scandinavian delegations jointly observed

> The UNV programme represents the complementarity that the recipient countries, in executing their own projects and programmes, can well utilize and appreciate.

The delegate from Sri Lanka observed that there will be a big demand for volunteers in the 1990s and that steps have to be taken to meet this challenge, as UNV should be in a position to meet the demand at short notice.

For the future, UNV was widely encouraged to continue its steady expansion.

The Governing Council's decision (90/38 of 22 June 1990) again noted the role of the UNV programme as an important instrument for development cooperation. It also noted the importance of the support provided by the UNV specialists to the relief and rehabilitation activities undertaken by the UNHCR and other U.N. organizations for refugees, displaced persons and returnees.

During the debates, many delegations underlined the particular value of the contribution of UNV specialists to development and humanitarian work, the "potent combination" of professionalism, flexibility, commitment and genuine concern for the well-being of the beneficiaries of the projects.

The U.N. Coordinator for Humanitarian and Economic Assistance relating to Afghanistan, Prince Sadruddin Aga Khan, expressed a view shared by many delegates from industrialized and developing countries alike when he stated that, while technical specialization clearly counts,

> in the field, nothing counts more than personal human qualities and empathy...It is important to have an understanding of the people they work with, of their culture and traditions, of their hopes and aspirations.

The delegate from Tanzania concurred:

> (UNVs) have a quality that is perhaps more important than their skills and professions—deep commitment.

There was wide endorsement from both donors and recipients for UNV involvement in post-crisis relief and rehabilitation endeavours: many delegates supported expanded recourse to UNVs for assistance to refugees, displaced persons and returnees[23].

UNV's Involvement in Humanitarian Assistance and Health Projects

UNV activities in the field of refugees started in 1974, when the first refugees from Rwanda were recruited as UNVs. The first contact between UNV and the UNHCR

---

[23] Internal UNV document.

was made in 1976 when the UNHCR requested the recruitment of a UNV for its activities in Sudan.

In 1980, the Governing Council of the UNDP authorized the Administrator to approve special projects to finance emergency assistance and to assist in the rehabilitation and reconstruction of stricken areas[24].

Two major UNHCR/UNV programmes were then initiated.

Under a 1980 project of "Support to Refugees in South East Asia" (Project RAS/80/002), 76 UNVs were assigned to Hong Kong, Indonesia, Malaysia, the Philippines, Singapore and Thailand.

Although the short-term humanitarian relief orientation of this project was not exactly in line with the traditional mandate of UNV development assistance, the acute refugee emergency situation in South East Asia prompted UNDP's support, on an exceptional basis, of these activities. In 1984, the UNDP contribution included cost-sharing with the U.S. Peace Corps for the funding of 35 UNVs of U.S. nationality. The volunteers were active in, *inter alia*, resettlement, counselling, social welfare, administration, water supply, nutrition, community development, cultural orientation, teacher training (languages). Outstanding contributions by UNVs in Pulan Bidong, Malaysia, were widely recognized. The project was phased out in 1984.

Another project of "UNV Assistance to Refugee Activities" in Somalia (SOM/81/001) assisted refugees in Somalia and promoted their self-sufficiency, together with the UNHCR, from 1981 to 1988. 42 UNVs carried out activities in logistics and distribution system for food and non-food items, self-sufficiency projects in agriculture, field programming and implementation of UNHCR activities and strengthening of the capacity of the National Refugee Commission in administration, finance, counselling and information. The total contribution to the project included cost-sharing with donor countries (mainly the U.S., then Finland and Norway) amounting to approximately $1 million. The average annual cost of each volunteer assignment, excluding internal transport and equipment costs, amounted to $16,000[25].

In 1984, the Governing Council of UNDP approved an allocation of $1.5 million for a regional project in Africa South of the Sahara to counter the effects of the natural disaster in the region, by providing U.N. volunteers. The Council thus endorsed the UNDP Administrator's initiative to channel on an immediate and exceptional basis an increased number of UNVs to the most severely affected countries in Africa. However, the Council's approval was only given on the understanding that this was not to be regarded as a precedent.

One year later, relenting on its previous caution, the Council expressed its satisfaction with the UNV programme in general, and in particular with the emergency relief provided by UNVs. It urged the UNDP Administrator to continue assisting

---

[24] Decision 80/48, 30 June 1980.
[25] Internal UNV document.

the governments of African countries affected by the emergency through, *inter alia*, the provision of UNVs beyond the duration of the regional emergency project. Recognizing the value of the programme for development and emergency projects, the Council urged donor governments and all U.N. organizations to consider the particular advantages of flexibility, speed and cost-effectiveness of using UNVs when making additional allocations to assist in the African emergency[26].

During the life of the UNV-executed project (RAF/84/024), "UNV Emergency Assistance to the Drought-Affected Countries in Sub-Saharan Africa", from 1984 to 1987, some 87 UNVs served under the project in 24 countries of the region. Their activities covered emergency aid cooperation, water supply and sanitation, health, livestock management, anti-desertification, forestry and administration.

Following the recurrence of drought and internal strife in the region, UNV was called upon, at the end of 1987, to provide additional emergency assistance to Angola and Ethiopia[27].

On 7 June 1989, a $4.4 million Agreement was signed in Geneva by the Executive Coordinator of UNV and the representative of Prince Sadruddin Aga Khan, the Coordinator of "Operation Salam", the U.N. Humanitarian and Economic Assistance Programme relating to Afghanistan. At the request of the U.N. Secretary- General and of the Prince, UNV will field 90 volunteer-specialists for relief and rehabilitation work arising from the Afghanistan conflict. The volunteers will work with U.N. agencies, including WHO, ILO, FAO, UNICEF, UNHCR and the World Food Programme, and NGOs in the field[28].

While this new programme tends to confirm the useful role of UNVs in emergency situations, the UNV Executive Coordinator has recently underlined the difference between emergency situations caused by catastrophes, such as wars, floods, earthquakes, etc., and others arising from disasters such as drought. The Coordinator felt that UNVs had proved to be more effective in emergency situations requiring longer-term assistance, ranging from 6 months to one year and beyond[29].

In the health field, UNV has initiated its own projects or has cooperated with WHO and UNICEF.

For instance, in order to meet Sri Lanka's shortage of health care personnel, the country's Ministry of Health called on UNV to provide volunteer-doctors as a temporary measure. The first group of UNV doctors, from India and the Philippines, arrived in Sri Lanka in November 1978, in time to provide medical assistance for victims of a devastating cyclone. By the Spring of 1980, nearly 150 Burmese, Filipino and Indian UNV doctors had been channelled into rural areas of Sri Lanka. The assistance of UNDP, which financed most of the costs, and of UNV helped the

---

[26] Decisions 84/18 and 84/119 of 29 June 1984, Decision 85/22 of 28 June 1985.

[27] U.N. Doc. DP/1988/46 of 4 March 1988, U.N. Volunteers, *Report of the Administrator*.

[28] UNV Announcement of 8 June 1989.

[29] Doc. DP/UNV/CM/1987/OSA/6/E, Consultative Meeting on Voluntary Service and Development, Geneva, 8–10 April 1987, p. 15.

Sri Lankan Government make qualified medical care available to some 18,000 patients a day. Furthermore, a number of pilot primary care projects were initiated[30].

In Yemen, a project channelling WHO, UNICEF, UNDP and UNV support to hospital administration and nursing services began in 1974. During the period 1975 to 1981, 27 UNV-nurses, one UNV-X-ray technician and one UNV-doctor served within the project. The volunteers—from Australia, Finland, India, Nepal, Norway, Pakistan, the Philippines, Sweden, the U.K. and the U.S.—helped local staff, reorganized hospitals, supervised the clinical teaching of students at the Health Manpower Institute and helped upgrade nursing standards[31].

Requirements for UNV Assignments and Conditions of Service

Applicants for UNV assignments must be professionally qualified persons willing and capable of making a contribution to the development efforts of host countries[32].

They must possess either a university degree or a higher technical diploma, as well as a minimum of two years of relevant professional experience after graduation. For skilled trades, applicants must have a diploma plus a minimum of five years of relevant experience.

Applicants are informed that dedication and commitment to the volunteer spirit are prime elements in being considered for a UNV assignment. They must be prepared to work under modest conditions of service.

They should not expect a career with the UNV programme nor a further appointment with a U.N. organization. UNV assignments are normally based on two-year contracts, with six consecutive years' service as a usual upper limit. Shorter-term assignments of three months and above may apply in relief and rehabilitation contexts.

There is no minimum age limit, although, in practice, the education and experience requirements set the minimum age within the twenties,—and there is no maximum age limit, thus allowing the use of "senior" volunteer specialists.

The programme is more flexible than other volunteer schemes in regard to the funding of accompanying dependents: in order to keep costs down, however, it will fund the costs of up to three dependents only—although other dependents may accompany at the volunteer's expense.

Applicants from a number of countries[33] must submit their application through

---

[30] *In partnership for better health—UNV in Sri Lanka*, 1979, pp. 3–4.

[31] *Development Microcosm-UNV in Yemen*, p. 23.

[32] Revised Instructions for Administration of UNVs effective 1 June 1981 and additional circulars.

[33] The countries concerned are Australia, Austria, Belgium, Canada, China, Cuba, Denmark, Finland, the Federal Republic of Germany, Ghana, India, Ireland, Italy, Japan, Luxemburg, the Netherlands, New Zealand, Norway, the Philippines, Poland, Spain, Sweden, Thailand, Tunisia, the U.K., the U.S.A., Vietnam, Yugoslavia and Zaire.

the appropriate cooperating organization in their country. Their application must therefore be accepted twice: first by their own national organization, such as the U.S. Peace Corps or the French "Volontaires du Progrès", and then by the UNV programme, while their final assignment is always subject to the approval of the host government.

Applicants of other nationalities are free to apply directly to the UNV programme in Geneva, or through the UNDP Resident Representative in their country of residence.

UNV conditions of service include a settling grant equal to 2 month living allowance, payable for contracts of two years. The monthly living allowance ranges from $457 to $1144 for single volunteers and from $622 to $1544 for volunteers with direct dependants, depending upon the cost-of-living at the duty station. The level of the monthly living allowance granted to UNV-DDS field workers is lower: it varies between $60 and $130, the rate being fixed in consultation with field offices[34].

A resettlement allowance is payable on return to the home country or place of recruitment, at a rate of $100 per month of service, after a minimum of 12 months of satisfactory service.

Adequate and simply-furnished accommodation, including utilities, is normally provided free of charge, as well as life, health and permanent disability insurance. Dependants residing with the volunteer are also covered by health insurance.

International travel on appointment and at the end of the assignment is provided by UNV or a cooperating organization to the volunteer and authorized dependants. Volunteers are entitled to take annual leave during the term of their assignment at the rate of 2 1/2 working days a month.

The UNV Programme Now

By 31 December 1989, 1801 UNVs from 101 different countries were serving in 108 developing countries, with nearly two-thirds (63 percent) of them located in the Least Developed Countries. Africa uses the largest share (49 percent) and, together with the Asia and Pacific region, accounts for 80 percent of the UNV total. The rest are found in the Arab States (13 percent) and in the Latin American and Caribbean region (7 percent).

The largest numbers of UNV specialists come from the developing countries of Asia and Africa (only 11 percent are nationals of industrialized countries), are mostly male (82 percent), married (36 percent are single) and are on average over 38 years old.

Of the serving UNV specialists at 31 December 1989, 61.7 percent had a first or second university degree, 3 percent a Ph.D, and 9.4 percent a medical doctorate.

[34] *UNVNews*, No. 45-E, June 1988, p. 15.

25.9 percent had an award from a higher professional/technical/vocational institution. 41 percent had from 6 to 10 years professional experience and 30.5 percent from 11 to 20 years experience.

About 85 percent of UNV specialists serve within projects funded by UNDP. About half serve in projects executed by 29 U.N. specialized agencies and related bodies, the largest being FAO (10 percent of the total serving UNV specialists) and ILO (8 percent) The other main users were U.N., WFP, UNIDO, UNESCO, UNICEF, WHO and UNHCR[35].

The total number of UNVs *in situ* at year end were:

— in 1971: 35
— in 1981: 975
— in 1989: 1801

while the aggregate numbers of UNVs serving in the given year were:

— in 1971: 35
— in 1981: 1330
— in 1989: 2355

The total number of UNVs engaged between 1971 and 1989 was 6.690.

The total number of candidates with confirmed availability at the end of 1989 was 5.900.

At the end of 1989, 3.9 percent of UNVs were working on humanitarian aid and relief, 16 percent on health, and the rest on agriculture, forestry and fisheries, social conditions, development, education, natural resources and energy, etc.

The estimated expenditure on the UNV programme in 1989 amounted to $36.8 million. In addition, 1989 contributions made to the UNV Special Voluntary Fund amounted to $1.1 million, and special purpose contributions, $3.1 million.

In 1986, the UNV headquarters in Geneva was employing 19 professional officers (the Executive Coordinator is graded D.2) and 32 general service staff. In 1990, the staffing was 34 professional officers and 55 general service staff. In addition, the Governing Council decided in 1988 (Decisions 88/38 and 88/46) to establish a cadre of 40 UNV programme officers under the administrative budget to support those UNDP offices managing substantial numbers of UNV specialists, giving them an enhanced role in programme planning and support role. In June 1990, the UNDP Governing Council, at its 37th Session, approved a field budgetary allocation to add 20 more UNV programme officers with an equal number of support staff. At the end of 1990, 60 UNV-funded programme officers were in position, plus 13 funded by bilateral national schemes.

---

[35] *UNV and the appropriate role of volunteers in development*, by Dr. B. G. McSweeney, Executive Coordinator, UNV, as part of a UNITAR publication in preparation.

Characteristics and Trends

The main difference between UNV and government-sponsored national volunteer schemes and volunteer-sending NGOs is that the UNVs are the only volunteers to operate under U.N., global, auspices. They do not represent their country of nationality, their role is not to promote the interests, culture and prestige of that country in the host country. During their assignment, their allegiance is to the U.N. while work-related instructions may be received from the host government authority, in accordance with the "Pledge of Commitment of UNVs" (see Table 8.2) and the UNV Rules of Conduct. The Rules include the following obligations:

C.9.a. U.N. Volunteers will discharge their functions and regulate their conduct with only the interest of the U.N. in view.

   b. In accordance with the ideals of volunteer service, U.N. Volunteers will be guided solely by the motivation to devote their knowledge and abilities, without regard to financial benefit, to realization of the broad objectives laid down by the U.N. Charter for the economic and social advancement of humanity.

   c. U.N. Volunteers will not engage in any activity that is incompatible with the proper discharge of their duties.

   d. Although U.N. Volunteers are not expected to relinquish national sentiments or political and religious convictions, they will not engage in any political activity that might be inconsistent with the independence and impartiality required of persons affiliated with the U.N. Furthermore, U.N. Volunteers will avoid any action and, in particular, any public statement which may adversely reflect on their special international status as U.N. Volunteers.

   e. During their assignment, U.N. Volunteers will not, except in the normal course of official duties or with the prior explicit approval of the UNV Executive Coordinator and/or the UNDP Resident Representative, issue statements to the press or other agencies of public information; release visual information for publication; submit articles, books or other material for publication; or take part in mass communication activities such as film, radio or television productions which are in any way related to project activities or to the aims, activities or interests of the U.N. or the host country.

   f. U.N. Volunteers will at all times respect the laws, moral codes, and traditions prevailing in the host country.

   11. In the performance of their duties, U.N. Volunteers shall neither seek nor accept instructions from any government or from any other authority external to the U.N. system, including representatives of cooperating organizations. U.N. Volunteers assigned to host-government projects, institutions or departments, however, will receive work-related instructions from designated government officials as appropriate.

The "Oath of Office" of U.N. staff members requires them not to "seek or receive instructions from any government or from any other authority external to the Organization" in the performance of their duties (Art. 100.1 of the U.N. Charter).

UNVs are not fully assimilated to international civil servants and do not benefit from the latter's total statutory independence from governments, including the host government. Their status is that of international operational, rather than advisory, personnel, placed at the disposal of the host government and allowed to receive instructions from that government's authorities. However, if they work in a U.N., or a U.N. specialized agency team, their instructions would come from the U.N. team leader, and not directly from the government authorities.

UNVs represent the universality of the U.N. and the U.N.'s political "neutrality". While most volunteer-sending agencies recruit their volunteers from their own national base, UNVs are recruited from more than 100 countries.

As an organization administered by the UNDP, the UNV programme is intimately linked to the U.N. mandate, status, regulations and hierarchy, particularly in field activities. This has the advantage of giving UNVs the protection of a worldwide established international structure, formally recognized by each host government under the terms of formal agreements.

Table 8.2. Pledge of commitment of United Nations Volunteers

I pledge to exercise with dedication, discretion and conscience such duties as shall be entrusted to and undertaken by me as a United Nations Volunteer, to comport myself in accordance with the standards of conduct of United Nations Volunteers, to work for social and economic development of the country of assignment in accordance with the principles of the United Nations Charter and not to seek or accept instructions in regard to the performance of my duties from any authority external to the United Nations System with the exception of work related instructions from the specific host Government authority to which I may be attached.

(Signature)　　　　　　　(Date)　　　　　　　(Place)

Source: UNV Form VC 2-2/Rev.1

A disadvantage is the possible lack of operational and administrative independence, and freedom of action, which may be enjoyed by NGO volunteers.

Administratively, the whole UNV programme is submitted to the constraints of 3 or 4 bureaucracies: the UNDP, with its administrative, personnel, budgetary and financial rules and regulations, its reporting requirements and its diplomatic obligations with regard to both donor and recipient countries, — the national donor bureaucracy which, in a number of countries, provides "cleared" volunteers and funds, — where applicable, the U.N. executing agency which programmes and selects U.N. volunteers, and decides on their assignment in close cooperation with the UNV administration, — and the receiving country which agrees to the inclusion of one or several UNVs in a project document, reviews the personal résumés of the three offered volunteers for a specific post, selects the preferred one, and, during his assignment, monitors his performance and conduct.

The interaction between these bureaucracies may explain some of the delays and problems of "fielding" volunteers.

Another characteristic of the UNV programme, as noted in a recent UNV Programme Advisory Note[36], is that the U.N. system use of volunteers is essentially demand-driven, based on requests formulated by governments which have found their way in most cases into the UNDP Country Programmes. There has therefore been so far, little scope, within the UNV programme, for any policy input to the process of determining how volunteers may best be used at the country level. However, the presence of UNV programme officers in an increasing number of UNDP Resident Representatives Offices may promote a more effective participation of the UNV Programme at the planning stage at national level.

Many other volunteer-sending agencies give considerable freedom to their field directors to identify promising areas for endorsement by the host government. Some do not even require government clearance for particular volunteer assignments, beyond standard immigration formalities.

The multinational composition of UNVs provides an enormous resource pool: it also produces special challenges in terms of organization, selection and procedures. The multinational composition of U.N. teams may bring, together with the richness of diversity, potential problems of communication, and frictions of professional and cultural background that call for special qualities of management.

Most international volunteers are recruited in OECD (Organization for Economic Cooperation and Development) countries: UNV, on the other hand, as the only multilateral volunteer-sending agency, is the single large exception which provides opportunities for volunteers from developing countries to serve abroad. This fact has changed the overall staffing characteristics of UNVs: in general, developing countries' volunteers have a distinct profile, which is reflected in the data given above. Additionally, many of them have served previously with their government, or are on leave from it. Older than most of the Western countries' volunteers, they have larger families as well as important extended family obligations. They are, of course, used to developing countries' conditions of life and work. In general, volunteers' entitlements compare favourably with home country salaries in the public service.

Altogether, the higher qualifications and longer professional experience, as well as the dedication, of most UNVs explains the increasing appreciation of the programme by recipient countries in the last decade.

Furthermore, UNVs "cost-effectiveness" is a powerful argument in favour of their increasing use, as a replacement for or in addition to the more "expensive"

---

[36] *UNV Programme Advisory Note—The appropriate use of volunteers in development*, May 1990, p. 28.

U.N. expert. In comparison with the U.N. expert or consultant, the unit delivery costs of an international UNV range from $12,000 to 25,000 p.a., while the former may cost $100,000 p.a. or more. The costs of a UNV-DDS field worker may amount to less than $5,000 p.a.

In Tanzania in 1988, the cost of technical assistance for some 1,000 expatriate professionals amounted to three times the total payroll of the entire civil service, including teachers and health workers[37].

As stated in the 1990 UNV Programme Advisory Note, these staggering figures raise very serious questions concerning the cost-effectiveness of traditional international technical cooperation today, giving urgency to the search for alternative approaches.

UNVs are generally perceived as willing performers in difficult circumstances, as task-oriented problem solvers who learn the local language and adjust to the local political, social, cultural and administrative circumstances. They work hand-in-hand with local personnel and are often effective on-the-job trainers.

The Sana'a Symposium of 1982 acknowledged that there was a vast and largely unfilled need for middle-level operational expertise to support economic and social development activities in developing countries. The Paris Conference, held in 1981, estimated the requirements for middle-level technicians in the order of 20,000 per year in the 1980s, probably a conservative estimate.

Considering the probable extensive needs of developing countries for such technicians in the 1990s, and the almost unlimited number of qualified candidates available for UNV service, and the fact that many volunteers may prefer to serve as an international, rather than as a national volunteer, one could envisage a significant growth of the UNV programme in the forthcoming decades.

The success of the UNVs interventions in relief and rehabilitation could also well justify allocating an increased share of the programme's resources to such humanitarian activities, while also increasing the UNV more traditional development projects.

A former UNV, Joseph Stimpfl, wrote[38] that UNV has the unique distinction of having an international constituency, composed of many nations, including the receiving country.

> This means that there is no self-serving or self-interest involved in the selection and evaluation of the work. UNV has no axe to grind, no politicians or agency bureaucrats analyzing success in terms of the interests of an organization or country that may conflict with the goals of the country receiving aid.

In his experience as UNV English Teacher in Malaysia, he found that a UNV can comfortably settle into the identity of an international volunteer, a citizen of the world, because of UNV's "neutral" identity.

[37] Ibid., p. 2.
[38] *UNV Newsletter*, No. 43-E, Oct.-Dec. 1987, pp. 3–4.

No government could ask the question: "Just what do they want to get from us? What is the danger in a cooperation agreement with them? What do we lose by letting them help us? Governments who accept technical assistance from UNV have nothing to lose but everything to gain.

While UNV is part of a large bureaucracy with its own organizational interests, it is true that its activities are non-political, non religious and extend well beyond national borders and parochial interests. Even though it still is a small organization, the UNV programme is a symbolic demonstration of international, non partisan, solidarity.

PART III

INTERNATIONAL HUMANITARIAN LAW
AND STATUS

In this Part, we will attempt to review and assess the present state of international humanitarian law insofar as it defines and affects the legal status of international humanitarian volunteers and their protection. Do the volunteers benefit from an established, recognized and respected international status, or should one be initiated and submitted to countries and intergovernmental organizations for adoption?

The legal position of U.N. Volunteers is related to that of their employing U.N. body: they benefit, by extension, from the well-defined privileges, immunities and facilities granted to U.N. officials under the Convention on the Privileges and Immunities of the U.N., the Convention on the Privileges and Immunities of the Specialized Agencies and other basic texts.

The specific status of the ICRC, a non-IGO and a very special NGO, is related to its statutory role under the Geneva Conventions: it affects the status of ICRC delegates who have acquired, while on mission, privileges and immunities comparable to those of U.N. officials.

Other NGOs have a national legal status, even if the scope of their activities is international. Their volunteers do not therefore benefit from any international protection, except for that accorded under the Geneva Conventions and Additional Protocols. Is there a need for an international status for NGOs, which might facilitate their international operations and give better protection to their members on mission?

The Geneva Conventions and Additional Protocols provide a specific protection to medical personnel under specific conditions. One of those conditions is the respect of medical ethics. Their employing organization must qualify as an impartial humanitarian body. Various proposals have been initiated to reinforce the protection of the volunteer doctor, including a "Charter for the Protection of Medical Missions" and a Council of Europe Resolution 904 (1988) "on the protection of humanitarian medical missions".

Are international humanitarian interventions legitimate under international law and international humanitarian law, and if so, under what conditions? Some recent examples of such interventions have been the object of either international condemnation, measured criticism or discrete approval. The related problem of the prompt delivery of relief assistance across borders and the persistent conflict between humanitarian needs and demands, and the reality of national sovereignty and pride have triggered recent proposals to create a generous but impossible, or premature "right of international humanitarian intervention".

We will consider in Chapter 9, the legal status and the protection of international humanitarian volunteers,—in Chapter 10, medical missions: the protection of the volunteer doctor,—and in Chapter 11, international humanitarian intervention.

THE LEGAL STATUS AND THE PROTECTION OF INTERNATIONAL HUMANITARIAN VOLUNTEERS

The status of international humanitarian volunteers is linked to the status of their employing organizations.

These organizations may be intergovernmental, in which case the organization's status is generally well defined under its Constitution and complementary international instruments, such as the 1946 Convention on the Privileges and Immunities of the United Nations, the 1947 Convention on the Privileges and Immunities of the Specialized Agencies, headquarters or host agreements, or project documents. The U.N. Convention endows the organization with international juridical personality, defines the extent of its legal capacity and specifies those privileges and immunities granted to the organization as well as to Member States' representatives and the organization's staff members. Such privileges and immunities are granted to the organization's staff in order to facilitate the fulfilment of the organization's mission and to guarantee the independence of the international civil service in relation to governments' authorities. Most of the international civil servants do not enjoy "full diplomatic status", but only a limited functional protection, granted in the interests of the organization only, and not for the personal benefit of the individuals themselves. Additionally, the International Court of Justice has clarified or confirmed the legal nature of the organization as well as some of its rights and obligations in relation to its Member States and its staff members.

U.N. Volunteers are employed by a U.N. organization but are not "international civil servants": do they have the same legal status as U.N. organizations' staff members and do they benefit from the same protection?

Similarly, the status of the delegates of the International Committee of the Red Cross (ICRC) is dependent on the legal status of the Committee.

If the status of the ICRC is considered to be only that of a "normal" Swiss nongovernmental organization (NGO), like that of any other Swiss humanitarian NGO (such as Caritas, Terre des Hommes or Médecins Sans Frontières, Switzerland), the status of the ICRC delegate would be simply that of a Swiss citizen working in his country or abroad. In the latter case, his protection would be assured by his own government and its diplomatic envoys, and by the government of the host country.

However, the legal nature of the Swiss ICRC is in fact affected by the international public mission entrusted to it under the Geneva Conventions, the Committee's direct relations with governments and its role as guardian and promoter of international humanitarian law. While the ICRC cannot be defined as an IGO, some of its characteristics would tend to place it in an intermediate, somewhat hybrid, status, between that of an IGO and that of an NGO. The fact that the protection of the ICRC, Swiss, delegates is in theory an exclusive responsibility of the Committee, and in fact a dual responsibility of the ICRC, as the employing international organization, and of the Swiss authorities, as the protecting power of Swiss citizens, demonstrates the ambiguous, *sui generis*, nature of this "quasi-IGO", the ICRC.

In principle, the legal position of NGOs is unambiguous: national or international NGOs only have a national legal status. They usually have to be declared or recognized in one or several countries, even if they belong to the same international humanitarian movement, such as the Salvation Army or Médecins Sans Frontières. The legal protection of NGO volunteers is then entirely dependent on their own government's diplomatic support and intervention and political influence, and on the host government's goodwill and ability to ensure protection.

However, NGOs performing services on behalf of IGOs may be granted privileges, immunities and facilities accorded by the host government to the IGO, insofar as NGO employees and volunteers may be considered as "agents" of the IGO.

The impressive growth of NGOs engaged in international humanitarian or development work in many countries since World War II has shown the need to define an international legal status for NGOs and their volunteers. This raises considerable problems at the global level. Even at the more homogenous European level, little progress has been achieved.

The Legal Status and Protection of U.N. Volunteers

Under its U.N. General Assembly mandate (Resolution 2659(XXV) of 7 December 1970—see Chapter 8), the U.N. Volunteer Programme (UNV) is administratively part of the United Nations Development programme (UNDP), which is itself part of the U.N.

U.N. Volunteers (UNVs) are not "officials" of the Organization, in the sense of Article 105 of the U.N. Charter which states that

> ... officials of the Organization shall similarly enjoy such privileges and immunities as are necessary for the independent exercise of their functions in connection with the Organization.

UNVs are not "staff" members of the U.N. secretariat, under Articles 100 and 101 of the Charter. They are not subject to the U.N. Staff Rules and Regulations.

UNVs are not "experts on mission for the U.N.": these are persons who are performing functions or assignments for the U.N. without being members of the staff. Examples of such experts are military observers on peace-keeping missions, and persons serving in their individual capacity on certain subsidiary bodies of the U.N. without being either officials (staff members) or representatives of member States.

However, UNVs may be considered as "agents" of the U.N.

UNVs are contractually responsible to the UNV Programme, represented in the country of assignment by the UNDP Resident Representative[1].

UNVs are recruited and employed by a U.N. body, under a contract of employment, for a specific duration, a contract which provides them with various allowances and benefits. During their UNV assignments, they are "agents" of the U.N., even if they do not enjoy the status of "international civil servants". Their employment by a subsidiary body of the U.N. creates an employer/employee contractual relationship with relevant rights and obligations on both sides. One of the obligations of the U.N., as an employer, is the obligation of protection.

The International Court of Justice (ICJ), in its Advisory Opinion of 11 April 1949, "Reparation for Injuries Suffered in the Service of the U.N."[2], has established the need of protection for the agents of the organization, as a condition of the satisfactory performance of their duties. The organization's right of functional protection of its agents is also an obligation:

In order that the agent may perform his duties satisfactorily, he must feel that this protection is assured to him by the Organization, and that he may count on it. To ensure the independence of the agent, and, consequently, the independent action of the Organization itself, it is essential that in performing his duties he need not have to rely on any other protection than that of the Organization (save of course for the more direct and immediate protection due from the State in whose territory he may be). In particular, he should not have to rely on the protection of his own State. If he had to rely on that State, his independence might well be compromised, contrary to the principle applied by Article 100 of the Charter.

The Court thus confirmed that

Both to ensure the efficient and independent performance of these missions and to afford effective support to its agents, the Organization must provide them with adequate protection.

The Court stated that, as a subject of international law and capable of possessing international rights and duties, the U.N. has the capacity to maintain its rights by

---

[1] Instructions for Administration of UNVs—p. 4, para. 10. See also U.N. Doc. CCAQ/PER/R.132, Annex A, 22 Jan. 1980, "Memorandum on the U.N. legal rights when a staff member or other agent of the U.N., or a member of their family, is arrested or detained.

[2] *ICJ Reports*, 11 April 1949, pp. 174–188.

bringing international claims. More precisely, the Court affirmed that the Organization has the capacity—to bring an international claim for adequate reparation against one of its Members which has caused injury to it by a breach of its international obligations towards it,—to negotiate,—to conclude a special agreement,—and to prosecute a claim before an international tribunal.

The Court noted that in view of its purposes and missions, the U.N. finds it necessary to entrust its agents with important missions to be performed in disturbed parts of the world, many missions involving the agents in "unusual dangers".

Whatever the relative importance of the missions entrusted to its agents and the relative danger of these missions, UNVs as U.N. employees are under U.N. protection and enjoy some of the privileges and immunities accorded to U.N. "officials" and "experts" under the U.N. Conventions. These privileges and immunities have been adapted from the customary and conventional diplomatic privileges and immunities.

Diplomatic Privileges and Immunities

The Preamble of the Vienna "Convention on Diplomatic Relations", which was adopted on 16 April 1961 by the U.N. Conference on Diplomatic Intercourse and Immunities[3], recalls that

> peoples of all nations from ancient times have recognized the status of diplomatic agents.

For instance, in Roman times, envoys from foreign states enjoyed protection of a religious nature.

An essential justification for the diplomatic privileges and immunities is to provide the diplomats with the necessary protection to enable them to fulfil their functions in full independence, without interference from the local authorities. Some of the customary immunities and privileges were considered imperative: those related to the personal inviolability and immunity of the diplomatic agent. Some were considered as matters of pure courtesy, such as the fiscal immunities[4].

From customary law, the diplomatic privileges and immunities became conventional law with the adoption of the Vienna Convention.

The general objective of the Convention is

> to contribute to the development of friendly relations among nations, irrespective of their differing constitutional and social systems.

The purpose of the protection provided by the diplomatic privileges and immunities listed in the Convention is to ensure the efficient performance of the functions of diplomatic missions as representing States, and not to benefit individuals.

---

[3] U.N. Doc. A/CONF. 20.13.

[4] Ch. Rousseau, *Droit international public*, Sirey, Paris, 1953, p. 342.

Finally, the international law principle of reciprocity applies: the establishment of diplomatic relations between States, and of permanent diplomatic missions, takes place by mutual consent.

Most provisions apply to a "diplomatic agent", defined as the head of a mission or a member of the diplomatic staff of the mission.

The Convention provides, in summary, the following main privileges and immunities:

1. Right to use the flag and emblem of the sending State on the premises of the mission, including the residence of the head of mission, and on his means of transport.
2. Inviolability of the premises of the mission. Immunity of these premises from search, requisition, attachment or execution. Inviolability of the archives and documents of the mission. Similar inviolability of the private residence, papers and correspondence of a diplomatic agent.
3. Freedom of movement and travel in the territory of the receiving State, subject to national security laws ånd regulations.
4. Freedom of communications for all official purposes, inviolability of the official correspondence of the mission, including the contents of the diplomatic bag.
5. Inviolability of the person of a diplomatic agent: he is not liable to any form of arrest or detention. Immunity from the criminal jurisdiction of the receiving State and qualified immunity from its civil and administrative jurisdiction. Exemption from social security provisions.
6. Qualified exemption from dues and taxes. Exemption from customs duties and taxes on articles for the official use of the mission or for the personal use of a diplomatic agent or family member.

All persons enjoying such privileges and immunities have the duty to respect the laws and regulations of the receiving State, and not to interfere in its internal affairs.

Such diplomatic privileges and immunities have served as a basis for the formulation of the privileges and immunities which have been granted to IGOs and their personnel.

Privileges and Immunities of U.N. Staff

Diplomatic privileges and immunities have been extended to intergovernmental organizations (IGOs), representatives of their member States and their staff

as are necessary for the independent exercise of their functions[5].

The rationale is that IGOs represent the collectivity of their member States and should be able to operate independently from the control or intervention of any one

---

[5] U.N. Charter, Art. 105.2.

State, and in particular, from the control of the State hosting the organization's headquarters or one of its offices or projects. Such privileges and immunities are deemed "functional", i.e. they are intended to ensure the independence of the organization's employees in the exercise of their official functions, and thus facilitate the operations of the organization.

Following the precedent of the League of Nations[6], the U.N. and its specialized agencies, their member States' representatives and the organizations' officials have been granted diplomatic privileges and immunities.

The basic texts governing the status, privileges and immunities of staff members of U.N. organizations are found in the U.N. Charter and the constituent instruments of the other U.N. organizations, the Convention on the Privileges and Immunities of the U.N. of 13 February 1946, the Convention on the Privileges and Immunities of the Specialized Agencies of 21 November 1947, the Standard Basic Assistance Agreements of the UNDP and host agreements concluded between the organizations and the country of the organization's headquarters[7].

Under Article 105.2 of the U.N. Charter, the "necessary" privileges and immunities are granted to "officials" of the organizations.

The U.N. Administrative Committee on Coordination, a body composed of the executive heads of the U.N. system of organizations, has given an extensive definition of those "officials" covered by the U.N. protection: staff members, experts on mission, locally recruited employees and, in general, all persons performing functions or services for the U.N. system[8].

The 1946 and 1947 Conventions on Privileges and Immunities prescribe that all officials of the U.N. and U.N. specialized agencies, irrespective of grades, shall

1. be immune from legal process in respect of words spoken or written and all acts performed by them in their official capacity;
2. be exempt from taxation on the salaries and emoluments paid to them by the U.N. organization;
3. be exempt from national service obligations.

Other privileges and immunities refer to immigration restrictions and alien registration, exchange facilities, repatriation facilities in time of international crisis, duty-free import of furniture and personal effects.

The Conventions provide that the organizations may issue U.N. laissez-passer to their officials: these laissez-passer "shall be" recognized and accepted as valid travel documents by the authorities of Members. Experts and other persons travelling on the business of the organizations may be accorded a U.N. Certificate.

---

[6] *La Charte des Nations Unies*, Economica, Paris, 1985, Art. 105 by Philippe Cahier, pp. 1387–1398.

[7] Yves Beigbeder, *Threats to the International Civil Service—Past pressures and new trends*, Pinter, 1988, pp. 121–122.

[8] U.N. Doc. A/C.5/36/31, para. 3.

Senior officials of the organizations are granted the same facilities for travel as are accorded to officials of comparable rank in diplomatic missions.

The Conventions specify that the privileges and immunities are granted to officials in the interest of the U.N. organizations and not for the personal benefit of the individuals themselves[9]. The organizations must

> cooperate at all times with the appropriate authorities of Members to facilitate the proper administration of justice, secure the observance of police regulations and prevent the occurrence of any abuse in connection with the privileges, immunities and facilities mentioned in this Article[10].

The rights of functional protection and of intervention have been further elaborated by the organizations[11]. The organizations assert that when a governmental authority arrests or detains a U.N. staff member, whether internationally or locally recruited, a representative of the organization has the right to visit and converse with the staff member, to be apprised of the grounds for the arrest or detention, including the main facts and formal charges, to assist the staff member in arranging for legal counsel and to appear in legal proceedings to defend any U.N. interest affected by the arrest or detention. The distinction between acts performed in an official capacity and those performed in a private capacity, which lies at the heart of the concept of functional immunity, is a question of fact which depends on the circumstances of the particular case. The position of the U.N. is that it is exclusively for the Secretary-General to determine the extent of the duties and functions of U.N. officials. The executive heads of the U.N. specialized agencies have adopted the same position.

Standard Basic Assistance Agreements between a government and the UNDP include "volunteers" among "all persons, other than government nationals employed locally, performing services on behalf of the UNDP, a Specialized Agency or the IAEA", to whom the same privileges and immunities as U.N. officials, as well as facilities, are granted by the host government.

UNVs are thus assimilated to U.N. staff members insofar as privileges and immunities are concerned, and are placed under the protection of the U.N. The UNDP Resident Representative is responsible for all arrangements relating to the security and protection of UNVs and their families in emergency situations arising from political and other crises, including natural disasters. While the UNV is not entitled to a U.N. Laissez-Passer, he is given a U.N. Volunteers Identity Card. The UNV or his family may receive compensation for injury or death attributable to

---

[9] The U.N. Convention may be found in *ICJ Acts and Documents Concerning the Organization of the Court*, No. 3, 1977, pp. 163–175, the Convention of the Specialized Agencies, in WHO *Basic Documents*.

[10] Art. V, Sections 17 to 21 of the U.N. Convention, and Art. VI, Sections 18–23 of the Convention of the Specialized Agencies.

[11] U.N. Doc. A/C.5/36/31.

UNV service, as well as compensation for loss of or damage to personal effects due to emergency situations[12].

As U.N. "agents", UNVs enjoy the protection of the world network of UNDP Resident Representatives under the international legal instruments applicable to the U.N. and to its employees.

Receiving governments are responsible for according the UNVs such facilities and immunities as are covered by the UNDP Standard Basic Agreement and /or Basic Agreements concluded by U.N. specialized agencies. In particular, receiving governments are expected to facilitate the expeditious entry and exit of UNVs to and from the country of assignment as well as their movements within the national territories, as required by their duties[13].

The Legal Status and Protection of ICRC Delegates

The ICRC is not an IGO: it has not been founded by states' governments, its statutes are not an international treaty or convention, approved by states: the ICRC is a Swiss association, with legal personality, governed by Article 60 and following of the Swiss Civil Code. The ICRC statutes are approved and revised by its Assembly, which is composed of members of the Committee, e.g. all Swiss private citizens and not government representatives.

Private citizens have created the ICRC and have run it since its creation. ICRC employees are not international civil servants nor government civil servants: they are private sector employees employed under Swiss law (in Switzerland), in accordance with a Collective Labour Convention[14].

The Convention, as a typical Swiss Labour Agreement, covers such areas as the rights and obligations of the employees, employment and working conditions, salaries and social security, duration of work and leave conditions.

However, three provisions in the Convention are specific to the ICRC, by underlining its specific mission and related exigencies of service.

One provision, in the Preamble, recalls that the aim of the ICRC is to ensure the protection of and assistance to the victims of international or other armed conflicts or internal strife, and that the exigencies ensuing from that aim must remain constantly present in the minds of the parties (employer and employees).

A second provision acknowledges that the status of the ICRC is particular, as it is a private body, dependent on private contributions, exercising an activity which

---

[12] As an example of a Government/UNDP Agreement, see "Agreement between the Government of Zimbabwe and the UNDP" of 26 May 1980 — Doc.UNDP/ADM/LEG/SBA/83 of 14 Feb. 1984. Instructions for Administration of UNVs, p. 52 and Annexes IV and VII.

[13] See "WHO Guidelines for the Programming and Employment of UNVs in WHO Projects", para. 3.4 and UNDP, "Project for Sub-Saharan Africa", Project Document, p. 5, para. G.1.

[14] *Compendium of Reference Texts on the International Red Cross and Red Crescent Movement*, 1990, Statutes of the ICRC, pp. 63–68, and "Convention collective", Jan. 1988.

makes it similar to a public service, and which has received a mandate from the international community.

A third provision is contained in the "Commitment to Discretion", which is to be accepted and signed by new employees, on the basis that the ICRC needs, at all times, the confidence of governments and victims, in the ultimate interest of the victims (see Chapter 4).

While the ICRC is a private Swiss NGO, it is also a constituent part of the International Red Cross and Red Crescent Movement, in which governments participate.

The Geneva Conventions are reviewed and approved by States in the Diplomatic Conferences, then ratified by States. The Conventions are international public law treaties. Revisions to the Conventions are prepared by government experts, with the assistance of the ICRC: for such revisions, the ICRC specialists play a role similar to that played by IGO staff members in assisting government experts or representatives in drafting an international convention or treaty.

The International Conference of the Red Cross and the Red Crescent, which generally meets every four years, brings together the components of the Red Cross Movement—the ICRC, the League and the National Societies—with the representatives of States Parties to the Geneva Conventions and Protocols. As the supreme deliberative body for the Movement, the International Conference contributes to the development of international humanitarian law and has sole competence to approve and amend the Statutes of the International Red Cross and Red Crescent Movement. States have therefore a joint responsibility for major policy options on questions of principle and in the field of international humanitarian law, together with the Red Cross and Red Crescent Movement components, which are international and national NGOs.

The States Parties to the Conventions and Protocols cooperate with and support the work of the components of the Movement. Each state promotes the establishment on its territory of a National Society and encourages its development. The Movement components support as far as possible the humanitarian activities of the states.

Besides their own responsibilities under the Conventions and Protocols, the states are to respect at all times the adherence by all the components of the Movement to the Fundamental Principles[15].

The Red Cross system therefore associates in a common Movement with common objectives an independent Swiss NGO, independent National Societies and their Federation (national and international NGOs),—and governments.

The functions of the Swiss ICRC are international, not national. The ICRC, as formally recognized in the Geneva Conventions and by the International Conference of the Red Cross, is entrusted with tasks of assistance to victims and monitoring of the states' obligations under the Conventions. Its role, in part, is

---

[15] *Compendium*, op.cit., Statutes of the International Red Cross and Red Crescent Movement, Art. 2, pp. 13–14.

to undertake the tasks incumbent upon it under the Geneva Conventions, to work for the faithful application of international humanitarian law applicable in armed conflicts and to take cognizance of any complaints based on alleged breaches of that law[16].

As a neutral intermediary between the victims which have rights and the states which have obligations, the ICRC has direct relationships with government authorities, as well as international legitimacy conferred by the Geneva Conventions and the International Conference resolutions. The status of the ICRC in relation to states in implementing and monitoring international humanitarian law is more comparable to that of IGOs, such as the ILO or the IAEA, than to the status of a NGO, such as Amnesty International or the World Council of Churches.

Dominicé[17] has found a similarity between the ICRC's behaviour in its relations with states, in spite of a very different legal nature, and the behaviour of IGOs. The ICRC is recognized as having an international legal personality in international public law, because it has acquired the capacity to negotiate international treaties and the capacity to entertain diplomatic relations: IGOs such as U.N. organizations or the European Economic Community have such legal capacity.

Plattner[18] has noted that the legal status of the ICRC delegate has been affirmed in positive law since the Second World War, under the impetus of two determining factors:—the exercise by the ICRC of its protection in favour of its agents,—and the conclusion of host agreements defining the immunities and privileges of the ICRC delegations and of the ICRC delegates. Without changing the legal nature of the ICRC from a Swiss (international) NGO into an IGO, this evolution has sanctioned in international law the functional independence of the ICRC.

Knitel[19] has listed the essential prerogatives of a "legal personality" in international law:

1. the right of active and passive legation.
2. various privileges relating to the status of representatives and delegates (for instance, tax exemption).
3. capacity to conclude international agreements, treaties and conventions.
4. the right to issue passports.
5. exterritoriality of the institution's headquarters and of its delegations.
6. other prerogatives, such as the issue of stamps or money, etc.

---

[16] Ibid., Art. 5.c.

[17] Christian Dominicé, "La personnalité internationale du CICR, in *Studies and Essays on International Humanitarian Law and Red Cross Principles in Honour of Jean Pictet*, ICRC/Nijhoff, 1984, pp. 663–673.

[18] *Studies and Essays*, op.cit., Denise Plattner, "Le statut du délégué du CICR sous l'angle du principe de l'inviolabilité de sa personne", pp. 761–769.

[19] Hans G. Knitel, *Les délégations du CICR*, Etudes et Travaux de l'Institut Universitaire de Hautes Etudes Internationales, Geneva, 1967, pp. 38–39, 63–64, 92–93, 100, 115.

He asserted that the ICRC has enjoyed *de facto*, at given times, almost all these privileges and rights. In his view, the ICRC has a *de facto* international legal personality and its delegates may be considered as international civil servants with a national status. He proposed to confirm *de jure* the international legal personality of the ICRC as a subject of international law with a *sui generis* limited capacity.

Swiss or ICRC Protection?

The first two Red Cross delegates, Dr. Appia (a Swiss citizen) and Dr. van de Velde (Dutch), sent respectively to the Schleswig and Denmark in 1864, were given an official letter of recommendation of the Swiss Federal Council. During their mission, they received, without difficulties, the necessary laissez-passer[20].

The three members of the ICRC mission sent to Montenegro in 1875–1876 also received letters of recommendation from the Swiss Federal Council, which were "highly useful". The delegates were instructed "to present these credentials" to the Chief of State. Considering that, in diplomatic practice, such credentials attest that the bearer is entitled by his government to fulfil his diplomatic functions, it appears that the ICRC delegates, during that mission, enjoyed a quasi-diplomatic status, as quasi- (Swiss) diplomats.

In letters prior to the mission, the ICRC had laid as a *sine qua non* condition that the Montenegro government would commit itself to facilitate in all manners the delegates' mission, notably regarding the guarantee of their personal safety.

During the Balkans War, on 2 November 1912, the ICRC sent Dr. C. de Marval as delegate. For the first time, an ICRC delegate received, at Dr. de Marval's request, a Swiss diplomatic passport, while the ICRC issued his credentials in order to accredit him to the governments and Red Cross and Red Crescent Societies of the Parties to the conflict.

In 1945, for the first time, the ICRC initiated a procedure of functional protection of its agents.

Dr. Matthaeus Visscher and his wife had been executed by the Japanese on 20 December 1943 in Borneo, where Dr. Visscher had been ICRC delegate since the Spring of 1942. His appointment had been agreed by the Dutch authorities. Dr. Visscher had been accused by the Japanese of espionage, while he was only giving relief to civilian internees in Borneo. The ICRC, for reasons of opportunity, asked the Swiss government to submit its claim for compensation to the Japanese authorities through diplomatic channels.

On 13 December 1961, an ICRC delegate, Georges Olivet (Swiss) and two voluntary workers of the Katanga Red Cross were killed in a Red Cross ambulance in Katanga, during the U.N. intervention in the ex-Belgian Congo (now Zaire). The ICRC then decided to submit a claim for compensation and proposed that an inde-

---

[20] Knitel, op.cit., pp. 16–17, 26–28.

pendent commission be formed for the purpose of enquiring into the circumstances of the case. On 8 June 1962, the Commission's report was officially submitted to the ICRC and to the U.N. On the basis of this report, both organizations concluded an arrangement according to which the U.N. would pay a lump sum amount to the ICRC, while not recognizing any responsibility for the events.

The legal, autonomous, capacity of the ICRC to initiate a process of functional protection for its agents had thus been recognized by the U.N., without assistance or intervention by the Swiss government[21].

Recent examples of abductions of ICRC delegates show, to a certain extent and with due regard to the statutory discretion of the ICRC and the diplomatic reserve of the Swiss government, the interaction between the ICRC and the Swiss authorities in protection efforts on behalf of delegates.

On 17 November 1988, an ICRC delegate, Peter Winkler, was abducted in Saïda, Lebanon, probably by a non-PLO Palestinian group. On 2 December, Winkler wrote that he had been abducted, not as an ICRC delegate, but as a Swiss citizen. This seemed to be related to the detention in Switzerland of Ali Mohamed Hariri, who had hijacked a plane and killed a French passenger, before being arrested at Geneva airport.

Both the ICRC and the Swiss government intervened with, among other contacts, Yasser Arafat, the PLO Chairman, in order to obtain Winkler's release, which occurred on 16 December 1988.

During two weeks after the abduction, the ICRC in Geneva took various initiatives with various governments, and its delegation in Lebanon made contacts with several local guerrilla groups. After two weeks, the Swiss government authorities intervened and took advantage of the U.N. General Assembly session held in Geneva from 13 to 15 December 1988 to multiply formal and informal contacts with Member States representatives and with the PLO Chairman. After the release of Winkler, both the ICRC and the Swiss government denied that any "negotiations" had taken place and that any compensation, such as the payment of a ransom, had been delivered.

In this instance, the "protection" of the delegate had been assured by two parallel entities: his own organization, the ICRC, and his government.

The President of the ICRC said in an interview on 19 December 1988 that Bern (the Swiss capital) and Geneva operate in a real "reciprocal independence". Each has its diplomatic channels, even though information is exchanged between the Committee and the Federal Department of Foreign Affairs. The fact that the kidnappers wanted to apply pressure on the Swiss government, and apparently not on the ICRC, justified the intervention of the Swiss authorities.

At the same time, in the words of a Swiss journalist[22], one felt that

---

[21] ICRC *Annual Report*, 1961, pp. 11–14, 1962, pp. 14–15, and Plattner, op.cit., pp. 761–762.

[22] *Le Monde*, 18–19 Dec., 22 Dec. 1988, — *Journal de Genève*, 19 Dec. 1988, ICRC *Bulletin*, No. 156, Jan. 1989.

The great Red Cross, with its emblem, sign of its absolute neutrality, and there-fore of a very great prestige in the world, is a small institution which had to be helped by the powerful Ministry of Foreign Affairs of its country.

In March 1989, four ICRC agents (one Swiss ICRC delegate, a West-German relief coordinator, a Dutch nurse and a representative of the Mozambique Red Cross Society) were captured by the Mozambique National Resistance, RENAMO. The armed opposition Movement alleged that the ICRC representatives had been cap-tured because they did not observe a "neutral" position during a fighting episode near Memba, and had adopted, during their mission, a behaviour politically favourable to FRELIMO, the party in power. This allegation was rejected by the ICRC.

After two weeks' detention and following discreet interventions by the ICRC, the four agents were released. It was then said that the capture had not been aimed particularly at the ICRC: they had been captured in error[23].

Two other ICRC delegates disappeared briefly in Mozambique in June 1990, leaving behind their burned car. Following an allegation by the Mozambique gov-ernment that they had been abducted by RENAMO, the delegates re-appeared 18 days later, saying that they had entered a zone controlled by RENAMO of their own free will, in order to assist isolated populations suffering from malnutrition[24].

During this ill-explained incident, as well as in the previous 1989 Mozambique abductions, the ICRC appears to have intervened alone, with a successful outcome.

On 6 October 1989, two ICRC orthopaedist specialists (Swiss) were abducted from their car, bearing Red Cross markings, in Saïda. One of them, Emmanuel Christen, was set free on 8 August 1990, and his colleague, Elio Erriquez, on 13 August 1990.

According to press reports, both the ICRC and the Federal Department of Foreign Affairs intervened actively. The ICRC acted on three levels:—in Lebanon itself, to inform and influence Lebanese public opinion, with the full support of the local press,—in extending contacts with the actors of the Lebanese conflict,—and in interventions with all interested foreign governments, including Syria, Iran, Libya, Egypt, Algeria, and the PLO.

In early 1990, a French lawyer, acting as an intermediary, informed the ICRC of the kidnappers' claim: $4 million. The Committee refused to negotiate. Following this refusal, the Swiss Federal Department of Foreign Affairs then assumed a more active role.

The final release of the two ICRC workers was attributed by the American tele-vision channel, CNN, to the payment of a ransom of $3 million. This was denied by both the Swiss government and the ICRC.

A French Foreign Ministry spokesman attributed the release to a decision by President François Mitterrand to pardon a convicted, pro-Iranian Lebanese assassin,

[23] *Journal de Genève*, 22 March, 23–24 March 1989,—*La Tribune de Genève*, 5 June 1990.
[24] *La Tribune de Genève*, 20 June 1990.

Anis Naccache, on 27 July 1990. Naccache had served ten years of a life sentence for killing two people in an abortive attempt to murder the former Iranian Prime Minister, Chapour Bakhtiar, near Paris. It was said that Iran had offered, in exchange, to facilitate the release of one or two Europeans held in Lebanon[25].

Whatever the circumstances and motivations of these various incidents, they show:

— that ICRC delegates and other Red Cross and Red Crescent employees are not immune from attacks, abduction, prolonged detention or murder in spite of the proclaimed and applied neutrality, independence and impartiality of the Movement. The Red Cross humanitarian role of assisting the victims is not always respected by the parties to an external or internal conflict;
— that the protection of ICRC delegates should normally be assumed exclusively by the Committee, but that it is in practice a dual responsibility of the Committee and of the Swiss government.

The reason for this dual responsibility is that the ICRC *is* a Swiss organization and that its delegates *are* Swiss citizens, even though the institution's mandate, objectives and activities are international.

Viewed from this perspective, the uninational ICRC does not possess all the attributes of an IGO, which is statutorily and exclusively responsible for the protection of its multinational staff.

Other aspects of the relations between the ICRC and Switzerland have been related in Chapter 2.

Headquarters Agreements

In 1970, the ICRC opened its first regional delegation in the Cameroon. The delegate negotiated locally the content of the agreement, considered necessary to facilitate the fulfilment of the tasks of the delegation. These contents were modelled on those of headquarters or host agreements of IGOs.

On 23 March 1973, the ICRC concluded its first "headquarters agreement" with the Government of the Cameroon.

Concerning the legal status of the ICRC delegate, its text is very similar to that of the 1946 Convention on the Privileges and Immunities of the U.N. Among other provisions, the delegate enjoys

personal immunities of arrest, detention and seizure of personal baggage and immunity from legal process in respect of acts performed by him in his official capacity, including words spoken or written (Art.7, a. and b.).

---

[25] ICRC *Bulletin*, No. 166, N—ov. 1989,—*La Tribune de Genève*, 20 June,—*La Suisse, Journal de Genève, International Herald Tribune*, 10 Aug.,—*Journal de Genève*, 14 Aug. 1990.

This precedent created a practice. By 1990, the ICRC had concluded 29 headquarters agreements. The Cameroon agreement served as a model regarding the personal status of delegates.

The agreements generally recognize the legal personality of the ICRC delegation or office, the inviolability of its premises, the usual functional immunities and privileges, related to the performance of official duties, tax exemption on ICRC salaries, exemption from customs duties, freedom of entry into the country, freedom of movement and communications, freedom to transfer funds. The ICRC delegates are authorized to display the emblem of the Red Cross. They receive, in some countries, identity documents

like those issued to officials of international organizations

In some agreements, reference is made to

privileges and immunities normally accorded to similar functionaries of international organizations

thus assimilating the legal status of the ICRC to that of IGOs and the legal status of ICRC delegates to those of IGO international civil servants[26]. The Agreement with the Government of Honduras grants to the ICRC delegation, to the Head of the Delegation and to the Delegates all the immunities granted by the Vienna Convention on Diplomatic Relations (Art. 7), thus granting diplomatic status to the ICRC. This same Agreement (Art. 5) recalls some of the Fundamental Principles of the Red Cross, and in particular the Delegation's obligation to act in accordance with the duties of impartiality and neutrality.

The ICRC headquarters agreements, like those of IGOs, are considered as international treaties concluded between a government and a public international organization.

A Public International Organization

During World War II, a number of governments accorded to the ICRC a status corresponding to that of a public international legal personality.

For instance in Hungary, during the period March-November 1944, the ICRC delegation attempted, with a degree of success, to protect the Jewish population. On 30 October 1944, Hungarian authorities broadcast by radio the following communiqu)

...the buildings of the ICRC delegation as well as those of the institutions placed under ICRC protection will—like diplomatic legations—enjoy the privilege of exterritoriality...

---

[26] Headquarters Agreement between the Federal Military Government of the Federal Republic of Nigeria and the ICRC, 5 July 1988, Art. XIII.

326

Thus the Hungarian Government then recognized the ICRC delegation as a "quasi-diplomatic legation" and granted it the privileges of diplomatic representations[27].

Most States tend to consider ICRC delegations as diplomatic missions, assimilated to IGOs.

Even without headquarters agreements, according to a survey undertaken in 1981, ICRC delegates enjoy a privileged status, due to the courtesy of the authorities and as a result of the assimilation of the ICRC to an IGO.

The President of the ICRC, when he is officially invited by a country's government, is sometimes treated as a chief of state, or at least as a chief of government. At the Geneva headquarters of the ICRC, credentials of chiefs of permanent missions accredited to the U.N. Office and other international organizations in Geneva often include the ICRC among the "other" international organizations. Courtesy visits of newly arrived chiefs of missions to the President of the Committee have become customary.

The U.S. Congress has formally recognized the ICRC's

unique status as an impartial humanitarian body named in the Geneva Conventions of 1949 and assisting in their implementation...

By amendment to the International Organizations Immunities Act (new section 13), the ICRC

shall be considered to be an international organization for the purposes of this title and may be extended the provisions of this title in the same manner, to the same extent, and subject to the same conditions, as such provisions may be extended to a public international organization in which the United States participates pursuant to any treaty or under the authority of any Act of Congress authorizing such participation or making an appropriation for such participation[28].

At the multilateral level, the ICRC has been granted the status of "guest" by the Non-Aligned Movement, status granted also to States such as Austria, Finland, Sweden and Switzerland, and IGOs such as the UNHCR. The ICRC has been granted a "special status" by the Council of Europe. The Intergovernmental Organization for Migrations has placed the ICRC in a separate category of "observers", between IGOs and NGOs.

On 16 October 1990, the U.N. General Assembly conferred observer status in its proceedings to the ICRC in a resolution sponsored by 138 of the U.N.'s 159 member states and adopted by consensus. This status was granted in consideration of the special role and mandates conferred upon the ICRC by the 1949 Geneva Conventions: speakers said that it should not be seen as a precedent for other NGOs to seek that status.

[27] Knitel, op.cit., p. 63.
[28] Executive Order 12643 of June 23, 1988.

The explanatory memorandum submitted together with the draft resolution recalled that the treaties of international humanitarian law assign duties to the ICRC that are similar to those of a Protecting Power responsible for safeguarding the interests of a State at war, in that the ICRC may act as a substitute for the Protecting Power under the Geneva Conventions and Additional Protocols. The ICRC has the same right of access as a Protecting Power to prisoners of war (Third Convention) and civilians (Fourth Convention). The promoters of the resolution noted that the tasks of the ICRC and the U.N. increasingly complement one another and cooperation between the two institutions is closer, both in their field activities and in their efforts to enhance respect for international humanitarian law. They also noted the close cooperation of the ICRC and the U.N. on legal matters, with the ICRC contributing to the U.N. in this field[29].

In fulfilling its functions — particularly its humanitarian action in favour of victims of armed conflicts — conferred on it by the Geneva Conventions, the ICRC acts as a subject of rights and obligations at the international level. Its general mandate of protection and assistance to civilian and military victims of armed conflicts as well as its capacity to act under certain circumstances as substitute of a Protecting Power and its capacity to offer its good offices constitute some key elements of its international status, with a functional international personality.

The ICRC, a Swiss NGO, is also a quasi-public international organization, with functions and attributes similar to those of IGOs. Its hybrid Swiss/international, NGO/IGO characteristics are unique in the realm of international relations and are unlikely to be duplicated. It is to be placed, in its own, unique and separate position, between IGOs and NGOs.

The status of ICRC delegates is becoming more formalized and standardized as a result of the formulation and conclusion of headquarters agreements. These tend to grant delegates privileges and immunities similar to those of IGO international civil servants.

The Legal Status and Protection of NGO Volunteers

National and international NGOs are created under national law: there is no international legal regime governing the status and activities of NGOs. Except for a regionally-limited Convention of the Council of Europe, there is no international, global convention granting NGOs a single legal personality and capacity over the territories of all states where they have staff and activities, — no more than there are any such agreements for the multinational activities of profit-making transnational

---

[29] IOM Council Resolution No. 753 (LVIII), 29 Nov. 1988 and internal ICRC Doc., — U.N. Doc. A/45/191 of 17 Aug. 1990 and U.N. *Press Release* DH/747 of 16 Oct. 1990. Intergovernmental organizations such as the European Community, the Arab League and the Organization of African Unity have been granted observer status, as well as Liberation Movements such as the Palestine Liberation Organization.

corporations. Médecins Sans Frontières (MSF)/France is a French association, as Ford/France is a French business company. MSF/Belgium and MSF/Switzerland are independent Belgian and Swiss associations, although their creation followed, and was initially inspired by and modelled on the French initiative. All MSF national associations have generally the same humanitarian philosophy and apply similar methods of action: like other international NGOs with national branches in several countries, they engage in joint planning and activities, sometimes joint financing, and benefit from each other's experience.

Unlike IGOs, international NGOs have not been granted an international legal personality, with the exception of the ICRC, as suggested above.

NGOs having a national legal status—that of their place of legal establishment and recognition —, their protection and the protection of their personnel and volunteers can only be provided by their national governmental authorities and those of the receiving country. In some cases, however, they may enjoy a degree of protection from their association with an IGO.

There is therefore a major contradiction between a NGO's international vocation and the national legal status in which it is confined.

Various National Legal Status of International NGOs

Merle[30] has identified three possible solutions to the problem of the national status of NGOs.

The first solution is a discriminatory system whereby the establishment and operation of international NGOs is made subject to conditions more restrictive than those applied to national associations. Until 1981, this was the French solution under the terms of a decree of 1939: associations deemed to be foreign on account of the composition of their governing bodies, could not be created without prior authorization and could be dissolved by a simple administrative decision.

Secondly, under a non-discriminatory system, international NGOs are assimilated in status to national associations as regards both the conditions of formation and dissolution and the rules under which they operate. This situation prevails in countries with a liberal tradition. In France, the Law of 9 October 1981 has repealed the 1939 decree: thus a NGO may now be created and form an association on French territory simply by means of a "declaration" published in the "Journal Officiel". Once declared, the NGO enjoys the same rights as any other association set up in France by French nationals.

However, in France and in some other countries, the legislation on associations contains a number of restrictions which turn NGOs into second-class entities in comparison with commercial companies or trade unions.

---

[30] Marcel Merle, "International NGOs and their legal status", Appendix 3.5 to *International Association Statutes Series (1988)*, Union of International Associations.

A more serious drawback to the assimilation to national associations is that national regulations may not necessarily meet the specific requirements of international NGOs, their interaction with other national branches and their assistance beyond borders, which may require quick communications, international financial transaction facilities, the purchase and shipment of material and the dispatch of teams of volunteers from and to various countries.

The third national solution to the status of international NGOs is to give them a preferential treatment, as set up in the Belgian Law of 25 October 1919. With the aim of encouraging the establishment of NGOs in Belgium, the Law grants legal personality to associations open to Belgians and to aliens which have as executive a permanent institution or committee with its seat in Belgium with an administration including at least one Belgian member. The more advanced provision in the Law is to allow

> international associations with their registered offices abroad which are governed by a foreign law but which meet (various) conditions . . . and without prejudice to public order, exercise the rights accruing from their national status. It is not essential that the administration shall include at least one Belgian member[31].

As noted by Merle, if a similar measure were adopted by the legislation of other countries, it would open the way to multilateral "transnationality", without the need to adopt an international NGO status.

NGOs' Consultative Status with IGOs

A number of IGOs have granted "consultative status" to a number of NGOs, which has allowed NGO representatives to contribute actively to IGO programmes, to collaborate with the international secretariats and to represent various non-diplomatic, non-official currents of opinion throughout the world.
For instance, Article 71 of the U.N. Charter provides that

> the Economic and Social Council may make suitable arrangements for consultations with non-governmental organizations which are concerned with matters within its competence.

Pressures from representatives of such ·non-profit groups as the Carnegie Endowment for International Peace led the 1945 San Francisco Conference to adopt Article 71.

Consultation arrangements are governed by ECOSOC Resolution 1296 which makes provisions for NGOs to be placed in consultative status with the Council as well as for them to hold consultations with the secretariat. The decision to place

---

[31] *Statutes Series*, op.cit., "Status of International Associations under Belgian Law, Fiche Info No. 7, July 1989.

NGOs in consultative status is made by the Council upon recommendation of its Committee on NGOs.

At the U.N., NGOs are provided access to open meetings of U.N. bodies, invitations to briefings, seminars and consultations, conferences on political, economic, social and humanitarian issues, documentation.

Many NGOs have worked with U.N. bodies on technical cooperation and development programmes, and on relief and rehabilitation.

848 NGOs were in consultative status with the Economic and Social Council in 1989.

U.N. specialized agencies also maintain consultative relationships with NGOs, which are formalized in their Constitutions, as well as regional organizations such as the Council of Europe and the European Economic Community.

While the grant of consultative status to an NGO is a recognition of international legitimacy, it has limitations.

Consultative status is only granted to a minority of NGOs.

Consultative status only governs relationships between an IGO and an NGO: it does not confer any right on an NGO capable of being exercised before any other national or international authority. As stated by Merle[32]

> The fact of belonging to that category of privileged bodies does provide a kind of badge of respectability and leaders of NGOs are jealously devoted to the granting and maintaining of such status, but access to consultation has only limited effects and under no circumstances can it amount to legal status in the full meaning of the term.

The extent of the NGO participation in the IGO's work and debates is essentially dependent on the goodwill or interest of the international secretariat and on the support or tolerance of Member States' representatives. Many NGOs are confined to a role of recipient of information and are legally powerless to demand an effective part in consultation and participation.

The different levels of consultative status which have been introduced in most IGOs (for instance, Categories I, II and Roster in the U.N.) establish another form of discrimination among NGOs.

Consultative status is granted at the discretion of IGOs and may be withdrawn on the same basis. Such decisions are based on certain criteria such as the relevance of the NGO's objectives and activities to the IGO's mandate, to the NGO's acceptance of the IGO's strategy and policies, to the NGO's international scope, to the NGO's actual contributions to the IGO's programmes, to the respect by the NGO of procedural requirements, and in some cases, to its ideological conformity with the IGO's policies and resolutions.

In summary, the consultative status offered and controlled by IGOs cannot give

---

[32] Merle, op.cit.

NGOs the protection and guarantees they need to carry out, in full independence, the international functions which they have assumed.

To strengthen the position of NGOs vis-à-vis the IGOs and to facilitate their work on an international basis, the only solution is to give them an international status guaranteeing them minimum rights and a degree of freedom of action vis-à-vis the various national and international authorities with which they have relations.

An International Status for NGOs

Two European IGOs, the Council of Europe and the European Economic Community have initiated texts to extend the recognition of the legal personality of an international NGO established in one member State to other States, members of the same organization, in order to facilitate their work at the European level.

The Council of Europe approved on 24 April 1986 the European Convention on the recognition of the legal personality of international non-governmental organisations.

The Convention recognizes that international NGOs carry out work of value to the international community, particularly in the scientific, cultural, charitable, philanthropic, health and education fields, and that they contribute to the achievements of the aims and principles of the U.N. Charter and the Statute of the Council of Europe.

Consequently, the Contracting Parties agree to recognize "as of right" the legal personality and capacity, as acquired by an NGO in the State in which it has its statutory office.

The Convention applies to associations, foundations and other private institutions which satisfy the following conditions:

— have a non-profit-making aim of international utility;
— have been established by an instrument governed by the internal law of a member State;
— carry on their activities with effect in at least two States;
— have their statutory office in the territory of a Contracting State and the central management and control in that State or in another Contracting State.

The Convention establishes rules on the proof to be furnished before the authorities of the Contracting State where the recognition is sought and sets down exceptional cases in which a Contracting State may refuse recognition: for instance, when the NGO invoking the Convention, by its object, its purpose of the activity which it actually exercises, contravenes national security, public safety, or is detrimental to the prevention of disorder or crime, the protection of health or morals, or the protection of the rights and freedoms of others, or jeopardises relations with another State or the maintenance of pease and security.

The Convention has been signed by Austria, Belgium, Greece, Portugal,

Switzerland and the U.K. The U.K., Greece, Belgium and Switzerland have ratified the Convention, which has entered into force in January 1991[33].

On 13 March 1987, the European Parliament adopted a Resolution on non-profit-making associations in the European Economic Community.

In its Preamble, the Resolution recalled that the freedom of association was an essential democratic right which should not merely be guaranteed in principle but be given the necessary means for its exercise. It also emphasized the outstanding service which associations perform for the community by developing the spirit of initiative, responsibility and solidarity of their members, by setting up active centres of democratic life, by efficiently serving the common interest as a supplement to State measures, and by fulfilling an irreplaceable role with regard to conciliation, exchanges and social equilibrium.

The Resolution, *inter alia*, requested that all discriminatory measures based on nationality that affect the right to belong, to form or administer an association be rapidly abolished throughout the Community, in respect of citizens of Member States.

With a view to harmonizing legislations and conditions for recognition of international associations in the European Community Member States, the Resolution requested that associations which have some legal recognition in the Member State in which they have their head office, should have the same recognition in other Member States.

The European Parliament called on the Commission to submit a proposal for a directive making provision for such mutual recognition.

The Resolution also proposed special tax concessions to non-profit-making associations as a means of mitigating the fact that their resources are too often "meagre and precarious", as well as the harmonization of such provisions.

The proposal to harmonize the conditions for legal recognition and tax concessions in the Member States would be beneficial to the associations: it would need to be approved by the European Commission as a directive.

The ultimate objective would be, as mentioned by the Rapporteur, to draw up a Community-wide statute for associations[34].

In November 1987, a draft proposal for the creation of a "European association" as a Regulation of the Council of Ministers of the European Communities, was submitted by Louis Eyraud, member of the European Parliament, to NGO federations established in Brussels, Paris and Geneva.

According to this draft text, a European association would be constituted by at least three persons, two of whom being citizens of at least two Member States, or at least three associations established in at least two Member States, or two or more European associations.

---

[33] Council of Europe *Press Release*, 302 (90) of 4 Sept. 1990 and Notification of Switzerland's ratification of 24 Sept. 1990.

[34] *Statutes Series*, op.cit., Appendix 4.12: European Parliament, *Texts adopted by the European Parliament*, Vol. 3/87, March 1987, pp. 94–96.

The intention to create a European association would be notified to the Commission of the European Communities for approval.

The European association would have a legal personality distinct from that of its members. The European association would be entitled, on the whole territory of the Community, to go to courts as plaintiff or defendant, to acquire movable and real property, to receive donations, to employ personnel, to open a bank account in each of the Member States and to transfer funds from one State to another. The European association would be exempted from income tax and value-added tax.

This interesting proposal could serve as blueprint for considering a possible international status for international NGOs.

However, the fact that, even at the relatively homogeneous West European level, it has not yet been possible to adopt a "European Statute" for associations, shows the difficulty, if not impossibility, of trying to design such a statute at the global level[35].

At the European level, the approach adopted by the Council of Europe may be the more practical and acceptable one: it would apply to more countries than the Twelve of the European Community. The European Convention on the recognition of the legal personality of international NGOs is the first international instrument on this subject to enter into force.

The Protection of NGO Humanitarian Volunteers

Volunteers sent on missions to foreign countries by humanitarian NGOs do not normally enjoy any international status and protection. Their protection is a responsibility of their own country's authorities as well as a responsibility of the host country vis-à-vis foreign nationals under international law.

Suy[36] has proposed that the two States concerned should conclude a bilateral agreement, either *ad hoc* or an umbrella agreement, under which the two governments, and particularly the host government, would grant to the humanitarian volunteers of the other Contracting Party a specific status.

In the case of armed conflict not of an international character, a frequent case where international humanitarian volunteers may be called upon to intervene, the Geneva Conventions (Art. 3/3/3/3) provide protection to "persons taking no active part in the hostilities". In particular, the following acts are prohibited with respect to these persons:

a. violence to life and person, in particular murder of all kinds, mutilation, cruel treatment and torture;
b. taking of hostages;

[35] *Statutes Series*, op.cit., Appendix 4.13.
[36] Erik Suy, "La protection des volontaires humanitaires dans les conflits armés non internationaux et dans les opérations de secours en cas de catastrophes", *Des menschen Recht zwischen Freiheit und Verantwortung*, Duncker and Humblot, Berlin, 1989, pp. 173–182.

c. outrages upon personal dignity, in particular humiliating and degrading treatment;

d. the passing of sentences and the carrying out of executions without previous judgment pronounced by a regularly constituted court, affording all the judicial guarantees which are recognized as indispensable by civilized peoples.

Under Art. 9 of Additional Protocol II, medical and religious personnel "shall be respected and protected". Art. 18 provides that relief societies located in the territory of the High Contracting Party, such as Red Cross or Red Crescent organizations, may offer their services for the performance of their traditional functions in relation to the victims of the armed conflict. Relief actions for the civilian population which are of an exclusively humanitarian and impartial nature and which are conducted without any adverse distinction need the consent of the receiving country's authorities.

Suy has suggested that any action envisaged by an NGO in a case of non-international armed conflict should be preceded by a careful evaluation of the situation and of the possible risks to which the relief volunteers could be exposed. The NGO should consider the conclusion of an arrangement, either with the State, or with the faction or authority on whose territory it wishes to operate. Such a non-legally binding arrangement, subject to the consent of the other party, would include details on the number of persons authorized to work on the territory, on the nature of the relief to be provided, the transportation methods, freedom of movement or restrictions thereto, methods of communications, etc.

The 1971 U.N. General Assembly resolution which created UNDRO (Resol. 2816 (XXVI) invited recipient governments, *inter alia*, to consider appropriate legislative or other measures to facilitate the receipt of aid including "necessary privileges and immunities for relief units".

Another protection method is for the NGO to conclude an agreement with an IGO with which it is operationally associated in order to extend the IGO's privileges and immunities to the NGO, its personnel and volunteers.

A complementary agreement would need to be negotiated with the host country government receiving a humanitarian assistance or disaster relief unit. Where the unit is a subsidiary organ of the U.N., for instance, the agreement would be concluded between the U.N. and the government of the receiving country. Where the unit has a legal status separate from that of the U.N. (for instance, Médecins Sans Frontières, a French association, working under a contractual agreement with the UNHCR), the U.N., if associated in the provision, administration or coordination of the relief services, may also be party to the agreement. Such agreements would provide, among other matters, for the coordination of the work of the disaster relief unit with the work of other bodies engaged in the relief services and for the privileges and immunities to be accorded to the disaster relief unit in the receiving country in accordance with, or by assimilation to, the Convention on the Privileges and Immunities of the U.N.[37].

---

[37] U.N. Doc. E/4994 of 13 May 1971, "Assistance in cases of natural disaster", Annex III, "Legal status of disaster relief units made available through the U.N.".

The UNDP Standard Basic Assistance Agreements with governments include NGOs retained by the UNDP among "persons performing services" who may be granted by host governments the same privileges and immunities as U.N. officials. Thus NGOs and their personnel, if sub-contracted by the UNDP, would enjoy such privileges and immunities on that basis.

The benefit of receiving protection through association with an IGO has to be weighed against the cost of partial loss of autonomy and independence of the NGO, its assimilation to an intergovernmental organization and its diplomatic and political problems, and a blurring of its own image.

An unusual agreement has been concluded in 1983 between the Government of Togo and a national grouping of NGOs active in that country, which makes provision for the activities of foreign NGOs. The agreement provides that the NGO grouping (CONGAT, the French acronym for Council of NGO in activity in Togo) will support Togo's development efforts and any programme of education and training in such fields, among others, as health, education and culture. The government will grant to CONGAT and its members, among other provisions:

— tax- and custom-free import of material, equipment or vehicles imported by an NGO in the exercise of its activities, and by non-Togolese members of NGOs within six months of their installation;
— exemption for non-Togolese staff and families from all restrictions concerning registration, transport, entry visas, work permits and similar formalities[38].

Rather than initiating a multilateral effort to codify the international status of volunteers, Suy suggests that the NGOs concerned could try to formulate the principles which they apply, and which they expect the host governments also to apply.

Such principles would include the following points:

— humanitarian assistance is part of the international law of solidarity;
— States should take all necessary means to facilitate the dispatch, transport and delivery of humanitarian assistance to those in need;
— humanitarian volunteers should have freedom of access and movement including protection measures (insurance, visas, distinctive signs, privileges, facilities etc.);
— humanitarian volunteers should be able to communicate freely with their organizations, the diplomatic and consular authorities of their own country as well as with the local authorities;
— the question of civil and penal jurisdiction applicable to international volunteers should be considered;
— a mechanism should be introduced to control the implementation of these provisions.

These commendable principles and desirable practices would need to be negotiated by the NGO concerned and the host government and then formulated in a written agreement or exchange of letters. A case by case approach does appear more

---

[38] *Statutes Series*, op.cit., Appendix 6.4.

acceptable and effective than another multilateral effort, probably doomed to failure.

In Conclusion

Diplomatic privileges and immunities are a fragile armour against terrorism, state or individual violence, abductions, arbitrary detention, torture or murder. In times of social unrest, civil or external war, and particularly in non-democratic countries, even the diplomats of powerful nations are not immune from violations of diplomatic conventions, human rights instruments, humanitarian law or other specific international agreements.

The Convention on the Privileges and Immunities of the U.N. did not protect Lieutenant-Colonel William Richards Higgins from being murdered. Higgins, an officer of the U.S.A., was serving as the Chief of a group of U.N. military observers assigned to the U.N. Interim Force in Lebanon when he was abducted on 17 February 1988. On 31 July 1989, an announcement at Beirut by his captors stated that he been killed.

In the period July 1988 to June 1989, 157 UNRWA staff were arrested or detained. On 8 June 1989, a locally-recruited WHO staff member, Ms. Ghennet Mebrahtu, was arrested in Addis Ababa without charges. She is still detained in spite of many appeals to the Ethiopian Government[39].

Neither the Red Cross emblem nor headquarters agreements have prevented the deaths of these ICRC delegates, among others: André Tièche and Alain Biéri, and their African colleague, murdered in Rhodesia/Zimbabwe while on mission, in May 1978, — in December 1985, an ICRC radio-operator, killed in Angola in an armed attack during his first mission, — Peter Altwegg, killed in Somalia in October 1990[40].

On the other hand, international agreements and an international legal status for NGO international volunteers would provide a legal basis for their access, presence and activities in a foreign country, for negotiations with the host country government and for possible discreet or public pressures against that government. It would also provide a legal basis for the NGO to claim compensation.

While it is most unlikely that governments will approve, in the foreseeable future, an international status for international NGOs and international NGO volunteers, it is advisable that international NGOs conclude agreements directly, or under the auspices of an IGO, with host governments on the modalities of humanitarian assistance and on the status and protection of international volunteers.

[39] U.N. Doc. A/C.5/44/11 of 2 Nov. 1989, and *U.N. Special*, Geneva, July 1990.
[40] ICRC *Press Release* No. 1329 b, 25 May 1978, *International Review of the Red Cross*, Jan. Feb. 1986, No. 250, pp. 53–54, *Tribune de Genève*, 9 Oct. 1990.

CHAPTER 10

MEDICAL MISSIONS: THE PROTECTION OF THE VOLUNTEER DOCTOR

Medical doctors play an important role in relief assistance, alongside other health and relief workers.

Their dedication to the care and welfare of others, to the succour of the sick and the wounded, to the alleviation of suffering, to the fight against death, their obligation of discretion place them in a special category among other relief workers.

The original task of the Red Cross was to aid the sick and the wounded of armed forces, by assisting and complementing the work of the Military Medical Services. Its early work in this connection was therefore medical.

As noted by Schoenholzer[1], this aspect of its work has never ceased to be characteristic of all the activities which it has successively assumed in the extension of its care from the wounded in armed conflicts to all the victims of social scourges, war, natural disasters or illness. Doctors and the Red Cross have the same objective: the alleviation of human suffering.

> The Red Cross without the doctors would be powerless; and the doctors are indebted to the Red Cross for having imposed upon the world a principle of which they (the doctors) had been for a long time the sole champions—the principle, namely, of the equality of all men in relation to suffering. The doctors further owe to the Red Cross a legal status which protects them in the exercise of international activities, and an emblem, the Red Cross emblem, which shields them on the battlefield.

The Red Cross has always realized the important part that medical personnel have to play, and from the very start it has ensured that such personnel, who are responsible for helping the wounded and the sick in the midst of battle should be respected and protected in the same way as religious personnel. The latter's task is complementary (but not necessarily consecutive) to that of the medical personnel, for they bring succour to the dying.

---

[1] Jean-Pierre Schoenholzer, "The Doctor in the Geneva Conventions of 1949", *International Review of the Red Cross*, Feb. March 1953, pp. 1–2.

What is the extent of the protection granted by the Red Cross Conventions and the Additional Protocols to medical doctors, including civilian volunteer doctors? What are the conditions required to benefit from this legal status?

Is there a need to complement and develop the existing Red Cross protection to new situations and new types of NGOs?

The Red Cross Conventions and Additional Protocols

These instruments relate to both international and non-international armed conflicts, where problems of protection arise[2].

Protected medical personnel can be either military or civilian. However civilian personnel are not covered as such by international humanitarian law unless they have received an assignment from the Party to the conflict to which they belong. Thus a civilian doctor, who continues to practise during an armed conflict without having received a specific assignment from his country, is not included in the protected medical personnel. This restriction is justified by the fact that medical personnel enjoy certain privileges, and that since the country at war is responsible for any abuses which might occur, it must exercise a certain control over the persons to whom these privileges are granted[3].

Besides the national medical personnel of the parties to the conflict, foreign medical personnel can also provide their services in the event of armed conflict. Such personnel can be placed at the disposal of a Party to the conflict by a State which is not a Party to the conflict, or by a relief society (such as the National Red Cross and Red Crescent Societies) of such a State, or they can be medical personnel working under the responsibility of the ICRC. The second category of medical personnel is the one most frequently found in practice, placed at the ICRC's disposal by National Red Cross and Red Crescent Societies.

The Red Cross Conventions and Protocols define rights and duties incumbent on medical personnel: their purpose is to enable them to perform the humanitarian tasks entrusted to them, namely to help the victims of armed conflicts whenever such conflicts occur.

Duties of Medical Personnel

These duties are directly linked with the rights of the protected persons placed in their care. Thus the duty to give humane treatment to a wounded person is linked with the right of such a person to receive humane treatment.

---

[2] The following developments are based on the *Manual on the Rights and Duties of Medical Personnel in Armed Conflicts*, by Dr. A. Baccino-Astrada, ICRC and the League, Geneva, 1982.

[3] The definition of medical personnel is in Art. 8, Protocol I.

The main general principles follow:

— Wounded, sick and shipwrecked persons, prisoners of war and civilians exposed to the consequences of an armed conflict, i.e. all persons who by their situation are outside the conflict or who do not take a direct part in it, must be treated humanely under all circumstances[4];
— The protection of medical personnel is not a personal privilege accorded to them, but is a natural consequence of the requirements designed to assure respect and protection for the victims of armed conflicts;
— Medical personnel must abstain from all acts of hostility;
— Medical personnel must be identifiable, through the display of the red cross emblem and identity cards. Protocol I has introduced a new protective sign for members of civil defence organizations, a blue equilateral triangle on an orange background[5].
— Medical personnel who commit abuses or breaches of international humanitarian law are subject to punishment[6].

Medical Ethics

Medical personnel who provide their services in armed conflicts must respect the principles of medical ethics in the same manner as in peacetime[7].

The principles of medical ethics (the duties of the doctor in the exercise of his profession), originally set forth in the "Oath of Hippocrates", control the medical function both in times of peace and in times of war.

In September 1948, the World Medical Association, which represents over a million doctors worldwide, developed a modern version of the oath, called the "Declaration of Geneva"[8]. By accepting the Declaration, the doctor makes the following promises (among others):

...

I will practise my profession with conscience and dignity;
The health of my patient will be my first consideration;
I will respect the secrets which are confided in me, even after the patient has died;

...

I will not permit considerations of religion, nationality, race, party politics or social standing to intervene between my duty and my patient;

---

[4] Art. 3, G I,II,III,IV, Art. 12, G I and II, Art. 13, G III, Art. 27, G IV, Art. 10, P.I, Art. 4, 7, P.II.

[5] Art. 40 and 41, G I, Art.42, G II, Art. 20, G IV, Art. 18, 66, 67 and Annex I, P.I, Art.12, P.II.

[6] Art. 3, 44, 49 to 54, G I, Art. 3, 44, 45, 50 to 53, G II, Art. 3, 13, 129 to 132, G III, Art. 3, 146 to 149, G IV, Art. 11, 18, 85 and 86, P.I, Art. 4 and 5, P.II.

[7] Art. 16, P.I, Art. 10, P.II.

[8] The 1948 Declaration of Geneva was amended in 1968 and in 1983. See *The World Medical Association, Handbook of Declarations*, 1985, p. 3.

I will maintain the utmost respect for human life from its beginning, even under threat, and I will not use my medical knowledge contrary to the laws of humanity.

In October 1949, the same Association adopted an "International Code of Medical Ethics"[9]. Among the doctor's general duties, the Code prescribes that he should provide competent medical service in full technical and moral independence, with compassion and respect for human dignity. He has the obligation of preserving human life. He is obligated to give emergency care as a humanitarian duty unless he is assured that others are willing and able to give such care.

In October 1956, the Association adopted "Regulations in time of armed conflict"[10] which affirm that medical ethics in time of armed conflict are identical to medical ethics in time of peace. The primary obligation of the doctor is his professional duty and his supreme guide is his conscience. The primary task of the medical profession is to preserve health and save life. In emergencies, the doctor must always give the required care impartially and without consideration of sex, race, nationality, religion, political affiliation or any other criterion.

Under the "Rules governing the care of sick and wounded, particularly in time of conflict", which are part of the "Regulations", the members of medical and auxiliary professions must be granted the protection needed to carry out their professional activities freely. Free passage should be granted whenever their assistance is needed. The fulfilment of medical duties and responsibilities shall in no circumstances be considered an offence. The Rules also provide an identification for the medical and auxiliary professions when fulfilling their professional duties, other than the red cross emblem: a red serpent and staff on a white field.

On 18 December 1982, the U.N. General Assembly adopted the "Principles of Medical Ethics relevant to the role of health personnel, particularly physicians, in the protection of prisoners and detainees against torture and other cruel, inhuman or degrading treatment and punishment" (Resol. 37/194). The Executive Board of the WHO had endorsed in January 1979 the draft of principles on this subject, which had been prepared by the Council for International Organizations of Medical Sciences. The Principles list a number of activities which health personnel should not engage in, as they would be in contravention of medical ethics.

While these texts are not legally binding, they are widely recognized and accepted as international recommendations by the health professions, in particular by the medical profession.

Baccino-Astrada[11] notes that although the main principles of medical ethics are almost universally accepted, medical standards still vary considerably from one region to another. International humanitarian law accordingly does not demand the application of universal standards and limits itself to calling upon the Parties to a

---

[9] Ibid., p.4. The Code was amended in 1968 and in 1983.

[10] Ibid., p.5 and 6. The Regulations were amended in 1957 and 1983.

[11] Baccino-Astrada, op.cit., pp. 38–39.

conflict to apply to protected persons in their power the generally recognized medical standards which they would apply in comparable medical circumstances to their own countrymen living in conditions of freedom.

Other Duties

Persons who do not take a direct part in hostilities and those placed "hors de combat" shall be treated humanely[12].

Care must be given without any distinction based on other than medical criteria. This principle of non-discrimination is based both on medical ethics and on one of the Fundamental Principles of the Red Cross, impartiality. Only reasons of medical urgency may justify priorities in treating people. Special attention is justified for persons in a state of weakness, such as children, old people or pregnant women.

It is prohibited to subject protected persons to any medical procedure which is not indicated by their state of health and to carry out on them any medical, biological or other scientific experiments[13]. This prohibition is directly related to some of the atrocities committed during World War II in Europe and in the Far East. International humanitarian law considers as a "grave breach"—and therefore as a war crime to be prosecuted at any time and at any place—any wilful act or omission which seriously endangers the lives of protected persons in the hands of a Party to the conflict which is not their own country. Medical personnel must in addition avoid any affront to the dignity of protected persons, any humiliating or degrading treatment. They must also make sure that the protected persons are not subject to any intimidation.

The will of the wounded and the sick in relation to medical or surgical treatment must be respected[14].

Medical personnel may be called upon to enter besieged or encircled areas to provide care, supply medical material or evacuate the wounded and sick, and also, if civilians are in the area, invalids, old people, children and women in labour. The Conventions call upon Parties to conflicts to make local arrangements to allow such medical missions[15].

All means of medical transport must be exclusively assigned to medical purposes in order to be entitled to protection. Medical transportation means the conveyance by land, water or air of wounded, sick or shipwrecked persons, medical and religious personnel and medical material[16]. Belligerents have the obligation to respect and protect means of medical transport, provided that these are identified by the distinctive emblem of the red cross or red crescent on a white field.

---

[12] Art. 3, G I, Art. 3, 12, G II, Art. 3, 13, 14, G III, Art. 3, 16, 27, G IV, Art. 10, 75, P.I, Art. 4, 5, 7, P. II.

[13] Art. 3, G I, II, III and IV, Art. 12, G I, G II, Art. 13, G III, Art. 32, G IV, Art. 11, P.I.

[14] Art. 11, P.I.

[15] Art. 15, G I, Art. 18, G II, Art. 17, G IV.

[16] Art. 8, P.I.

Medical units shall at all times be respected and protected[17]. In order to enjoy this right, the medical units must fulfil two conditions:

— apart from the units administered by the ICRC, they should be attached to the medical services of the armed forces or, for civilian units, be recognized and authorized by the competent authority of the Party to the conflict under which they are operating, or be placed under the responsibility of these authorities (where units have been provided by a State not a Party to the conflict or by a voluntary agency of such a State). In all cases, the authorities of a Party to the conflict having jurisdiction over a medical unit entitled to protection—and consequently to use of the distinctive emblem—are therefore responsible for it and must make sure that the unit is properly used in conformity with its purpose, that is, principally, that it fulfils the following second condition;
— they must not be used to commit acts harmful to the enemy.

Medical units must be clearly identified[18].

Rights of Medical Personnel

International humanitarian law provides that the medical personnel called upon to serve in the event of armed conflict shall be respected and protected[19].

Members of medical personnel may in no circumstances renounce any of the rights conferred on them by international humanitarian law. This injunction is intended to prevent pressure being exerted on medical personnel to make them renounce their rights, and to preclude justification of a breach on the grounds that the victim had given his consent[20].

Members of medical personnel are empowered to require the authorities to provide the means and facilities necessary to ensure that the victims are cared for in the best possible manner[21].

In order that they should help the wounded and sick with efficiency, medical personnel shall have access to the places where their services are essential, subject to such supervisory and safety measures as the relevant Party to the conflict may deem necessary[22].

Medical personnel shall not be punished or importuned for having discharged medical functions compatible with medical ethics, regardless of the person benefitting therefrom. This provision tends to prevent violence, threats, persecu-

---

[17] Art. 19, 20, 21, 22, G I, Art. 23, G II, Art. 18, 19, G IV, Art. 11, P.II, Art. 12, 13, P.I.

[18] Art. 42, 43, G I, Art. 43, G II, Art. 18, G IV, Art. 12, P.II, Art. 18, Annex I, P.I.

[19] Art. 24–27, G I, Art. 36–37, G II, Art. 20, G IV, Art. 15, 62, 67, P.I, Art. 9, P.II.

[20] Art. 7, G I, G II, and G III, Art. 8, G IV.

[21] Art. 15, P.I, Art. 9, P.II.

[22] Art. 15 and 28, G I, Art. 18, G II, Art. 33, G III, Art. 15, P.I.

tions or punishments in the case of medical care given to the wounded or sick of the adverse Party[23].

Medical personnel shall not be compelled to act contrary to medical ethics, other medical rules or to the provisions of the Conventions and Protocols[24].

Medical personnel shall not be compelled to give information about the wounded and sick in their care[25].

Medical personnel of a State not a Party to the conflict, or of a relief society of such a State made available to one of the Parties to the conflict, who are in the hands of the enemy of the Party to which they have been made available, shall be authorized to return to their own country or even to the Party in whose service they were carrying out their activities, as soon as a route for their return is open and military considerations permit.

Medical personnel working under the responsibility of the ICRC must be either immediately repatriated or assigned once again to their work for one of the Parties to the conflict, in accordance with an agreement concluded by those persons, the ICRC and the Party or Parties to the conflict.

Permanent military medical personnel, the medical personnel of national voluntary aid societies (e.g. National Red Cross or Red Crescent Societies) of a Party to the conflict, attached to that Party's Army Medical Service, the civilian medical personnel of a Party to the conflict are in principle exempt from capture, but may be retained under certain conditions[26].

Conditions Required for Medical NGOs To Benefit from International Humanitarian Law

We have seen that any intervention by a relief society is subject to state recognition and consent. For instance, under Art. 27 of the First Geneva Convention,

A recognized Society of a neutral country can only lend the assistance of its medical personnel and units to a Party to the conflict with the previous consent of its own Government and the authorization of the Party to the conflict concerned. That personnel and those units shall be placed under the control of that Party to the conflict.

The neutral Government shall notify this consent to the adversary of the State which accepts such assistance. The Party to the conflict which accepts such assistance is bound to notify the adverse Party thereof before making any use of it.

---

[23] Art. 18, G I, Art.16, P.I, Art. 10, P.II.
[24] Art. 15 and 16, P.I, Art. 9 and 10, P.II.
[25] Art. 16, P.I, Art. 10, P.II.
[26] Art. 32, G I, Art. 36, G II, Art. 28, G I.

In no circumstances shall this assistance be considered as interference in the conflict.

The members of the personnel named in the first paragraph shall be duly furnished with the identity cards provided for in Article 40 before leaving the neutral country to which they belong.

Under Art. 9.2.c) and 12 of the First Protocol, civilian medical units shall be respected and protected at all times and shall not be the object of attack provided that they belong to one of the Parties to the conflict, that they are recognized and authorized by the competent authority of one of the Parties to the conflict, or that their personnel is made available to a Party to the conflict for humanitarian purposes by a neutral or other State which is not a Party to the conflict.

There is therefore a double possibility of control, at least through the delivery of an identity card,—by the State of origin of the relief society,—by the State which accepts the services of the society.

In situations of international armed conflict, medical NGOs have to obtain the consent of the State party to the conflict before they can intervene. The same applies to

armed conflicts in which peoples are fighting against colonial domination and alien occupation and against racist régimes in the exercise of their right of self-determination, as enshrined in the Charter of the United Nations and the Declaration on Principles of International Law concerning Friendly Relations and Cooperation among States in accordance with the Charter of the United Nations.

under Art. 1.4. of the First Protocol. The movement which participates in such a conflict is bound to abide by the provisions of the Conventions and Protocol I.

In situations of non-international armed conflicts, if the medical NGO wishes to intervene on the part of the territory which is controlled by the legitimate Government, the Government's agreement will be required. If the medical NGO wishes to intervene in the part of the territory controlled by rebels, the rebels' authorities will have to give their approval.

Under Art. 3 common to the four Conventions,

An impartial humanitarian body, such as the International Committee of the Red Cross, may offer its services to the Parties to the conflict.

As mentioned by Torrelli, this Article allows in practice the ICRC (or any other impartial humanitarian body) to intervene in a territory without the agreement of a Government, when that part of the national territory is not controlled by the Government. Acting prudently, the ICRC attempts to obtain the consent, even if it is only tacit, of the Government, before giving relief to the rebels; this agreement will generally remain confidential.

In other cases, the formal agreement of both parties is sought. In October 1990, the ICRC obtained the agreement of both the Angolan Government and UNITA, the rebel movement, to provide 260 tons of foodstuffs and other emergency equipment to populations in the territories held by both parties[27].

Medical NGOs do not necessarily follow the same practice, at the risk of antagonizing the legal authorities, if they are captured by Government forces. The NGO's recourse to Art. 3 in order to justify their "offer of services" to a Party to the conflict may be rejected by some Governments.

Humanitarian and Impartial Organizations

In order to benefit from the protection accorded by the Geneva Conventions and Additional Protocols in armed conflicts situations, an NGO which sends doctors and other health personnel to such areas must qualify as an "impartial humanitarian body" as referred to in Art. 3 of the four Conventions.

Other references to those requirements are found in the Conventions and Protocols: for instance, in Art. 9/9/9/10 of the Conventions:

> The provisions of the present Convention constitute no obstacle to the humanitarian activities which the International Committee of the Red Cross or any other impartial humanitarian organizations may, subject to the consent of the Parties to the conflict concerned, undertake for the protection of wounded and sick, medical personnel and chaplains, and for their relief (Conv. I), — and shipwrecked persons (Conv. II), — for the protection of prisoners of war (Conv. III), — for the protection of civilian persons (Conv. IV).

Art. 81.4. of the First Protocol states that:

> The High Contracting Parties and the Parties to the conflict shall, as far as possible, make facilities similar to those mentioned in paragraphs 2 and 3 available to the other humanitarian organizations referred to in the Conventions and this Protocol which are duly authorized by the respective Parties to the conflict and which perform their humanitarian activities in accordance with the provisions of the Conventions and this Protocol.

In accordance with Art. 70 of the First Protocol,

> 1. If the civilian population of any territory under the control of a Party to the conflict, other than occupied territory, is not adequately provided with the supplies mentioned in Article 69, relief actions which are humanitarian and impartial in character and conducted without adverse distinction shall be undertaken, subject to the agreement of the Parties concerned in such relief actions. Offers of

---

[27] Maurice Torrelli, "La protection du médecin volontaire", *Annales de Droit international médical*, Monaco, 1986, pp. 53–73. Developments in this section are based in part on this report. On Angola, see ICRC *Bulletin*, No. 178, Nov. 1990.

such relief shall not be regarded as interference in the armed conflict or as unfriendly acts.

...

Under Art. 18.2 of the Second Protocol:

> If the civilian population is suffering undue hardship owing to a lack of the supplies essential for its survival, such as foodstuffs and medical supplies, relief actions for the civilian population which are of an exclusively humanitarian and impartial nature and which are conducted without adverse distinction shall be undertaken subject to the consent of the High Contracting Parties concerned.

The Fundamental Principle of Humanity includes the following three elements[28]: to prevent and alleviate suffering, to protect life and health and to assure respect for the individual. Humanitarian law affirms that the victims of conflict are first of all men and that nothing, not even war, can deprive them of the minimum requirements needed out of respect for the human person. The principle of humanity requires that the victims shall be respected, protected and humanely treated.

As medical ethics have similar requirements, all medical relief assistance NGOs should qualify as "humanitarian" organizations.

However, all humanitarian NGOs are not necessarily impartial.

The Red Cross Fundamental Principle of "Impartiality" involves three elements[29]:

1. It forbids discrimination as to nationality, race, religious beliefs, class or political opinions, and any other similar criteria. It applies to the giving of care and distribution of relief and the provision of the same humane treatment to all victims.
2. Under the principle of proportionality, it endeavours to relieve the suffering of individuals in proportion to the degree of their suffering and to give priority according to the degree of urgency, in relation to the availability of assistance.
3. The third element requires not to take sides, either for reasons of interest, prejudice or sympathy. Impartiality is closely associated here with the principle of neutrality which requires the Red Cross not to take sides in hostilities or engage at any time in controversies of a political, racial, religious or ideological nature. The purpose of these two Principles (impartiality and neutrality) is to enable the Red Cross to enjoy the confidence of all governments and other authorities, a condition necessary for the fulfilment of its humanitarian mission in the interest of the victims.

While all medical NGOs apply the principles of non-discrimination and proportionality, some of them (such as the French "no-border" associations) have, on occa-

---

[28] Jean Pictet, *The Fundamental Principles of the Red Cross—Commentary*, Henry Dunant Institute, Geneva, 1979, pp. 22–27.

[29] Ibid., pp. 37–51.

sions, "taken sides" and engaged in public political controversies or denunciations. Those doing so would no longer qualify for the protection of the Geneva Conventions and Protocols. Impartiality and neutrality have to be continually demonstrated.

Torrelli concluded his study on "The protection of the volunteer doctor"[30] in acknowledging the "weakness" of this legal protection.

In order to reinforce this protection, the International Federation of Human Rights submitted a draft "Charter for the Protection of Medical Missions" at a Conference held in Strasbourg on 28 and 29 February 1984.

The Proposed "Charter for the Protection of Medical Missions"

The proposal had been initiated by "Médecins Sans Frontières" and other French humanitarian NGOs, and endorsed by the International Federation of Human Rights. Their arguments for a Charter follow[31].

Several humanitarian medical associations have decided to help civilian populations denied of assistance throughout the world. They consider that it is a basic human right for people to benefit from medical assistance wherever and whoever they are, and that this right should not be limited by borders. They ignore any governmental prohibitions by giving medical assistance in countries or areas where other organizations cannot go, where medical needs are particularly urgent. They intervene in numerous regions of conflict, sometimes openly and legally, sometimes illegally and therefore without protection. For example, more that 200 doctors and nurses from the "no border" NGOs have worked in the rebel-held regions of Afghanistan since the Soviet invasion in December 1979.

The associations' medical missions have however been confronted with serious difficulties (capture, detention, acts of violence against their members, murders, bombing of their medical aid centres, etc.) which have underlined the lack of organized international protection to international health volunteers belonging to medical NGOs.

The laws of war have changed. Nowadays, conflicts no longer take place, as in the past, between regular armies, leaving the civilians behind. In Africa, Asia or Latin America, war is carried out by guerrillas. The theory of a "guerillero as a fish in the water among the population" has been created and applied by the Chinese Communists. The leaders of authoritarian countries have found a simple and definitive solution to stopping an armed rebellion: one has to empty the bowl in order to catch the fish. The effective response to guerrilla warfare consists in massive retaliation against the population, sometimes including the extermination of large segments of the population (Cambodia, Afghanistan, Ogaden, Timor...). Such a strategy needs secrecy, among other conditions, for its success: international

---

[30] Torrelli, op.cit., p. 70.
[31] Documentation "Médecins Sans Frontières".

public opinion would never accept such actions if properly informed. Therefore borders are firmly closed to both news reporters and members of humanitarian organizations. Those who dare defy the prohibition are chased and punished.

For the promoters of the Charter, the provisions of the Red Cross Conventions and Protocols do not adequately protect medical and other health volunteers of the new "no-border" organizations. Staff protected under these instruments have to be recognized and authorized by governments, or to work under the responsibility of the ICRC, which precludes members of NGOs which do not accept such conditions.

Accused of law-breaking, organizations such as Médecins Sans Frontières reply that their work in some countries is not unlawful but only in advance of a constantly changing International Law: events unavoidably precede law. On the one hand, their is a "lex lata", an existing law, determined in conventions and treaties. On the other hand, there is a "lex ferenda", a law to develop step by step according to the events and which, in turn, will be the "lex lata" of the future. Medical organizations believe that the time has come to protect all humanitarian teams giving assistance in such conditions.

Accused of interfering in governments' domestic jurisdiction, the medical associations reply that in this area two concepts are in conflict: medical deontology or ethics, which obligates doctors to give assistance to anyone in danger, and international law, which protects states' national sovereignties under the non-intervention principle. It is no wonder that medical associations have chosen the first concept as a moral imperative, against the second, a political argument. Furthermore, NGOs are not bound by the non-intervention principle in view of their non-governmental nature. Finally, the presence of doctors and nurses with their medicaments and medical equipment as their only weapon cannot be considered as a threat or an aggression against the host country.

The proposed Charter would therefore include both rights and obligations:

— a right for the civilian population to be cared for by medical staff offering guarantees of competence and impartiality. These guarantees could be formally recognized by an international body such as the ICRC;
— a right to protection for medical personnel during their missions. This protection would not be a personal privilege, but the necessary counterpart of rules guaranteeing the respect and protection of the endangered civilian population. Medical personnel should not be punished for their medical activities, they should have a right of access to where they are needed, they should not be forced to give information about the people they have assisted. If, due to medical activities, a member of the medical staff is arrested by the authorities of the country where he is on mission, or by rebel authorities, he must be set free and sent back to his home country without delay.
— Medical personnel have the usual obligations under the recognized codes of medical ethics. They should be identifiable by way of a professional card delivered by a recognized international body such as the ICRC.

The Council of Europe Resolution 904 (1988)

Following on the French medical associations' proposal, the Parliamentary Assembly of the Council of Europe approved on 30 June 1988 a Resolution "on the protection of humanitarian medical missions" (its text is in Table 10.1). The text of the Resolution includes some of the French associations' themes, such as the "right to life" and the "right to health", and a consequent "duty of solidarity" and a "duty to cooperate". However, it gives due regard to the "invaluable humanitarian activities carried out by or under the auspices of the ICRC", the work of the other organizations' medical missions being "complementary" to the ICRC activities. It also urges these missions to refrain from using the ICRC's emblem for non-medical activities and from using it without the consent and supervision of the authorities controlling the territory, so as not to diminish the protective value of the emblem. Its reference to assistance "in a neutral and impartial way" pays homage to two of the Red Cross Fundamental Principles, and does not support the claim of some of the medical associations that their moral responsibility is, when needed, to "take sides".

The Resolution recommends that a charter for the protection of medical missions be drawn up in the U.N. and thus be given the same universal recognition as the Geneva Conventions and Protocols. The rights and obligations of medical personnel on mission are defined in the Appendix to the Resolution.

Table 10.1. Parliamentary Assembly of the Council of Europe. Resolution 904 (1988) on the protection of humanitarian medical missions

---

The Assembly,
1. Convinced that every human being should be entitled to be cared for by medical personnel offering the guarantees of competence and impartiality;
2. Considering that this expectation derives from the right to life and the right to health as guaranteed by several international legal instruments;
3. Believing that the unrestricted exercise of the right to care implies a duty of solidarity among all states of the world, particularly a duty to cooperate in accordance with the Charter of the United Nations;
4. Anxious to support the various humanitarian medical organizations which have set themselves the task of assisting afflicted civilian populations throughout the world in a neutral and impartial way;
5. Being aware that the personnel of medical missions operating in countries in a state of strife (civil war, armed conflict) are often exposed to dangers (abduction, detention, murder) which jeopardize their ability to provide medical assistance as well as their physical safety;
6. Considering that the dangerous circumstances in which these medical missions operate have highlighted the insufficiency of organized international protection for medical personnel belonging to non-governmental organizations;
7. Wishing to support the efforts being made in particular by the International Humanitarian Centre (IHC) in Paris to improve the legal protection of medical missions;
8. Considering that the work of these medical missions is complementary to the invaluable humanitarian activities carried out by or under the auspices of the International Committee of the Red Cross (ICRC);
9. Underlining the necessity for such medical missions not to take any action which might be detrimental to the ICRC's work, and urging these missions to refrain from using the ICRC's emblem (the

350

red cross or the red crescent) for non-medical activities, and without the consent and supervision of the authorities controlling the territory, so as not to diminish the protective value of this emblem;

10. Bearing in mind that the Additional Protocols (1977) to the Geneva Conventions (12 August 1949) afford protection to medical personnel intervening in conflicts of a non-international character, and sincerely hoping that these protocols will soon be ratified by all the states of the world;

11. Emphasizing, however, that:

    a. the protected status provided for in these texts applies solely to medical personnel working under the aegis of the International Committee of the Red Cross (ICRC) and to personnel employed by a state;

    b. these protocols have not yet been accepted by all countries and therefore are not in force everywhere in the world;

    c. the application of these texts does not always cover cases of internal conflict not recognized by the legal government in whose territory the medical personnel of non-governmental organisations operate with increasing frequency;

12. Having regard to its Recommendations 714 (1973) and 945 (1982), on international humanitarian law, and its Resolutions 823 (1984) and 881 (1987) on the activities of the International Committee of the Red Cross (ICRC);

13. Wishing that a charter for the protection of medical missions be drawn up in the United Nations and thus be given the same universal recognition as the Geneva Conventions of 1949 and their Additional Protocols of 1977,

14. Earnestly calls upon all states of the world to respect:

    a. the right of all civilian populations to be cared for by medical personnel offering guarantees of competence and impartiality;

    b. the right of medical personnel to be protected during their missions in the manner specified in the appendix hereto;

15. Instructs its President to forward this resolution to the Secretary-General of the United Nations in support of any action to improve the protection of humanitarian medical missions.

APPENDIX

The rights of medical personnel on mission are as follows:

1. Medical personnel must be protected and respected. They may not be punished or molested for having engaged in medical activity, whoever the beneficiaries of such care may be.
2. Medical personnel must be afforded access to all places where medical care is needed.
3. No member of a medical staff may be compelled to provide information concerning the persons to whom he has given assistance, with the exception of information concerning contagious diseases.
4. If a member of a medical staff is, on account of his medical activities, arrested by the authorities of the territory in which he is carrying out his mission or by a party opposed to such authorities, he must be released and repatriated without delay.

These rights are accompanied by the following obligations on the part of medical personnel:

1. Medical personnel providing assistance must scrupulously respect the rules of medical ethics and may not refrain from performing acts required by these rules.
2. The assistance provided must be based on purely medical criteria of a humanitarian kind.
3. The wishes of persons receiving care must be respected.
4. Medical personnel must offer guarantees of competence and impartiality. They must be identifiable. For this purpose they may carry a professional card issued by an international body such as the International Humanitarian Centre (IHC) in Paris or any other health organisation expressly designated and accredited to such international organizations as the United Nations, the World Health Organization or the Council of Europe.

Source: Council of Europe, Fortieth Ordinary Session of the Parliamentary Assembly, Text adopted by the Standing Committee, acting on behalf of the Assembly, on 30 June 1988.

An Assessment

The Council of Europe's Resolution is a constructive compromise between the traditional values and practices of the Red Cross and the more activist and impatient demands of the "no border" Movement leaders. It acknowledges the essential humanitarian role and activities of the ICRC, a role "complemented" by the work of the "new" medical missions.

The adoption of the Resolution by a European IGO, however, does not predict its adoption by the U.N. General Assembly without substantial amendments to emphasize national sovereignty. In particular, the "right of access" of medical personnel "to all places where medical care is needed (Art. 2 of Appendix) would not be accepted by a majority of U.N. member States.

While the Resolution has a geographically-limited scope, its adoption is still important in the sense of giving international legitimacy to the role of the new medical missions and to the need to provide additional legal protection to their medical personnel.

It also confirms the Red Cross conditions for such protection: that the relief societies, or medical NGOs, should be humanitarian and impartial, as well as professionally competent.

An unresolved question is that of the authority which should decide whether an NGO fulfils, or not, these requirements.

One option is that this should be decided by the national state authorities of the country of origin of the NGO. However, this national decision may be challenged by other states, including the recipient country.

The credentials of an international NGO working in various countries should preferably be reviewed and assessed by a specialized international body.

The Council of Europe Resolution suggested that medical personnel with guarantees of competence and impartiality should carry a professional card issued by an international body such as the International Humanitarian Centre in Paris or any other health organization expressly designated and accredited to such international organizations as the U.N., the WHO or the Council of Europe.

In spite of its humanitarian experience and competence, the ICRC is not a medical organization as such. It is also unlikely that the Committee and its governing bodies would accept this new responsibility, which may affect the neutrality of the ICRC and interfere with its traditional statutory obligations and activities.

It is doubtful that any other international NGO or group or federation of NGOs would have sufficient authority to provide this international legal legitimacy.

The formal recognition given by the U.N. Economic and Social Council and the WHO in granting consultative status to a number of NGOs does not include a specific assessment of medical NGOs qualifications as humanitarian, impartial and competent.

A possible solution would be to create a joint IGO/NGO specific body of international, independent health specialists for this purpose, by a common decision of the U.N. General Assembly and of the World Health Assembly, in close consultation with the ICRC and the League of Red Cross and Red Crescent Societies.

In the meantime, in the present state of international humanitarian law, the only international legal protection available to medical volunteers is that provided by the Geneva Conventions and Additional Protocols.

CHAPTER 11

INTERNATIONAL HUMANITARIAN INTERVENTION

International humanitarian assistance is provided to recipient states and populations at the request or with the consent of the recipient states' government authorities.

Government approval or consent is required to allow the entry into the country of relief material and equipment, foodstuffs, medicaments, transport and communications support. It is also required for the entry of bilateral, intergovernmental or non-governmental organizations (IGOs or NGOs) aid workers in the country. It is required in order to facilitate the aid workers' access to the victims, under a government disaster plan, if any, or under IGO/NGO coordination arrangements which may have been approved.

Official bilateral aid and IGOs operate only through bilateral diplomatic or multilateral channels with recipient government authorities. The UNHCR, UNICEF, UNDRO, WHO and other U.N. bodies providing humanitarian assistance, as well as NGOs working in official association with such IGOs, are bound to fully respect the international law principles and diplomatic rules of national sovereignty, and non-intervention into another state's territory without that state's request or consent.

The International Committee of the Red Cross (ICRC), the League of Red Cross and Red Crescent Societies and the National Societies are also required to abide by these principles and rules in their dealings with governments, and in particular with the Contracting States of the Geneva Conventions. The Red Cross organizations operate with government approval and support.

Most international NGOs are also respectful of the authority of established governments with which they negotiate the conditions and modalities of their humanitarian assistance to the local populations.

The "French Doctors' no-borders" movement was created in the 1970s in part as a protest against the Red Cross alleged excessive respect for governments' exigencies and the Red Cross rule of discretion when faced with government violations of human rights and humanitarian law. It was also a protest against some governments' policies or practices of selective aid, and against the obstacles set by some governments to the delivery of aid to their population. When diplomacy fails, the French Doctors' associations claim that it is not only their right but their obligation to take immediate relief action and, if necessary, bypass official channels.

Organizations such as Médecins Sans Frontières, Médecins du Monde or Aide Médicale Internationale (MSF, MDM or AMI) thus chose, at times, to denounce publicly government active or passive violations of human rights, at the risk of being expelled from the assisted country. They also took bigger physical risks by crossing borders illegally and giving relief to populations in need, in areas in rebellion against the established government, such as in Sudan, Ethiopia, Afghanistan and in Latin American countries.

Building on these illicit "across borders" operations, French jurists and humanitarian organizations leaders have formulated a theory of an international "right" of victims to assistance and of an international "duty" to assist them (so far, in line with the Red Cross principles), culminating in an international "right" of international humanitarian intervention—the latter "right" being considered as unrealistic and unacceptable to states by Red Cross leaders.

The French Government's attempt to include such a concept in a U.N. resolution in 1988 was defeated by government representatives who insisted that the principles of national sovereignty and non-interference had to prevail over the ill-defined and controversial "right" of international humanitarian intervention.

This defeat has not resolved the inherent conflict between international humanitarian assistance and national sovereignty: on the one hand, the need to give victims of war and natural disasters prompt and adapted relief assistance, and, on the other hand, the need to obtain permission from the recipient government before such assistance may be given, when some governments may deny, against all evidence, that their country needs international assistance, or may delay this assistance, or may use it selectively, thus increasing unnecessarily the suffering of the victims and the number of casualties.

The fundamental issue is similar to that raised by the international protection of human rights: this regime implies an intervention of other states, IGOs and NGOs into the "domestic jurisdiction" of sovereign states.

In the human rights domain, at the global level, the legally acceptable intervention is mostly rhetorical: it may include reports, resolutions publicly condemning states violating their own commitments to abide by human rights conventions and other instruments. It may also include enquiries and visits by fact-finding missions, observers and rapporteurs. Under the European Convention on Human Rights, states may be condemned and sanctioned by the European Court.

However, in the course of history, states or groups of states have intervened by force in other countries in order to protect their own citizens or even the local populations against human rights abuses.

In the humanitarian domain, international assistance cannot remain rhetorical: it involves the provision of finances, material, equipment and personnel by the donors and it requires the crossing of borders in order to reach those in need. Whether this delivery should be implemented, assisted or conveyed by military forces is a controversial issue.

In the human rights domain, the conflict is between morality, responsibility and solidarity on the one hand, and the principles of national sovereignty and non-intervention on the other,—or between the respect of individual life, dignity ~ fundamental freedoms on the one hand, and the protection of the territorial integrity and political independence of states on the other.

In the humanitarian domain, the conflict is between the immediate exigencies of "charity", in a broad sense, or "the ethics of the extreme emergency", as expressed by the French Doctors' group, and the same principles.

We will first recall the principles of international law applicable to international intervention, as formulated in the U.N. Charter and confirmed by the International Court of Justice.

The conflicting positions of the International Red Cross and of an advocate of a qualified "right of humanitarian intervention" by force will be examined.

Are the principles of non-intervention respected? Past cases of international military humanitarian interventions by states will be summarized, together with the apparent justifications for these interventions.

The utilization of national military units specialized in relief assistance will then be considered.

The recognition given recently to the U.N. peace-keeping forces has raised the proposal that the forces could assume humanitarian assistance functions in addition to their now traditional missions.

The problem of delivery of relief and access of international humanitarian assistance to those in need in recipient countries will then be reviewed on the basis of a number of Red Cross and U.N. Declarations, Resolutions and other texts.

Is there a need for another international Resolution or Convention on this question? The frustrated French initiative of 1988 seems to indicate that the answer should be in the negative.

Humanitarian Intervention under International Law: The Principles

The U.N. Charter

The main and determining motivation in the creation of the U.N. was

> to save succeeding generations from the scourge of war, which twice in our life time has brought untold sorrow to mankind[1]

and the maintenance of peace and security is one of its essential missions: hence the confirmation in the Charter of the basic principle of non-use of force in relations between nations. Under Art. 2.4.

> All Members shall refrain in their international relations from the threat or use of force against the territorial integrity or political independence of any state, or in any other manner inconsistent with the Purposes of the United Nations.

---

[1] *U.N. Charter*, Preamble.

Under Chapter VI, states are required to first seek a solution to international disputes by peaceful means of their choice.

Enforcement measures under Chapter VII can only be taken under the authority of the Security Council. States retain the inherent right of individual or collective self-defence in case of an armed attack against one U.N. Member, but only until the Security Council has taken measures necessary to maintain international peace and security. Self-defence measures must be reported to the Security Council which retains its authority and responsibility to take any necessary action in order to maintain or restore international peace and security (Art. 51). Any enforcement action taken under regional arrangements or by regional agencies must be authorized by the Security Council. Only the Security Council can "intervene" by calling upon the parties to settle their dispute by peaceful means, by investigating disputes or situations which might lead to international friction or give rise to a dispute, by making recommendations, or by making decisions on what measures will be taken to maintain or restore international peace and security (Art. 33.2, 34, 36 and 39).

The principle of non-use of force, except as measures of collective security under the authority of the Security Council, thus prohibits any forceful "intervention" of a state or group of states, for whatever reason, in the territory of another state.

This principle is reinforced by the principle of the sovereign equality of all Member states (Art. 2.1) and broadened by the principle of non-intervention by the United Nations in matters which are essentially within the domestic jurisdiction of any state, without prejudicing the application of enforcement measures under Chapter VII (Art. 2.7).

In 1970, the "Declaration on Principles of International Law concerning Friendly Relations and Cooperation among States in accordance with the Charter of the United Nations" (Resol. 2625 (XXV) of 24 October 1970) reaffirmed even more forcefully the non-intervention principle by recalling:

> ...(that) the strict observance by States of the obligation not to intervene in the affairs of any other State is an essential condition to ensure that nations live together in peace with one another, since the practice of any form of intervention not only violates the spirit and letter of the Charter, but also leads to the creation of situations which threaten international peace and security,
> ...the duty of States to refrain in their international relations from military, political, economic or any other form of coercion aimed against the political independence or territorial integrity of any State,
> ...the basic importance of sovereign equality
> ...the duty not to intervene in matters within the domestic jurisdiction of any State, in accordance with the Charter—No State or group of States has the right to intervene, directly or indirectly, for any reason whatever, in the internal or external affairs of any other State...

On the other hand, the purposes of the U.N. are not limited to the maintenance of peace and security: they include international cooperation in solving international problems of an economic, social, cultural, or humanitarian character and encouraging respect for human rights and for fundamental freedoms for all (Art. 1.3).

The mission given to the U.N. of achieving international cooperation and the "wide international responsibilities" entrusted to the U.N. specialized agencies in such fields entail some degree of international intervention through reports, monitoring, advisory and operational assistance. While all bilateral or multilateral activities in those fields may be carried out within a national territory only at the request or with the consent of recipient states, it is in the nature of such activities as the international protection and promotion of human rights to override considerations of national sovereignty. The recent supervision of national elections in Nicaragua by the U.N., even though this was requested by the Government authorities, shows that there is a growing, albeit reluctant, acceptance of an international legitimacy beyond and above the parochial interests of states. The requirements of the growing world economic and social interdependence are necessarily eroding the principles of national sovereignty and non-intervention.

In situations of external conflicts, internal strife or natural disasters, should the interest of the victims prevail over the traditional legal restrictions of national domestic jurisdiction?

The International Court of Justice

Two Judgments of the Court have given support to a strict interpretation of the fundamental international law principle of non-intervention.

In its Judgment of 9 April 1949 in the Corfu Channel Case[2], the Court stated that it

> can only regard the alleged right of intervention as the manifestation of a policy of force, such as has, in the past, given rise to most serious abuses and such as cannot, whatever be the present defects in international organization, find a place in international law. Intervention is perhaps still less admissible in the particular form it would take here; for, from the nature of things, it would be reserved for the most powerful States, and might easily lead to perverting the administration of international justice itself.

> ...

> Between independent States, respect for territorial sovereignty is an essential foundation of international relations.

The veiled reference to gunboat diplomacy exercised by former colonial powers under the guise of humanitarian intervention could only elicit support from the less powerful States, and as from the 1960s, from the newly independent countries

---

[2] *ICJ Reports*, The Corfu Channel Case (Merits), Judgment of April 9th, 1949, p. 35.

which feared and rejected the power and influence of the "imperialist" and "neo-colonialist" Western countries.

In its Judgment of 27 June 1986 in the "Case Concerning Military and Paramilitary Activities in and against Nicaragua" (Nicaragua v. United States of America)[3], the Court again confirmed the same principles of non-intervention, of non-use of force and respect for State sovereignty. It found that

> ... no such general right of intervention, in support of an opposition within another State, exists in contemporary international law. The Court concludes that acts constituting a breach of the customary principle of non-intervention will also, if they directly or indirectly involve the use of force, constitute a breach of the principle of non-use of force in international relations.

The Court found that the support given by the U.S., up to the end of September 1984, to the military and paramilitary activities of the "contras" in Nicaragua constituted a clear breach of the principle of non-intervention.

It also held that the use of force could not be the appropriate method to monitor or ensure respect for human rights.

> With regard to the steps actually taken, the protection of human rights, a strictly humanitarian objective, cannot be compatible with the mining of ports, the destruction of oil installations, or again with the training, arming and equipping of the "contras".

The Court noted that, from 1 October 1984, the U.S. Congress had restricted the use of the funds appropriated for assistance to the "contras" to "humanitarian assistance". It then stated:

> There can be no doubt that the provision of strictly humanitarian aid to persons or forces in another country, whatever their political affiliations or objectives, cannot be regarded as unlawful intervention, or as in any other way contrary to international law.

However, the Court criticized the U.S. for having given this aid to only a selected group in Nicaragua, thus in disregard for the Red Cross Fundamental Principle of Impartiality, which provides that

> It makes no discrimination as to nationality, race, religious beliefs, class or political opinions. It endeavours to relieve the suffering of individuals, being guided solely by their needs, and to give priority to the most urgent cases of distress.

The Court stated that an essential feature of truly humanitarian aid is that it is given "without discrimination" of any kind:

> In the view of the Court, if the provision of "humanitarian assistance" is to escape condemnation as an intervention in the internal affairs of Nicaragua, not

[3] *ICJ Reports*, Case concerning military and paramilitary activities in and against Nicaragua (Nicaragua v. U.S.A.), Merits, Judgment of 27 June 1986.

only must it be limited to the purposes hallowed in the practice of the Red Cross, namely "to prevent and alleviate human suffering", and "to protect life and health and to ensure respect for the human being"; it must also, and above all, be given without discrimination to all in need in Nicaragua, not merely to the "contras" and their dependants.

The Position of the Red Cross

The same international law principles of non-use of force, non-intervention and national sovereignty are found in some of the basic documents of the International Red Cross and Red Crescent Movement.

The Preamble of the First Protocol[4] recalls that every State has the duty, in conformity with the Charter of the U.N., to refrain in its international relations from the threat or use of force against the sovereignty, territorial integrity or political independence of any State.

Art. 3 of the Second Protocol[5] states:

1. Nothing in this Protocol shall be invoked for the purpose of affecting the sovereignty of a State or the responsibility of the government, by all legitimate means, to maintain or re-establish law and order in the State or to defend the national unity and territorial integrity of the State.
2. Nothing in this Protocol shall be invoked as a justification for intervening, directly or indirectly, for any reason whatever, in the armed conflict or in the internal or external affairs of the High Contracting Party in the territory of which that conflict occurs.

Art. 2.5 of the Statutes of the International Red Cross and Red Crescent Movement[6] states that

The implementation of the Statutes by the components of the Movement shall not affect the sovereignty of States, with due respect for the provisions of international humanitarian law.

Art. 70 of Protocol I[7] provides that if the civilian population of any territory under the control of a Party to the conflict, other than occupied territory, is not adequately provided with essential supplies, relief actions will be undertaken subject to the

---

[4] Protocol Additional to the Geneva Conventions of 12 August 1949, and relating to the protection of victims of international armed conflicts (Protocol I) of 8 June 1977, in *International Red Cross Handbook*, 1983, p. 216.

[5] Protocol additional to the Geneva Conventions of 12 August 1949, and relating to the protection of victims of non-international armed conflicts (Protocol II), of 8 June 1977, ibid., p. 287.

[6] *Compendium of Reference Texts on the International Red Cross and Red Crescent Movement*, Geneva, 1990, Statutes of the International Red Cross and Red Crescent Movement, Art. 2.5, p. 14.

[7] Protocol I, Art. 70, op.cit., p. 255.

agreement of the Parties concerned. Such actions would have to be humanitarian and impartial in character and conducted without adverse distinction.

As a "quasi-IGO", the ICRC deals essentially with governments, the Contracting Parties to the Geneva Conventions. Maintaining normal diplomatic relations with governments is a prerequisite to obtaining access to the victims. The close links of the National Red Cross and Red Crescent Societies with their own government make it unlikely that any Society, or the League, would not deal exclusively with legitimate government authorities.

However, the Red Cross Movement mission is to prevent and alleviate human suffering "wherever it may be found" and one of the functions of the League is to bring relief by all available means "to all disaster victims"[8]. This duty therefore extends the Red Cross organizations missions to authorities other than legitimate government authorities, as seen during the Biafra War, when the ICRC provided relief both to Nigeria and to Biafra, under an agreement with the Nigerian Government (see Chapter 7).

For Sandoz[9], the ICRC is obviously not tempted by any (forceful) humanitarian intervention, as it does not have the means to carry it out. This weakness is also a strength: one accepts aid more easily from the "weak", which does not constitute a threat. The ICRC has voluntarily not used, save in exceptional cases, its only weapon, the public denunciation of a State's violation of humanitarian law. This self-limitation has helped to promote the idea that the humanitarian action of such bodies as the ICRC is more effective, at the purely humanitarian level, than armed "humanitarian interventions".

A Right of Humanitarian Military Intervention?

Teson[10] has argued that there is a right of humanitarian intervention, in the sense of a forcible transboundary action undertaken for the purpose of protecting the rights of individuals against violations by their own governments. He sets aside the more limited type of humanitarian intervention, e.g. the one undertaken by a state (or by a group of states) to protect its (their) own nationals, whose rights are being violated by the target government—the "rescue mission". It is doubtful that the rescue mission is truly humanitarian as it may be conceived as based on either self-defence principles or the law of diplomatic protection of nationals.

Teson's thesis is founded on the assumption that morality matters in international relations. He finds it morally intolerable that the international community, in

---

[8] Statutes of the International Red Cross and Red Crescent Movement, Art. 6.4 c), op.cit., p. 18.

[9] *Annales de droit international médical*, No. 33, 1986, Monaco, "L'intervention humanitaire, le droit international humanitaire et le CICR", Yves Sandoz, pp. 43–51.

[10] Fernando R. Teson, *Humanitarian Intervention: An Inquiry into Law and Morality*, Transnational Publishers, Inc., New York, 1988, pp. 4, 5, 15, 16, 111–123.

the name of the non-intervention rule, is impotent to combat massacres, acts of genocide, mass murder and widespread torture.

He defines humanitarian intervention as

> the proportionate transboundary help, including forcible help, provided by governments to individuals in another state who are being denied basic human rights and who themselves would be rationally willing to revolt against their oppressive government.

The ethical theory of international law defended by Teson is based on the following norms (summarized hereunder):

1. From an ethical standpoint governments are, internationally and domestically, mere agents of the people. Consequently, their international rights derive from the rights of the individuals who inhabit and constitute the state. Only governments that are representative and respect human rights have these international rights. The states' rights to political independence and territorial integrity derive from the rights of individuals, as the reason for creating and maintaining states and governments is to ensure the protection of the rights of individuals. Thus states and governments do not exist primarily to ensure order, but to secure natural rights: the proper philosophical justification of the state presupposes some form of social contract.
2. A justifiable intervention must be aimed at dictators for the purpose of putting an end to human rights violations. The intervening state must aim its military action at stopping human rights deprivations by governments, which includes overthrowing dictatorial governments where necessary.
3. Humanitarian intervention is governed by the interplay of the principles of proportionality and restoration of human rights. The seriousness of the reaction against human rights abuses must be proportionate both to the gravity of the abuses and to the probability of remedying the situation. If an oppressive government can be forced to enact democratic reforms through economic or political pressure, those measures should be tried first. Military intervention, as a remedy against human rights violations, should only be resorted to when all peaceful means have failed or are likely to fail.
4. The victims of oppression must welcome the foreign intervention, a requirement which is met when subjects are actually willing to revolt against their tyrannical government or would be willing to revolt if they were fully autonomous.

These "norms" are in support of democratic principles, national legitimacy and respect of human rights by governments and international morality: they do not accord with traditional international law and the U.N. Charter, which do not generally admit forcible intervention, except for self-defence and under the authority of the Security Council.

Although human rights violations are more likely to be committed by undemocratic states, the overthrow of a despotic government and the removal of a dictator by foreign military forces have never been legitimized by international law and justice.

Some practical questions arise as to how to assess the potential welcome by victims of oppression and their potential willingness to revolt.

In a more traditional framework, Lévinet[11] has formulated a few basic conditions for humanitarian interventions, without recognizing their international legality:

— they have to be justified by particular serious, massive and systematic violations of human rights;
— the intervening state(s) should not have any direct interest or stake in the matter;
— the mandate of the intervening state(s) should come from the international community: no one state should assume the role of the world's policeman, or democracy's armed guardian;
— there should be proportionality between the degree of violations and the means of intervention;
— the intervention should be limited in time, and it should avoid causing other violations of human rights.

The Practice: Past Cases of International Humanitarian Interventions

Humanitarian interventions in the 19th and the present century have been initiated mainly, but not exclusively, by European states and the U.S.A.: in 1976, the Entebbe raid was carried out by Israeli forces to save Israeli nationals, and in 1979, Tanzania and Vietnam also launched humanitarian interventions respectively in Uganda and in Cambodia. Humanitarian considerations have usually been associated with other reasons or arguments, such as self-defence against an aggression, national political or economic interests, hegemonic ambitions, the overthrow of a despotic leader or government, or of a communist government, anti-colonialism and self-determination.

Early humanitarian interventions were based on notions of promoting a mission of civilization among "inferior" peoples, and in particular the protection of the Christian religion[12].

For instance, in 1827, the U.K, France and Russia, under the auspices of the Treaty of Locarno, took military action to protect Christians in a conflict between Turkey and Greece, which ultimately led to Greek independence[13]. In 1860, thou-

---

[11] Michel Lévinet, "Réflexions sur la résurgence de l'intervention d'humanité)", *Trimestre du Monde*, 2e Trimestre 1990, pp. 97–113.

[12] Lévinet, op.cit., pp. 100–101.

[13] Teson, op.cit., p. 157.

sands of Christians were massacred by the Druzes in Syria. With the consent of other Western powers, France dispatched 6,000 troops to put an end to the atrocities.

U.S. Humanitarian Interventions

The U.S. have a tradition of interventionism, particularly in Latin American countries, under the Monroe doctrine.

In 1898, when the people of Cuba rebelled against Spanish domination, President McKinley and the U.S. Congress declared their right to intervene and later sent an armed force to assist the rebels.

The U.S. sent armed forces into Honduras in 1905, Cuba in 1906, Panama -the first of four invasions in a decade—in 1908, Nicaragua in 1912, Haiti in 1914 and the Dominican Republic in 1916 and in 1965[14].

On 25 October 1983, a joint military force composed of a U.S. contingent of 8,000 troops and 300 men from six Caribbean countries landed in the island of Grenada[15]. After three days of fighting at a relatively small cost (18 Americans died), the invaders deposed the new self-appointed Revolutionary Military Council. The legality of the intervention in Grenada has been defended by the U.S. government under three headings:—that it was legitimized by a lawful invitation by the Grenadian Governor-General,—that it was a regional peace-keeping action authorized by the competent regional treaties, in turn based on Art. 52 of the U.N. Charter,—that it was a lawful use of force in protection of U.S. nationals. After the intervention, the more fundamental motive was expressed by President Reagan, that of restoring democratic institutions and rights to the Grenadians, thus saving them from repression. In her address to the U.N. General Assembly, Jeanne Kirkpatrick, the U.S. Permanent Representative to the U.N., said:

> We believe that the use of force... was lawful under international law and the U.N. Charter... because it was carried out in service of the values of the Charter, including the restoration of the rule of law, self-determination, sovereignty, democracy, respect of the human rights of the people of Grenada[16].

On 20 December 1989, President George Bush launched the biggest U.S. military operation since the Vietnam war: the invasion of Panama by more than 20,000 troops backed by war planes. Bush ordered the attack after General Noriega said that Panama was in a state of war with the U.S. and after the shooting to death, the week-end before, of a U.S. Marine lieutenant.

In a nation-wide television address, Bush said that he sent U.S. forces into a sur-

[14] Ibid., p. 158 and *The Guardian*, 21 Dec. 1989.
[15] Teson, op.cit., pp. 188, 189, 193.
[16] Ibid. , p. 194.

prise overnight attack in Panama to end a "dark chapter of dictatorship" by General Noriega and forestall a "grave danger" to the 35,000 Americans living there. Secretary of State James A. Baker 3rd said that there was more risk to American citizens from inaction than there was from action[17].

The initial public motivation for the intervention was therefore, first to overthrow a dictatorship and restore a democracy,—secondly, to protect U.S. citizens in a foreign country, the traditional and basic justification for a military humanitarian intervention.

However, Bush also said that the chief goal of the invasion of Panama was to capture General Noriega and to bring him to trial in the U.S. (by force, and not by legal and implausible extradition) under an indictment for trafficking in Colombian cocaine[18].

Observers said that fundamental U.S. interests, such as the safeguarding of the Panama Canal or regional interests, were not at stake. The intervention, aimed at restoring a democracy, on the Grenada model, and at capturing an alleged drugking, was deemed to be aimed primarily at U.S. public opinion[19].

Internally, the U.S. intervention received quick bipartisan support from the U.S. Congress and from U.S. public opinion. Externally, the intervention was praised by Margaret Thatcher as a courageous decision and condemned by the USSR and Latin American countries.

On 23 December, France, the U.K. and the U.S. vetoed a draft resolution by which the U.N. Security Council would have demanded the immediate cessation of the U.S. intervention in Panama and the withdrawal of its armed forces. It would also have strongly deplored the intervention as a flagrant violation of international law and of the independence, sovereignty and territorial integrity of states. Canada also voted against the draft resolution, and Finland abstained.

During the meeting, the U.S. representative said that he was not claiming the right of the U.S. to intervene where it was not welcome. The U.S. had acted in Panama in self-defence and to protect the Panama Canal. The U.S. action had been welcomed overwhelmingly by the people of Panama[20].

On 29 December, the U.N. General Assembly condemned the U.S. intervention in the same terms as those in the vetoed Security Council draft resolution (Resol. 44/240), by 75 votes for, 20 against and 40 abstentions—a relatively mild response.

Public opinion in Latin American countries condemned the U.S. operation as an act of "arrogance" in the region, no different from countless similar episodes in the past. The major nations in the sub-continent voted — with the exception of Venezuela — in favour of a resolution in the Organization of American States "regretting" the intervention: only the U.S. opposed the resolution[21].

---

[17] *International Herald Tribune*, 21 Dec. 1989.
[18] *Time*, 15 Jan. 1990.
[19] *The Economist*, 6 Jan. 1990.
[20] U.N. *Press Release* SC/212 of 23 Dec. 1989.
[21] *Time*, 1 Jan. 1990, *Newsweek*, 8 Jan. 1990.

However, the intervention was generally welcome in Panama and a more democratic government was installed in the country.

On the negative side, the costs were relatively high: during the five-day intervention, 23 American soldiers were killed and 300-odd wounded,—between 300 to 800 Panamanians were killed and the country suffered $2 billion in economic damage[22].

On 5 August 1990, 225 U.S. Marines launched a daylight helicopter operation from U.S. ships off the coast of Monrovia in order to rescue Americans from the midst of the Liberian civil war. In two days, 74 people, including 62 Americans, were evacuated with neither resistance nor human losses[23].

French Humanitarian Interventions

France has also been active in military or non-armed humanitarian actions, particularly in its former African colonies. Some were joint actions with the Belgians in former Belgian colonies.

On 19 May 1978, in order to stop massacres of civilians by "rebels" coming from adjoining countries, in the mining city of Kolwezi in Zaire, France landed paratroopers, followed on 20 May by Belgian paratroopers. This intervention had been initiated following an appeal for assistance by the Zaire government[24].

On September 20–21, 1979, the dictator Jean-Bedel Bokassa, self-proclaimed Emperor of the Central African Republic, was overthrown by a group of citizens with the active support of a contingent of 1,800 French troops. The U.N. and the Organization for African Unity had remained silent and passive during the atrocities committed by Bokassa, who had been supported politically and financially by France, until its later decision to overthrow the despot. The French-initiated coup was bloodless and received few international criticisms[25].

On 5 October 1990, following an attack by Tutsi rebels crossing over from Uganda into Rwanda, French and Belgian troops flew into the former Belgian colony, at the request and with the approval of the Rwanda government, in principle only to protect French and Belgian citizens and facilitate their safe departure. However, by militarily securing the airport and the roads to it, the heavily armed humanitarian forces appeared to give support to the established government[26].

A Non-Military French Humanitarian Intervention
In April 1989, a French governmental initiative to give humanitarian assistance to the Lebanese foundered when Syria and its Moslem allies condemned the plan as a move to help only the Christians.

[22] *Time*, 8 Jan. 1990.
[23] *International Herald Tribune*, 6–7 Aug. 1990.
[24] *Le Monde*, 30 Aug. 1990.
[25] Teson, op.cit., pp. 175–176.
[26] *The Economist*, 13 Oct. 1990.

France has had long relationships with Lebanon's Christians, especially the Maronite Catholics, the largest Christian group. Lebanon and Syria were entrusted to France in 1919 as League of Nations mandates. They both became independent in 1941.

Lebanon's continuing internal strife had become a political issue in France, when French conservative politicians and intellectuals vocally demanded action by the French Socialist government to help the Maronites, subjected to artillery bombardment by Syria and its Lebanese allies. General Michel Aoun, commander of the Christian-dominated portion of Lebanon and then Prime Minister of its Christian enclave, had launched in mid-March a war of "national liberation" against Syria's 40,000 man force, which had entered Lebanon ten years before as an Arab League peace-keeping force[27].

At the initiative of Bernard Kouchner, the French Secretary of State for Humanitarian action, President Mitterand sent a hospital ship and a French navy ship carrying fuel to assist the besieged Christian Lebanese and offered to mediate in the Lebanon conflict.

Syria and its allies reacted strongly against this new "crusade" of the former colonial power in favour of the Christian Maronites, considered to have exorbitant and unjustified privileges. More bombing of the Christian enclave followed and Syria threatened to fire on the French ships.

President Mitterand then changed direction: he stated that France was, and wanted to remain a friend to all Lebanese, of all religions, of all communities. Kouchner said in Lebanon that

a misinterpreted humanitarian assistance would be totally deviated from its purpose ... France's humanitarian help is intended for all Lebanese and could not be successful without the agreement of all[28].

In turn, the Christian Lebanese took the French evolution towards a neutral, impartial stance as an abandonment of France's traditional role of protector of Christianity in the Middle East.

The failed French attempt to mediate in Lebanon was more appropriately taken over by the Ministerial Committee of the League of Arab States, with the support of the U.N. Security Council and, in particular, of the U.S.A.[29].

In May, the State Department announced that the Bush Administration had allocated $200,000 for disaster relief efforts for Lebanese affected by the recent fighting in Lebanon. Medical supplies and food were intended for "all segments of the affected population"[30].

---

[27] *International Herald Tribune*, 15–16 Apr. 1989.

[28] *Le Monde*, 12 Apr. 1989.

[29] *Press Release*, Security Council, U.N. Doc. SC/192 of 31 March 1989 and U.S. Mission (Geneva) *Daily Bulletin*, 24 Apr. 1989.

[30] U.S. *Daily Bulletin*, 22 May 1989.

The French humanitarian initiative in Lebanon was criticized for being hasty and politically poorly conceived: quick, improvised action, a characteristic of NGO action, with its inherent risks, cannot be applied by states without more important potential consequences. The risks taken by an NGO only affect its own private organization, possibly its prestige and its capacity to attract funds. The risks taken by a state in launching a humanitarian intervention may have serious political, and possibly military consequences without relation to the potential positive returns expected from the operation.

The French initiative was also perceived as being initially partial towards one part of the Lebanese population, a cardinal sin for any humanitarian operation. The Red Cross principles of neutrality and impartiality are critical requirements for humanitarian access and effectiveness.

Cambodia and Uganda

In December 1978, Vietnam invaded and occupied Cambodia, ousting the Pol Pot's Khmer Rouge regime, which brutally ruled the country from 1975 to 1978, causing the deaths of one to two million Cambodians from starvation and executions and the suffering of many others. The legalistic and immoral position adopted during several years by the U.N. General Assembly, including the Western countries, was to condemn the Vietnamese intervention and occupation and to continue to recognize a delegation to the U.N. which included Khmer Rouge representatives, and to ignore the result obtained by the military intervention in eliminating a despotic and criminal leadership[31].

In April 1979, the brutal rule of President Idi Amin of Uganda came to an end as a result of his overthrow by Tanzanian troops. One can but agree with Teson's assessment[32] that the Tanzanian intervention was a legitimate use of force to stop ongoing serious deprivations of the most fundamental human rights.

The Use of National and International Military Forces for Humanitarian Assistance

The international humanitarian interventions related above (except for the non-military French intervention in Lebanon)' were military operations which included a partial humanitarian objective, but only one among other political, military, territorial, ideological objectives.

An alternative, which has been applied in the past and whose use could be expanded, is to employ national or international military forces trained and specialized in relief assistance for non-military humanitarian interventions.

---

[31] *International Herald Tribune*, 29 Aug. 1990.
[32] Teson, op.cit., pp. 159, 174.

This appears to be a contradiction in terms: is there not a patent incompatibility between the main justification for military forces, e.g. the preparation, organization and implementation of military action aimed at attack or defence at the cost of human lives and material destruction, and the utilization of these forces for relief assistance aimed at saving lives and caring for the victims?

On second thoughts, armed forces may prove useful to stop fighting, re-establish public order, protect civilian lives, protect civilian relief workers, assist relief action with their substantial material and human resources, and more specifically by providing direct assistance by specialized military medical and relief units.

The détente between East and West, the reduction of armaments agreements may allow some of the military forces to develop a more peaceful and constructive use of their resources in situations of armed conflict (in which the contributing forces are not directly involved) and in natural disasters.

Such contributions have in the past, and could in the future usefully complement the limited resources of IGOs and NGOs in the humanitarian field.

National Military Relief Assistance Forces

Transport, communications and medical services form an integral part of any modern military force.

France set up the "Force d'action humanitaire militaire d'intervention rapide" (called "Force" hereafter) in 1983, whose mission is to undertake medical, surgical or biological assignments anywhere in the world. The Force, a direct heir of France's colonial past in the medical and epidemiological fields, is part both of the army and of the scientific and medical community.

The Force has three elements:

— a small surgical paratroopers' unit capable of carrying out about 15 major surgical interventions per day;
— a military medical unit, which can be transported by cargo planes and helicopters. It can assume surgical, medical, hospitalization and evacuation tasks, as well as laboratory examinations;
— a biological unit (Bioforce) which may provide quickly scientific and technical assistance to states, by request to the French government,—or deal with an epidemiological crisis. The Mérieux Institute (in Lyons) and the Pasteur Institute (in Paris) collaborate with the French Ministry of Defence and the Ministry of External Relations in the missions of Bioforce.

International assistance may be provided by the Force only at the request of the government of the state concerned, and with the authorization of the French authorities.

The intervention of the Force during an armed conflict is subject to the provisions of the Geneva Conventions and Additional Protocols. In particular, the Force's health personnel

— must abstain from any hostile action and maintain a strict neutrality in avoiding all interference, direct or indirect, in military operations,
— must respect the principles of the "Declaration of Geneva" adopted by the World Medical Association (see Chapter 10),
— must respect the principles of impartiality and non-discrimination.

The Force considers its action as a complement to the activities of civilian humanitarian NGOs, such as Médecins Sans Frontières, even though its own logistical, financial, medical and scientific resources by far exceed those of most NGOs.

The Force has carried out interventions:

— in relation to armed conflicts, for instance in Biafra (1968–1970), during the Palestinian-Jordanian conflict (September 1970) under the auspices of the Red Cross, during the Civil War in Chad (March-July 1980),
— in relation to natural disasters, for instance following the Peru earthquake in June 1970,
— in relation to epidemics, for instance, in assisting the WHO-sponsored smallpox eradication campaign in Somalia in 1970 and 1977, in dealing with a cholera epidemic in the Comoros in March 1975 and with an epidemic of cerebrospinal meningitis in Guinea, in April 1985[33].

Sweden and Switzerland have also set up specialized military units[34]: also dedicated only to emergency humanitarian services, they are designed to take on only short-term tasks such as restoring communications, managing relief logistics, provision of emergency medical care and delivery of high priority supplies. The units can be dispatched within hours or days to the scene of an emergency after an appropriate request is received. Their officers and men have undergone special training. Such units served during the refugee emergency in Somalia in 1980, and elsewhere in a variety of natural disasters (most recently in Armenia).

The contribution of military units specialized in humanitarian emergencies offers the advantage of prior planning and organization, trained, competent and motivated personnel, significant material resources, sophisticated equipment, efficient transportation and communications support, readiness and speed of action.

Some of the limitations of the use of national military relief units include the following:

— possible political, ideological or cultural differences between the donor's and the recipient country's governments and populations;

---

[33] Unpublished report "Les missions humanitaires du service de santé des armées: La force d'action humanitaire militaire d'intervention rapide", by Michel Deyra.
[34] *Humanitarian Emergencies and Military Help in Africa*, Edited by Thomas G. Weiss, Macmillan/International Peace Academy, 1990, pp. 16–17.

— the fact that only Western industrialized countries have, at present, the capacity and the willingness to provide this type of military assistance, which restricts the freedom of choice of the recipient countries;

— resistance or fear on the part of recipient governments or populations to offers of aid by military units, whose humanitarian missions may not be perceived as clearly separated from the military, forceful, operations of their brothers-in arms, nor necessarily devoid of covert efforts to exert power and influence;

— the military units' sophisticated equipment and procedures may have the effect of supplanting local adaptive practices in emergencies and creating dependency on outside assistance: however this argument may also apply to external civilian assistance;

— recipient governments' concern that such bilateral aid may be "tied", and would later require various concessions to the donor country.

"Humanitarian" U.N. Peace-Keeping Forces

While a number of "civilian" U.N. bodies are specialized in humanitarian relief assistance (see Chapter 1), the role of U.N. peace-keeping forces is to separate combatants, enforce cease-fires, and, recently, to organize and/or monitor elections: they were not created, in principle, to give humanitarian assistance.

As stated by the U.N. Secretary-General, Javier Perez de Cuellar, when he accepted the Nobel Peace Prize on 10 December 1988 on behalf of the U.N. peace-keeping forces

> The technique, which has come to be called peace-keeping, uses soldiers as the servants of peace, rather than as the instruments of war. Never before in history have military forces been employed internationally, not to wage war, nor to establish domination, and not to serve the interests of any power, or group of powers, but rather to prevent conflict between people[35].

Soldiers who do not wage war and do not represent national interests are international soldiers of peace who can assume impartial and neutral humanitarian missions in addition to or separately from their more traditional functions, without fear of being associated with forceful nationalistic or ideological ambitions.

In practice, such forces as the U.N. Peace-keeping Force in Cyprus and the U.N. Interim Force in Lebanon have assumed subsidiary relief assistance tasks, such as protecting civilians, relocating refugees, providing medical and food assistance, rebuilding infrastructure. Many of the national contingents in U.N. peace-keeping forces, including Sweden, Finland, Austria and France, regularly provide medical services to local populations[36].

---

[35] U.N. Publication *The Blue Helmets—U.N. Peace-keeping Forces*, UNPA, 1988.
[36] Weiss, op.cit., pp. 17, 122.

In March 1989, 40 experts in humanitarian assistance to civilian victims met in Harare under the auspices of the International Peace Academy and the University of Zimbabwe to consider the delivery of humanitarian assistance in African armed conflicts[37].

They asked how the deliverers should react if denied access, forcibly restrained, or attacked. The responses ranged from moral implorations, prolonged negotiations with the parties, political pressure from the international community, unauthorized cross-border delivery, and bilateral military air transport to calls for direct military assistance to repel attackers.

In between a negotiated passage (the Red Cross approach) and forced intervention, the provision of humanitarian assistance by U.N. personnel in peace-keeping operations was envisaged. Participants wondered whether a lightly armed escort under strict peace-keeping rules of non-engagement, namely to fight only in self-defence, would inhibit hostile action and ensure delivery.

The Harare group then considered the possible creation of a new type of U.N. force. In addition to unarmed military observers and lightly armed peace-keeping forces, the third type of U.N. operation would be called "humanitarian support operation". Three steps would be required:

1. the codification of evolving practices and ethics into a new international norm to guarantee the rights of civilians to have access to humanitarian relief;
2. the willingness to call governments as well as insurgents publicly to task and thereby to use the U.N. to embarrass any party which denied humanitarian aid to civilians for any purpose;
3. the operational military capacity to ensure delivery of such assistance when international pressure failed which, given the potential risks, would probably require the establishment of a volunteer force under U.N. auspices[38].

In another meeting held in Niinsalo, Finland, in October 1989, under the auspices of the International Peace Academy and of the Finnish Ministry of Foreign Affairs, the workshop participants recommended that the "third type" of U.N. peace-keeping forces should, like the other two, be placed under the authority of the U.N. Secretary-General. This type of operation would also require broad agreement by governments, especially the permanent members of the Security Council and the parties directly concerned. The proposed U.N. humanitarian force should be perceived as non-provocative, and should have clear, precise specifically-limited mandates[39].

[37] Ibid., pp. 118–120.
[38] Ibid., p. 129.
[39] Workshop on "Humanitarian Emergencies and Armed Conflict: The possible contribution of outside military forces", Concluding Statement, Co-sponsored by International Peace Academy, New York, and Ministry of Foreign Affairs, Helsinki,—Niinisalo, Finland, October 24–26, 1989.

The Delivery of Relief Assistance

Effective international relief assistance requires that supplies and personnel are able ·to bring relief to the victims promptly, without undue interference or delays on the part of the recipient country's authorities.

Under the principle of national sovereignty, recipient countries are "masters at home" and thus free to authorize, delay or refuse the import of foodstuffs, medicaments or equipment, or the entry of international NGO volunteers, Red Cross teams, IGO staff members, bilateral aid workers, or any other relief personnel.

Any delays in the delivery of relief assistance to the victims of internal or external armed conflicts or natural disasters may cause unnecessary grief and suffering and additional deaths.

The moral duty of giving assistance and the humanitarian "right" of victims to receive assistance is liable to conflict with the legal protection of sovereign states against undue intervention and interference.

International organizations have attempted to bridge the gap between these two imperatives by adopting international conventions, recommendations or resolutions aimed at facilitating the access of international humanitarian assistance to the victims. These are found essentially in the Red Cross Conventions and Additional Protocols, Resolutions of the International Conference of the Red Cross and in U.N. resolutions and other texts.

The 1949 Geneva Conventions and 1977 Additional Protocols

Art. 9 of the First Geneva Convention refers generally to

the humanitarian activities which the ICRC or any other impartial humanitarian organization may, subject to the consent of the Parties to the conflict concerned, undertake for the protection of the wounded and sick, medical personnel and chaplains, and for their relief.

Art. 59, 61 and 62 of the Fourth Convention are more specific:

If the whole or part of the population of an occupied territory is inadequately supplied, the Occupying Power shall agree to relief schemes on behalf of the said population and shall facilitate them by all the means at its disposal.

Such schemes, which may be undertaken either by States or by impartial humanitarian organizations such as the ICRC, shall consist, in particular, of the provision of consignments of foodstuffs, medical supplies and clothing.

All Contracting Parties shall permit the free passage of these consignments and shall guarantee their protection.

. . .

Such consignments shall be exempt in occupied territory from all charges, taxes or customs duties unless these are necessary in the interests of the economy of the territory. The Occupying Power shall facilitate the rapid distribution of these consignments.

All Contracting Parties shall endeavour to permit the transit and transport, free of charge of such relief consignments on their way to occupied territories.

Art. 108 and 110 of the same Convention allow internees to receive individual parcels or collective shipments containing foodstuffs, clothing, medical supplies etc. and provide that all relief shipments for internees "shall be" exempt from import, customs and other dues.

Art. 70 of Protocol I, on the protection of victims of international armed conflicts, provides that relief actions which are humanitarian and impartial in character and conducted without adverse distinction in favour of the civilian population, in case of inadequate supplies, "shall be undertaken", subject to the agreement of the Parties concerned in such relief actions. Offers of such relief shall not be regarded as interference in the armed conflict or as unfriendly acts. The Parties to the conflict and each High Contracting Party "shall allow and facilitate" rapid and unimpeded passage of all relief consignments, equipment and personnel provided, even if such assistance is destined for the civilian population of the adverse Party.

Art. 71 provides that where necessary, relief personnel may form part of the assistance provided in a relief action, in particular for the transportation and distribution of relief consignments. The participation of such personnel is subject to the approval of the Party in whose territory they will carry out their duties. Such personnel "shall be" respected and protected.

Under Art. 81, the Parties to the conflict "shall grant" to the ICRC and to the Red Cross and Red Crescent Societies the facilities necessary to carry out their humanitarian activities. Similar facilities are accorded to other humanitarian organizations.

Art. 18.2 of Protocol II, on the protection of victims of non-international armed conflicts, provides that

If the civilian population is suffering undue hardship owing to a lack of the supplies essential to its survival, such as foodstuffs and medical supplies, relief actions for the civilian population which are of an exclusively humanitarian and impartial nature and which are conducted without any adverse distinction shall be undertaken subject to the consent of the High Contracting Party concerned.

These provisions, which relate to international or non-international armed conflicts, generally authorize relief actions under two conditions: — that they should be humanitarian and impartial and conducted without adverse distinction, — and that they are subject to the consent of the Parties concerned.

Under such conditions, the Parties should allow and facilitate rapid passage of all relief equipment, foodstuffs and personnel. Relief consignments should normally be exempt from taxes and other duties.

Other Declarations, Resolutions and Texts

A number of Resolutions and other texts were initiated, in turn, by U.N. bodies and International Red Cross Conferences.

In 1968, Resolution 2435 of the U.N. General Assembly invited governments to make preparations at the national level to meet natural disasters. Noting this Resolution, the XXIst International Red Cross Conference meeting in Istanbul in 1969, urged all governments which had not already done so to prepare and to pass the necessary legislation enabling immediate and adequate action to be taken, in conjunction with the Red Cross, along the lines of a pre-established plan based on the disaster relief rules adopted by the Conference (Resol. XXV). The same Conference adopted a "Declaration of principles relating to relief actions for the benefit of civilian populations in disaster situations" which stated, *inter alia*:

> Relief by impartial international humanitarian organizations for civilian populations in natural or other disaster situations should as far as possible be treated as a humanitarian and non-political matter and should be so organized as to avoid prejudicing sovereign and other legal rights in order that the confidence of the parties to a conflict in the impartiality of such organizations may be preserved.

States and authorities should facilitate the transit, admission and distribution of relief supplies provided by impartial international humanitarian organizations for the benefit of civilian populations in disaster areas[40].

The same Conference also requested airline companies to transport relief supplies under conditions in no way prejudicial to the conveyance of such supplies, and in particular to reduce freight charges (Resol. XXIII).

In 1971, the U.N. General Assembly Resolution which created UNDRO[41], *inter alia*, invited potential recipient Governments to consider appropriate legislative or other measures to facilitate the receipt of aid, including overflight and landing rights and necessary privileges and immunities for relief units (Art. 8.(e)).

In 1977, in Bucharest, the XXIIIrd International Conference of the Red Cross noted that the plight of the victims depends to a large extent on the speed with which adequate help arrives and that there are still too many obstacles and difficulties which slow down the movement of international relief supplies and relief personnel to the detriment of those in urgent need of assistance. The Conference then supported the joint recommendations adopted by the League of Red Cross Societies and UNDRO on "Measures to expedite International Relief" and urged National Societies, Governments, IGOs and NGOs concerned with relief operations to implement these recommendations to the fullest possible extent (Resol. No. VI and Annex).

---

[40] This Resolution has been amended in 1973, 1977, 1981 and 1986. The present text of "Principles and Rules for Red Cross Disaster Relief" is found in *Compendium*, op.cit., pp. 157–163.

[41] Resol. 2816 (XXVI) of 14 Dec. 1971.

Among the proposed measures, it was recommended that potential recipient governments waive specific import/export requirements with respect to relief consignments, including food imports, that they ensure that their customs authorities receive standing instructions to expedite processing of relief shipments, that they waive requirements for transit, entry and exit visas for relief personnel acting in their official capacity as representatives of internationally-recognized relief agencies and that they facilitate their internal and external communications, that they authorize their national airlines to accord free transportation or transportation at reduced rates for relief consignments and relief personnel.

In the same year, the U.N. General Assembly adopted the same "Measures to expedite International Relief"[42].

In 1982, UNITAR (U.N. Institute for Training and Research) published its "Model Rules for Disaster Relief Operations"[43]. The purpose of the Rules was to contribute to closing a lacuna in international humanitarian law regarding assistance to victims of disasters: while the law of armed conflict sets out rules for protection and assistance to victims of armed conflicts, UNITAR noted that no such body of law existed to cover other disaster situations. In the case of natural disasters, there were no guidelines.

UNITAR had envisaged different formats which could be used to regulate disaster relief operations, including:

1. The conclusion of a multilateral agreement on disaster relief assistance. The advantage of this approach is its universal and non-discriminatory regulation of disaster relief assistance on the basis of standard legal rules rather than *ad hoc* diplomacy. Its disadvantage is the expected reluctance of governments to commit themselves in any substantial degree, in a multilateral form, with respect to relief assistance in advance of a disaster. This would probably result in an agreement that would reflect the lowest common denominator among the parties.

2. The conclusion of regional or sub-regional agreements on relief assistance. The advantage of this approach would be its practical feasibility, especially in regions where a close degree of cooperation already exists, and its adaptability to the characteristics of each region. However, an agreement among donors (in the European region, for instance) would not cover recipient governments (in Africa, for instance). Furthermore, a number of regions may consist of States that are not in a position to provide effective assistance to one another.

3. A stand-by agreement to be concluded on a bilateral basis in anticipation of a disaster situation. The approach has the advantage of flexibility, but its effectiveness depends on the conclusion of a potentially large number of bilateral agreements by the foreseeable parties.

---

[42] Resol. A/RES/32/56 (1977).
[43] UNITAR, *Policy and Efficacy Studies*, No. 8.

4. A set of model rules for bilateral agreements which can be circulated in advance to all prospective parties and which can be referred to in requests and offers of assistance. These model rules would have no legal effect in themselves. They would merely provide a text for incorporation into a specific agreement, which, when approved by the parties concerned, would constitute a legal instrument.

These formats are not mutually exclusive, and UNITAR suggested that multiple approaches might be pursued.

However, given the existing political and legal circumstances, UNITAR considered that Model Rules for bilateral agreements were the most practical and feasible at this stage. Such bilateral agreements could be concluded at the outset of a disaster situation or in anticipation of it. The rules refer to three types of relations:—(A) relations between an assisting State and a receiving State,—(B) relations between an assisting organization and a receiving State,—(C) relations between an assisting State or organization or a receiving State and a transit State.

Considering only (B), e.g. relations between an assisting organization, such as a U.N. organization, some other IGO or an NGO and the receiving State, some of the recommendations include the following provisions, which tally with and amplify the 1977 "Measures to expedite International Relief":

— Absolute priority shall be granted to relief supplies;
— The receiving State shall exempt the designated relief supplies from customs duties, fees or tolls chargeable by reason of importation;
— The receiving State shall take all possible measures for its airlines to provide transport on a priority basis for designated relief personnel and relief supplies, —such transportation will be provided free or at minimal rates;
— The receiving State shall authorize the designated relief personnel in the performance of their duties to use on a priority basis, free or at rates not higher than the rates applied by the receiving State, telex, cable, wire, telephone, and other means of communications;
— The receiving State shall allow the relief organization to maintain bank accounts and to convert currency held by it into local currency as necessitated by the relief function and at the most favourable rate of exchange;
— The receiving State shall extend to disaster relief units that are subsidiary organs of the U.N., or are made available through the U.N., specific privileges and immunities under the Convention on the Privileges and Immunities of the U.N. Similar privileges and immunities shall be granted to disaster relief units that are subsidiary organs of the U.N. specialized agencies;
— The receiving State shall extend to designated relief personnel the necessary facilities with a view to securing the expeditious performance of relief functions;
— The receiving State shall waive requirements for entry and exit visas, provide with minimum delay visas at points of entry and exit or issue multiple entry and exit visas for designated relief personnel;

— The receiving State shall permit the designated relief personnel freedom of access to, and freedom of movement within, disaster-stricken areas that are necessary for the performance of their specifically agreed functions;
— The receiving State shall take all necessary measures to ensure the security and safety of the designated relief personnel and of all the premises, facilities, means of transport used in connection with relief activities.

The UNITAR Model Rules are primarily designed to regulate the emergency phase of the disaster when time is recognized to be the critical factor. They do not deal with other aspects of disaster relief such as disaster prevention and rehabilitation. Their scope of application extends to natural and man-made disasters.

The Model Rules are practical, concrete recommendations along the lines of previous recommendations of the League of Red Cross and UNDRO: like those, they do not attempt to challenge existing principles and practices of international law. They fully respect the principle that relief will only be provided at the request or with the consent of the recipient country.

UNDRO's Draft Convention (1984): An Aborted Initiative

In 1984, UNDRO submitted to the U.N. Economic and Social Council a "Proposed draft convention on expediting the delivery of emergency relief"[44].

Although UNDRO had not been specifically requested by ECOSOC or the General Assembly to prepare a draft convention, it based its initiative on an ECOSOC Resolution of 1977[45], which requested the U.N. Disaster Relief Coordinator

> To continue (his) efforts and, in cooperation with Governments, U.N. bodies and appropriate intergovernmental organizations and voluntary agencies, and particularly the International Red Cross, to pay special attention to the promotion of measures designed to remove obstacles and to expedite international relief assistance.

Concerned only with the delivery of assistance following natural disasters (excluding an ongoing situation of armed conflict), the draft convention emphasized the traditional principles of respect for the sovereignty of the receiving state and non-interference in its internal affairs, cooperation with its appropriate authorities, respect for and observance of its laws. It established that the receiving state "shall have", within its territory, responsibility for facilitating the coordination of operations to meet the situation created by the disaster. The draft convention was to apply to all assistance provided by an Assisting State or organization to a Receiving

---

[44] U.N. Doc. A/39/267/Add.2—E/1984/96/Add.2 of 18 June 1984.
[45] ECOSOC Resol. 2102 (LXIII) of 3 Aug. 1977, endorsed by the General Assembly in Resol. 32/56 of 8 Dec. 1977.

State. It included provisions concerning the conditions for the delivery of assistance, exchange of information, protection and facilities, communications, notification, qualitative nature of assistance, packaging, labelling and marking, identification, exportation, importation, financial provisions, transport and liability.

This initiative had started in August/September 1983 when UNDRO asked a group of experts to propose a set of simple principles likely to be acceptable to governments.

The five NGOs forming, with the League of Red Cross and Red Crescent Societies, the "Licross/Volags Steering Committee for Disasters"[46] wrote a letter to the U.N. Disaster Relief Coordinator to express their concern at the draft text of the proposed convention and their surprise and regret that their organizations and other NGOs well-known as active practitioners of emergency assistance had not been invited to participate in discussions concerning the proposed convention. On 10 January 1984, the ICRC and the League sent a detailed memorandum to UNDRO to explain the grounds of their concern.

The basis of the Red Cross and Red Crescent Movement's attitude to the UNDRO proposal, with the full support of NGOs in the Steering Committee, was that no standard-setting in the humanitarian field can be justified unless it is likely to lead to an improvement in the condition of the victims of disasters. The existing standards are in the Geneva Conventions of 1949 and the Additional Protocols of 1977, the practical recommendations in the Red Cross Disaster Relief Handbook of 1970, revised in 1976 and 1983, and the 1977 "Measures to expedite International Relief" adopted both by the International Conference of the Red Cross and the U.N. General Assembly.

The memorandum recalled that one of the central problems in international relief action arises from the excessive invocation of national sovereignty which sometimes paralyses action. The prevailing international climate hardly seemed favourable to greater flexibility in this respect and a convention which would result in a reinforcement of the obstacles caused by the over-emphasis of national sovereignty would in no way improve matters.

It would be more profitable to concentrate on securing the fuller implementation of existing instruments and resolutions on disaster relief.

For these reasons, the ICRC and the League felt that a convention, by its very nature, would not at that time be opportune. Some other formulation, such as a Declaration, or an improved version of the 1977 Resolutions would probably be preferable.

With regard to the text of the proposed convention, the Preamble sees disaster aid as being provided to countries, states and governments, without mention of the victims of disasters themselves, an essential and regrettable omission.

In draft Art. 3 and 4, it is assumed that relief assistance is provided to a State

[46] Members are Caritas Internationalis, Catholic Relief Services, the Lutheran World Federation, Oxfam and the World Council of Churches.

rather than to disaster victims. According to the Red Cross organizations, experience amply demonstrates that governments often cannot or will not assume the "responsibility for facilitating the coordination of operations". The control of distribution by a neutral State or organization is in certain circumstances a right recognized by international humanitarian law. Governments may not have the necessary financial resources or administrative infrastructure to coordinate relief operations; they may be unwilling to acknowledge the existence of a disaster, in order not to discourage tourism or fearing to show themselves publicly incapable of dealing with the disaster; internal conflicts, discrimination in giving assistance or corruption may also argue against the distribution of relief assistance through official channels. In summary, the overriding interest of the disaster victims should prevail: the delivery of relief assistance should not depend exclusively upon the goodwill or unilateral decision of the receiving government[47].

During the discussions in the Economic and Social Council, in July 1984, many serious reservations were expressed by delegates concerning the proposed draft convention. The Council's Resolution on UNDRO

> takes note of the reports of the Secretary-General on a proposed draft convention on expediting the delivery of emergency relief and on the implementation of the medium-term and long-term recovery and rehabilitation programme in the Sudano-Sahelian region and decides to transmit them to the General Assembly.

The draft Convention was then referred to the 6th Committee of the General Assembly, "from which hopefully it will never emerge", in the words of a Geneva observer.

It emerged, to the chagrin of the Geneva NGOs, in a Resolution adopted in September 1988 by the 80th Inter-Parliamentary Conference in Sofia, recommending

> the creation of a working group composed of the representatives of the main universal and regional organizations providing assistance in the event of natural or other disasters (International Movement of the Red Cross and the Red Crescent, UNHCR, UNDRO, EEC, OAU, etc.), to coordinate and hasten the preparation of an international convention to provide swift and effective relief to the victims of disasters, both natural or caused by man[48].

The Resolution had been introduced by the French delegation.

It is however likely that the ICRC and the League will be able to resist any further progress in the drafting of yet another convention.

---

[47] See ICRC/League internal document "UNDRO Convention: Draft letter to certain National Societies". Some of the arguments against the draft convention are summarized from the Annex dated 17 Oct. 1984.

[48] Operative paragraph 5, Resolution B, "With regard to the international cooperation in the humanitarian field", adopted by the September 1988 Session of the Inter-Parliamentary Union in Sofia.

A Misdirected French Initiative for a U.N. Resolution

On 8 December 1988, a Resolution on "Humanitarian assistance to victims of natural disasters and similar emergency situations" was adopted by the U.N. General Assembly without a vote.

In its Press Release following this decision, the U.N. said that the Resolution

> reaffirmed the sovereignty of countries affected by natural disasters, declaring that they had the primary role in the initiation, organization, coordination and implementation of humanitarian assistance in such circumstances.
>
> ...
>
> The resolution was adopted without vote, with some delegates commenting that the text was, in some respects, ambiguous and emphasizing the need to ensure that provision of humanitarian assistance was not used as a pretext for interference in the internal affairs of an affected country[49].

The final text of the Resolution was therefore in total contradiction with the intent of its French proponents, which was to affirm the human right of disaster victims to receive assistance: this was replaced by the "divine" right of governments to control all cross-border movements under a re-confirmed national sovereignty principle.

Bernard Kouchner, who was at the origin of the Resolution, had founded both Médecins Sans Frontières (MSF) and Médecins du Monde (MDM), and had been appointed as France's Secretary of State for Humanitarian Affairs. He said in 1988:

> The suffering of a population does not belong to the government that harbours it or provokes it. Humanitarian organizations must be allowed to care for the wounded on the other side of frontiers[50].

Under the influence of Kouchner, the Socialist French Government encouraged initiatives directed to establish an international right and duty to take humanitarian action.

In January 1987, MDM and the Faculty of Law of a Paris University organized an international conference on "Law and Humanitarian Ethics" in Paris[51].

Reviewing the history of humanitarian assistance, Kouchner identified three phases. First, there was Henry Dunant's creation of the Red Cross and assistance to wounded people and prisoners. Basically, the charitable drive, the desire to assist, is always present, as several speakers reminded the audience. A second generation of altruists began carrying out humanitarian activities during the 1960s—doctors and nurses who both treat those in need and bring their plight to the attention of the rest

---

[49] U.N. *Press Release*
[50] *Time*, 9 Jan. 1989.
[51] *International Review of the Red Cross*, March-April 1987, No. 257, pp. 226–229.

of the world. Finally, recent years have seen the advent of movements which to a great extent depend on media coverage, reporting "live" from the scene and becoming embroiled in polemics. In view of these excesses, Kouchner felt that the time had come for all humanitarian organizations

> to come together and elaborate a code of ethics, a charter of basic rules for humanitarian aid.

Recalling that the most fundamental human right was the right to life and that our primary duty was to assist people in danger, President François Mitterand underlined the challenge facing the humanitarian organizations of today—how to "reconcile" the law, recognized principles and the assistance required with the complexity of government structures, regulations, prohibitions and suspicions. The humanitarian organizations—those who uphold "the ethics of the extreme emergency"—must ensure that

> international law show increasing recognition of the rights of the individual human being and that individual rights be not denied in the course of everyday life, that they be not denied by the law of States.

It was noted that an increasing number of NGOs feel that they have a "right to take humanitarian action", whereas any unilateral, unauthorized cross-border intervention is illegal because it violates national sovereignty. Professor Mario Bettati felt that the victims of conflicts had an inalienable right to receive assistance when that assistance was purely humanitarian and intended to protect the right to receive care and the right to life. He felt that such a right should now be formally recognized by the international community for the following four reasons:

— the scope of armed conflicts and natural, industrial and nuclear disasters;
— the speed and efficiency of private assistance;
— the practical application of the right to life and the right to health (Art. 3 of the Universal Declaration of Human Rights) and,
— the right to humanitarian assistance which is a corollary of the duty to show solidarity. This duty implies, among other things, the duty to cooperate in accordance with the U.N. Charter (Art. 55 and 56). He therefore proposed that the participants adopt a resolution referring, *inter alia*, to the existing rules of international humanitarian law and affirming

> that both the right of victims to humanitarian assistance and the obligation of States and non-governmental organizations to contribute to and facilitate that assistance should be acknowledged by all the members of the international community in a single international instrument.

On 29 September 1988, President Mitterand referred in his statement to the U.N. General Assembly to a "right to humanitarian assistance".

On 19 October, the French Delegation to the U.N. submitted the first draft of a Resolution on "Humanitarian assistance to victims of natural disasters and emergency situations". Referring to the Universal Declaration of Human Rights and international instruments relating to human rights, it re-affirmed the sovereignty of states and their primary role in caring for victims of catastrophes and emergency situations occurring on their territory. However, the draft Resolution recognized that in such cases, the principles of humanity, neutrality and impartiality, on which rests humanitarian assistance, must prevail on all other considerations. It also asked states to facilitate the access to victims by governmental and non-governmental organizations for their relief operations.

Kouchner's intention was to establish, internationally, the human right of victims to receive assistance, the duty of IGOs and NGOs to provide such assistance, and the obligation of recipient governments to facilitate the access of the relief workers to the victims. In the same way as the international defence and promotion of human rights know no borders, humanitarian assistance should also be "sans frontières".

This generous initiative met with strong opposition in the Third Committee. The original version of the French Resolution had been toned down before presentation to the Committee to eliminate several references to human rights. The principles of national sovereignty and non-interference in internal affairs were again and again put forward by the delegations of Brazil, India, Pakistan, Mexico, Chile, Nicaragua, Peru, Ethiopia and Sudan.

As a result of these interventions,

— the scope of the Resolution was restricted to "natural disasters and similar emergency situations", instead of "other emergency situations";
— the reference to national sovereignty was placed higher in the text, the "major role" of the state becoming the "primary role";
— all references to the U.N. Charter, the Universal Declaration of Human Rights and other international instruments relating to human rights were deleted.

France had to accept several amendments which resulted in stressing national sovereignty, thus destroying any illusory "right of access" and watering down any "rights" of victims to receive acceptance.

After the consensus approval of the revised Resolution in the Third Committee, several delegates re-affirmed their concerns.

The delegate from Brazil said that (contrary to Kouchner's thesis) emergency assistance was not to be considered as an obligation of States, IGOs and NGOs, but rather as a moral duty of international solidarity. However, this type of assistance could not be given without the approval of the country concerned, otherwise, it could be considered as interference in a country's internal affairs. The delegate from Mexico said that there had been cases in which, under the description of humanitarian assistance, aid had been given to armed groups with a view to destabilizing the situation in a country. The Ethiopian delegate felt that the Resolution was ambiguous and it was not clear what it was intended to achieve. All relief activities carried out by expatriates in any country must be governed by domestic law and not by resolutions or decisions of bodies or institutions which were "inconsistent" with the sovereignty, territorial integrity or security interests of the affected country. Delegates from Peru, Sudan, Nicaragua and Chile again spoke against any potential interference in the internal affairs of States[52].

Was the vote a defeat or a victory for those who submitted the Resolution?

The French promoters of the Resolution felt that it was a success insofar as the Resolution emphasized the need for victims to receive prompt assistance, the importance of humanitarian assistance and the role played by NGOs.

In the view of the Geneva NGOs, the submission of the well-meaning French Resolution was

an object lesson in how not to use U.N. machinery.

On 8 March 1989, in a UNDRO Working Group, the representative of the same six members of the Geneva Licross/Volags Steering Committee for Disasters, which are also members of the International Council of Voluntary Agencies, re-affirmed that a new international Convention or Declaration on disaster relief was neither necessary nor desirable. They believed that such an initiative was not desired by the International Community.

On the other hand, the organizations made three proposals:

1. Governments should be reminded of the international undertakings which they have adopted already, and particularly General Assembly Resolution A/RES/32/56 of 8 December 1977 which endorsed the "Measures to expedite International Relief". Implementation of what has already been agreed should be the primary goal.

2. Governments, IGOs, the League of Red Cross and Red Crescent Societies and NGOs should make further efforts to help improve preparedness arrangements at the national level in disaster-prone countries and at the international level. UNDRO could play a useful role in this area in the context of the International Decade for Natural Disaster Reduction.

3. A major international effort should be undertaken to convince donors to make a more judicious selection of relief supplies so that they correspond more accurately to needs assessed at the disaster site. For instance, draft guidelines are being prepared by UNDRO, WHO, UNICEF, the League and "Food for the Hungry International" and will be submitted to other interested U.N. and non-governmental organizations and concerned governments before being finalized[53].

In a more specialized field, UNDRO convened in March 1990 an International Conference on Telecommunications for Disaster Management attended by 83 par-

[52] U.N. Doc. A/C.3/43/SR.49 of 22 Nov. 1988.

[53] Unpublished document, "UNDRO Working Group: 8 March 1989—Statement by Mr. Robert T. Quinlan".

ticipants from 54 organizations. Recommendations called on UNDRO to be the focal point in promoting the use of communications and remote-sensing technology in disaster relief, preparedness and prevention. In particular, UNDRO should take the lead role in obtaining international agreements facilitating entry and operations of communications equipment by relief teams in stricken countries, with the assistance and cooperation of the International Telecommunications Union[54].

In Summary

Leaving aside the special case of humanitarian intervention by military force, international humanitarian intervention requires the consent of the recipient state, or needs to be requested by that state. Supplies and personnel may enter the recipient state only with its permission.

Rather than trying to "force" an impossible U.N. Resolution on an illusory "right" of humanitarian intervention, the Red Cross and other NGOs have chosen to encourage states to implement what they have already agreed to in various international instruments.

Rather than demanding a "right of access", they believe that discreet negotiations and pressures can be more effective than public denunciations.

Their gradualist approach, based on long and direct experience of international humanitarian work, seems more appropriate to the present state of international relations, where states, and particularly potential recipient states in the Third World, are not prepared to willingly relinquish, formally and publicly, any part of their national sovereignty.

As a separate issue, the use of national or international military units specialized in relief assistance is already a fact. In particular, national units play a role in complementing or supplementing the assistance provided by IGOs and NGOs.

The limitations in the use of national military units, related essentially to possible political differences between donor and recipient countries, would be alleviated, or would disappear, if they were placed under U.N. sponsorship. The creation of a "third type" of U.N. peace-keeping forces, the humanitarian support forces, should be seriously envisaged. Their mandate would have to be carefully designed, under the authority of the Security Council, and their assignment directed by the U.N. Secretary-General. The financing of these new "forces" would also need to be considered.

---

[54] U.N. *Press Release* ND/272 of 23 March 1990.

CONCLUSION

Since the creation of the Red Cross Movement in 1863, international humanitarian assistance has grown considerably: it is now recognized as a legitimate and important aspect of international relations and an indispensable demonstration of international solidarity.

The increased focus on human rights as one of the objectives of the United Nations has been due to a large extent to the public and discreet pressures of NGOs, such as Amnesty International, the International Commission of Jurists and many others, on individual governments and in the various U.N. human rights bodies.

Similarly, the campaigns and field activities of such NGOs as Save the Children Fund, Oxfam, religious organizations and the French Doctors, have attracted the attention, aroused the emotions and obtained the support of a large public, mainly in Western countries. The support needed was, and is, mainly financial, but it also attracted volunteers of all ages who gave administrative, secretarial and professional support to NGOs headquarters and other offices, managed gift shops and raised funds in the home countries,—and for those having the necessary skills and spirit of adventure, gave direct relief and assistance to those in need wherever such assistance was needed.

The ICRC and its delegates, the League of Red Cross and Red Crescent Societies, the National Societies, their doctors, nurses and other volunteers, were the pioneers of modern international humanitarianism: the central role of the International Red Cross Movement in international humanitarian law and assistance remains essential.

Most other humanitarian NGOs were created after War World I, and mainly after World War II to alleviate the suffering and distress of war victims, refugees, displaced persons, children, who needed shelter, clothing, food, security and sympathy. While the NGOs' work, like that of the IGOs created during and after World War II, was initially addressed to European populations, the later "discovery" of the Third World through decolonization, local or regional conflicts and natural disasters in poor nations, gave a new priority to relief assistance to donor governments, U.N. and other IGOs, and NGOs and their volunteers. It also encouraged NGOs to add development assistance to their still essential emergency relief activities.

The continuing need for NGOs in relief and development assistance has been amply demonstrated, in part because of the useful financial, material and human resources which they offer in complement to the official governmental and intergovernmental aid. They also have specific assets related to their different nature: their autonomy and independence from state powers and administrative authorities, their capacity to act quickly, their commitment to the poor, their work with local people at the grassroots level, their diversity, their practical, activist altruism.

Most of the Red Cross Fundamental Principles have been adopted and practised by humanitarian NGOs. In particular, the principles of humanity, independence and voluntary service are shared by all NGOs. However, some have questioned whether it was right, or even tolerable, to be "impartial" and "neutral" (and discreet) in the face of flagrant and repeated violations of human rights conventions and humanitarian law. Should NGOs have to choose, like the Red Cross, between charity and justice? Should they assert and actively support the rights of the politically, economically, socially and culturally oppressed people in the foreign societies where they work?

The answer to this dilemma may only be found case by case by each organization, possibly by reference to the general criteria applied by the Red Cross: (1) consider first the interests of the victim (2) allow that organization to continue to give relief and assistance. The argument of "special purposes" organizations is also valid: relief organizations should give relief and human rights organizations should promote human rights and denounce human rights violations, it being understood that there are constant communications, exchange of information and interaction between the two types of organizations.

Is there a duty and a right to international humanitarian assistance?

There is a moral duty of humanitarian assistance, a duty which extends to the international level on the grounds of human solidarity. Whether its motivation is religious, moral, philosophical, political or ideological, the extraordinary expansion of voluntarism at national and international levels is a proof of its vitality. Voluntarism for relief assistance and for development is based on an individual urge to help directly those in need, at home or in foreign countries, even if the results are limited in scope: it is a concrete sign of mutual assistance, and a symbol of interdependence.

While governments are primarily responsible for the welfare of their people, government administrations and agencies cannot always respond effectively to all human consequences of man-made or natural disasters. Voluntary national and international agencies and their volunteers play a useful role in assisting, complementing, or sometimes replacing governmental services and efforts.

Is there a right to receive assistance?

The sick and the wounded have a right to be cared for: the counterpart of this right is the medical obligation to cater to such needs under clearly defined medical ethics. National legislations ensure that the sick and the wounded are given prompt assistance by public services and officials or by private individuals.

At the international level, the Geneva Conventions provide that persons not directly taking part in hostilities and those put out of action through sickness, injury, captivity or any other cause must be respected and protected against the effects of war; those who suffer must be aided and cared for without discrimination. The Additional Protocols extend this protection to any person affected by an armed conflict. The Conventions and Protocols also provide that medical personnel should be respected and protected.

Does this right to receive assistance extend to international assistance provided in situations other than armed conflicts? In other words, do NGOs and their volunteers have a duty and a right to give assistance to those in need in foreign countries, without regard to national borders and national sovereignty requirements? Under international law, the answer is clearly in the negative, whatever the moral and humanitarian imperatives which may be invoked.

Sovereign countries may accept or reject international offers of humanitarian assistance. They may accept such offers under unacceptable conditions of discrimination as to the recipients of aid. They may accept assistance in principle but raise procedural and practical obstacles to the delivery of aid and the entry of foreign workers. They may assert that they are capable and well equipped to deal, by themselves, with problems of shelter, food, medicaments and health care. Such assertions may be based in part on realistic assessments of the country's capacity, or on a fear of opening a closed political or religious society to foreign eyes and influence, or on fears of revealing national or local inadequacies, discrimination or other abuses.

While it is unlikely that an international right of humanitarian intervention could be formally recognized by the international community in the foreseeable future, a number of factors may lead to a slow and gradual evolution and a progressive erosion of the traditional principles of international law concerning the national sovereignty of states, in this particular domain of international relations. These factors include the growing feeling of international human solidarity, quicker and more open communications and exchange of information on disaster situations, more effective, enterprising or even adventurous humanitarian organizations, and the reality of interdependence. Additionally, the progress, in the last few decades, of the international promotion and defence of human rights, which requires an intervention "in matters which are essentially within the jurisdiction" of states (Art. 2.7 of the U.N. Charter), may serve as a basis, an example and a hope for the promoters of a right and duty of international humanitarian intervention.

Are expatriate relief workers and volunteers still needed and are they still welcome in recipient countries?

Under the self-reliance concept, it has become axiomatic that the former benevolent paternalistic assistance given by Northern "experts" and other "do-gooders" to "under-developed" countries is no longer productive nor acceptable. Many developing countries have a large number of well-educated specialists, in part due to previous international efforts, and no longer need international experts. On the other hand, as noted in Chapter 8, the requirements for expatriate middle-level technicians have been estimated to be in the order of 20,000 per year in the 1980s, an estimate which can well be projected into the 1990s. The growth of national and international volunteer programmes tends to respond to these needs, as well as the development of South-South mutual assistance.

The concept of "partnership" between North and South institutions aims at creating a relationship of equality, thus avoiding vertical links and dependency. The objective is to help the people to help themselves on a local community basis.

Many Northern NGOs have decided to employ only a limited number of expatriate staff in selected field offices, and to mainly train and employ nationals and national volunteers in their national and local programmes.

However, international relief workers and volunteers still have a role to play in emergency situations, usually on a short-term basis, provided that they understand that effective aid cannot be imposed, that their usefulness lies mainly in training others and in acting as facilitators[1].

A Realistic Humanitarian Strategy

In its Report of 1988[2], the Independent Commission on International Humanitarian Issues has stressed the lack of humanitarian protection during internal disturbances and tensions, despite the adoption of Protocol II in 1977, as well as the weakness of institutional means in the face of increasing violations of humanitarian law:

> Political considerations prevail over humanitarian requirements and humanitarian concerns are used to further political aims.
> ...There is a need to reinforce and revitalize rules of humanity which are often blatantly disregarded. But it is clear that to have any effect, solutions must be realistic and take into account the international climate.

The Commission felt strongly that it was not by adopting new sets of rules of humanitarian law that better compliance would be achieved. Indeed, codification may have reached saturation point. What is lacking is simplicity, clarity and, above all, efficient and effective implementation. To these ends, the Commission proposed the following general measures:

a. A clear and concise restatement of the fundamental rules of humanity, combining fundamental principles of humanitarian law and human rights, including

---

[1] *Imposing Aid—Emergency Assistance to Refugees*, B.E. Harrell-Bond, 1986, Oxford University Press, pp. 363–366.

[2] *Winning the Human Race?*, The Report of the Independent Commission on International Humanitarian Issues, 1988, Zed Books Ltd, London and New Jersey, pp. 69–77. The Commission was established in 1983, outside the U.N. framework. Its 29 members were chosen among leading personalities in the humanitarian field or having wide experience of government or world affairs. Its Co-Chairmen were Sadruddin Aga Khan and Hassan bin Talal.

The right to life; dignity of the human person; no unlimited choice of the means used to maintain law and order; prohibition of acts of terrorism and of indiscriminate violence; prohibition of torture and degrading treatment; respect for the injured and protection of medical action; prohibition of forced or involuntary disappearances; fundamental judicial guarantees; special protection of children; dissemination and teaching of these fundamental rules.

b. International and regional organizations should encourage ratification of the 1977 Additional Protocols and ensure wider dissemination of humanitarian norms, as has been done in the field of human rights. The U.N. and human rights organizations should assure supplementary protection on the basis of human rights Conventions, especially in situations of internal conflict where humanitarian law has not yet been much developed, as well as in situations of internal disturbances and tensions where it does not apply at all. Violations of humanitarian rules should be publicized and denounced similarly to the publicity given to violations of human rights.

A Need for Operational Leadership

It is well known that the international humanitarian relief network, based on voluntary initiatives, autonomy of the organizations and a spirit of generosity, lacks coordination and leadership.

Criticisms are being periodically levelled at the organizational chaos that sometimes occurs during relief operations. As recently reported by *International Management*[3],

In the race to help, duplication of aid often floods relief channels, overburdening supply operations. Agencies compete for the maximum media visibility to reach potential donors.

In its report on the international response to the Mexico earthquake of 1985, the Regional Office for the Americas of the World Health Organization characterized the influx of well-intentioned rescue personnel as a "second disaster". Some agencies rushed to intervene without the necessary expertise or equipment.

In December 1988, much of the 40,000 tons of second-hand clothing sent to Armenia after its earthquake could not be used and had to be burned, according to the Red Cross.

The U.N. has declared the 1990s as the Decade for Natural Disaster Reduction in an attempt to focus attention on the need for improvements in relief coordination and the long-term development of disaster preparedness.

Donor governments, IGOs and NGOs should complement rather than compete with each other. But who will organize, lead, decide on priorities, approve, select or reject specific offers of help?

---

[3] *International Management*, Nov. 1990, pp. 23–24.

In 1975, the Tansley Report[4] proposed that the Red Cross should seek to establish itself firmly as the leading non-governmental assistance organization within whatever international disaster relief system would evolve in the coming years. The League of Red Cross and Red Crescent Societies replied that this could be the result of effective work by the Red Cross Movement, but that it was inappropriate to think of pre-eminence as an aim in itself.

The reticence of the League to assume leadership in disaster situations, at least for the NGO group and subject to their agreement, does not augur well for any future leadership, or even coordination of the "non-system".

The position is not much better at the U.N. level, where UNDRO has not been able to assume effectively a leadership role. The appointment of *ad hoc* Representatives of the U.N. Secretary-General for specific disaster situations is at least a palliative remedy.

The Independent Commission on International Humanitarian Issues has recommended[5] that the U.N. should designate a central coordinating body which should be fully recognized as *primus inter pares* for a predetermined period of time bringing the full potential of the international network to a particular disaster. It should have acknowledged authority to declare a disaster and to intervene effectively. During the disaster period, this body should have the authority to coordinate the receipt and disbursement of emergency funds based on pre-arranged formulae with donors and recipient officials and be empowered to establish priorities after assessing actual human needs. It should also have recognized authority to coordinate emergency relief provided by IGOs and NGOs concerned for a pre-determined period in order to ensure complementary responses.

This commendable recommendation should be seriously considered and pursued, in spite of the resistance to be expected from both IGOs and NGOs.

A Need for Evaluation

In OECD countries, samples of development projects co-financed with NGOs undergo systematic evaluation by the official aid agency, sometimes with participation of NGO representatives on the evaluation team. According to a 1988 OECD Report[6], available evaluations tend to confirm the comparative advantage of NGOs in their ability to work at the grass-roots level, to address basic human needs and to operate in remote areas often unserved by national governments or official donors. However, studies reveal that the NGO record is uneven, differing from country to country, from NGO to NGO and from sector to sector.

[4] *The ICRC, the League and the Report on the Re-Appraisal of the Role of the Red Cross*, Reprinted from the *International Review of the Red Cross*, March-April 1978, Jan. Feb. 1979, Geneva.

[5] *Winning...*, p. 178.

[6] *Voluntary Aid for Development—The role of NGOs*, OECD, 1988, Paris, pp. 102–106.

Limitations, weaknesses and constraints have been identified in a number of cases, indicating that there is still scope for clarifying goals and improving effectiveness.

According to a Canadian study, the most relevant standards of efficiency for NGOs are: their ability to mobilize private resources; the long-term impact of their projects as measured by: a) sustainability and, b) extent of replication; and the effectiveness of cooperation among agencies.

A wide-ranging evaluation was initiated in 1985 by the Commission of the European Economic Community based on findings of 32 project evaluations in 17 different countries in Africa, Asia and Latin America. The study used the following criteria:

— effectiveness, which compared the actual project performance with targets formulated initially. However, the concept was not applicable to such projects as those promoting social consciousness as well as multipurpose and nonproductive projects.
— efficiency, which measured tangible results against the means employed to achieve them (cost-efficiency). Even where efficiency was measurable in this sense, the analysis was generally thwarted by the failure of project management to measure the financial value of recurring inputs, and more importantly, of outputs.
— viability, considered the most important, was defined as the capacity of the project to sustain itself after external funding ended.
— impact, which encompassed the general developmental consequences for different groups of people and institutions.

The analysis based on these four criteria showed that there was clearly scope for substantial project improvement. The study identified certain common features pertaining to the more successful projects:

— conduct preliminary investigations to determine how they can intervene in response to the priority needs of intended beneficiaries;
— start with the ends and then proceed to identify the appropriate means to attain them;
— possess the technical knowledge to respond to needs or seek it from other agencies;
— develop sufficiently comprehensive approaches;
— facilitate the development of strong indigenous institutions.

Finally, the study reflected a general weakness in the capacity and will of development NGOs to monitor and evaluate their own progress, or to use these processes for internal management.

The evaluation of humanitarian NGOs faces similar problems, with some reluctance on the part of NGOs themselves and even on the part of their IGO partners to consider that evaluation is important and to take steps to initiate the evaluation process.

According to Smyke[7], about 400 international NGOs work exclusively in humanitarian work. The UNHCR works with 200 NGOs as implementing partners: yet, the UNHCR does not evaluate their performance. Most humanitarian NGOs giving emergency relief in disaster situations, and those working for refugees, give all their energy and time to respond to immediate, urgent, human needs: the need for evaluation is seen by them as a wasteful bureaucratic effort, only justified to pacify international or national donors.

Smyke has designed an evaluation methodology on humanitarian NGOs aimed at providing information and at improving NGO performance. While donor evaluation practice tends to contract evaluation tasks to academic teams, he suggests that humanitarian evaluations should be fully participatory. Evaluation team selection, for instance, would include representatives from IGOs and Third World NGOs with humanitarian aid experience in operations, administration and management, the donor being represented by a senior official. The participatory approach would apply to the selection of the country or project, special donor needs, the type of evaluation and its purpose.

One possible methodology would be to centre on the recipient as the object (or subject) of humanitarian aid: for instance, refugees could well assess the quality of services provided by U.N. organizations and their operating partners. The evaluation would then be carried out by a completely independent body, such as a local university. The assessment team would include refugees, as well as other representatives from the donor, IGOs, international and indigenous NGOs.

A "real life" evaluation of a major humanitarian operation, Operation Lifeline Sudan, has been carried out recently[8]. The Lifeline experience confirms, in a dramatic way, that humanitarian action can never be divorced from politics, which may both constrain and enhance responses to human need.

Rather than denying political realities, those committed to humanitarian values need to work to make the concern for human welfare a more potent political force in its own right.

The Lifeline review has suggested that agencies specializing in one particular area, whether humanitarian assistance, peace, human rights, or development, need to be more catholic in their concerns, even if their programmes retain a more specialized focus.

---

[7] "NGOs Involved in Humanitarian Assistance", Raymond J. Smyke, *Transnational Associations*, 4/1990, pp. 233–239.

[8] *Humanitarianism Under Siege—A Critical Review of Operation Lifeline Sudan*, by Larry Minear, The Red Sea Press, Trenton—Bread for the World Institute on Hunger and Development, Washington, D.C., 1991.

A Bigger Role for the U.N.

The present role of U.N. organizations in humanitarian assistance has already been described, particularly in Chapters 1 and 8.

Additionally, the Independent Commission on International Humanitarian Issues has proposed[9] that the U.N. establish a Central Office for Humanitarian Issues, close to the Secretary-General. This Office would help in coordinating policies and programmes of the U.N. system and provide policy guidance in regard to specific humanitarian issues, including those which are not adequately covered by existing agencies.

The Commission has also recommended that the U.N. elaborate and promote a special legal, administrative, financial and operational code of conduct to regulate the management of disasters:

> The cornerstone of the code should be the increasingly recognized principle that, during a disaster, humanitarian criteria ought to prevail over any political or sovereignty constraints for the limited period of the emergency. In practice, this will include concepts such as "mercy corridors" entailing, to the extent compatible with minimum standards of hygiene and national security, relaxed procedures for the entry of relief personnel and import of goods to ensure unhindered access of assistance to victims.

The possible creation of "humanitarian" U.N. Peace-Keeping Forces has been discussed in Chapter 11.

An Appeal to the World

The World Campaign for the Protection of Victims of War was approved by the Council of Red Cross Delegates in 1989. The Campaign will take place in 1991, with the following goals:

— to ensure, in places where there is fighting, that both combatants and civilians know the rules of warfare, and their rights. Dissemination work of the Movement will be stepped up;
— in countries which are not at war, to mobilize public support for both protective and assistance roles. In 1990, a list of humanitarian projects has been prepared to illustrate how increased assistance can bring real help and it is hoped that a number of National Societies will adopt them.

Finally at the International Conference of the Red Cross to be held in October 1991, there will be a debate on the conditions of war victims.

---

[9] *Winning ...*, p. 177, 195.

The text of the Appeal follows[10]:

The world has never been closer to peace. But war has never been more destructive.

Nine out of ten of its victims today are civilians.

The suffering of these people is an insult to humanity. It is in the power of mankind, and is the duty of states, to put an end to the spiral of violence which leads to war and internal conflicts.

We appeal to governments, to governmental and non-governmental organizations as well as to the leaders of combatants on all sides, and to the people of the world:

— to respect the fundamental human rights of individuals at all times, in all places and in all circumstances.
— to live up to their international undertakings and responsibilities, to enable all necessary humanitarian aid to be made available to victims of conflict and to ensure that they can seek and receive such aid.
— to recognize that the life of each human being is the concern of all.

War is an obsolete and absurd means of settling disputes. However, so long as it persists, the plight of its victims is of universal concern.

We must not remain silent.

We must reach out to succour every suffering man, woman and child.

We must urge governments, as an act of humanitarian consensus, to make available the necessary resources to protect and assist the victims of man's violence to man, thereby enabling them to live a life worth living.

After centuries of conflict let us dare, in the name of those victims, to conceive of a world without enemies.

The U.N. Secretary-General, J. Perez de Cuellar, commented that today's Solferinos occur mainly within the borders of a country, where brother fights brother and the innocent victims are women, children and old people.

International assistance and solidarity should apply to all victims, whether victims of wars or natural disasters.

In this effort, national and international NGOs play a vital role, which is increasingly being recognized.

They need and deserve our support.

---

[10] *Red Cross, Red Crescent*, May-Aug. 1990.

BIBLIOGRAPHY

Armstrong, J.D., "The International Committee of the Red Cross and Political Prisoners", *International Organization*, Vol. 39, No. 4, Autumn 1985, p. 621.

Arnould, F., "Les Casques Bleus du développement", *Croissance des jeunes nations*, No. 317, June 1989—NGO Supplement, French Association of Progress Volunteers.

Baccino-Astrada, A., *Manual on the Rights and Duties of Medical Personnel in Armed Conflicts*, ICRC—League of Red Cross and Red Crescent Societies, Geneva, 1982.

Barnes, C., *Army without Guns*, The Salvation Army, 1986.

Beigbeder, Y., *Threats to the International Civil Service—Past Pressures and New Trends*, Pinter, 1988.

Ben-Tov, A., *Facing the Holocaust in Budapest—The ICRC and the Jews in Hungary, 1943–1945*, H. Dunant Institute, Nijhoff, 1988.

Berlin, A. and Rocha Grimoldi, J.A., *Combining Professionalism with Voluntarism* (working paper), H. Dunant Institute, Geneva, 1988.

Bettati, M., and Dupuy, P.M., *Les O.N.G. et le Droit International*, Economica, Paris, 1986.

Bettati, M. and Kouchner, B., *Le devoir d'ingérence*, Denoel, Paris, 1987.

Brodhead, T., "NGOs: In One Year, Out the Other?", *World Development*, "Development Alternatives: the Challenge to NGOs", Vol. 15, Supplement, 1987.

Brodhead, T. and O'Malley, J., "NGOs and Third World Development: Opportunities and Constraints", WHO Doc. GPA/GMC(2)/89.5, Dec. 1989.

Brodhead, T and Brent, H.C., *Bridges of Hope: Canadian Voluntary Agencies and the Third World*, North-South Institute, Ottawa, 1988.

Browne, S.G., "The Leprosy Mission—A Century of Service", *Leprosy Review*, 1974/45.

Cahier, P., "Article 105", *La Charte des Nations Unies*, Economica, Paris, 1985.

Charities Aid Foundation, *Charity Trends*, 12th Ed., Tonbridge, 1989.

Commission Coopération Développement, *Petit guide du volontariat et du bénévolat*, Paris, 1989.

Condamines, C., *L'aide humanitaire entre la politique et les affaires*, Editions L'Harmattan, Paris, 1989.

Deeny, J., *To Cure and to Care*, The Glendale Press, Dublin, 1989.

Delcourt, R., *L'Armée du Salut*, Presses Universitaires de France, Paris, 1988.

Dodd, E.M., *The Gift of the Healer*, Friendship Press, New York, 1964.

Dominicé, C., "La personnalité juridique internationale du CICR", *Studies and Essays on International Humanitarian Law and Red Cross Principles in honour of Jean Pictet*, ICRC, Nijhoff, 1984.

Egan, E., *Catholic Relief Services—The Beginning Years*, CRS, New York, 1988.

Elliott, C., "Some Aspects of Relations between the North and South in the NGO Sector", *World Development*, "Development Alternatives: the Challenge to NGOs", Vol. 15, Supplement, 1987.

Favez, J.C., *Une mission impossible—Le CICR, les déportations et les camps de concentration nazis*, Payot, Lausanne, 1988.

Feld, W.J. and Jordan, R.S., *International Organizations—A Comparative Approach*, 2nd Ed., Praeger, 1988.

Forsythe, D.P., "Humanitarian Mediation by the ICRC", *International Mediation in Theory and Practice*, S. Touval and I.W. Zartman Ed., Conflict Management Studies, SAIS, Westview Press, 1985.

Forsythe, D.P., *Humanitarian Politics: The International Committee of the Red Cross*, The Johns Hopkins University Press, 1977.

Freeman, K., *If Any Man Build—The History of Save the Children Fund*, Hodder and Stoughton, London, 1965.

Harrell-Bond, B.E., *Imposing Aid—Emergency Assistance to Refugees*, Oxford University Press, 1986.

Hoekendijk, L., "Which work ought to be paid?", Volonteurope, *The Journal*, No. 5.

Holzer, B. and Lenoir, F., *Les risques de la solidarité*, Fayard, Paris, 1989.

Howell, L., *People are the subject—Stories of Urban Rural Mission*, World Council of Churches, Geneva, 1980.

Independent Commission on International Humanitarian Issues, *Winning the Human Race?—The Report of the Independent Commission on International Humanitarian Issues*, Zed Books Ltd, London and New Jersey, 1988.

Institut Universitaire de Hautes Etudes Internationales, *Les organisations non gouvernmentales en Suisse*, Colloque des 8 et 9 juin 1972, Genève, 1973.

International Committee of the Red Cross—League of Red Cross and Red Crescent Societies, *International Red Cross Handbook*, Geneva, 1983.

International Committee of the Red Cross—League of Red Cross and Red Crescent Societies, *Compendium of Reference Texts on the International Red Cross and Red Crescent Movement*, Geneva, 1990.

International Committee of the Red Cross—League of Red Cross and Red Crescent Societies, *Inter Arma Caritas—The Work of the ICRC during the Second World War*, 2nd Ed., Geneva, 1973.

International Committee of the Red Cross—League of Red Cross and Red Crescent Societies, *Red Cross Disaster Relief Handbook*, The League of Red Cross and Red Crescent Societies.

International Committee of the Red Cross—League of Red Cross and Red Crescent Societies, *Report of the ICRC on its activities during the Second World War (September 1, 1939—June 30, 1947)*, Geneva, 1948.

International Committee of the Red Cross—League of Red Cross and Red Crescent Societies, *Report on the First World Meeting on Red Cross Voluntary Service*, Mexico, The League of Red Cross and Red Crescent Societies, Geneva, 1983.

International Committee of the Red Cross — League of Red Cross and Red Crescent Societies, "The ICRC, the League and the Report on the Re-Appraisal of the role of the Red Cross", *International Review of the Red Cross*, from March-April 1978 to January-February 1979.

International Council of Voluntary Agencies (ICVA), "Relations between Southern and Northern NGOs: Effective Partnerships for Sustainable Development", 1989 (unpublished).

International Council of Voluntary Agencies (ICVA), "Voluntarism within the Red Cross" (working document), Third Conference of National Red Cross and Red Crescent Societies of the Balkan Countries, Athens, Doc. DD/SND-9, 1979.

International Council on Social Welfare, *Justice in the Aid Relationship—A Dialogue on Partnership*, ICSW, Vienna, 1988.

International Court of Justice, *ICJ Reports*

International Court of Justice, The Corfu Channel Case (Merits), Judgment of April 9th, 1949.

International Court of Justice, Reparation for injuries suffered in the service of the U.N., Advisory Opinion of April, 11, 1949.

International Court of Justice, Case concerning military and paramilitary activities in and against Nicaragua (Nicaragua v. U.S.A.), Merits, Judgment of 27 June 1986.

International Foundation for Development Alternatives (IFDA), *Dossier 67*, Sept. Oct. 1988.

Jacobson, H.K., *Networks of Interdependence—International Organizations and the Global Political System*, Knopf, New York, 1984.

Jaeger, G., "Participation of NGOs in the Activities of the UNHCR", in Willetts, see *infra*.

Kalshoven, F., Ed., *Assisting the Victims of Armed Conflict and Other Disasters*, Nijhoff, 1989.

Kent, R. C., *Anatomy of Disaster Relief—The International Network in Action*, Pinter, London, 1987.

Kimble, G.H.T., *Tropical Africa*, Twentieth Century Fund, New York, 1960.

Knitel, H.G., *Les délégations du Comité International de la Croix-Rouge*, Institut Universitaire de Hautes Etudes Internationales, Geneva, 1967.

Korten, D.C., "Micro-Policy Reform—The Role of Private Voluntary Development

Agencies", *Community Management—Asian Experience and Perspectives*, Korten Ed., Kumarian Press, 1986.

Kouchner, B., *Charité Business*, Le Pré aux Clercs, Paris, 1986.

Kue-Hing Young, T., "Manchu Anatomy—how China missed the Vesalian Revolution", *CMA Journal*, Sept. 21, 1974, Vol. III.

Le Net, M. and Werquin, J., *Le volontariat—Aspects sociaux, économiques et politiques en France et dans le monde*, La Documentation française, Paris, 1985.

LeRoy Bennett, A., *International Organizations*, Prentice-Hall, Englewood Cliffs, 1984.

Lévinet, M., "Réflexions sur la résurgence de l'intervention d'humanité", *Trimestre du Monde*, Paris, 1990/2.

Lewin, H., *A Community of Clowns—Testimonies of People in Urban Rural Mission*, WCC Publications, Geneva, 1987.

Lissner, J., *The Politics of Altruism—A Study of the Political Behaviour of Voluntary Development Agencies*, Lutheran World Federation, Geneva, 1977.

Macalister-Smith, P., *International Humanitarian Assistance—Disaster Relief Actions in International Law and Organizations*, Nijhoff/H. Dunant Institute, Geneva, 1985.

Merle, M., "International NGOs and their Legal Status", Appendix 3.5 to *International Association Statutes Series (1988)*, Union of International Associations.

Meurant, J., *Red Cross Voluntary Service in Today's Society*, H. Dunant Institute, Geneva, 1985.

Michanek, E., "Democracy as a Force for Development and the Role of Swedish Assistance, *Development Dialogue*, Uppsala, 1985/1.

Minear, L., *Humanitarianism Under Siege—A Critical Review of Operation Lifeline Sudan*, The Red Sea Press, Trenton,—Bread for the World Institute on Hunger and Development, 1991.

Moreillon, J., "Suspension of the Government Delegation of the Republic of South Africa at the Twenty-Fifth International Conference of the Red Cross, Geneva 1986—Different perceptions of the same event", *International Review of the Red Cross*, Mar.- Apr. 1987, No. 257.

Organization for Economic Co-operation and Development (OECD), *Report, Development Assistance Committee*, 1989, Paris.

Organization for Economic Co-operation and Development (OECD), *Voluntary Aid for Development—The Role of Non-Governmental Organisations*, 1988, Paris.

Pictet, J., *The Fundamental Principles of the Red Cross—Commentary*, H. Dunant Institute, Geneva, 1979.

Plattner, D., "Le statut du délégué du CICR sous l'angle du principe de l'inviolabilité de sa personne", *Studies and Essays on International Humanitarian Law and Red Cross Principles in Honour of Jean Pictet*, ICRC, Nijhoff, 1984.

Puchala, D.J. and Coate, R.A., *The Challenge of Relevance—The U.N. in a Changing World Environment*, The Academic Council on the U.N. System, 1989–5.

Regis Polcino, Sister M., "The Medical Mission Sisters", *Transactions and Studies of the College of Physicians of Philadelphia*, Vol. 35, No. 1, July 1987.

Rousseau, C., *Droit international public*, Sirey, Paris, 1953.

Sandoz, Y., "L'intervention humanitaire, le droit international humanitaire et le CICR", *Annales de droit international médical*, Monaco, 1986.

Schoenholzer, J.P., "The Doctor in the Geneva Conventions of 1949", *International Review of the Red Cross*, Feb. March 1953.

Siedentopf, H., "Decentralization for Rural Development: Government Approaches and People's Initiatives in Asia and the Pacific", *Planning and Administration*, 1989–2.

Sigmund, P.E., *Liberation Theology at the Crossroads—Democracy or Revolution?*, Oxford University Press, 1989.

Simonnet, J., "Le Jansénisme humanitaire d'Aide Médicale Internationale", *Documentation française*, No. 148, 1989.

Smyke, R.J., "NGOs Involved in Humanitarian Assistance", *Transnational Associations*, No. 4, 1990.

Suy, E., "La protection des volontaires humanitaires dans les conflits armés non internationaux et dans les opérations de secours en cas de catastrophes", *Des menschen Recht zwischen Freiheit und Verantwortung*, Duncker and Humblot, Berlin, 1989.

Swinarski, C., *Studies and Essays on International Humanitarian Law and Red Cross Principles in honour of Jean Pictet*, ICRC, Geneva—Nijhoff, Dordrecht, 1984.

Tansley, D.D., *Final Report: An Agenda for the Red Cross*, Joint Committee for the Reappraisal of the Red Cross, Geneva, 1975.

Teson, F.R., *Humanitarian Intervention—An Inquiry into Law and Morality*, Transnational Publishers, New York, 1988.

Thierry, H., and Decaux, E., *Droit international et droits de l'homme*, Centre de Droit international de Nanterre, CEDIN, Montchrestien, Paris 1990.

Torrelli, M., "La protection du médecin volontaire", *Annales de droit international médical*, Monaco, 1986.

UNESCO, *International Dimensions of Humanitarian Law*, H. Dunant Institute, Geneva,—UNESCO, Paris,—Nijhoff, Dordrecht, 1988.

UNITAR *Model Rules for Disaster Relief Operations*, New York, 1982.

Union of International Associations, *Yearbook of International Organizations, 1989–1990*, Brussels.

United Nations, *Basic Facts about the U.N.*, 1980.

United Nations, *The Blue Helmets—U.N. Peace-keeping Forces*, UNPA, 1988.

United Nations High Commissioner for Refugees (UNHCR) *Handbook for Emergencies*, Geneva, 1982.

United Nations Volunteers (UNV), *International Volunteer Service and Development Cooperation*, U.N. Doc. UNV/SYM/REP/2, 1982.

United Nations Volunteers (UNV), *2nd UNV High-Level Intergovernmental Meeting on International Volunteerism and Development*, U.N. Doc. UNV

II/1986/REP/1/E, 1986.

United Nations Volunteers (UNV), *Consultative Meeting on Volunteer Service and Development*, Geneva, 20–22 April 1988, U.N. Doc. DP/UNV/CM/1988/OSA/6/E, 1988.

United Nations Volunteers (UNV), *Development Microcosm—UNV in Yemen*, undated.

United Nations Volunteers (UNV), *In Partnership for Better Health—UNV in Sri Lanka*, 1979.

United Nations Volunteers (UNV), *Programme Advisory Note—The Appropriate Use of Volunteers in Development*, 1990.

United Nations Volunteers (UNV), *UNV and the Appropriate Role of Volunteers in Development*, by Dr. B.G. McSweeney, Executive Coordinator, UNV, as part of a UNITAR publication in preparation.

United Nations Volunteers (UNV), *UNV at a Glance—The Key Statistics*, 1990.

Van Boven, T.C., "Some reflections on the principle of neutrality", *Studies and Essays on International Humanitarian Law and Red Cross Principles*, ICRC, Nijhoff, 1984.

Vichniac, I., *Croix-Rouge—Les stratèges de la bonne conscience*, A. Moreau, Paris, 1988.

Weiss, T.G., Ed., *Humanitarian Emergencies and Military Help in Africa*, Macmillan—International Peace Academy, London, 1990.

Willetts, P. Ed., *Pressure Groups in the Global System*, Pinter, London, 1982.

Wiseberg, L.S., "Humanitarian Intervention: Lessons from the Nigerian Civil War", *Human Rights Journal*, Vol. VII-1, Pedone, Paris, 1974.

Wood, D., *The Background to Quaker Work at the U.N.*, Quaker U.N. Office, Geneva, 1987.

World Council of Churches, *The Role of the World Council of Churches in International Affairs*, 1986.

World Health Organization (WHO), *The Work of WHO, 1986–1987*.

World Medical Association, *Handbook of Declarations*, 1985.

Yourilin, S., "Volunteer work in the USSR", *State and Civil Society: Voluntary Work in Eastern and Western Europe*, Volonteurope, 1989.

Zarocostas, J., "Church Organizations Involvement in International Affairs", *Report of the Seminar*, Centre for Applied Studies in International Negotiations, Geneva, 1987.

LIST OF TABLES

LIST OF ABBREVIATIONS

AFSC	American Friends Service Committee
AMI	Aide Médicale Internationale
AMREF	The African Medical and Research Foundation
CCIVS	Coordinating Committee for International Volunteer Service
CDAA	Churches' Drought Action on Africa
CICARWS(WCC)	Commission on Inter-Church Aid, Refugee and World Service
CIDSE	International Cooperation for Socio-Economic Development
CRB	Commission for Relief in Belgium
CRS	Catholic Relief Services
DP	Displaced Persons
EEC	European Economic Community
FAO	Food and Agriculture Organization of the United Nations
FF.	French Francs
FSC	Friends Service Council
FWCC	Friends World Committee for Consultation
IAVE	International Association for Voluntary Effort
ICEM	Intergovernmental Committee for European Migration (see IOM)
ICIHI	Independent Commission on International Humanitarian Issues
ICJ	International Court of Justice
ICM	Intergovernmental Committee for Migration (see IOM)
ICRC	International Committee of the Red Cross
ICVA	International Council of Voluntary Agencies
IGO	Intergovernmental Organization
INGO	International Non-Governmental Organization
IOM	International Organization for Migration
IRO	International Refugee Organization
IRU	International Relief Union
ISCA	International Save the Children Alliance
JRP	Joint Relief Partnership

403

LIVE	Learn through International Voluntary Effort
LWF	Lutheran World Federation
MDM	Médecins Du Monde
MSF	Médecins Sans Frontières
NGO	Non-Governmental Organization
OAS	Organization of American States
OAU	Organization of African Unity
OFHOM	Oeuvres Hospitalières Françaises de l'Ordre de Malte
PCR(WCC)	Programme to Combat Racism
PLO	Palestine Liberation Organization
QPS	Quaker Peace and Service
QUNO	Quaker U.N. Office in Geneva
RENAMO	Mozambique National Resistance
SCF	Save the Children Fund
SWAPO	South-West Africa People's Organization
Sw.F.	Swiss Francs
U.N.	United Nations
UNDP	U.N. Development Programme
UNDRO	Office of the U.N. Disaster Relief Coordinator
UNESCO	U.N. Educational, Scientific and Cultural Organization
UNHCR	The U.N. High Commissioner for Refugees
UNICEF	U.N. Children's Fund
UNITA	National Union for the Total Independence of Angola
UNITAR	U.N. Institute for Training and Research
UNRRA	U.N. Relief and Rehabilitation Administration
UNRWA	U.N. Relief and Works Agency for Palestine Refugees in the Near East
UNV	U.N. Volunteers Programme
WCC	World Council of Churches
WFP	World Food Programme
WHO	World Health Organization
WMO	World Meteorological Organization
WVI	World Vision International

POSTSCRIPT

On 5 April 1991, the U.N. Security Council adopted Resolution 688: this adoption was hailed by the French government which had initiated it as a major break-through in the formal recognition of an international right of humanitarian intervention.

The Gulf War had ended on 28 February 1991. On the same date, Iraq formally accepted the twelve Resolutions of the Security Council imposed against it after its invasion and occupation of Kuwait in August 1990. On 11 March, Iraq renounced its annexation of Kuwait.

Encouraged by the defeat of the Iraqi Army, Iraqi Shiite Moslems in the South and Kurds in the North started a rebellion against the central power in order to acquire a degree of political, cultural and religious autonomy or independence.

These uprisings were forcefully repressed by the Iraqi troops, tanks and heli-copters, resulting in massacres in both minorities and streams of refugees trying to escape from the terror by taking refuge in Turkey or Iran.

The Western Allies in the Coalition rejected all calls to intervene militarily against the Iraqi Army in defence of the Shiites or Kurds. The U.S. rationale for not intervening, openly expressed by President Bush and undoubtedly shared silently by the British and the French governments, was based on the following arguments:

— no more Vietnam: Iraq's internal problems should be solved by the Iraqis them-selves. The "precious" lives of American (British, French) soldiers should not be placed at risk in an intervention in Iraq itself.
— while the Coalition military intervention was justified in order to restore the independence, sovereignty and integrity of Kuwait, the unity and territorial integrity of Iraq itself should not be jeopardized by minority movements.
— U.S. (British, French) troops should be withdrawn promptly from the area.

In spite of these realpolitik considerations, the suffering of the populations moved public opinion particularly in Western countries, while Turkey and Iran called for financial and material assistance to cope with the influx of refugees.

On 2 April, France called on the Security Council to take action to stop the "brutal repression" being carried out by Iraqi troops against Shiite Muslim and Kurdish rebels and communities.

On 3 April, the Council adopted Resolution 687 approving a cease-fire under stringent conditions to be unconditionally accepted by Iraq.

On 5 April, the Council adopted Resolution 688 by ten votes in favour, 3 against (Cuba, Yemen and Zimbabwe) and two abstentions (China and India).

The French draft Resolution had been supported by the U.S., the U.K. and Belgium. Turkey, not then a member of the Council, had first asked for an emergency meeting of the Security Council to deal with the problem of Kurdish refugees.

Countries with nationality or minority problems showed hesitations (the USSR) or expressed reservations (India, Zimbabwe): Romania, with its Hungarian minority, agreed to vote for the Resolution only when a reference to Article 2.7 of the U.N. Charter was inserted in the text: it also insisted that the Resolution was not to constitute a precedent.

In support of the draft Resolution, France, the U.S. and the U.K. argued that the situation in Iraq had given rise to worldwide concern so that it was no longer an internal matter.

Resolution 688

In this Resolution, the Council stated that it was

> *Gravely concerned* by the repression of the Iraqi civilian population in many parts of Iraq, including most recently in Kurdish populated areas which led to a massive flow of refugees towards and across international frontiers and to cross border incursions, which threaten international peace and security in the region,

The Council was

> *deeply disturbed* by the magnitude of the human suffering involved

The Council condemned the repression of the Iraqi population and demanded that Iraq

> immediately end this repression and expresses the hope in the same context that an open dialogue will take place to ensure that the human and political rights of all Iraqi citizens are respected;

The Council "insisted"

> that Iraq allow immediate access by international humanitarian organizations to all those in need of assistance in all parts of Iraq and make available all necessary facilities for their operations;

The Council requested

the Secretary-General to pursue his humanitarian efforts in Iraq and to report forthwith, if appropriate on the basis of a further mission to the region, on the plight of the Iraqi civilian population, and in particular the Kurdish population, suffering from the repression in all its forms inflicted by the Iraqi authorities;

and "demanded"

that Iraq cooperate with the Secretary-General to these ends;

The Iraqi Ambassador to the U.N. declared that this Resolution was a blatant interference in Iraq's internal affairs. His Government had invited a U.N. mission to investigate locally the fate of the Kurds who, in his view, were in no way the object of persecutions.

An Assessment

The motivation for the French-inspired Resolution stemmed in part from a humanitarian, popular response to the human tragedy experienced by hundreds of thousands of civilian people, including women, children and old people, subjected to a cruel and indiscriminate repression and killing.

The support for the Resolution was also motivated by governments' feelings of guilt in the face of atrocities committed by a dictator whom they had combatted in order to liberate Kuwait, but had allowed to continue his despotic and inhuman leadership in his own country over his helpless population.

The humanitarian response only addressed the dramatic consequences of a monumental misunderstanding. The future victims felt encouraged in their claims for autonomy, independence or revolt by Bush's calls for toppling Saddam Hussein, by the Allies' victory and by their own mistaken belief that their struggle would be supported by the Allies' military might.

How were they to know that the new "World Order" only applied to States, and not to political and human rights and self-determination within one's own country, even though this country was the U.N.-condemned aggressor?

The impact of the Security Council Resolution was to explicitly link a humanitarian crisis (a massive flow of refugees, human suffering) to its direct cause (the internal repression of its own population by the government of a Member State), and to condemn this repression.

The Resolution justified the Council's intervention by the international consequences of this internal conflict.

On the other hand, the Resolution did not demand but "insist" on immediate access by international humanitarian organizations to all those in need of assistance in Iraq.

While "insists" is a stronger term than the following terms used in the U.N. General Assembly Resolution 43/131 (see Chapter 11) invites all States...to facilitate the work of these organizations...appeals...to all States to give their support...urges States...to participate closely...

the Council's Resolution does not formally establish an "international right of humanitarian intervention" across borders, as desired by its promoters: approval by the receiving country is still required, even if this approval is given only under threat of military enforcement or under pressure of international public opinion.

In fact, as for Resolution 43/131, national sovereignty is emphasized in the Council Resolution by reference to Article 2.7 of the U.N. Charter and in

> reaffirming the commitment of all Member States to the sovereignty, territorial integrity and political independence of Iraq and of all States in the area,

The Council Resolution which constituted a flagrant breach of Iraq's national sovereignty is Resolution 687 which, in part, established a demilitarized zone extending 10 kilometers into Iraq (and 5 kilometers into Kuwait), decided that Iraq unconditionally accept the destruction, removal, or rendering harmless, under international supervision of all chemical and biological weapons and ballistic missiles with a range greater than 150 kilometers, under the inspection of a Special Commission, and decided that Iraq unconditionally agree not to acquire or develop nuclear weapons.

While the latter Resolution was approved, as a consequence of Iraq's military defeat, by 12 members of the Security Council, including all permanent members (only Cuba voted against, and Yemen and Ecuador abstained), states are still unwilling to formalize and approve an international right of humanitarian intervention. It is very unlikely that even the terms of Resolution 688 could have been approved by a two-third majority in the General Assembly.

The last General Assembly Resolution on humanitarian assistance (Resolution 45/100), adopted on 14 December 1990, considered favorably the possibility of establishing "relief corridors" for the distribution of emergency medical and food aid: however these were to be established by means of "concerted action" by affected governments, IGOs and NGOs, and not as a "right" of international humanitarian intervention. The Resolution reaffirmed

> the sovereignty of affected States and their primary role in the initiation, organization, coordination and implementation of humanitarian assistance within their respective territories.

On 8 April 1991, the Council of Heads of States and governments of the European Community endorsed a British proposal (inspired by the Turkish President) to seek a U.N. enclave in Northern Iraq as a sanctuary for fleeing Kurds.

Rejected by Iraq as a

> part of the chain of plots against Iraq's sovereignty

this proposal met reservations from the USSR, China and the U.S. The European powers then shifted their position: the best solution would be for the U.N.

Secretary-General to "persuade" Iraq to allow a semi-permanent U.N. humanitarian presence in Kurdish areas.

If Iraq is not "persuaded" to accept an international, extra-territorial enclave on its territory, who will enforce the plan? Presumably not the Allied Forces, whose governments initially refused any further military role and involvement within Iraq. U.N. peace-keeping forces are traditionally not mandated to use force, except in self-defence. Their military capacity may not match Iraq's remaining military strength. The use of force by U.N. peace-keeping forces would require the approval of the Security Council, which is unlikely to be obtained.

Another objection is that a permanent settlement of Kurdish refugees in a protected territory might be a first step towards the creation of a Kurdish state, a prospect which all countries with Kurdish minorities reject.

It was feared that such a settlement might create another chronic refugee problem similar to that of the Palestinians, as well as a base for a liberation movement on the lines of the PLO.

At the time of writing this Postscript (end April 1991), the Allies were creating "safe havens" for displaced Kurds in Northern Iraq under their military protection and against Iraq's protests. In parallel, refugee relief was being negotiated by U.N. envoys with Iraqi authorities: humanitarian centers would be set up and operated by U.N. civilians, in Northern and Southern Iraq, with Iraq's agreement. The later announcement, received with some skepticism, that President Saddam Hussein had agreed to Kurdish autonomy in Iraq would, if this agreement is applied, resolve the refugee crisis.

National sovereignty is still strongly defended. At best, Security Council Resolution 688 should be taken as another step towards the desirable, progressive recognition of an international right and duty of humanitarian assistance, but not of a right of intervention.

Notes

See *Le Monde* of 5, 6, 7 and 8, 9 and 11 April, *International Herald Tribune* of 3, 4, 5, 6 and 7, 8, 9, 10, 11 and 25 April 1991, and *The Economist* 20 April 1991.

OTHER BOOKS BY YVES BEIGBEDER

La représentation du personnel à l'Organisation Mondiale de la Santé et dans les principales institutions spécialisées des Nations Unies ayant leur siège en Europe: Libriarie générale de droit et de jurisprudence, Paris, 1975, 290 p.

Management Problems in United Nations Organizations: Reform or Decline?: Frances Pinter Publishers, London, 1987, 174 p.

Threats to the International Civil Services—Past Pressures and New Trends: Pinter Publishers, London, 1988

INDEX

LEGAL ASPECTS OF
INTERNATIONAL ORGANIZATION

1. S. Rosenne: *Procedure in the International Court*. A Commentary on the 1978 Rules of the International Court of Justice. 1983   ISBN 90-247-3045-7

2. T. O. Elias: *The International Court of Justice and Some Contemporary Problems*. Essays on International Law. 1983   ISBN 90-247-2791-X

3. I. Hussain: *Dissenting and Separate Opinions at the World Court*. 1984
ISBN 90-247-2920-3

4. J. B. Elkind: *Non-Appearance before the International Court of Justice*. Functional and Comparative Analysis. 1984   ISBN 90-247-2921-1

5. E. Osieke: *Constitutional Law and Practice in the International Labour Organisation*. 1985   ISBN 90-247-2985-8

6. O. Long: *Law and Its Limitations in the GATT Multilateral Trade System*. 1985   ISBN Hb: 90-247-3189-5; Pb: 0-86010-959-3

7. E. McWhinney: *The International Court of Justice and the Western Tradition of International Law*. The Paul Martin Lectures in International Relations and Law. 1987   ISBN 90-247-3524-6

8. R. Sonnenfeld: *Resolutions of the United Nations Security Council*. 1988
ISBN-90-247-3567-X

9. T.D. Gill: *Litigation Strategy at the International Court*. A Case Study of the Nicaragua versus United States Dispute. 1989   ISBN 0-7923-0332-6

10. S. Rosenne: *The World Court*. What It is and how It works. 4th revised ed. Prepared with the assistance of T.D. Gill. 1989   ISBN 90-247-3772-9

11. V. Gowlland-Debbas: *Collective Responses to Illegal Acts in International Law*. United Nations Action in the Question of Southern Rhodesia. 1990
ISBN 0-7923-0811-5

12. Y. Beigbeder: *The Role and Status of International Humanitarian Volunteers and Organizations*. The Right and Duty to Humanitarian Assistance. 1991
ISBN 0-7923-1190-6